GREATEST
BATTLES
OF WORLD WAR II

GREATEST BATTLES OF WORLD WAR II

Bison Books Limited

This edition published 1982 by
Bison Books Limited
4 Cromwell Place
London SW7

ISBN 0 86124 062 6

Printed in Hong Kong

Page 1: US Marines raise the 'stars and stripes' after landing on a Japanese-held Pacific island in 1944.
Pages 2/3: The *USS West Virginia* blazes fiercely following the Japanese attack on Pearl Harbor on 7 December 1941. Hit by bombs and a torpedo, she sank but was later raised, repaired and saw service at the Battle of Leyte Gulf in October 1944.
These pages: Armorers rearm a Spitfire Mark 1 of 19 Squadron at RAF Duxford during the Battle of Britain.

CONTENTS

Battle of Britain *Norman Franks* 10
Pearl Harbor *H P Wilmott* 73
Midway *Lt Col A J Barker* 137
D-Day *Brigadier Peter Young* 201
Battle of the Bulge *John Pimlott* 265
Okinawa *Lt Col A J Barker* 329
Index 391

INTRODUCTION

Greatest Battles of World War II is an analysis in depth of six of the most significant battles of the war, written by a team of highly-skilled military historians. The book shows how the course of the war was decisively changed by the outcome of six battles. The Battle of Britain ensured the survival of the United Kingdom, which eventually served as a base for the invasion of occupied Europe. Pearl Harbor brought the United States into the war, thus enabling the Allies to build up sufficient resources to defeat the Axis Powers. Midway halted the tide of Japanese conquest in the Pacific, launching the Americans onto the offensive. The D-Day invasion was the beginning of the campaign which led Allied armies into the heart of the Reich. The Battle of the Bulge saw the destruction of Hitler's last reserves and finally sealed the fate of the Third Reich. Okinawa led to the fateful decision to drop the atom bomb on Japan.

The Battle of Britain was the first turning point of the war. Up until the summer of 1940 Hitler's forces had swept all before them in the brilliant and unstoppable blitzkrieg campaigns against Poland, Norway and Denmark, the Low Countries and France. It was only the formidable anti-tank barrier of the English Channel which prevented Britain from sharing the fate of her Continental allies. In order to mount a seaborne invasion of southern England, Hitler had first to neutralize Britain's air and naval defenses. He believed that once RAF Fighter Command had been destroyed, the Royal Navy could be effectively neutralized by the Luftwaffe's bombers. The key to the defeat of Germany's remaining enemy lay therefore in the destruction of the RAF's fighter force and so the stage was set for the first major air battle in the history of warfare.

The Battle opened with probing attacks by the Luftwaffe against ports, coastal convoys, foreward airfields and, for a short time, radar stations. The latter targets were Fighter Command's Achilles' heel, had German Intelligence but realized it. Radar stations were sited in exposed positions on or near the coast and were highly vulnerable to bomb damage. If the Luftwaffe had concentrated their bombing effort against them, Fighter Command would have been denied the vital advanced warning of attack on which the defenses relied. Even with the advantage of early warning, the defenders became increasingly hard-pressed to find the pilots and fighter aircraft to meet the German attacks, especially when these switched to Fighter Command's own airfields. By early September the RAF was facing defeat in the air and it was only Hitler's miscalculated decision to send his bombers against London which gave Fighter Command the necessary respite to regain the initiative. As a result of the Luftwaffe's failure to defeat the RAF, Hitler indefinately postponed the invasion of Britain. The following year he launched his attack on the Soviet Union with an undefeated enemy to his rear.

Although Germany had suffered her first defeat in the Battle of Britain there seemed no prospect of halting Hitler's stream of conquests. In 1941 German armies swept through the Balkans as a preliminary to the invasion of the Soviet Union. It was the entry of the United States into the war, with the promise of her enormous industrial and manpower resources being brought to bear against the Axis, which changed the course of the war. Germany's Axis partner Japan precipitated this change in fortune by her surprise attack on the US Pacific Fleet at Pearl Harbor on 7 December 1941.

Japan saw war with the United States as unavoidable if she was to realize her ambitions in the Pacific. Her master strategist, Admiral Yamamoto, saw that Japan could not hope to win a prolonged war with the United States and the Pearl Harbor *coup de main* was his solution to the problem. If the US Pacific Fleet could be eliminated at a single blow the United States would be forced to come to terms. The attack was vigorously executed by the airmen of the Japanese Navy's highly-trained carrier air groups and the US battleship force was all-but wiped out. However the Americans were not disposed to seek terms from Japan and in the aircraft carriers which had escaped the carnage at Pearl Harbor the US Navy had a weapon which could halt the tide of Japanese conquest. Far from eliminating the United States as an obstacle to Japanese ambitions in Asia, the Day of Infamy was to lead to the total collapse of Axis power in the Pacific and in Europe.

US 105mm M3 Howitzer during the Battle of the Bulge.

Yet before the United States could mobilize her vast potential, the flood tide of Japanese conquest had to be stemmed by the often inadequate resources which were to hand. In the wake of the Pearl Harbor attack Japan occupied the Philippines, the Netherlands East Indies, Malaya and Burma. Her forces seemed invincible. In the South Pacific they threatened the mainland of Australia and advanced to the borders of India to the west, while in the Central Pacific naval forces were thrusting toward Midway Island and Hawaii, beyond which lay the western seaboard of the United States.

The Battle of Midway marked the turning point of the Pacific War. The three United States aircraft carriers, *Yorktown, Enterprise* and *Hornet*, formed the backbone of the Pacific Fleet after the loss of the battleships. Admiral Yamamoto knew that Midway Island was of such strategic importance that the United States must commit these precious ships to its defense and he intended to wipe them out before new construction from American shipyards could rebuild the Pacific Fleet. To achieve this aim the Japanese assembled a force of 162 warships and auxiliaries, which included four large aircraft carriers. The American defenders had 76 ships, including the carriers, backed up by Army Air Force and Marine Corps aircraft operating from Midway. The United States commander, Admiral Chester Nimitz, had one more priceless asset, because thanks to the work of American cypher-breakers he knew the Japanese plan of attack.

On the morning of 4 June 1942 Japan opened the battle with an air strike against Midway Island. The riposte from the American carriers came after this force had returned to the Japanese carriers and was being refuelled and rearmed. Within the space of six minutes US Navy Dauntless dive-bombers set three of the Japanese carriers ablaze and they later sank taking with them their valuable aircraft and aircrews. *Hiryu*, the surviving Japanese carrier, took her revenge by inflicting serious damage on the *Yorktown*, which was finished off by a Japanese submarine two days later. *Hiryu* herself did not long survive this success, as she came under attack from a second striking force of US Navy Dauntlesses which speedily sent her to the bottom. In a single day the hitherto invincible Japanese Navy had lost four of her modern carriers together with 250 aircraft and most of their highly-trained crews. It was a defeat that could not easily be reversed and thenceforth it would be the Japanese who were the defenders in the Pacific.

In spite of Allied victories in North Africa, the invasion of Italy and the hard-won Russian victories at Stalingrad and Kursk, it was not until the second front was opened in Western Europe that the defeat of Nazi Germany was within sight. Plans for the cross-Channel invasion had been maturing since the Casablanca Conference in

Above: US and British landing craft (LSI's) disgorge their cargo onto Omaha Beach shortly after D-Day, June, 1944.

Left: German infantry during the Ardennes offensive, December, 1944.

January 1943, but such was the complexity of assembling the largest amphibious assault force in history, that the landings did not take place until June 1944. Even with such meticulous preparation the result on D-Day was not a foregone conclusion. Hitler's vaunted Atlantic Wall defenses had to be spread thin, as the Allies were careful to give no clue as to where the invasion would come. Yet until a secure bridgehead was established in Normandy the invaders would be vulnerable to counterattack.

Allied supremacy in the air and at sea was essential to the success of the landings. Preliminary bombardment of the defenses helped to establish the assault forces ashore. Even so on Omaha beach the US 1st Division met stiff opposition and suffered heavy casualties. Yet the German reaction was too slow to check the landings decisively. Rommel, the commander of German forces in Northern France, was on leave in Germany on D-Day. Airborne landings inland from the beaches and attacks on transportation targets by Allied bombers and resistance fighters all helped to isolate the battlefield from reinforcements. By 12 June the five bridgeheads were linked into a continuous front 60 miles long and over 326,000 troops had been put ashore. The Allies had secured a springboard for the liberation of Western Europe.

Once Allied forces were firmly established in Normandy, the reoccupation of France proceeded systematically against a stiff German rearguard action. The landings in Southern France on 15 August 1944 hastened the process and ten days later Paris was liberated. If the Allies were disposed to write off the German Army as a spent force, then the bitter and costly defeat of the British 1st Airborne Division at Arnhem in September provided a sharp corrective. Yet it was undeniable that German forces were everywhere in retreat. On the Eastern Front the Soviet armies had reached the Danube in November and the war was approaching the borders of the Reich. A German counteroffensive seemed inconceivable.

Hitler's last offensive, the Battle of the Bulge, threatened to drive a wedge between the Allied armies by a thrust through the Ardennes to occupy the strategically-important port of Antwerp. Such an attack in midwinter, through difficult terrain caught the Allies totally unprepared. Intelligence had given no warning of the concentration of a German army 250,000 men strong on the Western Front. The offensive opened on 16 December and by Christmas Day had advanced some 50 miles almost to the River Meuse, but the attack had lost its momentum. Its failure was primarily due to the stubborn fighting qualities of the American soldier. Deprived of his accustomed air support by appalling weather conditions and quite unprepared for the German onslaught, he nevertheless stood firm. The rock-like defense of Bastogne by American airborne troops gave the Allied commanders time to prepare a counterattack. By the New Year Hitler's last reserve army was destroyed and all he had achieved was to delay the Allied advance by some six weeks. In the east the Soviet winter offensive opened on 12 January. Hitler had made his last gambler's throw and lost; the fate of the Third Reich was sealed.

On 1 April 1945 when US Marines stormed ashore on Okinawa they did not realize that the final decisive battle of the Pacific War had opened. Okinawa was but the final stepping stone to the Japanese home islands. The fighting seemed a grim foretaste of what was to come. The landings were preceded by a prolonged naval barrage which proved largely ineffective as the Japanese defenders had abandoned the beaches and moved inland to a labyrinth of fortified bunkers which the Americans had to reduce one by one at a heavy cost in casualties. By the time that Okinawa was completely overrrun the US Tenth Army had lost some 7600 men killed and a further 31,800 wounded. Offshore the United States and Allied navies had faced an equally grim ordeal from Kamikaze suicide attacks, with 34 vessels sunk and 4900 men killed.

If it was clear that the defeat of Japan was inevitable, then it was equally apparent that the Japanese forces would defend their homeland with fanatical courage and a terrible price would be exacted from the invaders. President Truman's awesome decision to sanction the dropping of atomic bombs on Japanese cities can be seen as a response to this threat. In helping to lead to the bombing of Hiroshima and Nagasaki, the Okinawa battle was decisive not only to the outcome of World War II in the Pacific, but also was to effect the lives of generations as yet unborn.

BATTLE OF BRITAIN

NORMAN FRANKS

Pages 10/11: Hurricane in 111 Squadron markings.
These pages: Ian 'Widge' Gleed, DFC, of 87 Squadron, leading a Hurricane formation from Exeter to Bibury in September 1940.

RAF FIGHTER COMMAND
COMMAND HEADQUARTERS
GROUP HEADQUARTERS
SECTOR STATION & BOUNDARY*
FIGHTER STATION
LOW-LEVEL RADAR STATION
HIGH-LEVEL RADAR STATION
COMMAND BOUNDARY
TOWNS BOMBED
LUFTWAFFE BASES
BOMBER
STUKA (DIVE-BOMBER)
FIGHTER (Bf109)
TWIN-ENGINED FIGHTER (Bf110)
COMMAND BOUNDARY
MILES
0
100
KILOMETRES
0
150
*11 Group only
FIRTH OF FORTH
GLASGOW
BELFAST
NEWCASTLE
SUNDERLAND
Fighter Command 13 Group (Saul)
MIDDLESBROUGH
Luftflotte 5 (Stumpf) (from Norway and Denmark)
NORTH SEA
HULL
Cover of low-level radar (500 ft)
Cover of high-level radar (15,000 ft)
LIVERPOOL
MANCHESTER
SHEFFIELD
NOTTINGHAM
Fighter Command 12 Group (Leigh-Mallory)
NORWICH
BIRMINGHAM
COVENTRY
Duxford
Debden
IPSWICH
Martlesham
SWANSEA
CARDIFF
Stanmore
Northolt
LONDON
North Weald
Uxbridge
Rochford
Hornchurch
Croydon
THAMES ESTUARY
Eastchurch
Biggin Hill
Kenley
Manston
BRISTOL
Ball
BATH
Andover
Middle Wallop
Fighter Command 11 Group (Park)
Redhill
West Malling
Detling
CANTERBURY
Lympne
Hawkinge
Fighter Command 10 Group (Brand)
SOUTHAMPTON
EXETER
PLYMOUTH
Tangmere
PORTSMOUTH
VENTNOR
ENGLISH CHANNEL
ROTTERDAM
ANTWERP
GHENT
BELGIUM
CALAIS
LILLE
Luftflotte 2 (Kesselring)
AMIENS
CHERBOURG
LE HAVRE
FRANCE
PARIS
Luftflotte 3 (Sperrle)
RENNES

1. THE BUILD UP

Below: Air Chief Marshal Sir Hugh C T Dowding, AOC in C, RAF fighter Command, during the battle of Britain.

Above: The distinctive outline of the Spitfire.

Britain was alone. The debris of Dunkirk had disappeared and those soldiers who were still in France were either dead or in prison camps. Western Europe was now under the heel of the German jackboot.

In an astonishingly short space of time France, Belgium and Holland had fallen to the German's lightning attack – their now famous Blitzkrieg tactic. In that time the British army had been forced out of France, the Royal Air Force had been overwhelmed, and Britain's allies had been defeated and forced to surrender their arms and their countries. In one month Hitler's forces, already victors in Poland and Norway, had achieved what the Kaiser's armies had failed to do in the four years between 1914–18.

Anyone standing on the south coast of England in mid-June 1940, and looking out across the English Channel toward France could feel tangibly that he and his country were alone. True, Britain still had her Commonwealth, but although some of its fighting men were in the Mother country, Canada, South Africa, Australia, New Zealand and so on were too far away to be of any real help. They could send more men and supplies but that was all. Britain was still alone and it was obvious to everyone that the Germans' next conquest must be the British Isles. In their way stood Air Chief Marshal Hugh Dowding, Commander in Chief of Britain's Fighter Command, and his fighter pilots.

Right: Hermann Wilhelm Goering, the 'supremo' of the Luftwaffe throughout its existence.
Far right: A Lockheed Hudson of Coastal Command approaching Dunkirk on a reconnaissance patrol.
Bottom: Part of the armada which rescued the BEF standing off Dunkirk.
Below: The forlorn remains of a Hawker Hurricane on Dunkirk beach, July 1940, epitomizing the utter defeat of Allied air forces in France during the Blitzkrieg.

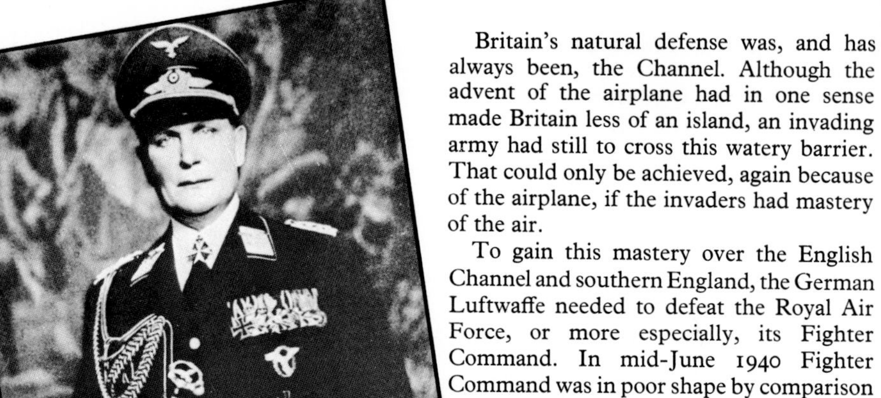

Britain's natural defense was, and has always been, the Channel. Although the advent of the airplane had in one sense made Britain less of an island, an invading army had still to cross this watery barrier. That could only be achieved, again because of the airplane, if the invaders had mastery of the air.

To gain this mastery over the English Channel and southern England, the German Luftwaffe needed to defeat the Royal Air Force, or more especially, its Fighter Command. In mid-June 1940 Fighter Command was in poor shape by comparison

with the attackers. Losses over Dunkirk and in the Battle of France had seen to that. It is said that one can prove anything with figures and various accounts of comparative strengths of the RAF and the Luftwaffe do differ.

The Luftwaffe, under the command of Hermann Wilhelm Goering, a former fighter pilot of World War I, had been building its strength for a number of years. By August 1938 it had nearly 3000 aircraft, and the total had increased to 3750 by the time Poland was attacked on 1 September 1939, which plunged the world into World War II. Despite losses sustained in Poland, and later over Norway in April 1940, the Luftwaffe mustered nearly 5000 aircraft by May 1940. Of this total 3900 were in the two Air Groups, *Luftflotte* 2 and *Luftflotte* 3, which were poised to lead the Blitzkrieg in the west.

Although the Air Forces of France, Belgium and Holland could field a large number of fighting aircraft, the RAF in France had only four squadrons of Hawker Hurricanes and two of Gloster Gladiator fighters in France during the period known as the 'Phony War' – September 1939–May 1940. When the Germans invaded France and the Low Countries on 10 May, reinforcements of RAF aircraft were sent to France but in 10 days it was obvious that there was no stopping the German advance. The RAF gave a good account of itself in France, its pilots fighting themselves to a standstill. Yet finally those who survived had to be evacuated back to England. It was because of Hugh Dowding that Britain's fighter force had not been completely whittled away in the French campaign.

A scheme approved in 1935 promised Fighter Command a minimum of 53 squad-

Above left: Hurricane 1, N2479 of 56 Squadron at dispersal.
Left: Spitfire of Pilot Officer Colin Gray of 54 Squadron at Hornchurch in April 1940, armed, fuelled, and with trolley accumulator plugged in for immediate start up.

Left: Hurricane marked as the aircraft flown by Squadron Leader R R S Tuck, DSO, DFC, OC 257 Squadron in 1940–41.
Below: The sturdy Hurricane was the mainstay of RAF Fighter Command throughout the Battle of Britain.

rons by 1939 with which to defend the British Isles. In 1936, when Dowding became Commander in Chief, he only had 15 regular and three auxiliary squadrons. This was increased to only 24 regular and six auxiliary units by 1938 – and every one was equipped with a variety of outdated biplanes.

When the German offensive began on 10 May 1940, the RAF had 2750 front-line aircraft, of which just over 1000 were fighter types. In the first two days of the offensive four more fighter squadrons were sent across to France and on the 13th a further 32 Hurricanes and pilots flew over. Dowding had now been forced to commit around a third of his fighter force to France. Clearly this could not continue if he was to retain sufficient fighters to defend Britain.

He put his case forward forcibly at a Cabinet meeting, illustrating with graphs that if the present rate of attrition continued for a further two weeks the RAF would not have a single Hurricane left in France – or Britain! He followed this with his now famous and courageous letter to the Under Secretary of State for Air, setting out his fears and asking for the Air Ministry to commit itself as to what it considered the level of strength needed to defend Britain. This in itself won him few friends in high places but it eventually did the trick. Shortly afterward came the order from Winston Churchill that no more fighters would leave the UK, whatever France's need.

The Royal Air Force eventually lost over 1000 airplanes in France and Norway, half of which were fighters. This represented two-thirds of all aircraft delivered to the RAF since the war began. Even more serious was the loss of so many valuable aircrew, both regular air force men and peacetime trainees. Their loss was not in vain for not only did they inflict considerable damage on the Luftwaffe, thereby reducing the number of aircraft which would eventually be used against Britain, but those who survived to return to Britain had gained immeasurable experience. The Dunkirk evacuation cost the RAF 100 fighters and about 80 pilots, leaving Fighter Command with roughly 470 serviceable aircraft by early June, of which just 330 were Hawker Hurricanes and Supermarine Spitfires. There were only 36 more in immediate reserve.

Left: Air Marshal Keith Park, the brilliant New Zealander who commanded the vital 11 Group, Fighter Command during the battle.
Bottom: Chain Home (CH) radar, 1940. The three towers at left are the transmitters; those at right are receivers.
Below: A Heinkel He III, one of the Luftwaffe's main bombers in 1940.

Right: Junkers 88 bombers played a relatively small part in the battle, but were to be used in a host of operational roles by the Luftwaffe throughout World War II.
Below right: The Messerschmitt Bf 109E, the only single-seat fighter type used by the Luftwaffe throughout the battle.

A month later, the first week in July, with both sides about ready to meet each other in deadly action, *Luftflotte* 2 and *Luftflotte* 3 numbered 2075 aircraft, of which 900 were fighters, 875 bombers and 300 dive bombers. *Luftflotte* 5, based in Norway, threatened the eastern side of England and Scotland and had 123 bombers and 34 twin-engined fighters. The RAF at this moment had just 46 fighter squadrons plus two equipped with Defiants (soon to be relegated to night fighting only) with four more squadrons in course of formation. The total number of aircraft was between 600–700 with 1253 pilots – 197 short of establishment. With this number, Fighter Command had to defend all of Britain, not just the south, although it was anticipated that the main assault would take place in the south.

Those in command viewed the coming battle with a good deal of foreboding. The task of defending Britain with such a small force against a victorious Luftwaffe was daunting. The pilots who would fight the battle viewed the coming struggle in a variety of ways. Some who had been in France felt utterly devastated at being on the losing end, a few even felt that Britain too must fall. Others were keen to hit back, to have another go. Many others, having tasted action above Dunkirk, were equally eager to have another crack at the Germans. Those pilots still to see action were, in the main, raring to go. Yet by far the majority believed they would prevail – defeat was unthinkable. This was perhaps a testament of youth, for most of Britain's fighter pilots were young. However young, they were the professionals, led by professionals. The wartime trainee pilots were not in evidence in any great number as yet. Whatever thoughts went through their minds, everyone was keen to 'get stuck in.' Yet within a few short weeks, those who were still alive were physically and mentally exhausted and any excuse for a rest was gratefully taken. If rain or bad weather stopped flying it was a godsend. However, as July began each one of them stood ready.

One asset that the defenders had was Britain's advanced radar system, which was far in advance of the Germans' own development. When the battle started it gave the fighter pilots advanced warning of the approach of flying raiders, an estimate of their number and, with a degree of accuracy, their height. With help from the Observer Corps, 30,000 civilian volunteers, Britain had a good chance of knowing where the enemy was coming from and where it was heading.

Although as yet the air force had little chance to test its fighter defenses in nine months of war, the success in intercepting these few raiders that had made flights over Britain was encouraging. It was a practiced art and one that had been practiced often enough. This was due to the energies of the leader of Fighter Command, Hugh Dowding. His devotion to the concept of total defense of his country brought success although often his approach did not help his subsequent career. Even to his pilots he was an aloof figure – only later would they appreciate his great qualities of leadership.

Dowding's principal air leaders were the three Group Commanders whose squadrons would bear the brunt of the coming attack. All three had served in the air force in World War I. In the southeast of England was 11 Group, commanded by Air Vice-Marshal Keith Park, a New Zealander. North of the River Thames, covering most of Essex, Suffolk and Norfolk, was 12 Group, controlled by Air Vice-Marshal Trafford Leigh-Mallory. Air Vice-Marshal Sir Christopher Quintin Brand, a South African, commanded 10 Group in the southwest.

Left: Messerschmitt Bf 110 two-seat escort fighters which proved of little value during the assaults on England in 1940. Illustrated are Bf 110s of ZG 79 *Haifischgruppe* (Shark Group) with their distinctive 'teeth' markings.

Opposing them was Reichsmarschal Hermann Goering and his three main air group commanders. *Luftflotte* 2 was led by Generalfeldmarschal Albrecht Kesselring, a soldier turned airman, while *Luftflotte* 3 was headed by Generalfeldmarschal Hugo Sperrle. Sperrle had commanded the Condor Legion during the Spanish Civil War, where the Germans had gained considerable experience fighting for General Franco's forces. *Luftflotte* 5 in Norway was under the command of Generaloberst Hans-Jurgen Stumpf, a former staff officer.

Historians have conveniently divided the Battle of Britain into five phases although at the time, to the ordinary fighter pilot, there seemed to be a general buildup from about 10 July, as the Luftwaffe stepped up its attacks, until October/November when they began to cease.

As July began, the RAF was still licking its wounds after the French and Dunkirk campaigns. Dowding's strength was far from 100 percent; several units had lost much of their equipment in France and were not fully operational. The Luftwaffe had moved rapidly into bases in Belgium, Holland and northern France, had been reinforced from Germany and now stood ready to take the offensive against Britain. By mid-July Luftwaffe strength was in the region of 2000 aircraft. Keith Park's 11 Group had just 190 or so day fighters and as it was the RAF's most vulnerable sector, the odds against it were considerable.

The RAF's main antagonists in the battle were Heinkel 111, Dornier 17 and Junkers 88 bombers, Junkers 87 'Stuka' dive bombers and Messerschmitt 109 and 110 fighters. All had had their successes in Poland, Norway and France, but over Britain their shortcomings soon became evident. The three bombers were all twin-engined craft with relatively short ranges when fully laden. In daylight raids they were vulnerable to fighter attacks and close escort by fighters proved essential as the battle progressed. The Ju 87, while successful in the Blitzkrieg type of action when it could accurately blast a path for advancing ground troops, quickly proved extremely vulnerable in actions over southern England and had to be withdrawn from major involvement by mid-August. The Messerschmitt 109E single-seat fighter was a dangerous adversary for RAF pilots, but it was hampered by its short range. Often it had only a short time in the combat zone, usually measured in minutes, and its pilots were ever mindful of their fuel levels. The twin-engined, two-seat Me 110 was also dangerous but it had already proved vulner-

Below: The effect of eight Browning guns is well illustrated on this Dornier Do 17 (3Z + GS) of 8/KG77 (Obltn Gillios) which was hit by fighters, then downed by antiaircraft guns near Dover on 1 July 1940.

Above: A Hurricane landing.
Right: Bf 109E brought down in southeast England on 11 July 1940.

P3602

Above left: Pilots of 32 Squadron at Hawkinge, 31 July 1940. From left: R Smythe, J Procter, K Gillman, P Gardner, P Brothers, D Grice, A Eckford. All but Gillman, who was killed in action on 25 August 1940, survived the war. In background is Hurricane I, P3522, GZ-V.
Below left: Luftwaffe crews taking their meals. The order to attack can come at any moment.

Above: Flight Lieutenant A W A Bayne, DFC, of 17 Squadron in the cockpit of his Hurricane. Note rear-view mirror at top of canopy.
Below: One of the many AA units firing at night at Barry, near Cardiff.

able in combat over France. Pilots often had to resort to flying in defensive circles when under attack, thus leaving the bombers open to attacks by British fighters.

The Luftwaffe was organized principally for use as a direct support of an advancing land army. It was, therefore, totally unsuited for an offensive war involving distances such as France to Britain.

Both fighters and bombers were equipped with the 7.9mm machine gun, roughly equivalent to the RAF's Browning .303-inch machine gun, but in addition the Messerschmitts carried 20mm cannons which were much heavier hitting guns and could cause considerable damage to RAF Spitfires and Hurricanes. The RAF was experimenting with its own 20mm cannon but trials were not immediately successful.

The RAF's fighter tactics left much to be desired at this time. Squadrons flew in sections of three: a leader and two wing men. The problem was that although the leader was free to scan the sky for hostile aircraft, his two wing men were kept busier watching their leader and trying not to collide with him. Thus they were not totally concentrating on the sky around them. This rigid, inflexible formation took some time to change and even when more-discerning air fighters and leaders began to adopt a more open formation, and sections of four rather than three, others still continued in the old prewar formation. Even when proved effective there was no immediate directive from Fighter Command Headquarters to change to the new formation. Fortunately air fighters who had found over Dunkirk that flexibility made for more effective and less cumbersome attacks, put their theories into practice. Men whose names would soon be well known to the RAF and to the general public were emerging from the crowd: 'Sailor' Malan, Douglas Bader, Al Deere, Johnny Peel, Bob Tuck and Ginger Lacey.

German fighter pilots had discovered in Spain the advantages of a more open formation and flew in sections of four which split down into two-man elements once action was joined. In this way the leader was able to concentrate on an attack while his number two protected his tail. Already the Germans were producing ace pilots on their side of the Channel: Werner Mölders, Helmut Wick, Gunther Lützow, Walter Oesau, Rolf Pingel and Adolf Galland.

As Hitler hoped that Britain would soon request peace now that her European neighbors had been overrun, he had no wish to endanger a decision by attacking British towns and civilians. The opening phase of the battle was directed against Channel convoys and ports while the full German strength was being assembled in northern France. The German aims were to test Dowding's air defenses and to force him to use up his precious reserves.

On Wednesday 10 July 1940, the day that has become the official date of the commencement of the Battle of Britain, the first encounter of the day was made by a section of Spitfires from 66 Squadron based at Coltishall in 12 Group. Scrambled at 0440 hours, they intercepted a Dornier 17z of *Kampfgeschwader* 3 (KG3), 20 miles out to sea and shot it down. The successful pilots were Pilot Officers C A Cooke, J A P Studd and Sergeant F N Robertson.

The day's main activities centered around the Channel convoys which resulted in several air fights. At the end of the day, nine German aircraft had been shot down, with others damaged, for the loss of one RAF pilot who had collided with a Heinkel 111 over the sea. Six RAF fighters had been damaged.

The battles over the coastal convoys were vicious and costly to both sides. Several young, inexperienced pilots were lost chancing their arm against the Luftwaffe, some chasing Germans back toward France, only to be jumped by Messerschmitt 109s over the sea.

Over a convoy on the 12th, Dorniers and Heinkels of II/KG2 and III/KG53 were intercepted by Hurricanes of 17, 85, 151 and 242 Squadrons from Martlesham, Debden, Coltishall and North Weald. One pilot in 17 Squadron, Flying Officer Count M B Czernin, spotted 12 Heinkel 111s coming in fast from the east at 8000 feet. He immediately went into a climbing turn to the left, then, stick over and a kick on the left rudder and he was plunging down to attack. The Station Commander at North Weald, Wing Commander F V Beamish, flying with 151 Squadron, was also on hand. Attacking three Dorniers, he was:

'. . . met by heavy crossfire with much tracer. After a long burst at the left hand Dornier, his port engine blew up and stopped, his undercarriage dropped down and he broke away from the formation.'

Meanwhile, Czernin and one of his section, Pilot Officer D H W Hanson, had broken off the first action and followed Beamish's attack on the three Dorniers. They attacked the leading bomber and sent it into the sea. Its pilot was the Staffelkapitan of KG3, Hauptmann Machetski.

Later in the day three pilots of 74 Squadron took off to investigate a raid plotted 15 miles northeast of Margate. They saw anti-aircraft fire coming from a ship, exploding around a Heinkel 111. The section leader, Flight Lieutenant A G Malan DFC, opened fire from 300 yards and silenced the rear gunner, allowing his two wingmen to finish it off.

Sailor Malan was again in evidence on 28 July when he and his men tangled with Werner Mölder's JG51. No 74 Squadron was using Manston as a base and had been scrambled at 1350 hours when a raid had been reported approaching Dover. Malan's Spitfires went after the Messerschmitt escort, but the bombers turned away. The Spitfire pilots attacked the Me 109s; no less than three were destroyed and three others were damaged. One of those damaged was flown by Mölders himself. Malan reported the action:

'. . . turned on to their tails without being observed and led Red Section into the attack. Gave one enemy aircraft two-second bursts from 250 to 100 yards. He attempted no evasion tactics except a gentle right-hand turn and decreasing speed, by which I concluded he had at least had his controls hit (shot away). I then turned onto another 109 which had turned past my nose and I delivered three deflection bursts at 100 yards. He went down in a spiral.'

The squadrons that periodically used RAF Manston as a forward base were

Right: Flying Officer M B Czernin, DFC of 17 Squadron.
Above right: Pilots of 151 Squadron at North Weald, July 1940, including Wing Commander F V Beamish (fifth from left), and Squadron Leader E M Donaldson (forth from left), both of whom had several brothers in the RAF.
Far right: Spitfires of 66 Squadron get away from Coltishall in 'Vic' formation.
Below: Hurricanes of 56 Squadron at North Weald in July 1940.

constantly in the front line. Little wonder that this southeastern tip of England was soon called 'Hellfire Corner' by the pilots. It became liberally pitted with bomb craters as low-flying Me 109s were easily able to slip in to fly a strafing run over the base. Rochford (Southend) was another airfield and forward base similar to Manston and also used by squadrons from Hornchurch.

At Manston the pilots occupied a dispersal site on the far side of the airfield. They had some huts for both ground personnel and aircrew during readiness periods. This sometimes caused delays in bringing food and refreshments to dispersal as it was a long way from the domestic amenities of the camp. It was code named 'Charlie 3.' The typical routine for Manston, Rochford (and some others) was: Readiness at Dawn. Takeoff straight away to fly a convoy patrol. Refuel and return to immediate readiness until mid- or late afternoon taking part in whatever sorties might come along. Then back to the parent station, remaining at Readiness until finally released at dusk.

No 65 Squadron used Rochford during one period. The conditions were somewhat primitive. Their Spitfires were parked into the wind while the pilots used an old civilian clubhouse as flight hut, restroom and eating place. There they would wait for the call for action. Parked outside the clubhouse was a 15-hundredweight Bedford truck and a motorbike which was used to get to the aircraft in a hurry when the call came.

In the clubhouse was a single telephone which was answered by whoever was sitting nearest to it, while everyone else made for the door at top speed, aiming for the truck. 'Thumbs up' and away they went, leaving the chap on the phone to get the whole message then follow on the motorbike and pass on the message as they climbed away on takeoff. 'Thumbs down' stopped the panic and everyone settled

Above: A three-some Vic of 610 Squadron, AAF, on patrol, searching for the Luftwaffe.
Below right: A G 'Sailor' Malan of 74 'Tiger' Squadron who was recognized as possibly the finest fighter leader in the RAF, 1940–42.
Below: Wing Commander Brendan Finucane, DSO, DFC – 'Paddy' – who scored some 32 credited victories before his death in action in 1942.

down again.

One morning a young pilot named Paddy Finucane was nearest the phone and his sign sent everyone aboard the truck and away. As the pilots took to the air they looked down to see Finucane get onto the bike, fall off and try to climb back from the other side. With obvious signs of panic he jumped up and down as the others flew off without him. Upon landing it was discovered that Finucane could not ride a motorbike nor drive a car. They never let Finucane sit by the telephone after that.

The telephone became the center of attention in many crew rooms, dispersal huts and pilots' caravans over those summer months of 1940. The pilots would try to ignore its presence but as soon as it rang, their hearts missed a beat. Its message could send them racing to their waiting fighters, or it could be just an innocuous message, perhaps from the canteen, asking how many lunches were required, or the station commander wanting to speak to the commanding officer. The scenes at Manston and Rochford were repeated on a score or more fighter bases in southern England where the fighter pilots waited for the call for action.

As July gave way to August so too came the change of tactics by the Luftwaffe. The time of probing was at an end. If Hitler had any intention of invading Britain he had to attack in the summer, and before he did, Fighter Command had to be destroyed. On 19 July Hitler made his 'last appeal to reason' speech to the Reichstag – but he should have known Britain would in no way contemplate surrender. Hitler was confident of victory, for in his hands was the latest intelligence report comparing the Luftwaffe strength with that of the RAF. In its conclusion it showed that the Luftwaffe was clearly superior to the RAF in strength, equipment, training and command. In the event of intensive air warfare the Luftwaffe would be in a position to achieve a decisive effect in 1940 in order to support an invasion. What the report did not allow for was the dogged, stubborn attitude of the British in general, or the skilled determination of the pilots who stood in the way of German victory.

The first phase of the battle ended after the first week in August. In that phase the Luftwaffe lost nearly 200 aircraft, nearly twice as many as the Royal Air Force.

2. FIGHTER-VERSUS-FIGHTER

The second phase of the battle began on 8 August. The Luftwaffe now saw their task as mainly a fighter-versus-fighter conflict in order to destroy the British fighter force. The bombers which attacked British targets, mainly airfields, provided the bait to bring the Hurricanes and Spitfires to battle; then the Me 109 pilots could deal with them.

At the start of August there was a lull in Luftwaffe activity and it was clear to Dowding and to Keith Park that this had to mean that the enemy was regrouping ready for a massive all-out assault. Whether or not Hitler really meant to invade Britain, there can be little doubt that everyone in Britain did expect him to do so. Therefore, every pilot knew that destiny lay very much in his hands.

In the German Intelligence Appreciation of the RAF referred to above, the Luftwaffe underestimated the strength of the RAF fighters by half! This was to lead to various complications within the German High Command and the continuing shortcomings of Intelligence Reports led to much frustration among German aircrew who continued to meet strong resistance when they had been told that the RAF had been practically wiped out.

Dowding was a little more confident at this stage, for trained pilots were quickly making up the recent losses and he had now more than 1400 pilots; his only dilemma was that they lacked experience. Nearly 100 experienced regular squadron and flight commanders had been lost since May.

Of the many air actions which occurred on the 8th, two flown by Pilot Officer A N C Weir of 145 Squadron produced three victories. During the first part of the morning he shot down an Me 109 and a Ju 87. In a lunchtime battle he got another Me 109:

'Saw 110s in two groups five miles apart, flying in defensive circles low down. Three Hurricanes at 12,000 feet circled, wondering the best way to attack and asking for help. After ten minutes decided to dive when a 109 flew across in front of me – a decoy I thought. Pulled round to get on its tail and we flew round in circles till I was just gaining a position from which I could fire. He dived steeply and I fired from astern from 500 yards.'

Another pilot saw the Me 109 crash into the sea.

Goering had promised Hitler that his Luftwaffe would clear the sky of the RAF in readiness for invasion during early August. Now that his fliers had built up their strength, they were ready to go. His strength was 2250 serviceable aircraft between Cherbourg and Norway. Against this Dowding had 708 aircraft, an increase in the number he had started the battle with owing to the tremendous effort by aircraft factory workers.

As far as the Luftwaffe was concerned, the battle for Britain began on 8 August and Goering, head of the mightiest Air Force in the world, set 10 August as the date for his major assault, his *Adlertag* ('Eagle Day'). However, bad weather forced a postponement.

On the 11th heavy raids were directed against Portland, while a diversionary attack was mounted in the area of Dover. Three RAF Squadrons went up to engage the Dover attack while seven were scrambled to patrol Weymouth, near Portland. These found 150 German aircraft, Ju 88s and He 111s escorted by Me 109s and Me 110s. Huge dogfights began as the bombers pressed home attacks against the docks, oil tanks, gasworks and army barracks. At the end of the day the Germans had lost 38 aircraft but the RAF lost 32 precious fighters.

Above: Junkers Ju 88 of KG54 brought down by antiaircraft guns at Portland Bill during the Luftwaffe's raid on Weymouth on 11 August 1940. Note extended wing dive-brake slats.
Above left: Prominent among a galaxy of veteran German fighter pilots during the battle was Adolf Galland (in white jacket), who commanded JG 26 *Schlageter.*
Top: A Heinkel He III, victim of 'Sailor' Malan of 74 Squadron, erupts in flames.
Left: Messerschmitt Bf 109 bags a barrage balloon over Dover, August 1940. Such 'victories' counted as one-half when credited to Luftwaffe fighter pilots.

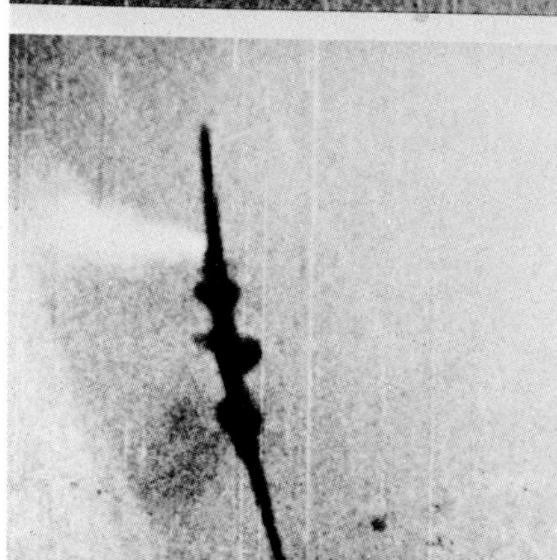

The next day was equally hard for the RAF defenders, as raids were directed against Portsmouth, radar stations and coastal airfields. The arithmetic was a little better. Some 31 Germans were shot down for 22 RAF fighters, although the Germans claimed 70 Spitfires and Hurricanes destroyed. These exaggerated claims did little to help German Intelligence reporting to the Luftwaffe High Command. The claims included the total destruction of one Spitfire squadron at Manston – 65 Squadron. They had been taxying out for takeoff when Dorniers of KG2 bombed the base, but most of them got off amid bomb bursts to join in the battle above.

RAF Hawkinge was also badly hit. Two hangars and the station workshops were destroyed and the stores building was damaged. Twenty-eight bomb craters pitted the airfield but it was operational next morning. The next morning was Eagle Day – 13 August.

The Germans were still not fully aware of how the operational structure of RAF Fighter Command worked, a fact borne out by the many attacks against airfields not even used by the defending fighter force. They were also unaware as to how the reporting chain from radar stations was coordinated. Their reconnaissance flight interpretation made some astonishing revelations, most of which were totally inaccurate and misleading.

Eagle Day saw heavy attacks on Eastchurch airfield in the morning and against Portland, Southampton and airfields in Hampshire and Kent during the afternoon. It was a massive effort; 1485 sorties were flown by the Luftwaffe crews, the highest number to date. B Flight of 65 Squadron scrambled from Manston at 1530 hours and off Dover they spotted 20 Me 109s. One of the pilots engaged was Pilot Officer B E Finucane:

'Saw three 109s flying in formation . . . and attacked number three, firing fairly long bursts from 300 to 75 yards. 109 burst into flames and dived into the clouds. I then spotted a lone 109 climbing up 400 yards ahead. Closed to 200 yards and gave it a burst. Drawing near could see the 109 had orange wing tips. 109 half rolled very slowly and seemed to shudder then slowly spin away. . . .'

Pilot Officer P C F 'Paddy' Stevenson of 74 Squadron was flying as Number Two to Sailor Malan and saw an Me 109 chase after his leader:

'He must have thought I was an Me 109 but when he suddenly dived away I followed him and gave a two-second deflection burst. The EA (enemy aircraft) lurched slightly and went into a vertical dive. I saw the EA dive straight into the sea 15 miles SE of Dover and disappear in a big splash.'

Stevenson climbed again and was about to engage more Me 109s when he was hit from behind. Looking back he saw a dozen Me 109s on his tail, half of whom seemed to be firing at him. His Spitfire was hit and he had to get out as he went into a dive:

'I pulled the hood back. I got my head out of the cockpit and the slipstream tore the rest of me clear out of the machine. My trouser leg and both shoes were torn off. I saw my machine crash into the sea a mile off Deal.'

The pilots of 609 Squadron got in among a formation of Ju 87s over Lyme Bay shortly after 1600 hours and shot down six of them without loss. Pilot Officer D M Crook, Number Three in Blue Section, saw several Me 109s pass right under his squadron:

'I immediately broke away and attacked one which was behind the rest. Fired a good burst from dead astern. He rocked violently and then turned over and burst into flames and crashed near Hardy's Monument behind Weymouth.'

Right: Out of ammunition and fuel, Hurricanes of 32 Squadron let down at Biggin Hill on 15 August 1940. Note airman with flag to guide aircraft through a network of bomb craters on the grass airfield.
Inset right: The parade ground at RAF Hemswell, Lincolnshire, receives a direct bomb hit on 27 August 1940.
Left: Junkers Ju 88, victim of the 13 August battles.
Above left: Messerschmitt Bf 110 at the receiving end of a Spitfire's guns.

Above: Airmen threading .303-inch ammunition belts into the wing boxes of a 610 Squadron, AAF Hurricane.
Above Left: Engine fitters testing the Merlin engine of a Hurricane. Note fabric-covered ports of the starboard wing's four-gun battery.

At the other end of the scale, the Hurricanes of 56 Squadron did not fare so well. They broke through some scattered cloud to meet between 12–20 Ju 88s, escorted by some 30 Me 109s with Me 110s above. Seeing the Hurricanes the Ju 88s began to jettison their bombs and turn over Canterbury – then the Me 110s came hurtling down and the air was full of twisting aircraft, Hurricanes, Me 110s and Me 109s. As one pilot put it:

'The 109s hurtle past and then up. Straight above are about 40 109s and one Hurricane. The whole sight is so commonplace and natural. Forty odd aircraft are wheeling aimlessly, slowly, like so many plovers on a windy day, yet it is a fight for life.'

Three Me 110s were claimed destroyed, but two Hurricanes went down in flames and their pilots were badly burned. Another also took to his parachute but was wounded, while a fourth crash landed at RAF Hawkinge. A fifth pilot hit an Me 110 but was blasted by another. He too left his crippled fighter, delayed deploying his parachute from 12,000–6000 feet in order to clear the battle area, and eventually landed in the sea two and a half miles from the beach, but successfully swam ashore.

At the end of this momentous day the statistics were better, 45 German aircraft brought down for the loss of just 13 RAF fighters. Ten of the pilots were saved

Below: Armorers working quickly to rearm a Spitfire of 19 Squadron at Duxford.

although some were wounded. Yet both sides exaggerated the claims; the Germans estimated the loss to the RAF to be at least 70 fighters and 18 Bristol Blenheims.

On the 14th raids were less intense but airfields were the main targets. Manston was bombed again by a sneak raid by Me 110s which destroyed four hangars. In the afternoon Middle Wallop was hit. No 609 Squadron's hangar was set on fire, and the main doors were blown down onto three airmen. Other, less-important airfields were also bombed. In the air only five RAF planes were lost as against 21 German machines.

The pressure continued unabated. On 15 August the Germans mounted massive attacks, with raids coming from all three *Luftflotten* in the greatest effort of the battle. Again it was RAF airfields which took the brunt of these assaults.

British radar detected a massive buildup of enemy aircraft all along the enemy coast in the late morning. Then they came. Over 100 headed in toward Hawkinge and Lympne. At 1140 hours Flying Officer A Eyre of 615 Squadron found enemy aircraft over Folkestone:

'Suddenly Blue 3 (Pilot Officer K T Lofts) noticed six 109s behind and above coming out of the sun. Blue 3 got onto the leading 109 and I gave him three bursts of five seconds, attacking from behind, above and below. He burst into flames about 8000 feet and baled out.'

Then in the north a raid was mounted by *Luftflotte* 5, hoping to meet little opposition while the defenders were busy over the south coast. An estimated force of over 30 raiders turned out to be 65 bombers and 34 Me 110s. The attacks were directed against Newcastle and Sunderland in the north, and Driffield further to the south. The radar had everything under control and far from having an easy time of it, this German force found Spitfires and Hurricanes waiting for them. They lost 16 bombers and seven fighters, and the RAF lost just one Hurricane and one pilot.

In the south Manston was raided again by low-flying Me 109s which destroyed two parked Spitfires. Then Martlesham was attacked by Stukas and Messerschmitts. At the same time 100 raiders headed in toward Deal, followed by 150 over Folkestone. Seven RAF squadrons intercepted them but the heavy fighter escort kept them occupied. Eastchurch was bombed as were factories at Rochester. Radar sites at Dover, Rye, Bawdsey and Foreness were attacked but without any real success. In the late afternoon some 250 raiders came in, crossing the coast near the Isle of Wight, spreading raids out over Hampshire and Wiltshire. Middle Wallop, Odiham and Worthy Down airfields were the targets. Eleven RAF squadrons intercepted this force, causing losses totalling 25 for the loss of 11 fighters. Nos 87 and 213 Squadrons up from Exeter engaged part of this raid, finding a huge formation of German aircraft coming in from the south; Ju 87s with Me 109s and Me 110s stacked up behind them. Squadron 87's Commanding Officer gave the order to attack and within minutes he was shot down and killed. Three others of the squadron went down in the fight, one pilot was killed, a second was wounded and the third baled out. Flight Lieutenant I R Gleed dived to the attack:

'I dived unseen by EA out of the sun, attacking a 110 which burst into flames. Broke away, climbed and dived for vertical attack on a 110. Starboard engine of 110 caught fire and it broke formation.'

He was then attacked by two Me 109s:

'They attacked me, one did a head-on attack, the other made for my tail. Got a good burst at engine and underside of head-on 109 then aileron turned vertically downwards.'

At 1815 hours another raid of over 70 aircraft approached Biggin Hill and Kenley but actually bombed West Malling and later Croydon. This was followed by an Me 110 raid on a factory just south of London near Croydon. Nos 32 and 111 Squadrons intercepted them to shoot down four.

By the end of the day, 182 German aircraft had been claimed by the RAF, with losses of 34 fighters. Actual German losses totalled 75, but it was still a significant victory. The Germans claimed 101 victories. The day's fighting had been ferocious; the Germans had flown 1786 sorties, the RAF 974. One outcome was that *Luftflotte* 5 made no further major contribution to the battle, its bombers going to *Luftflotte* 2 later in August. Another was that the Ju 87 and Me 110 were finally deemed to be inadequate for their allotted tasks. Owing to the bomber losses, the Me 109 pilots were subsequently not allowed a free rein to combat RAF fighters, being ordered to stay close to the bombers. This was totally against the purpose for which the Me 109 had been designed. In future, therefore, they had to await the assaults by Spitfires and Hurricanes rather than seek out their adversaries.

The Luftwaffe's fury continued the next day despite the losses of the 15th. Airfields were once again subjected to attack, while the RAF flung themselves at the raiding aircraft. All remained quiet until an hour before midday when a series of raids was flown over Kent and Norfolk. Manston and West Malling were bombed yet again. Three heavy raids were mounted at midday which made for the Thames Estuary, Dover and Southampton. This split the defending fighters – an estimated 350 German aircraft were reported. Twelve squadrons from 10, 11 and 12 Groups were scrambled to intercept. Tangmere, Gosport,

Above: Eric James Brindley Nicolson, VC, DFC, the only fighter pilot awarded a Victoria Cross during the war.
Right: H M Stephen, DSO, (left) and J C Mungo-Park, DFC of 74 'Tiger' Squadron, Summer 1940.

Lee-on-Solent and Brize Norton were all hit but only Tangmere was a fighter field. Flight Lieutenant R F Boyd of 602 Squadron based at Tangmere's satellite base at Westhampnett made what is probably the quickest kill of the battle. Scrambling when Tangmere was being bombed, he ran straight into a Ju 87, shot it down and was back on the ground in less than a minute after takeoff.

These raids cost the Germans a further 45 aircraft, the RAF losing 22 and eight pilots. One of these was the Hurricane flown by Flight Lieutenant J B Nicolson of 249 Squadron. He and his section became embroiled with German raiders over Southampton at 1245 hours. It was Nicolson's first taste of action. Following an abortive chase after three Ju 88s, he and his two wingmen were rejoining the main squadron formation when they were bounced by Me 109s. All three Hurricanes were hit; one pilot was forced to land at Boscombe, a second baled out only to have his parachute shredded by ground fire, sending him to his death. Nicolson's machine was set ablaze and he was wounded. He heard four big bangs as cannon shells from an attacking Me 109 hit home:

'The first shell tore through the hood over my cockpit and sent splinters into my left eye. One splinter I discovered later, nearly severed my eyelid. I couldn't see through that eye for blood. The second cannon shell struck my spare petrol tank and set it on fire. The third shell crashed into the cockpit and tore off my right trouser leg. The fourth shell struck the back of my left shoe. It shattered the heel of the shoe and made quite a mess of my left foot.

I was just thinking of jumping out when suddenly a Messerschmitt 110 whizzed under me and got right in my gun-sight. . . . I pressed the gun button for the Messerschmitt was in nice range; I plugged him first time and could see my tracer bullets entering the German machine.'

Despite the flames he continued to attack until he finally was forced to take to his parachute. Wounded and badly burned he survived to receive Fighter Command's only Victoria Cross of the war.

Hurricanes of 615 Squadron were in evidence during a raid near Brighton at 1615 hours. Pilot Officer J A P McClintock attacked one He 111 he found out of formation. He opened fire from 300 yards closing in to 50. The Heinkel's starboard engine began to pour out smoke, followed by flames, then it went down. Pilot Officer C R Young attacked two others, one of which he left smoking. The second, hit by a long burst, went down into cloud and Young followed it. Coming out he fired again from 100 yards. The bomber levelled out at sea level, streaming smoke, but a third burst sent it crashing into the sea leaving a large green swirl on the water.

Flight Lieutenant P C Hughes, an Australian with 234 Squadron, shot down two Me 109s at around 1830 hours south of the Isle of Wight. He saw 50 Me 109s circling above him and led his section in a climbing attack:

'I fired a deflection shot at the nearest 109 . . . it caught fire and blew up. I felt a jolt and turned sharply and found another 109 on my tail. He immediately climbed away in front of me where I shot him behind the cockpit. He caught fire and crashed into the sea. Four Ju 87s went by, heading south. I closed to attack but as I fired my tailplane got shot through by a 109. My aircraft dived and my tabs were shot away.'

The next major assault against RAF airfields came on the 18th. Kenley, Biggin Hill, Croydon and West Malling were all attacked. Some 100 bombs fell on Kenley,

destroying four Hurricanes, one Blenheim and three training types. Several hangars were destroyed and there were some personnel casualties. Kenley's 615 Squadron was attacked by Me 109s at high level. One pilot was lost, another baled out wounded and two more force landed, one being wounded.

Flying Officer F Gruska, a Polish pilot flying with 65 Squadron from Rochford, was reported missing at 1330 hours. His wrecked Spitfire with his body still in the cockpit was recovered from Stodmarsh near Canterbury, in July 1975 – 35 years later!

A massed Stuka attack on Ford and Thorney Island airfields was met by 152, 601, 602 and 234 Squadrons. Sixteen of the dive bombers were shot down, six more being damaged, two of which crashed at their base. Eight escorting Me 109s were also shot down but four Spitfires and two Hurricanes were lost.

Flying Officer W Rhodes-Moorhouse, son of the World War I VC winner, was a flight leader with 601 Squadron, although he often led the squadron in action. He got one of the Me 109s:

'There were two formations of Ju 87s, 20 machines in each, flying in close vic formation and stepped up in line astern was about 20 Me 109s above and to the sides. I gave the order for sections to form line astern and turning right I dived on the rear formation of Ju 87s making a head-on attack from the starboard bow. I saw no result from this attack. Passing quickly I became engaged with a lot of Me 109s at which I fired a number of short bursts . . . only one of these did I see crash as I had no time to follow or watch results of my attack.'

The day was another disaster for the Luftwaffe, 71 of their aircraft failed to get home. Twenty-seven RAF fighters and 10 pilots were lost. The 18th saw the death-knell of the Ju 87 over England, until late autumn at any rate. This made a total of 194 Luftwaffe aircraft lost between 15–18 August, with many more damaged.

Although the RAF was still suffering casualties it was nevertheless making its presence felt. Yet Keith Park was extremely conscious of the dangers his pilots were in and had to try and restrain their exuberance in engaging enemy fighters which in themselves posed no danger to Britain. His fighter strength had to damage the German bombers and stop them turning his fighter bases into rubble.

After the mammoth battles of the last few days there was a relative calm owing to bad weather between 19–23 August. The latter date ended the second phase of the battle which had cost the Luftwaffe in the region of 300 aircraft. The third phase began on the 24th. It was the crucial phase for Fighter Command – the Germans were after its blood – the RAF had to be destroyed.

Left: Cuthbert Orde sketch of Flight Lieutenant 'Willie' Rhodes-Moorhouse, DFC of 601 Squadron, AAF.
Below: Pilot Officer A N C Weir, DFC, of 145 Sqn, later killed in action.

Below: Max Aitken, DSO, DFC, son of Lord Beaverbrook, served in 601 Sqn.

Bottom: A victim of the clashes on 23 August, a Bf 110, goes on public display at Hendon Park.

3. AIRFIELDS ATTACKED

The fighter pilots of the RAF were tiring. The previous weeks had been a hard slog. Pilots in the south of England had already been called to perform Herculean tasks almost daily. Readiness was at dawn – always at dawn. Readiness states varied from cockpit 'standby' of two minutes or readiness in the dispersal hut (or outside it in the sunshine) of five minutes. From time to time the squadron might be put down at 15 or 30 minutes availability, which gave the pilots time to go for a wash or bath or a hot meal.

Pilot Officer H A C Bird-Wilson, a member of 17 Squadron based at Debden for the first two phases of the battle, remembers those moments which began with the telephone ringing at dispersal. Most rings meant 'scramble,' excitement, acceleration of heart beats and a dash to the aircraft. On a dawn scramble it was known

Left: Men of 74 Squadron at their dispersal hut. At left Henryk Szcesny, DFC from Poland, with J C Mungo-Park, DFC (center).
Below left: Spitfire pilots of 610 Squadron, AAF relax between sorties at Biggin Hill.
Right: The Operations Room at HQ Fighter Command, RAF Bentley Priory, Middlesex, in 1940, with controllers and WAAF plotters around the central plot table.

for some pilots to scramble in their pajamas. Takeoffs from the grass airfield were usually in squadron strength of four sections of three Hurricanes, from two different corners of the airfield. At times 12 Hurricanes approached each other in the center of the airfield, lifting up over each other. Somehow they got away with it. The climb-out vector was always to the southeast to the left of London. Climbs were always made flat-out and with full throttle. Their ground controllers were superb and information was continually passed to the pilots, such as, enemy formation of 160 plus approaching the south coast at 12,000 feet, and above there are more bandits joining up with them – so climb harder!

It was a strange phenomenon, but many individual squadrons scrambled flew on their own. Each climbed to engage the enemy as just one unit, but hoped that somewhere near would be at least one other 12-man squadron. (Harold Bird-Wilson recalls this feeling vividly.) In contrast, Pilot Officer H M Stephen who flew with 74 Squadron, remembers being too damn scared of his legendary Commanding Officer, Sailor Malan, to think of anything else than to climb hard and get stuck into the Germans.

If squadrons engaged alone there would be 12 against 100 or more aircraft. As they fought as small units they had little idea of what the overall picture was. They took off, flew hard, fought hard and those who got back waited for the next call. They learned little of what was going on outside their immediate circle of action. They heard the news bulletins, of course, and read newspapers, but it did not mean that much to them. Even their squadron commanders knew little more and they certainly did not know about the whole picture of the battle. The individual pilot merely lived from dawn readiness until released at dusk, and with dawn at 0330 hours or so, it was a long day. Little wonder they slept where they sat or lay between flights.

At their dispersal points the pilots had certain creature comforts. Some had easy chairs, others had camp beds pulled out into the sunshine. There was the inevitable record player and sometimes a radio. Twelve men would sit in the warm sun in a variety of uniform or flying clothing, Mae West life jackets on. Within a short distance stood their aircraft, trolley starter accumulator plugged in. Each fighter's ground crew sitting or lying nearby was ready to start the machine as soon as the yell galvanized their pilots into a run toward them.

Everyone's day started early. If the pilots were ready at dawn then the ground crews were up earlier, testing the engines, running them up and checking them over. Flight sergeants tried to get the most aircraft available following the previous day's battle damage. Each aircraft would have its daily inspection.

Most pilots were woken up still tired. Their cheery batmen would ignore the rude comments that would greet them as they woke their pilots. Once up those who could concentrate would gulp down mugs of tea before getting themselves down to the flights. They would look over their own aircraft, talk to the ground crew, ensure that their parachute was ready and that the flying helmet was in position, usually draped over the gun sight, ready to be pulled on as they sat in the cockpit and were strapped in by a crewman. Everyone hoped for bad weather but, generally speaking, the summer of 1940 was beautifully warm and sunny.

In the early days, many pilots were physically sick in the early mornings. In 74 Squadron for example, after they had washed, shaved and drunk a cup of tea, they would be off to the airfield. Before reaching dispersal, several of them were sick, usually getting rid of the last of the beer drunk the previous evening. Drinking the odd pint or two helped guarantee a few hours deep sleep – an important consideration. The squadron doctor wondered why this sickness occurred and discovered that being so early in the morning, coupled with nervous tension (this might be their last day on earth), the body's sugar content was low, and breakfast was still some hours away. The problem was solved by having a handy supply of barley sugar sweets to suck.

There was no special flying clothing in 1940, pilots simply flew in something comfortable; an old uniform, with perhaps a jumper or pullover, covered perhaps by an overall. Neither the Hurricane or Spitfire had any cockpit heating and within minutes a pilot could be at 30,000 feet where the outside temperature was a good deal colder than on the ground! Irvin jackets too, although bulky, helped keep the body warm.

Sitting in the sun was pleasant enough but the ever-present danger was often just minutes away. At dawn readiness the pilots usually nodded off to sleep right away, they were half asleep anyway. If there had been a binge the night before, the pilot might trot over to his airplane and take a whiff of oxygen. Another method of sobering up was used by the medical officer. He would give the pilot a special mixture tasting oddly of toothpaste, which some pilots thought it was anyway. The pilots had to be prepared to give their all in the coming battle.

Death and destruction for the RAF and the Luftwaffe continued with the commencement of the third phase of the battle on 24 August. The shortage of RAF pilots had recently become critical. Support came from the Fleet Air Arm, who lent 56 pilots during the battle. A further 30 or so came from Bomber and Army Co-operation Commands. Some new squadrons also became available, a Polish, a Czech and a Canadian squadron helped to swell Fighter Command's ranks or fill a gap left by a unit pulled out of the front line for a rest.

On Saturday 24 August, airfields were attacked in the southeast of England. Manston was evacuated and Portsmouth was hit heavily. North Weald was bombed by 20 bombers which hit station buildings, two messes, the married quarters and stores, but otherwise did not affect the efficiency of the base.

By midafternoon Keith Park had all his squadrons airborne and engaged, so he requested help from Leigh-Mallory's 12 Group. Leigh-Mallory had been keen to try and form his squadrons into wings in order to bring a larger force of fighters into action at one time. This made sense but unfortunately it took time to organize once they were in the air and more often than not in the days ahead, the raiders were on their way home before the 12 Group Wing could get at them. On the 24th only the Spitfires of 19 Squadron became engaged after the failure of the wing to form over Duxford. The six pilots of 19 Squadron were flying cannon-armed Spitfires which were suffering from gun-stoppages at this stage of RAF cannon development. However, Flight Lieutenant B J E Lane's guns scored:

'I climbed up and at approximately 1610 hours got astern of a ragged formation of about 40 Me 110s and Do 215s, escorted by ten Me 109s above and to the rear. I approached from below . . . and almost got within range when 110s saw us and turned towards us. A dog-fight ensued and I opened fire from below and astern of nearest 110 but was forced to break away as tracer appeared over my head from enemy aircraft astern. Got below another 110 and fired slight deflection burst at port engine and observed a large part of engine or mainplane fly off. Enemy aircraft dived and I observed it crash into the sea.'

Another pilot, Sergeant R F Hamlyn of 610 Squadron claimed the destruction of five German aircraft during the day, in three hectic sorties. Altogether the RAF flew 936 sorties on the 24th, and lost 22 aircraft. The Luftwaffe losses totalled 38 during 1030 sorties.

The following day *Luftflotte* 3 sent a large force toward Weymouth. Nos 17, 87 and 609 Squadrons engaged this raid, destroying several raiders. Flying Officer Count M B Czernin of 17 Squadron shot down two and shared a third with 609 Squadron despite seeing his Commanding Officer shot down ahead of him during a battle with a gaggle of Me 110s:

'One broke. Chased and fired from above. Nose went down, EA burst into flames and crashed straight into the sea. Climbed and resumed attack. Beam attack and 110 broke away pouring smoke and went into a vertical dive, burst into flames and crashed into the sea. Resumed attack and had to break off as Spitfire on its tail firing at him. Shook him off and attacked 110

Above: A Heinkel He III perfectly aligned in a Hurricane's gun sight.
Right: Another member of 43 Squadron was John Simpson, seen here at Buckingham Palace on 6 August 1940 for investiture with a DFC.
Top left: Sergeant, later Wing Commander, R F 'Ronnie' Hamlyn, AFC, DFM of 610 Squadron, AAF.
Top center: Squadron leader B J E 'Sandy' Lane, DFC, commander of 19 Squadron at Duxford in 1940.
Top right: Flight Lieutenants Peter Townsend, DFC (left) and Caesar Hull, DFC of 43 'Fighting Cocks' Squadron. Hull, a South African, commanded the unit briefly before his death.

and after a long burst from quarter astern, nose dropped and it lost height . . . and glided down with both engines out. Broke off as obviously it was going to crash and saw two Spitfires attack it again. One baled out and then EA nose dived into a wood two miles SE of Dorchester and burst into flames.'

No 609 Squadron were in the thick of it and shot down four Me 110s and damaged several others. No 87 Squadron got three escorting Me 109s but lost one pilot, Sergeant S R E Wakeling. His voice came over the radio that he had had his hand blown off by a cannon shell but he thought he would make it to base. He did not. He probably fainted from loss of blood.

The pace was beginning to tell in many squadrons. No 32 Squadron, based at Biggin Hill, had sustained a number of casualties since mid-August and on the 18th lost five of its Hurricanes with four pilots wounded or with burns. It lost one more on the 22nd and on the 24th lost another five of its aircraft with one pilot wounded. On the 25th it lost two aircraft and one pilot. This reduced 32 Squadron's effective strength to eight. It was pulled out of the battle area.

In recent raids by the Luftwaffe, bombs had been dropped upon the suburbs of London. Although this was not planned by Luftwaffe leaders it led to a reprisal raid by Bomber Command on the night of 25/26 August, Berlin being the obvious target. Little damage was inflicted but the effect upon German morale was considerable. However, it started a chain of events which led to London being a major target for Luftwaffe bombers and swung the weight of their effort away from Dowding's reeling fighter bases.

However, that was still a few days off and in the meantime, RAF fighter airfields continued to be the primary target. No 1 Canadian Squadron moved from RAF Northolt to North Weald and saw its first major action in the afternoon of 26 August. No 616 Squadron, who had been involved in the raid against the northeast on 15 August and who had now moved south to Kenley, were hit badly. Scrambled to intercept raiders over Dungeness they arrived too late to engage the bombers but were attacked by a large force of Me 109s. Six of their aircraft were shot down, two pilots were killed and three others wounded. Meanwhile the Canadians were vectored onto a raid of Dornier 17s, escorted by Me 109s, but it was the bombers which inflicted the damage. Three Hurricanes were hit by accurate return fire from the German air gunners, killing one attacking pilot and forcing two other pilots to crash land, their aircraft were written off. One of the latter was the Commanding Officer, Squadron Leader E A McNab.

Portsmouth was attacked at around 1600 hours when 50 He 111s escorted by more than 100 single- and twin-engined Messerschmitts came in near the Isle of Wight. Between them 10 and 11 Groups sent up eight squadrons but only 43, 602 and 615 Squadrons managed to intercept. One pilot of 43 Squadron, Pilot Officer H L North, was wounded but:

'. . . I echeloned my section to port and attacked head-on a formation of six He 111s. They were the lower layer of a much larger mass stepped up. I could only fire the briefest of bursts and broke away below without noticing any results. I climbed back to the attack and got in two long . . . bursts. Quantities of smoke was emitted, the undercarriage dropped, one person at least baled out and the enemy was last seen diving, but I got hit by explosive shell which went into my shoulder and arm.'

Despite this wound, Pilot Officer North used up the remainder of his ammunition on another Heinkel which went down with one engine trailing smoke. Then North, having been hit again from behind, was forced to bale out.

It was not a good day for the Kenley squadrons, for in addition to 616 Squadron being bounced around midday, 615 Squadron lost four aircraft in the late afternoon, again by Me 109s. Keith Park's express orders were for RAF pilots to avoid wasteful combats with German fighters and to get at the bombers but it was not always possible to totally ignore the deadly Messerschmitts.

In the final days of August, there was no let up by Luftwaffe aircraft in attacking airfields, indeed the action on 30 and 31 August was, according to some pilots, the bloodiest of the battle. In 1054 sorties and 978 sorties respectively, the RAF lost 25 fighters on the 30th with 10 pilots killed, and 39 on the 31st with 14 pilots lost – some of the heaviest casualties of the battle. On the same dates the Germans lost 36 and 41 respectively.

Detling was bombed on the 30th and so was Biggin Hill, which reduced the base to a shambles and left 39 dead and 26 injured. One of the casualties on the 31st was the Commanding Officer of 253 Squadron, Squadron Leader T P Gleave. Gleave had shot down four Me 109s on the previous day.

Having led seven Hurricanes off, which was all that was left of Gleave's unit, they engaged enemy bombers. Returning to his base at Kenley, Gleave was hit from behind and below by an Me 109, which set his Hurricane on fire. The first thing he knew of the enemy's presence was a shattering crash as the whole of the instrument panel disappeared in front of his eyes. Bullets hit the reserve gasoline tank located between the panel and the engine, setting it on fire and spraying 28 gallons of gasoline in his lap. Fortunately Gleave had his cockpit canopy locked open so he was able to quickly release his harness and push forward on the stick. As the burning Hurricane went over the vertical he was shot straight out. His clothes were on fire so he chose not to open his parachute for fear of it too catching fire. He fell a couple of thousand feet, felt cooler so pulled the ripcord. As luck would have it he had broken his goggles the day before and had not had time to replace them. Consequently, when his face was badly burned, his eyelids were stuck closed together. Yet he could clearly hear the unmistakable sound of a Messerschmitt's engine as it came near but luckily it was forced away by a Spitfire. With that danger passed he managed to prise his eyes open and shortly afterward hit the ground in a clearing in the middle of a wood. He was terribly burned. Apart from his face and eyelids, his trousers had been burned away and skin on both legs had lifted and draped his legs like outsize plus fours. His gloves had been almost burned off and the skin from his wrists and hands hung down like paper bags. The underside of his right arm and elbow were also burned. As he sat in the clearing he came to the conclusion that the services of a doctor might be necessary!

Another commander wounded on the 31st was Squadron Leader P W Townsend of 85 Squadron operating from Croydon. Bombs began to fall on the east side of the airfield as the Hurricanes became airborne.

They, like 253 Squadron, had been sent off too late. Climbing at full throttle and with black mushrooms of exploding antiaircraft shells staining the sky to the south above Biggin Hill, they could see Me 110s above. As he fight began, Townsend pushed his cockpit hood back so as to see the enemy better. Then Me 109s came diving down. Townsend fought one, sending it down belching smoke. Engaging another he could see an Me 110 heading toward him, its guns flashing. His Hurricane took hits and his left foot was knocked off the rudder pedals as gasoline gushed into the cockpit. His machine dived, trailing smoke but luckily it did not catch fire. In front of him his windshield was starred with bullet marks for the bulletproof screen had taken the enemy's slugs. Moments later he took to his parachute with a wounded foot.

At RAF Hornchurch that same day, raiders screamed in and caught 54 Squadron on the ground as they struggled to get airborne. An estimated 60 bombs hit along a line from the dispersal pens to the gasoline dump and beyond. The last three Spitfires were caught and all were totally wrecked, but all three pilots miraculously survived. Flight Lieutenant A C Deere had one wing and his propeller blown off, the machine turned over and plowed along the airfield on its back. Sergeant J Davis was blown across two fields and into a river while Pilot Officer E F Edsall was blown up but landed right side up. He scrambled clear to help Deere out of his smashed airplane as bombs continued to rain down. All three pilots were ready for action the next day.

As August ended it became evident to Luftwaffe commanders that despite the claims of its fighter pilots, the RAF was far from being knocked out of the sky. They also realized that the output of fighter production from British factories and from repair depots, had been considerably underestimated. The German bomber crews continued to report aggressive actions by RAF fighters. There was not the slightest sign that the British boys were relaxing in their determination to get to grips with the enemy.

Despite this view, Fighter Command's reserves were running dangerously low but it could just maintain support for 10, 11 and 12 Group's losses. Dowding's main concern was for pilots, especially leaders. A dozen squadron commanders had been killed or wounded and nearly 40 flight commanders had similarly been knocked out. On some sorties, sections, flights and, on occasion, even whole squadrons were led by junior officers and experienced non-commissioned officer pilots, such as Ginger Lacey (501 Squadron), Geoffrey Allard (85), Archie McDowell (602) and 'Grumpy' Unwin (19). Of all the experienced fighter pilots in Dowding's force, there were only about 500 officers or sergeants and each had to fly four, five or even six sorties each day.

It was inevitable that replacement pilots from training units had not the length of

Above center: Alan Deere (left) and Colin Gray, two New Zealanders who fought with 54 Squadron during the battle.
Above right: Flight Lieutenant Geoffrey 'Sammy' Allard, DFC, DFM of 85 Squadron. An ex-Halton aircraft apprentice, Allard fought in France and the battle over Britain, claiming two dozen victories; only to die in a simple flying accident in 1941.
Above left: J H 'Ginger' Lacey, DFM, one of the leading scorers during the battle, who flew with 501 Squadron, AAF.
Above: Pilots found the Spitfire highly maneuverable and easy to fly.
Left: Group of 19 Squadron Spitfire pilots at Duxford, 1940. Seated on the wing are Squadron Leader B J E Lane, DFC (OC) and Flight Sergeant 'Grumpy' Unwin, DFM.

training that would have been desirable. Some became easy prey to a still victorious Luftwaffe fighter arm. The squadrons were taking a battering. No 151 Squadron was pulled back from the front, down to 10 aircraft and 12 pilots. No 56, without a Commanding Officer and with only seven aircraft went to a quieter location. No 43 had lost two Commanding Officers and its third, Squadron Leader C B Hull, was to last just one week. No 610 Squadron was about to leave for the north and a rest. The fate of Britain now rested totally on the young shoulders of Fighter Command's fighter pilots as September began.

The first day of September saw the continuance of attacks on air bases with four major assaults. Biggin Hill was attacked for the sixth time in three days. No 79 Squadron was now Biggin's only defense and pilots returning from an interception found the airfield pitted with bomb craters, forcing them to divert to Croydon. Eastchurch, Detling and the docks at Tilbury were other targets. Over 120 raiders returned to these targets after lunch while two further raids went for Hawkinge, Lymne and Detling in the late afternoon. In the last raid Biggin was hit yet again, knocking out the operations room. Four Spitfires were also destroyed and the armory set ablaze.

On 2 September, there were four raids. This time Eastchurch, North Weald, Rochford and again Biggin Hill were attacked. The raiders totalled around 250 aircraft, an awe-inspiring sight for individual squadrons to see flying in.

Two tragic losses occurred on the 1st and 2nd. Two fighter-pilot brothers fell within hours of each other. On 1 September Flying Officer Patrick Woods-Scawen of 85 Squadron died when leading his section. No 85 Squadron was led by Flight Sergeant Allard against a vast armada of aircraft, but enemy fighters hurled themselves at the squadron to shoot down five of the Hurricanes. One pilot was killed, two wounded and one missing (the fifth crash landed unhurt). The missing pilot was Woods-Scawen who was found on the 6th – his parachute had failed to open. The next day his brother Tony, flying with 43 Squadron, was shot down by Me 109s just 24 hours after his brother. Both had won the DFC in the battle.

Also on the 2nd, Pilot Officer R H Hillary of 603 Squadron shot down two Me 109s, probably a third and damaged a fourth in three sorties. On the second sortie, just after midday:

'When five miles off Sheppey I saw a formation of 109s. I chased one over to France and fired at it. I saw the EA's perspex hood break up but as it was a head-on attack I was unable to see anything more of it. I then saw a squadron of 109s at the same height as myself, 23,000 feet . . . I attacked outside Me 109 with three short bursts and saw it spin down emitting black and white smoke. After a few seconds it caught fire.'

Sergeant J H Ginger Lacey, flying in 501 Squadron, also destroyed an Me 109. He saw three Messerschmitts about to dive on his squadron and climbed to engage them:

'I was able to get in a good burst of about five seconds at a red cowled Me 109, but the EA immediately turned and I was unable to bring my guns to bear, but after about 30 seconds of circling, the Me 109 pilot jumped out and did a delayed drop of about 5,000 feet before opening his parachute.'

The next day, the first anniversary of the war, more heavy attacks were directed against the southern airfields, the now familiar build up of aircraft over Calais coming onto the radar screens around 0800 hours. Their allotted targets were Hornchurch, North Weald and Debden, although North Weald was the only one reached by the raiders. One of the defending fighter pilots was the same Richard Hillary of 603 Squadron who had done so well the day before. He later wrote of his feelings as he sat in his Spitfire following the scramble call:

'I felt the usual sick feeling in the pit of my stomach, as though I was about to run a race, and then I was too busy getting into position to feel anything.'

Below: 'Red' Tobin, 'Shorty' Keough, and 'Andy' Mamedoff; three US pilots who fought in the Battle of Britain.

Above: A Heinkel He III has its starboard engine shattered by a Spitfire's guns.

Above right: Trio from 242 Squadron at Coltishall. Flight Lieutenant W L 'Willie' McKnight, DFC, Squadron Leader Douglas Bader, DSO, and Flight Lieutenant Eric Ball, DFC. McKnight and Ball were later killed on operations.
Below: Hurricanes of 242 Squadron.

Making the mistake of following a 109 for too long he was himself attacked from behind. His Spitfire burst into flames and for several agonizing seconds he was trapped in the blazing cockpit before the machine broke up and he was flung into space. He, like Tom Gleave, was very badly burned and spent months in hospital. Later he wrote his classic book *The Last Enemy*.

Sergeant D Fopp of 17 Squadron was also shot down and burned on the 3rd:

'We were scrambled late and did not get sufficient altitude to achieve a favourable attacking position from above, with the result that we had to attack head-on at about 20,000 feet, and hope to break up the large formation of Do 17s, with guns blazing which did separate them considerably. I had just put a Dornier's engine out and he was smoking badly when I saw three Me 110s coming in behind in line astern. By this time I had run out of ammunition but decided that as I could not match them for speed I would turn into them and simulate an attack. This I did and to my astonishment and joy they broke all round me so I immediately half rolled and dived for the deck. Unfortunately for me one of them was also below and behind out of sight and managed to put a cannon shell into my radiator, with the result that all I heard was a thump and the next second I was sitting in a ball of fire.'

Fopp managed to bale out and put out his smoldering tunic and trousers. He landed in trees but got out of his harness safely, walked out of the wood and met two farm laborers. In his condition he could have been any nationality but his language was such that they were quickly convinced that he was British!

Pilot Officer D W Hanson, also of 17 Squadron, shot down a Dornier in this action but his machine was hit by return fire. Hanson had difficulty in getting out of his Hurricane and when finally he succeeded he was only 100 feet up. His parachute failed to deploy in the short drop and he was killed when he hit the ground, almost at the same moment as his machine crashed on Foulness Island.

Honors were even on the war's first anniversary – 16 Germans shot down, for 16 RAF fighters and eight pilots.

It was slightly better the next day, 25 Germans for 17 RAF machines. The Germans went for sector RAF stations and the Vickers factory at Brooklands. A force of Me 110s got through the defenses by flying at low level and following the railroad track over Guildford. They hit Brooklands, where Wellington bombers were being built. Alert ground gunners shot down two Me 100s and others hurriedly got rid of their bombs, as Hurricanes of 253 Squadron got in among them, but nevertheless the Germans did considerable damage. Some 88 workers were killed and 600 were injured. Output almost stopped for four days as machine and erecting shops were badly damaged.

Several Me 110s were shot down by the Hurricanes.

No 253 Squadron was based at Kenley, sharing the base with 66 Squadron who did not have a good day. They lost five of their Spitfires and all the pilots involved were wounded. No 222 Squadron from Hornchurch lost three Spitfires and two pilots were killed. As if enemy fighters were not dangerous enough, Pilot Officer J M V Carpenter was hit by 'friendly' anti-aircraft fire over Kent and blown out of his cockpit. He landed in his parachute with only slight injuries.

The next day 66 Squadron lost three more aircraft, while 41 Squadron lost five including the squadron commander and one flight commander. No 19 Squadron also lost its commanding officer on the 5th.

On Friday 6 September, the final day of phase three, it was the Polish pilots of 303 Squadron who suffered at the hands of the Luftwaffe. Five of their aircraft were shot down although no pilots were killed. The Squadron's joint Commanding Officers, Squadron Leader R G Kellet, an Englishman, and Squadron Leader Z Krasnodebski, were both wounded. Both British flight commanders were also shot down and a Polish noncommissioned officer was wounded.

Four pilots from 601 Squadron based at Tangmere were shot down, two of whom were killed. One was Flying Officer C R Davis, an experienced South African pilot with several victories to his name, the other was Flying Officer Willie Rhodes-Moorhouse.

The Luftwaffe lost 378 of its aircraft during the third phase. The margin between victory and defeat was now very slender.

Below: Messerschmitt Bf 109E-4 of II/JG3 piloted by Oberleutnant Franz von Werra, shot down by 234 Squadron Spitfire over Kent in the afternoon of 5 September 1940.

Bottom: In theory the Spitfire was supposed to tackle the high-flying Messerschmitt cover formations and leave the bomber formations to the slower Hurricane.

Below: The erks (airmen) of 602 Squadron, AAF refuel and rearm a unit Spitfire.

4. THE BLITZ

The battle's fourth phase, marked by a change of tactics by the Luftwaffe, began on 7 September. It was clear now to the Luftwaffe High Command that RAF resistance was far from decreasing. During the period 24 August to 6 September, over 100 bombers had been lost despite the orders to German fighter pilots to stick close and defend the bomber formations. It appeared also that despite continual raids on RAF airfields, they were not being knocked out for any appreciable length of time.

Some believed that London should be the direct target, thereby causing the civilian population to crack and force the British Government to capitulate. Bombs had in fact been dropped on London by navigational error on the night of 25 August, which caused the reprisal raid already mentioned. Hitler gave Goering a free hand and it was just as well for Britain that he did, for Goering ended his attacks on RAF airfields in order to concentrate on the plum of a prize – London. It was to prove an incalculable error, but it saved Fighter Command. Plans were immediately put into operation to fly against London and the first assault took place on the 7th.

Prepared for further attacks on its airfields, the RAF were not even considering a raid on London when the radar screens showed a massive armada of aircraft heading toward the Thames Estuary – 300

Above: The aftermath of a raid on Coventry.
Left: London Docks after the first mass raid on London, 7 September 1940.

Right: The sky over Westminster recalls Stephen Spender's lines, '. . . and left the vivid air signed with their honour.'

bombers escorted by 600 fighters in two waves. The first wave flew direct to the Estuary, the other passed over Central London before turning back to the Estuary and the East End of London. Caught on the hop, the defending RAF fighters were unable to engage before many of the German aircraft had dropped their bombs. So while the airfields were being adequately defended, the road to London was open. Finally 11 Group got some units to intercept the huge armada and thereafter Hurricanes and Spitfires tried to nibble at them all the way back to the coast. It was to cost both sides dearly.

No 12 Group's Big Wing got into action, with 19, 242 and 310 Squadrons making preparations, when antiaircraft fire attracted them to part of the raid near North Weald. Squadron Leader B J E Lane, now Commanding Officer of 19 Squadron, saw them and attacked:

'A 110 dived in front of me and I led A Flight after it. Two Hurricanes were also attacking it. I fired a short burst as well as the other aircraft. Two baled out, one parachute failing to open. Enemy aircraft crashed one mile east of Hornchurch and one crewman landed nearby and was taken prisoner of war.'

Flight Lieutenant J H G McArthur of 609 Squadron went for a formation of bombers which he took to be Dorniers. (Dornier 17s and Me 110s were often confused during the battle):

'I went for the nearest bomber and opened fire at about 400 yards, meanwhile experiencing very heavy return crossfire from the bomber formation. After about 12 seconds smoke started to come from the port motor and it left the formation. . . . I waited until it got down to about 3000 feet

and then dived vertically on to it and fired off the rest of my ammunition. It kept going on down seemingly still under some sort of control, until it hit the water about 10 miles out from the centre of the Thames Estuary.'

Casualties among the RAF defenders totalled 28 fighters and 19 pilots. Some were experienced pilots and leaders. No 43 Squadron lost Ceasar Hull, who had won his DFC in the Norwegian campaign earlier in the year, and Flight Lieutenant R C Reynell, the Hawker test pilot who was flying operationally with the squadron. No

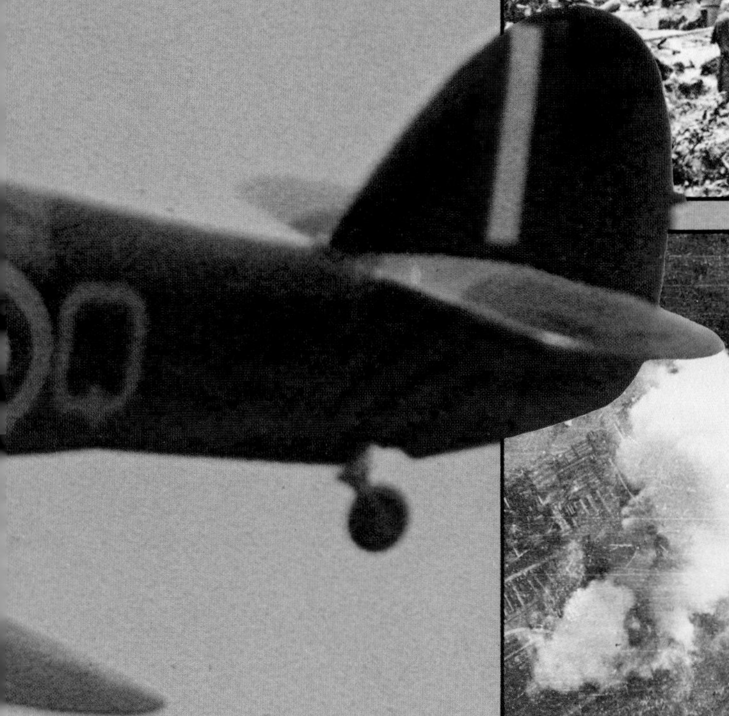

Above: Hurricane in markings of 111 Squadron.
Top right: The freak effect of a bomb blast on the night of 8/9 September 1940. Luckily the crew was in a nearby shelter.
Right: Dorniers from KG3 over Canning Town, London, on 7 September 1940.
Left: Air-to-air view of a Dornier bomber formation.

234 Squadron lost its Commanding Officer, Joe O'Brien, as well as its senior Flight Commander, Flight Lieutenant P C Hughes, DFC, who had claimed 16 victories in two months. Hughes was attacking a Dornier when its wing ripped off and smashed into his Spitfire, causing him to crash. No 257 Squadron was bounced by Me 109s and lost four aircraft and two pilots, including Flight Lieutenant H R A Beresford. It was not until 1979 that his remains and his shattered Hurricane were found in marshy ground on the Isle of Sheppey. No 303 Polish Squadron lost two aircraft with two more damaged. One of the damaged aircraft was flown by the British Flight Lieutenant A S Forbes who was slightly wounded. No 249 Squadron from North Weald lost six Hurricanes and one pilot plus three more wounded in fights with Me 109s.

German casualties totalled 41, of which 15 were Me 109s and seven were 110s. London had been heavily bombed and nearly 450 people had been killed in both central and suburban areas with over 1300 injured. The new phase in the Luftwaffe's offensive against Britain had begun. London and its populace would now have to 'take it' but at least the pressure was taken off Dowding's sorely pressed fighter bases. In addition the Luftwaffe began flying against London by night.

The next day the air action was light by recent comparisons and only night raids affected London, but on the 9th the battle flared again. London was bombed and raids were directed against factories in the Thames Estuary area as well as Brooklands. Some 28 German aircraft were shot down as against 19 British machines. Two days later, on 11 September, the losses were 25 German aircraft and a depressing 29 RAF aircraft with 17 pilots killed and six others wounded, during raids on London, Portsmouth and Southampton.

Keith Park was now, whenever possible, ordering paired squadrons to be used together. When squadrons at 'readiness' were sent against early raiders, the Spitfires would take on the escort fighters while an accompanying Hurricane unit went for the bombers. In their turn, the 'available' – 15 minutes – squadrons, brought to the 'readiness' state also in like pairs, to be ready to deal with subsequent waves of raiders. The 'available' – at 30 minutes – squadrons were then used singly to reinforce those units already engaged or to protect specific factory or airfield targets.

On the 11th, big enemy formations began to build up over Calais and Ostend in the early afternoon while others began to fly in from the Seine area and Cherbourg. Shortly afterward waves of Me 109s were in evidence over Kent. It was these Me 109s, as well as close escort 109s, that caused many of the RAF casualties.

Only two RAF pilots were lost on 12 September, but one was Wing Commander J S Dewar DSO, DFC, Wing Commander at Exeter and late Commanding Officer of 87 Squadron. He had been visiting friends at Tangmere and took off with them during

Above: Hurricanes of 303 *Kosciuszko* Squadron, Northolt in late September 1940.
Top right: Members of 303 (Polish) Squadron at Northolt, September 1940. From left: Z Henneberg, J A Kent (a Canadian Flight Commander) and M Feric.
Below: Hurricane pilots of 1 Squadron, RCAF at Northolt on 12 September 1940.

Right: Czech pilots of 310 Squadron at Duxford on 1 September 1940. Formed on 10 July, the unit flew its first combat sorties on 26 August. Kneeling, in RAF uniform, is Flight Lieutenant A Jefferies, DFC, an English Flight Commander. *Below:* Surviving crew members of a Heinkel He III being escorted from their crash at Burmash, Kent on 11 September – victims of a Spitfire pilot.

A view of a Hurricane coded in 242 Squadron markings.

Below: Heinkel He III crew survey bullet damage to their crashed bomber in France on return from a sortie.

Bottom: Hurricane RF-E, P3700, of 303 *Kosciuszko* Squadron at Northolt in September 1940.

Right: The remains of Hauptmann Ernst Püttman's KG3 Dornier Do 17Z-2 in the forecourt of Victoria Station, London on 15 September 1940.
Below right: Antiaircraft guns fire at the enemy in London.
Below: Sergeant Josef Frantisek, a Czech fighter who served with 303 (Polish) Squadron, scoring at least 16 victories. He was fated to die in a landing accident on 8 October 1940.

an alert. He failed to return and later his bullet-ridden body was found where he had fallen in his parachute. A few days later one of his old 87 Squadron's pilots chased a bomber 20 miles out to sea to shoot it down in personal revenge for Dewar's death.

The issue of shooting up pilots in their parachutes is a controversial one, but it did happen from time to time on both sides. One former Battle of Britain pilot told this author that in his squadron they had an unwritten law that if a German pilot was in his parachute over the French coast or within 10 miles of it they might have a go at him, but not if he was coming down over England or off the English coast. One of his companions was always for shooting them up wherever he found them!

The 13 September was also quiet, although one of the RAF's successful non-commissioned officer pilots, Ginger Lacey, had to take to his parachute after engaging an He 111 over Kent. It was a cloudy day and Lacey had volunteered to go up to try to locate a reported raider. Guided by ground control he found his prey and shot it down but his Hurricane was hit by return fire and he had to bale out. Later he was told that this Heinkel had bombed Buckingham Palace.

London was again attacked on the 14th although poor weather prevented any large-scale assault until the afternoon. A little after 1500 hours three raiders crossed the English coast and headed in along two routes – the Estuary and over Kent. Most of the raiders were fighters and in the scraps which occurred honors proved even, 14 to each side.

Yet it was to be the next day which turned out to be significant in many respects. For ever afterward, 15 September every year has been set aside as the Anniversary Day of the Battle of Britain. It saw the Germans heavily defeated in the air and ultimately the Germans were forced to change their policy against Britain.

For the Germans it was a repeat of the 7 September raid, in that it was supposed to be a prelude to invasion. Hitler had postponed his planned assault by sea and air, from early September to the 11th. Then he postponed it again to the 17th. However, the disastrous results of the 15th caused him to postpone the invasion indefinitely. While it is felt in some quarters that Hitler never seriously considered invading Britain, there is no doubt whatsoever that the people of Britain, and especially the war leaders, could see no other course open to Hitler.

By 1100 hours on Sunday 15 September mass formations of German aircraft clearly showed on the radar screens. Even at this stage the Germans had not totally realized how accurately the radar plots could identify size, course and height of their raids. No 11 Group scrambled 11 squadrons, 10 Group one and 12 Group its Big Wing of five squadrons.

As the Germans flew in from the coast toward London, in layers from 15,000–26,000 feet, they were continually harassed by RAF fighters whose young pilots flung themselves relentlessly at the vast horde of black-crossed bombers and fighters.

The tenacity of the RAF fighter pilots as well as the sheer number of fighters they could see, must have come as a great shock to many Luftwaffe flyers. It had been confidently predicted that Fighter Command was down to its last 'handful' of aircraft, and yet the Luftwaffe could see flight after flight, squadron after squadron, heading straight for them, their wing guns blazing. One of the attackers was Flying Officer J C Dundas of 609:

'(We) turned towards enemy aircraft which we identified as Dorniers and turned to intercept. There were many 109s on both sides of the bombers and above them. . . . I turned and attacked the EA in centre of formation from below and from the beam. As I passed I saw one of its motors stop. On breaking away I was attacked by a 109 from above and astern. . . . I was chased off by three 109s which peeled off from 20,000 feet above, but who gave themselves away by opening fire from excessive range.'

Squadron Leader J Sample, Commanding Officer of 504 Squadron also got in among the Dorniers. He attacked one which broke formation streaming smoke. Looking down he clearly saw the famous bend in the River Thames and also picked out the Oval cricket ground:

'I found myself below another Dornier which had white smoke coming from it. It was being attacked by two Hurricanes and a Spitfire. . . . I went to join in. I climbed up above and did a diving attack on him. Coming in to attack I noticed what appeared to be a red light shining in the rear gunner's cockpit but when I got closer I realised I was looking right through the gunner's cockpit into the pilot and observer's cockpit beyond. The red light was fire. I gave it a quick burst and as I passed him on the right I looked through the big glass nose of the Dornier. It was like a furnace inside. He began to go down and we watched. In a few seconds the tail came off and the bomber did a forward somersault and then went into a spin. After he had done two turns in his spin his wings broke off outboard of the engines.'

Sergeant R T Holmes of Sample's Squadron gained undying fame by shooting down a Dornier which crashed into the forecourt of Victoria Station. Holmes was hit by return fire and baled out, only to land ingloriously in a Chelsea garbage can.

As the assault continued into the afternoon, other units took to the air. One pilot airborne was the Station Commander of RAF Northolt, a fighter pilot from World War I, Group Captain S F Vincent. He was near Biggin Hill when he saw 18 Dorniers escorted by 20 Me 109s above:

'There was no other British fighters in sight, so I made a head-on attack on the first section of the bombers, opening fire at 600 yards and closing to 200 yards. I saw my DeWilde ammunition hit the EA. On breaking away I noticed that five of the bombers had turned round and were proceeding due south. I made further attacks on the retreating bombers . . . and could see the DeWilde hitting in each attack. One Dornier left the formation and lost height. With no ammunition left I could not finish it off.'

John Dundas was back in the air for another crack and again found Dornier bombers, this time above Rye:

'Red section attacked the rear wing of Dorniers and as they did so two Dorniers detached themselves from formation and tried to dive away. I selected one and went in after it had been attacked by a number of Red Section. Fired from 300 to 150 yards and closed to dead astern and slightly above. At first I experienced return fire and was twice hit. Then pieces began to fall off and flames came from its starboard wing and engine. After breaking away I saw EA spin down and members of the crew escape by parachute.'

Pilot Officer P S Turner, flying with 242 Squadron in 12 Group's Wing, was in the action, sending down an Me 109 probably destroyed before he attacked a Dornier from KG2:

'. . . observed a Do 215, attacked from abeam using full deflection. His starboard engine started to smoke, the 215 then slid into a gentle dive. It hit the ground and exploded between some houses on the north bank of the Thames east of Hornchurch. No people left the aircraft.'

Yet again German Intelligence estimates were wrong. The RAF's 'last 50 Spitfires' was only a figure on their reports. Although at the time an inflated figure of 185 German aircraft shot down put great heart into the British people and the RAF pilots, the true figure was 60. Even so, with damaged machines taken into account it was a savage blow to the Luftwaffe, particularly in view of recent air losses. The RAF lost 26 fighters.

Below: Messerschmitt Bf 109E of II/JG3 *Udet* after its ultimate sortie over England.

5. THE TURNING POINT

Although the battle was to rage for several more weeks and the RAF fighter pilots had to continue their constant air actions against the Luftwaffe, it has now become accepted that 15 September was the turning point. As if to accentuate the victory of the 15th, the skies over southern England stayed comparatively quiet on the 16th.

Goering called a conference with his air commanders. Although presumably shaken by the losses of the previous day he showed little sign of it and merely informed his commanders that there was to be a return to a policy of knocking out the RAF – a task he felt would now only take four or five days. In this he was supported by his Intelligence people who still continued to underestimate both the RAF's front-line strength and reserves. These reserves now numbered 160 with a further 400 available for delivery in seven days.

Goering also decided to reduce the bomber formations but to support them with maximum fighter cover in order to blast the British fighters as they came up to engage the raids. London would continue to be raided by night.

The 11 Group commander, Keith Park, was also adjusting his tactics. He felt that his squadrons could do better if more were able to engage the enemy. Specifically, he wanted the Spitfires from Biggin Hill and Hornchurch to engage the Me 109s, while Hurricanes, operating in groups of three if time allowed them to get together, from Northolt and Tangmere, went for the bombers. It also became clear that the claim of 185 kills on the 15th was not supported by crashed aircraft on the ground, and the figure was being revised.

Activity was still reduced on the 18th although it was obvious to the RAF that a large fighter sweep flown by the Luftwaffe in the afternoon was designed solely in order to produce a fighter-versus-fighter action. In an attempt to carry out Goering's directives, the Luftwaffe mounted another sweep the following morning, followed by a small raiding force of Ju 88s escorted by 100 Messerschmitts. This was ignored by the RAF as its intention was too obvious. Therefore, another force of Ju 88s was sent in. This was met by a large force of Hurricanes and Spitfires, including the 12 Group Duxford Wing. Nine Ju 88s were quickly destroyed by 92 Squadron and the Big Wing, although the Wing claimed 30 victories!

The most significant event on the 19th was that Hitler finally shelved his plans to invade England and ordered the prepared invasion fleet of barges and troops to be dispersed. This latter fact was confirmed by RAF reconnaissance who, naturally, had been taking a keen interest in watching this force grow in recent weeks in the Channel ports along the French coast.

Over the next few days Luftwaffe activity was slight, confined mostly to fighter sweeps. Then on the 27th the fury returned. At 0800 hours activity was recorded on Operations Tables – bomb-carrying Me 109s and Me 110s headed in toward London on a broad front from Dover to Brighton. The 11 Group fighters harried

Bottom: WAAFs plot the progress of the battle.
Below: Adolf Galland (center) and Werner Mölders talking with Ernst Udet, Chief of the Luftwaffe's Technical Branches, during a visit to the 'Channel Front' by Udet on 4 September 1940.

them all the way to the outskirts of London. The Germans remained over the southeast, trying to exhaust the defender's fuel and ammunition supplies preparatory to a raid by Ju 88s. However, the bombers failed to pick up their heavy escort and met over 100 defending fighters who promptly set about the raiders. Urgent calls for supporting Me 109s brought in a large force of Messerschmitts and both raiders and defenders suffered losses. Twelve Ju 88s went crashing earthward in this battle. One of the defending Me 109s was shot down by Pilot Officer R G A Barclay of 249 Squadron:

'I chased a 109 which dived very steeply. I had to use automatic boost cut-out to catch up the 109. I lost the 109 in haze owing to its camouflage against the ground, but it suddenly climbed almost vertically out of the haze. I closed to about 150 yards and fired about four bursts, one almost vertically up at the 109, one almost vertically down at the 109, two bursts from the beam. The EA poured glycol. The cockpit roof flew off. The pilot baled out successfully. The EA crashed on a farm SW of Ashford.'

Later, on the Squadron's third sortie of the day, Barclay destroyed a Ju 88 but had to force land at West Malling when his Hurricane was hit by an Me 109's snap burst. Pilot Officer A G Lewis of 249 claimed six victories on this day, three Me 109s, two Me 110s and a Ju 88. He also damaged another Me 109 and probably destroyed a Me 110. It brought his personal score to 18.

Further west 80 aircraft were heading for Bristol; He 111s and bomb-carrying Me 110s escorted by more Me 110s, came over the coast. This raid was met by five RAF squadrons. The Heinkels were split up and sent scurrying for the coast, the Me 110s pressed on to Bristol but were hotly engaged by RAF fighters. One escorting Me 110 was shot down by Pilot Officer M C Maxwell of 56 Squadron who wrongly identified it as a Dornier. Having scrambled with his squadron, Maxwell had to land again, but taking off shortly afterward he engaged the returning force on his own:

'At 16,000 feet saw a formation of about 25 EA ahead at 18,000 feet, climbed and made a stern attack on rear aircraft. I then broke away and saw EA losing height with black smoke emitting from port engine. Another Hurricane attacked EA which dived steeply and later I attacked again after Hurricane broke away, and saw EA with one engine stopped, crash after endeavouring to force-land.'

Total losses by the Luftwaffe numbered 55 including 21 bombers; the RAF lost 28 fighters. At the time the day ranked with 15 August and 15 September as a victory against the German Air Force.

In contrast the 28th saw a victory for the

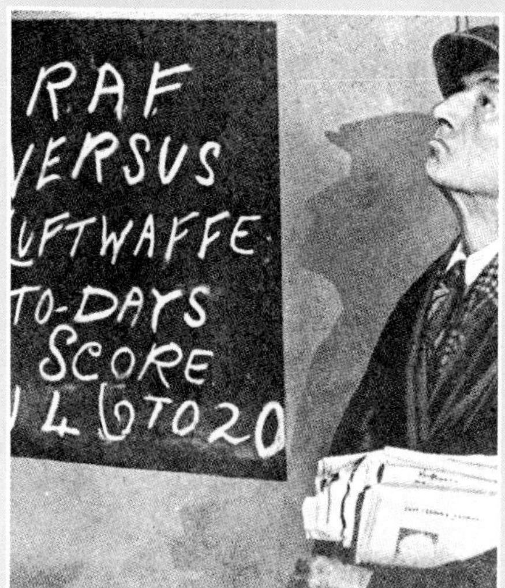

Left: Hermann Goering addresses his air crews.
Below left: British newspapers gave the score for each day.
Bottom left: Cockney humor and the carry-on spirit during the Blitz.

Above: St Clement Danes church, the RAF's church, after a bombing raid.
Left: Havoc in a London street which became a familiar sight to commuters.
Below: A mobile YMCA canteen at an antiaircraft-gun site.

Luftwaffe fighters, for during attacks on London and the Solent they shot down 16 RAF aircraft and only lost two of their own in actual combat. One of the RAF men shot down was A G Lewis who had scored so heavily the previous day. Me 109s hit him over Faversham – he baled out with burns.

The final fury of September came on the final day of the month when Me 109s flew sweeps toward London in the morning. No 229 Squadron suffered badly, losing four Hurricanes and four damaged in fights with Me 109s, with one pilot killed and three others wounded. This raid was followed by Me 109s and Me 110s attacking the Weymouth area and then after lunch Ju 88s and Me 109s again made for London. The final raid consisted of He 111s and Me 110s going for the Westland factory at Yeovil. No 56 Squadron was attacked by Me 110s, losing five Hurricanes with two others damaged, but luckily no pilots were lost. No 152 Squadron also tangled with the Me 110s, losing one pilot and aircraft and damaging four Spitfires. However, overall the Germans lost 47 aircraft during the day, to the RAF's 20. Most of the Luftwaffe's casualties were Me 109s.

We now realize that by the end of September the battle had effectively been won in the air. The German Luftwaffe could no longer sustain the losses which Fighter Command had inflicted upon it and tactics were again changed. The battle was continued by the Germans but now fighters generally flew alone, many carrying bombs. It became known as 'Messerschmitt Month.'

6. CLEARING THE SKIES

The October battles were in many ways more dangerous than the hectic days of the previous weeks. The Me 109s flew high, often above 25,000 feet, and the RAF fighters had to climb hard through hazy autumn sunshine and cloud to reach them. The advantage was usually held by the Me 109s above. During these weeks the RAF lost many veteran fighters in this moment of victory.

For the defenders it was impossible to know which of the Messerschmitts carried bombs and which did not. Also, once those carrying bombs had dropped them they became again a dangerous adversary.

One veteran pilot shot down and wounded on the very first day of October was Pilot Officer G H Bennions of 41 Squadron. Having already shot down 11 German aircraft plus five probables, he was due for leave but wanted to bring his score to a neat dozen. Flying high on patrol he became separated from his companions when he went after a bunch of Me 109s, one of which he destroyed. His machine was then hit and a cannon shell exploded by the left side of his face. His left eye was destroyed and a hole in his skull exposed his brain. In addition he sustained wounds to his right arm and leg. He managed to bale out and it was pure willpower that ultimately pulled him through.

Skirmishes occurred during the first week of October in poor weather. This improved on Monday the 7th, and the Luftwaffe sent an almost continuous stream of Me 109s over southeast England and later a Ju 88 raid was made against the Westland plant at Yeovil. Among the RAF scorers was the 'boss' of 609 Squadron, who had taken command of the squadron two days previously, Squadron Leader M L Robinson:

'It was extremely bright and as we were heading into the sun it was very difficult to pick out the EA which were now ahead of. . . . saw a circle of 110s directly ahead of us and proceeded to attack. I broke away downwards without seeing the result of the attack and I climbed up and attacked a separate 110 from astern. A Hurricane carried out a deflection shot between 110 and myself but I went on firing when the Hurricane broke away and the 110 dived vertically down with its port motor smoking.'

Minutes later he shot down a second 110 which dived into the ground north of the coastline. The day ended with 21 German and 17 RAF aircraft lost.

The RAF was now flying patrol lines in order to be in the air and ready to engage hostile raids. When the raids came in, other squadrons took off to be covered by those already airborne. Once the new squadron was at a good height, then the covering squadron could be sent to engage raiders or land to refuel as necessary. However, with Me 109s flying as high as 32,000 feet, it was a dangerous game, the Me 109s always holding the advantage of height. It took the average Spitfire Mk 1 18 minutes to climb to 25,000 feet, and 21 minutes for a Hurricane.

On 8 October the RAF lost only four aircraft but managed to shoot down 14 Germans. One of the Allied pilots lost was Sergeant Joseph Frantisek, a Czech pilot flying with 303 Polish Squadron. He had already destroyed 17 Luftwaffe aircraft during September, and was the highest scoring pilot of the battle. He had shot down 11 Germans in Poland and France – making 28 in total. He was killed in a crash at RAF Northolt. Another high-scoring pilot was shot down on the 10th, Pilot Officer R F T Doe of 238 Squadron. He baled out wounded near Poole. He had 15 victories.

Over the next few days Me 109s continued to try, and often succeeded, in penetrating to London where they dropped their bombs in random fashion. RAF fighters continued to climb up and engage these raiders but often combat claims of both sides were more or less even. However, night raids were on the increase. The RAF had won the day battle but it was weak in night defense. Despite Britain's preoccupation with building a night-bomber force to use against Germany, it had badly neglected a night-defense plan. Antiaircraft fire was really the first line of defense. Apart from this the RAF struggled along with Blenheims, Defiants, Spitfires and Hurricanes, but the latter, despite some successes, were not designed for this role. One day fighter pilot described a night sortie as trying to locate a fly in the Albert Hall, in the dark, without airborne radar!

The day fighting continued throughout the month, Spitfires and Hurricanes and

Above: Squadron Leader Michael Robinson, DFC of 609 Squadron, AAF.
Top: 'Stan' Turner of 242 Squadron, Coltishall in the summer of 1940.
Top right: Messerschmitt Bf 109E, 'Red 13,' shot down over Sussex on 25 October. Its pilot was 'captured' by a local farmer.
Above right: Spitfire pilot, 1940.

Above: Pilots of 46 Squadron at Stapleford Abbotts in October 1940 being debriefed after combat. From left: Ambrose, Young, Leggett, McGregor, Earp, Lefevre.

Messerschmitts tangling in the autumn sky. Pilot Officer A N C Weir of 145 Squadron wrote on 17 October:

'We generally get told to patrol at 15,000 feet below the Huns, who dive from the south straight out of the sun. Also, whatever we are told, we climb as high as we can, preferably inland first and then out to meet what is obviously fighters, though one has to go and make sure they are not bombers. I see no point in engaging 109s at 30,000 feet as they can do no harm up there.'

The 29 October brought the last big clash, with raids upon London and Southampton. No 602 Squadron, having managed to gain a tactical advantage of height and position, found themselves above the Me 109s for a change. In company with 222 Squadron they dived on the Messerschmitts from behind. Flight Lieutenant C J Mount was leading the squadron and in the initial attack and the subsequent chase when the 109s turned tail, they claimed eight of the German fighters shot down for no loss. The day's losses were 19 German to seven British.

The 30 October saw more fighter-versus-fighter actions, but overall activity was much reduced and it was not until late morning that the first plots appeared on the British radar screens. Ten RAF squadrons were on their patrol lines, and six sighted the raiding aircraft. Two Me 109s were shot down but 222 Squadron up from Hornchurch lost two pilots and a Spitfire was damaged. In the afternoon 130 Me 109s streamed in across the south coast, and some reached London. Half a dozen were shot down but the RAF lost four aircraft, and 602 Squadron who had scored so well the previous day lost two Spitfires. On the 31st air activity was practically nil. The Luftwaffe lost 325 aircraft during October. The RAF lost 100 pilots with a further 85 wounded. It had been indeed a dangerous sky.

Right: Hurricane P3886 of 601 Squadron, AAF being 'turned round' at Exeter, November 1940.

Below: Hurricanes of 615 Squadron, AAF get airborne from Northolt.

It was now evident to everyone that the battle was over. The raids were greatly reduced, the bombers were few and far between and with the coming of winter the Germans could no longer maintain an offensive in daylight. In any case they had been so badly mauled that they could not make an effective assault except by raiding at night.

The accepted casualty figures for the Battle of Britain, the first major battle fought solely in the air, and which officially lasted from 10 July to 31 October 1940 are:

Luftwaffe aircraft lost	1733
German aircrew lost	3089
RAF fighters lost	915
RAF aircrew lost	503

Claims by both sides were much exaggerated at the time, the RAF claimed to have shot down 2698 German aircraft, the Germans claimed 3058 Royal Air Force machines.

Undoubtedly the chief architect of the victory gained by Fighter Command was its Commander in Chief, Air Chief Marshal Hugh Dowding. His control was faultless. His foresight in designing and building his air-defense system saved Britain in its darkest hour. Laurels too must go to Air Vice-Marshal Keith Park who had so ably commanded 11 Group which daily took the brunt of the assault. He commanded his squadrons with remarkable insight and courage.

Despite the victory, there was little respite for the pilots of Fighter Command. November continued to see the fighters meeting in combat in the sky over southern England.

No 145 Squadron got themselves into a tight spot on 7 November near the Isle of Wight. On patrol they were surrounded by three large formations of Me 109s – totalling about 50. The Hurricane pilots were unable to engage or dive away without exposing themselves to attack but the Me 109s began to pick off the members of B Flight. Five were hit and sent down and one pilot, Pilot Officer A N C Weir, DFC, was killed.

Four days later came the famous action when the Italians raided in the locality of Harwich. Nos 17, 46 and 257 Squadrons were in the air. Flight Lieutenant H P Blatchford, leading 257 Squadron, gained fame by destoying one Fiat BR 20 bomber and probably a Fiat CR 42 fighter biplane which he hit with his propeller.

The Italians were to make only a few intrusions over England in 1940. Another raid occurred on 23 November. No 603 Squadron found them and gave the call that they had spotted the ancient-looking machines. Another squadron in the area asked where they could be found. Perhaps an indication of the vast numbers and caliber of the enemy the pilots of 603 Squadron had been used to engaging was their classic reply:

'Shan't tell you, we're only outnumbered three to one!'

Bottom left: Three WAAFs decorated with MMs during the battle of Britain.
Bottom center: Some of 257 Squadron's pilots at Martlesham Heath, after their successes against the Italian raids.
Bottom right: Italian Fiat BR20 bomber shot down by Pilot Officer P G Leggett of 46 Squadron on 11 November 1940, in Rendlesham Forest, Suffolk.

Below: Just three of the 3080 pilots involved in the defense of England in the high summer of 1940.

Left: Roof spotters watching the fires from Northcliffe House, London.
Above left: Flight Lieutenant John Dundas, DFC, of 609 Squadron, AAF whose 13th claimed victory was the Luftwaffe 53-victory ace, Helmut Wick, on 28 November 1940. Only seconds later Dundas was killed by Wick's wing man.
Right: Damage in the center of Coventry, 16 November 1940.
Top: Hurricanes of 85 Squadron, led by Squadron Leader Peter Townsend, DFC, patrol over England. The skies were relatively free of German aircraft by late 1940.

They shot down several of them. Before this, however, another veteran, Flying Officer M B Czernin, DFC, of 17 Squadron, was shot down. On the 17th he attacked a formation of Me 110s of EG210, hit one but was then shot down by the famed Adolf Galland. Count Czernin baled out successfully. Flight Lieutenant Blatchford, again leading 257 Squadron shot down an Me 109 on the same day after a bit of a chase. The Me 109 pilot shot down a Hurricane during the fight but Blatchford finally nailed him:

'He continued to dive and I followed behind and above. After 30 seconds when at about 1500 feet, he flattened out and I put the finishing touches on him. The EA did a cartwheel and the pilot was jettisoned into the sea, pilot and aircraft hitting the sea at the same time 30 yards apart.'

The dangers in the sky continued to the end of the month. On the 28th came the now famous action when Flight Lieutenant J C Dundas, DFC, was lost near the Isle of Wight after possibly shooting down one of the leading German pilots, Helmut Wick of JG2. Dundas died with the yell of victory on his lips. In the air too was 152 Squadron, which was attacked by Me 109s which screamed through their formation, shooting down veteran pilot Pilot Officer A R Watson who had flown all through the battle. He baled out but tore his parachute in doing so and fell to his death. Pilot Officer E S Marrs went after the yellow-nosed Me 109:

'I followed and caught it up about 10,000 feet at about 10 to 15 miles south of the Needles. I waited my time and closed to about 100 yards. EA was not turning or weaving at all and evidently did not suspect any pursuit. I gave a short burst from astern and slightly underneath and oil smothered over my windscreen. EA did a half roll and dived down. I broke away . . . and when I saw it again, pilot was floating down by parachute. EA machine was descending in flaming fragments, evidently exploded.'

Each summer we remember and recall with pride that summer of 1940 when a handful of gallant young men daily carried out feats of great valor above southern England. Many died in the battle, others were to die before the war finally ended nearly five years later. As we watch the fast jet fighter aircraft of today we know that the spirit which the 1940 pilots engendered then still lives on in the men who fly above us today. Churchill's famous 'Few' gave of their best then. Let us hope that the men of today never have to show the world again what an air war can mean, not just to them but to everyone.

APPENDIX

Luftwaffe aircrew casualties

Bomber crews	1,176
Stuka crews	85
Fighter-bomber crews	212
Fighter crews	171
Crewmen missing	1,445
	3,089

RAF fighter bases during the Battle of Britain, in Fighter Command's three main Fighter Groups.

(Names marked with an asterisk denote Sector Headquarters.)

10 Group HQ at Rudloe Manor, Box, Wiltshire.

Pembrey*	Bibury
Filton*	Colerne
Exeter	St Eval*
Roborough	Boscombe Down
Middle Wallop*	Aston Down
Warmwell	Sutton Bridge
	Hawarden

11 Group HQ at Hillingdon House, Uxbridge, Middx.

Debden*	Biggin Hill*
Castle Camps	Gravesend
Martlesham Heath	Redhill
North Weald*	Hawkinge
Stapleford	Lympne
Hornchurch*	Tangmere*
Rochford	Westhampnett
Manston	Ford
Kenley*	Northolt*
Croydon	Hendon
West Malling	

12 Group HQ at Watnall, Nottingham, Notts.

Duxford*	Speke
Coltishall*	Ringway
Wittering*	Church Fenton*
Digby*	Leconfield
Kirton-in-Lindsey*	Yeadon

Aircrew who took part in the Battle of Britain

	Total	Killed
British RAF personnel	2,384	398
Fleet Air Arm	57	9
Australians	21	13
New Zealanders	100	11
Canadians	87	20
South Africans	21	9
Rhodesians	2	—
Jamaicans	1	—
Irish	9	—
Americans	7	1
Poles	135	29
Czechs	85	8
Belgians	27	5
Israelis	1	—
French	12	—
	2,949	503

A 32 Squadron Hurricane taxies out from dispersal at the forward landing ground at Hawkinge, Kent on 31 July 1940.

Squadrons, flights and other units which took part in the Battle of Britain

Sqdn No	Aircraft				
1	Hurricane	87	Hurricane	263	Hurricane
1 RCAF	Hurricane	92	Spitfire	264	Defiant
3	Hurricane	111	Hurricane	266	Spitfire
17	Hurricane	141	Defiant	302	Hurricane
19	Spitfire	145	Hurricane	303	Hurricane
23	Blenheim	151	Hurricane	310	Hurricane
25	Blenheim	152	Spitfire	312	Hurricane
29	Blenheim	213	Hurricane	501	Hurricane
32	Hurricane	219	Blenheim	504	Hurricane
41	Spitfire	222	Spitfire	600	Blenheim
43	Hurricane	229	Hurricane	601	Hurricane
46	Hurricane	232	Hurricane	602	Spitfire
54	Spitfire	234	Spitfire	603	Spitfire
56	Hurricane	235	Blenheim	604	Blenheim
64	Spitfire	236	Blenheim	605	Hurricane
65	Spitfire	238	Hurricane	607	Hurricane
66	Spitfire	242	Hurricane	609	Spitfire
72	Spitfire	245	Hurricane	610	Spitfire
73	Hurricane	247	Gladiator	611	Spitfire
74	Spitfire	248	Blenheim	615	Hurricane
79	Hurricane	249	Hurricane	616	Spitfire
85	Hurricane	253	Hurricane	421 Flight	Hurricane
		257	Hurricane	F.I.U.	Blenheim

Main Luftwaffe units which took part in the Battle of Britain.

Kampfgeschwader 1	Heinkel 111 and Dornier 17
Kampfgeschwader 2	Dornier 17
Kampfgeschwader 3	Dornier 17
Kampfgeschwader 4	Heinkel 111 and Junkers 88
Kampfgeschwader 26	Heinkel 111
Kampfgeschwader 27	Heinkel 111
Kampfgeschwader 30	Junkers 88
Kampfgeschwader 51	Junkers 88
Kampfgeschwader 53	Heinkel 111
Kampfgeschwader 54	Junkers 88
Kampfgeschwader 55	Heinkel 111
Kampfgeschwader 76	Dornier 17
Kampfgeschwader 77	Junkers 88
Lehrgeschwader 1	Junkers 88, Junkers 87 and Messerschmitt 110
Lehrgeschwader 2	Messerschmitt 109 and 110
Stukageschwader 1	Junkers 87
Stukageschwader 2	Junkers 87
Stukageschwader 3	Junkers 87
Stukageschwader 51	Junkers 87
Stukageschwader 77	Junkers 87
Zerstörergeschwader 2	Messerschmitt 110
Zerstörergeschwader 26	Messerschmitt 110
Zerstörergeschwader 76	Messerschmitt 110
Erprobungsgruppe 210	Messerschmitt 110 and 109
Jagdgeschwader 2	Messerschmitt 109
Jagdgeschwader 3	Messerschmitt 109
Jagdgeschwader 26	Messerschmitt 109
Jagdgeschwader 27	Messerschmitt 109
Jagdgeschwader 51	Messerschmitt 109
Jagdgeschwader 52	Messerschmitt 109
Jagdgeschwader 53	Messerschmitt 109
Jagdgeschwader 54	Messerschmitt 109
Jagdgeschwader 77	Messerschmitt 109

Plus various reconnaissance, air-sea-rescue, coastal and night intruder Groups.

Squadron Leader Bob Stanford Tuck (right) and Flight Lieutenant P 'Prosser' Hanks examine an Italian aircrew helmet following 257 Squadron's successful interception of a raid on 11 November 1940.

PEARL HARBOR

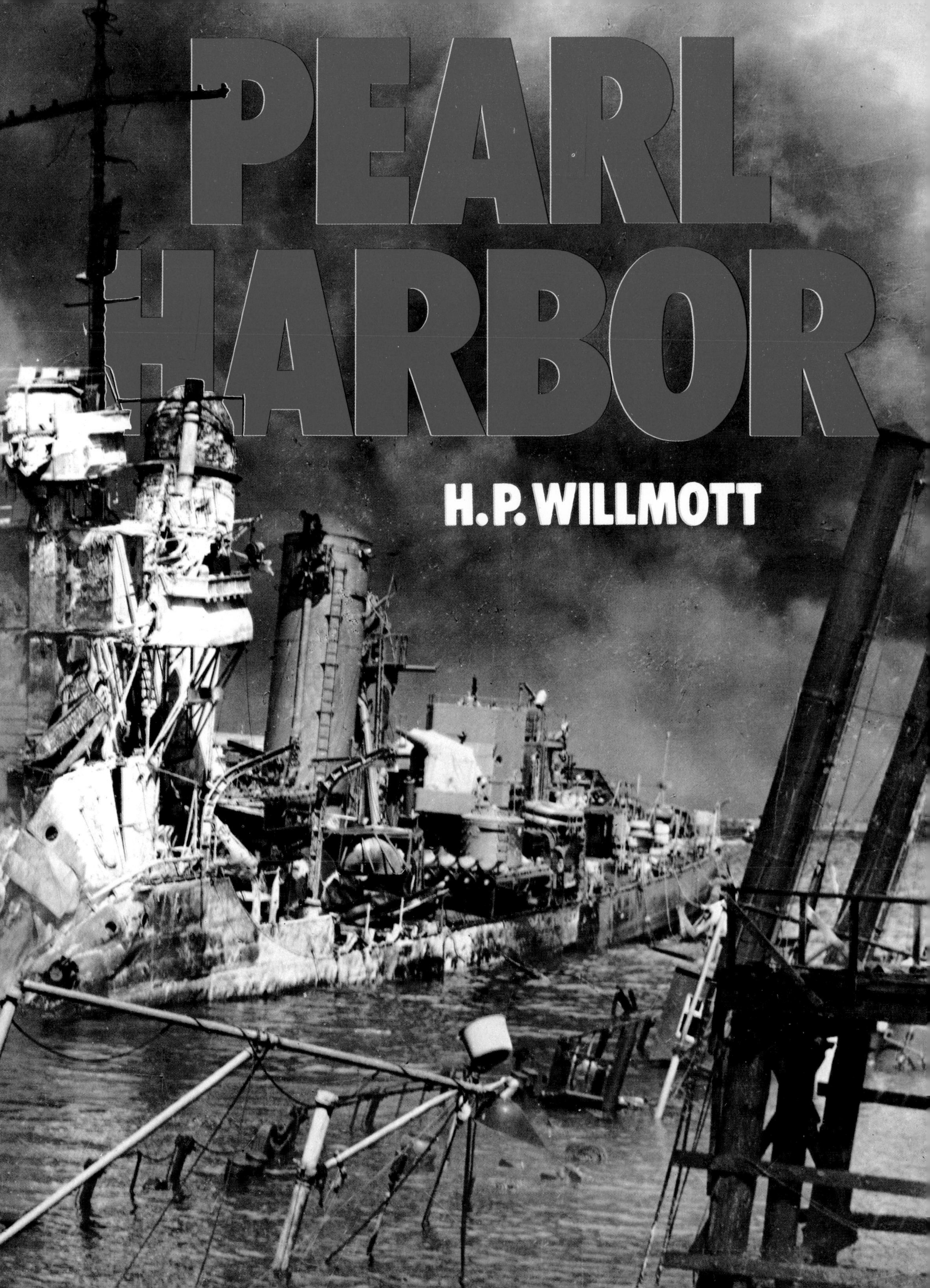
PEARL
HARBOR
H. P. WILLMOTT

Page 72: Pearl Harbor was quickly repaired and restored as a major US naval base after the Japanese attack. Here *USS Tinosa* returns from a successful war patrol.
Page 73: Disregarding the possibility of explosions, US sailors fight the flames on the doomed battleship *USS Virginia*.
Pages 74/75: The destroyer *USS Shaw* lies in a flooded floating drydock after an explosion caused by a bomb hit. She was later salvaged.
These pages: Sailors rearm clips and belts during the attack.

Slicks

1. THE QUEST FOR SUPREMACY

Mythology tells of Japan's divine origins and character. Ruled by a god-emperor, the Tenno, who was the direct descendant of the chief deity, Amaterasu, the sun-goddess, it was a land watched over by the lesser gods, and inhabited by a semi-divine chosen people. The Japanese, who saw death in the service of their Tenno as insufficient atonement for the debt they owed their homeland, regarded themselves as being charged with a divine mission. This mission, their manifest destiny, was the domination and leadership of eastern Asia.

Divinity, however, has its limits. Heavenly kingdoms may run on faith and worship, but earthly ones run on oil, and a whole host of raw materials without which ordered society cannot survive. Divine purpose, moreover, can be balked by the capriciousness of man. In the 1930s, as Japan sought to assume the leadership and control of eastern Asia by starting with the progressive and bloody conquest of China, it became increasingly obvious that not many people outside Japan shared her view of her heaven-sent mandate.

Fate dictated that Japan was forced to operate in a political and economic world order devised by and benefitting white imperialist nations – in the Far East these nations were Britain, France, the Netherlands and the USA. These states, through their colonial possessions, stood in the way of Japan's quest for domination of the Far East. Their territories contained all the raw materials Japan needed if she was to be self-sufficient and not dependent on the white nations for her means of existence. Rubber and tin from Malaya, iron ore from the Philippines, rice from Indo-China and Burma, oil, bauxite, coal, cobalt, copra, graphite, iron, lead, nickel, phosphates and potash from the Indies were the commodities Japan needed if she was to expand. The events of 15 May 1940 brought within Japan's grasp the glittering prospect of securing these territories and their resources.

On the outbreak of war in Europe in September 1939 Japan had declared her neutrality. It was in Japan's interest to wait upon events in Europe and see how they unfolded before committing herself. Being an expansionist power, she had little to gain, and possibly much to lose, by an Anglo-French victory, but this possibility was ended by the events of 15 May. When German armor ruptured the French positions overlooking the Meuse, it made a breach that the Anglo-French armies were unable to seal. Within six weeks Britain and France were hounded to decisive defeat; France to an armistice, Britain to ineffective defiance.

The humbling of France created an entirely new situation in the Far East of which Japan immediately prepared to take advantage. The French in the interwar period had placed their faith in a series of fixed defenses along their border with Germany. These defenses were known as the Maginot Line. At its first and only test it failed France because it was outflanked. The Maginot Line was much more than the shield of France alone. It had been the shield of the United States and the guarantee of American immunity from the malignancy of Nazism. It had also been the shield that had protected the British, Dutch and French possessions in the Far East which Japan coveted. Within a matter of weeks of the prostration of France, the Japanese made a series of moves to capitalize on the powerlessness of the European colonial empires.

In the van of these moves was the Imperial Navy which had long regarded Southeast Asia as the proper area of Japanese expansion because only there could Japan find the resources she needed to achieve autarky. The navy had small regard for the Imperial Army's invasion of China, which since 1931 had secured Manchuria, northern and central China and much of coastal southern China, but which showed no sign of achieving final victory over the Nationalist Government of Chiang Kai-shek. Despite the loss of its best armies and most productive areas, the Chinese government refused to come to terms with Japan. Japan therefore found herself with an open-ended commitment to a war which she could not win militarily. Japan was without the political, diplomatic and economic leverage to end the war by other means.

Top right: Japanese machine gunners man their post in northern China.
Top far right: This Chinese soldier was killed in Shanghai in 1932.
Right: Japanese infantrymen cry 'banzai' in China, summer 1937.

Up until May 1940 the army restrained the navy's desire for movement toward Southeast Asia. It had no wish to add further complications to an unfinished war and the sensitive uncertainties of Japanese–Soviet relations. With the humbling of France the army saw the chance to isolate China from outside support, either by securing Southeast Asia or by forcing Britain, the Netherlands and Vichy France into such concessions that the same result would be achieved by peaceful means. Thus at the fateful army–navy liaison meetings in June and July 1940 the army endorsed the navy's demands for a move on the south. The two services joined together to force the resignation of the cautious government of Admiral Mitsumasa Yonai when it showed signs of being alarmed by the implications of their demands. Prince Fumimaro Konoye was appointed in Yonai's place, but the services allowed him to take office only if he agreed to an alliance with Germany and Italy, a strengthening of the armed services and a more aggressive forward strategy in Southeast Asia.

The two armed services made clear to Konoye that in demanding expansion southward they recognized and accepted the possibility of a hostile American countermove designed to prevent Japan from securing resources that in future would make her invulnerable to any form of American pressure. The navy, particularly, realized that Japan's quest for self-sufficiency might provoke the type of economic blockade of Japan by the Americans that the quest itself was designed to forestall. Though in 1940 neither service anticipated that the Americans would go to war in the immediate future, both recognized that in the long term the United States was unlikely to stand aside tamely and abandon China and the European empires to their fate. American hostility to a rearming Japan was self-evident; the Japanese held no illusions on that matter. The Americans, by a variety of actions, had consistently belittled Japan as a nation and people. Both Japanese armed services were convinced that in the final analysis war was probable, and this was accepted as the only way Japan could hope to realize her ambitions and destiny.

A war with the broken powers of Europe held no terrors for Japan, but a war with the United States was not something that the Japanese considered lightly. A conflict with the United States was certain to be a hazardous undertaking because of the vast disparity of resources between the two nations. Paradoxically, however, it was this very disparity, because it threatened not to shrink but grow, that began to force Japan toward action before it became too late to act at all.

The fall of France had forced the Americans to define their security interests. As American opinion was heavily isolationist this was no easy task, but the framework had been established even before the war. The United States had recognized that the greatest danger to her security came from Germany. Before the fall of France the United States had thought in terms of fighting a two-ocean war in association with Britain and France. The defeat of France pushed the Americans into an increasingly heavy commitment to sustain a beleaguered Britain, but it also forced them to assume the role of restraining Japan – without any help from Britain and France. Yet in 1940 America was in a weak position. Years of interwar neglect of the armed services and the demands of two oceans meant that American military, naval and air power in the Pacific in 1940 were at abysmally low levels.

With the fall of France something close to real panic gripped the United States, Congress passed a series of measures designed to strengthen the American armed services. The strength of the army and navy and their air forces was to be greatly increased but the most significant measure was the Two-Ocean Naval Expansion Act. Under its terms the Americans, at a cost of $4,000,000,000, committed themselves to building seven battleships, 18 carriers, 27 cruisers, 115 destroyers and 42 submarines to add to the 130 warships already under construction and the 358 major units in commission.

The Imperial Navy appreciated that when the act's provisions were realized, the Americans would be so powerful at sea as to be unchallengeable. Japan in time would be reduced to the second or third rank, as the new ships would be more than double the size of the US Pacific Fleet. With every year that passed Japan's chances of avoiding defeat in a war with the Americans would lessen until they became nonexistent. At this time the Imperial Navy never considered itself capable of defeating the Americans, but it did believe that it was capable of fighting a successful defensive campaign in the western Pacific – among the Carolines and Marianas – that could lead to a profitable compromise peace. It believed that it could make the reduction of Japan and her conquests so costly that the Americans would accept a negotiated peace, especially if the European situation seemed likely to result in a total German victory.

The navy's interwar planning centered around the notion of a decisive naval engagement in the western Pacific. The Japanese were prepared for war with America, knowing that with every mile the drag of logistics, strain and dispersal would eat away at American strength. The orthodoxy of the day was that for every 1000 miles a fleet operated away from its base, it lost 10 percent of its effectiveness. It was believed that it was impossible for a fleet to operate more than 2000 miles away from its bases. The Imperial Navy calculated that as long as it could maintain itself at not less than 50 percent of American strength, and as long as its ships were qualitatively superior to those of the Americans, it had every chance of fighting a successful defensive campaign in the western Pacific. In 1940 the navy estimated that the balance of naval power was 10:7 against it. When this was adjusted to take into consideration the effect of the Atlantic on American dispositions, the balance in the Pacific was strongly in Japan's favor.

The Two-Ocean Act promised to undermine this favorable Japanese position. The Japanese calculated that to match new American construction their own scheduled building program for 1942 would have to be doubled, and this was impossible. The proposed 1942 program was far in excess of the current program, which in 1940 was encountering difficulties because it was too ambitious for Japan's slender resources. In 1941 the navy calculated that the Americans were building three tons for every ton in Japanese yards, and that by 1944 the balance of naval power would be a disastrous 10:3 against it. The Imperial Navy's long-term prospects were therefore bleak.

The key factor in this situation was time. The act would only produce ships from 1943 onward, and it was not due for completion until the period 1946–48. As Japan had entered the field of naval rearmament early, her 1937 and 1939 programs would allow her to stand at the peak of her strength relative to the Americans in late 1941 or early 1942. Thus certainly for a year, and for perhaps as long as two years, the Imperial Navy would be either superior or very close to American strength in the Pacific. Thereafter American dockyards would reduce the Japanese to a position of helpless inferiority and ineffectiveness as eloquently as any decisive defeat in battle could achieve.

This was the essence of Japan's strategic problem. She had to find a way of avoiding inevitable relegation to the second rank without abandoning her ambitions. In the event of her trying to secure Southeast Asia she faced a further strategic problem with regard to the Americans. Between Japan and the area of her ambitions lay the Philippines, an American colony scheduled for independence in 1944. The Philippines straddled Japanese lines of communication with Southeast Asia, and on the island group were American defense installations that could be reinforced to menace any Japanese deployment southward. Moreover, Japan's southern lines of communication were also straddled by the Hawaii–Wake–Guam–Luzon–China line, though this was not too serious a problem because in Oceania the Japanese held the stronger geographical position by virtue of their possessions in the Marianas, Carolines and Marshalls. If the Japanese moved against Southeast Asia they could not afford to leave these American positions unreduced, and they could not risk leaving the whole of their left flank, stretching across thousands of miles of ocean, bared to an intact and

Right: The US fleet lies at anchor at Cólon, which lies at the Caribbean end of the Panama Canal. This waterway provided a vital link between the Pacific and Atlantic.

Above: Japanese troops man their positions during the siege of Shanghai in the summer of 1937.
Right: Prince Konoye with members of his cabinet in 1937.

alerted US Pacific Fleet at its base in Pearl Harbor. This was the only force capable of offering effective resistance to Japan.

Japan's strategy was the responsibility of the Imperial Government and the Naval General Staff but in fact one man came to dominate the strategic planning of the Imperial Navy in the two years before the Pearl Harbor operation. That man was Admiral Isoruku Yamamoto, Commander in Chief of the Combined Fleet, the senior executive officer in the Imperial Navy. The plan to attack the US Pacific Fleet at its base in Pearl Harbor was his brain child, though he would have been the first to acknowledge the help he received in forming the plan – not least from American sources.

Yamamoto was a practical, realistic patriot. He shared Japanese ambitions in the Far East, but he knew from first-hand experience, gained as a student at Harvard and later as a naval attaché in Washington, of the awesome power and potential of American industry. He was outspoken in his opposition to a war with the Americans because he had no confidence in the ultimate outcome of such a conflict. He was trapped by the drift toward war, and he believed that war might be forced upon Japan if she was to retain her world position and self-respect. From the time of his appointment as Commander in Chief in August 1939, Yamamoto's mind turned to the problem the Americans posed to Japanese ambitions. His strategic acumen told him the obvious points: that he could not rely on American nonintervention in the event of a Japanese move on Southeast Asia; that he dare not leave an open flank across the width of the Pacific and that American construction was too great a long-term threat to be ignored. Increasingly he became convinced that if a war was inevitable then it was desirable that it be induced and not delayed. He was also increasingly convinced that the only way out of Japan's strategic difficulties was to find a way of striking a decisive blow that would crush the Americans and equalize accounts between the two nations either at the start of a war or shortly after.

This was just what the Japanese had done in 1904 against the Russians. Indeed, the Russo–Japanese conflict and the wars against China in 1894, 1931 and 1937, had certain points to offer Yamamoto as he

Below: A Japanese howitzer battery during the siege of Port Arthur in the Russo-Japanese War of 1904–05.

Bottom: The Russian defenders of Port Arthur in action against Japanese warships.

Bottom right: After the capitulation of the Russian garrison the defenders were allowed to evacuate the port, as depicted by this war artist's painting.

deliberated over the problem of the Americans. In all these conflicts the Japanese had attacked without the formality of a declaration of war. In the Russo–Japanese war the Japanese had started hostilities with a night attack on the main Russian fleet base at Port Arthur with their light forces. It was an attack from which the Russians never recovered, psychologically and materially. For the rest of the war the Russian battle squadron barely left harbor and finally succumbed to indirect fire from the Japanese army, attacking the harbor-fortress from landward.

The Russo–Japanese war, and the Sino–Japanese war of 1894, were major milestones in Japan's emergence as a major power, and the outcome of these wars, plus the manner in which she fought them, had major effects on Japan's political and strategic values and concepts. In both conflicts Japan fought and defeated nations that on paper were vastly superior to herself. From these wars Japan drew the confidence, which became dangerously unbalanced, that she need not fear superior numbers. Superior morale, it was believed, would see Japan through against the odds. Japanese martial prowess, *Nihon Seishin*, based upon an acceptance, even readiness, to die in imperial service, was the critical factor in the balancing of the odds. The planners were also aware that certain hard-headed military factors of a more orthodox and pragmatic nature were basic considerations in the triumphs on either side of the turn of the century.

Both the Sino–Japanese and Russo–Japanese wars had been primarily fought on land, but the basis of Japanese victory in both conflicts had been sea power. In these wars Japan's navy had been inferior to its enemies, but it had enjoyed local superiority because, unlike the Chinese and Russian fleets, it had been concentrated and held the advantage of superior geographical position. This local superiority, when combined with the use of surprise and offensive action, was the means by which the Imperial Navy fought for and secured command of the seas. In this process the Japanese used their battle fleet sparingly. The battle fleet was held back, ready to give battle if the need arose, but the need had to be urgent to justify its commitment. The brunt of the task of fighting for supremacy fell to Japan's light, expendable and easily replaced warships. These were entrusted with engaging and destroying enemy battle units; if that could not be achieved then Japan's light forces were charged with inflicting on the enemy disproportionately heavy losses that would either cause a faltering of enemy resolve or allow the battle fleet to join battle under conditions of maximum advantage and minimum risk to itself. The whole essence of Japanese naval policy in both wars was the use of cheap craft, capable of quick and easy replacement, to fight for and secure supremacy at the forward edge of the battle area. In both wars this basic naval blueprint served Japan well, and the master plan contained all the basic ingredients for a plan of attack on the Americans. Yamamoto was free to draw upon them if he was to persist in his notion of attacking the Americans before they became too strong to be challenged.

If the American fleet was crippled at the outset of a war then the Japanese would be free to conquer and then consolidate their gains in reasonable security. Moreover, if a surprise attack was successful American construction would not be additional to existing strength but replacement for losses. In this way the potential disparity between the American and Japanese fleets would not necessarily materialize, or if it did would not become too serious. The Americans would be forced to feed their newly commissioned ships into action in a piecemeal manner so the Japanese could hope to maintain themselves above the crucial 50 percent margin. Thereby a successful attritional campaign could be fought in the western Pacific with every confidence.

The Japanese plan of attack on Pearl Harbor has been called many things, few of which have been complimentary. It is normally portrayed as imbecilic or an act of suicide because it was certain to be self-defeating, but it was not necessarily any such thing. It was an action shaped and determined by Japanese historical experience and deeply entrenched in the mainstream of Japanese strategic and psychological values. It was the response to what was virtually an impossible strategic situation. The plan was logically conceived and carefully reasoned, and it formed part of an overall strategy which, despite its weaknesses and certain unrealities, was rational, calculated and ruthless.

2. PLANS AND PREPARATIONS

Detailed planning and preparation for the Pearl Harbor attack was extremely thorough. The problem of relating the plan's gestation, however, is that it separates into distinct parts, not all of which are in phase with one another. Firstly, there was the development and then the enunciation of the idea itself. The idea was mooted for the first time in November 1940. Secondly, there was the detailed planning stage. The initial plans were drawn up by March 1941 and, with the exception of certain very important details, were completed by May. Thirdly, predating both and continuing right up until the first week in November was the series of exercises to which the forces, particularly the aircrew, earmarked for the attack were subjected. Fourthly, from May onward there was a series of arguments within the Imperial Navy over whether or not to accept the plan. Formal endorsement of the plan was only given as late as 3 November by the Chief of the Naval General Staff, Admiral Osami Nagano. This was just three days before the final exercises before the attack and less than two weeks before the first units detailed for the attack sailed on their missions. Fifthly, there was the deteriorating international situation throughout 1941 which added urgency to the Japanese quest to solve their problem of if, when and how to go to war. Eventually on 23 November the main task force for the attack received its orders to sail and on 3 December it received confirmation of its orders to proceed.

The linking element in at least the first four points was Yamamoto. The plan to attack the American Fleet at its Pearl Harbor base was his. Though he drew his ideas from many sources and much of the detailed planning fell to Commander Minoru Genda, it was first and foremost Yamamoto's plan. It was Yamamoto who first formulated the concept and then forced it through to acceptance despite

Below left: As Chief of the Japanese Naval Staff, Rear Admiral Osami Nagano was responsible for the formulation of naval strategy.
Bottom: Rear Admiral Takajiro Onishi took a leading part in planning the Pearl Harbor raid.
Below: Among Japan's newest aircraft carriers in December 1941 was *Shokaku.*

opposition from many quarters. He did this because he considered it absolutely essential to Japan's conduct of a war against the Americans. Without his ruthless determination the plan would certainly have been shelved.

It is unclear when Yamamoto first considered the possibility of attacking Pearl Harbor. It may well have been the time when American exercises involving carrier-aircraft attacks on shore installations were carried out in the interwar period. The most notable of these exercises were those of 1932 and 1938, when Pearl Harbor itself was the target of attack, and both maneuvers were deemed to have ended with success for the carrier aircraft. Yamamoto, who made his reputation as an advocate of air power and was one of the very few senior admirals in any navy to wear pilot's wings, cannot have been unaware of these exercises. What is known for certain is that from the time he took up his appointment as Commander in Chief, Combined Fleet Yamamoto showed an extremely keen interest in Pearl Harbor and pushed through a series of measures which, in retrospect, might suggest that he was thinking of a preemptive attack on Pearl Harbor long before November 1940.

Almost as soon as he hoisted his flag his cabin in the *Nagato* housed specially marked maps and intelligence summaries of Pearl Harbor. As the months passed and American activity on Oahu increased so too did the amount of information at Yamamoto's fingertips. It is difficult to believe that this interest was merely casual. On taking up his appointment Yamamoto secured the agreement of the Naval General Staff to widen the Marianas–Carolines war zone to include the Marshalls. In view of the increasing range and speed of aircraft this amendment to Japanese plans was prudent, but Yamamoto used it as the first step in the extension of the war zone right up to Pearl Harbor itself. This, again, was sensible, though it was done without any commensurate increase in auxiliary vessels needed to make such an extension workable. An enemy coast is always one's own first line of defense, but Yamamoto's proposals were more than a recognition of the truth of this simple dictum. He planned to use submarines off Hawaii – an idea that accorded with Japanese use of 'cheap craft, capable of quick and easy replacement' at the forward edge of the battle area. The point is, however, that aircraft also fell into this category.

On his appointment Yamamoto also began to draw back naval aircraft and aircrew from China. Owing to their superior range over their army counterparts, naval aircraft were much in demand in China. Yamamoto began to recall naval aircraft and started a program of retraining crews for attacks on shipping – a very different proposition from attacks on land objectives. In April and May 1940, at Yamamoto's insistence, a series of war games was played involving attacks by carrier aircraft on shipping anchored in harbor. The results of these games were naturally open to dispute, but two general conclusions cautiously emerged. The first was that the torpedo would be the most effective weapon with which to attack anchored shipping. The second was that such attacks could prove decisive because moored ships could not evade a torpedo attack. Yamamoto argued a further point from these conclusions. He insisted that if surprise was achieved the results would, not could, be decisive.

Yamamoto's views were to be proved correct in November 1940 when a group of obsolete British carrier aircraft, far inferior to anything that the Japanese possessed, sank or severely damaged three Italian battleships at their moorings in Taranto Harbor. For the loss of just two aircraft the

Left: The carrier *Akagi* was launched in 1925 and underwent modernization in 1938. She is pictured during training for the Pearl Harbor strike in the summer of 1941.

Right: Japanese pilot selection and training standards were rigorous and exacting. Trainees are shown demonstrating their physical fitness.
Below: Trainees were prepared for the disorientation of aerobatic flying in the crude but effective contraption shown.

British decisively altered the balance of naval power in the Mediterranean. The lesson of the attack was there for all to see – carrier aircraft, attacking with the advantage of surprise, could achieve strategically decisive results. That month, after the attack, Yamamoto spoke for the first time of his idea of using carrier aircraft to attack the US Pacific Fleet at its Pearl Harbor base.

The first man Yamamoto consulted about his plan was his Chief of Staff, Admiral Shigeru Fukudome. Fukudome was unimpressed, and remained skeptical until the time he left the Combined Fleet in October 1941. In deference to his admiral he advised Yamamoto to consult Rear Admiral Takijuro Onishi, then Chief of Staff to the land-based XIth Air Fleet, and one of the most aggressive air-minded officers in the Imperial Navy. Onishi had already toyed with the idea of an attack on Pearl Harbor with aircraft. He had considered using land-based aircraft from the Marshalls, but he had had to abandon the idea because of the insurmountable distance problems involved. Onishi warmed to Yamamoto's idea, but his enthusiasm cooled distinctly with time. He suggested that they consult Genda, one of the ablest staff officers in the Navy. Genda was a firm believer in the value of air power, and he had been attaché in London at the time of the Taranto attack. He was privy to many aspects of the attack. After an initial consideration of Yamamoto's ideas, Genda told the admiral that the plan to attack Pearl Harbor was difficult, but not impossible.

Genda, however, immediately demolished two of Yamamoto's main proposals for an attack. Yamamoto singled out American battleships as the main objective of the attack. It has been suggested that Yamamoto considered the breaking of American battleship strength to be more psychologically devastating than attacks on carriers. Genda thought that this was nonsense. Either carriers were the decisive strike weapon at sea or they were not. If they were, then there could be no justification for using them against lesser weapons or secondary objectives. Genda firmly fixed attention on the main objective of the attack – the elimination of American aircraft carriers.

Genda also refuted Yamamoto's suggestion to use attacking aircraft on a one-way mission. Such an idea might appear ridiculous – though in keeping with Japanese ideas of expendable light units – but Yamamoto had good reasons for such a proposal. Land-based reconnaissance aircraft could sweep the seas around Pearl Harbor to a distance of up to 800 miles, far beyond the range of carrier aircraft. The carriers could not risk being compromised or advancing to a position where they could be counterattacked easily by shore-based aircraft. Using aircraft on a one-way mission and leaving submarines to pick up ditched aircrew would lessen the risks to the carriers. Genda would have none of this. For an attack on Pearl Harbor only the elite of the navy's aircrew could be used, and to risk losing them on the first operation of a war was a luxury Japan could not afford. Such a proposal was certain to be bad for morale, and writing off the aircrew would leave the carriers hopelessly vulnerable if a counterattack materialized. Genda argued that the risks of being compromised had to be accepted but that every effort had to be made to reduce the risks to a minimum.

Genda laid down three conditions for success. He calculated that at least 300 aircraft would have to be used in an attack – making it by far the greatest carrier operation ever carried out – and that this would involve the use of six fleet carriers and eight oilers. This would involve waiting until after the summer of 1941 when the new carriers *Shokaku* and *Zuikaku* entered service. This in fact fitted into Japanese preparations very well. The total mobilzation of the Imperial Navy had been ordered in October 1940, and this would not be complete until November 1941. As the new carriers would not be ready until that time Genda's condition posed no technical problem. Genda also insisted that only the very best aircrews should be selected for the operation and that security and surprise were absolutely essential to success.

Yamamoto accepted these points and Genda, with a very small team of officers, was charged with the drawing up of a plan of attack. Genda worked quickly, the draft was completed in March 1941. By May the final proposals were completed, but some of the technical problems Genda encountered were not solved until November. The problems involved in the operation fell into three main groups: those of the advance-to-contact phase (the time between the carriers leaving port and the aircraft taking off), the technical problems of armory, and the plan of attack itself once the aircraft reached their objective.

The advance-to-contact phase posed the most difficulties because so much had to be left to chance. The problem was the selection of a route to Hawaii and a flying-off point that would run the least risk of detection. Intelligence work, mainly based on radio intercepts, quickly established that American aircraft reconnaissance patrols concentrated on the waters west, south and east of Hawaii – along the major trade routes – but left northern waters relatively free from surveillance. An approach north of Hawaii recommended itself to the Japanese. By passing between Midway and the Aleutians – but out of range of patrols from both – the Japanese would have to sail some stormy and inhospitable waters, unfrequented by merchantmen. The bad weather conditions prevailing in the northern Pacific in the autumn and winter, when fog alternated with bad weather fronts that closed Hawaii from the north and northeast, would provide cover for the Japanese advance. These same rough conditions threatened refuelling and were certain to cause major navigational problems and difficulties in station keeping and time keeping. The final plan had a hairline schedule because it had to be synchronized with other operations; the Japanese could not afford delays. The carriers would have to refuel once and their escorts at least twice during their mission, and in the stormy north Pacific this would be difficult. Careful research, however, which included a liner, the *Taiyo Maru*, sailing most of the proposed route in October 1941, revealed that on seven days in a month weather conditions moderated sufficiently to permit refuelling at sea. These were not good odds but Genda and Yamamoto had to accept them because there was no alternative.

The technical problems involved in the plan to attack Pearl Harbor were formidable, but most of them were solvable. Most of the problems centered around the torpedo, accepted by Genda as the primary means of attack. Japanese aerial torpedoes were designed to be dropped at about 250 feet and at speeds of up to 150 knots. They generally plunged to about 14 fathoms before running to their required depth. They needed to run some 600 feet in water before arming themselves. Clearly there were problems because Pearl Harbor drew no more than eight fathoms and conventional torpedoes would run themselves harmlessly into the bed of the harbor unless they were modified. Moreover, the greatest expanse of water between the shoreline and where the Americans habitually anchored their capital ships was no more than 1600 feet – which represented less than six seconds of flight for a torpedo bomber. The amount of space and water available for a torpedo run was therefore much less than 1600 feet, and this posed obvious problems. In addition, the American practice of mooring ships in pairs meant that the ship standing out toward the deep water channel shielded its landward neighbor from torpedo attack. Obviously, torpedoes by themselves would not be enough.

These problems forced two considerations. Firstly, modifications to the torpedoes had to be made. The British attack at Taranto, in waters of eight fathoms, showed that there was a solution to this problem. Secondly, bombs would have to be used against the inner targets. These bombs would have to be much larger and more powerful than conventional bombs if they were to inflict telling damage on massive armored heavy ships.

The bomb problem proved relatively easy to settle. New armor-piercing bombs, weighing up to 1600 pounds and based on shells, could be fitted with special fins to give stability and enhanced penetrative powers. Such bombs were quickly manufactured, but new torpedoes could not be quickly improvised. It was not until September that tests were concluded and production started on torpedoes equipped with wooden fins which seemed capable of keeping the weapon shallow-running. Even then only an 80 percent efficiency rating was given to these weapons. The production run to meet the requirements of the Pearl Harbor attack was not complete until mid-November. One of the carriers involved in the operation, the flagship *Akagi*, had to wait behind to collect the full quota of torpedoes after the rest of the carriers had left for their operational base.

Even these torpedoes presented problems. In order to prevent them from diving deep they had to be launched by a bomber flying at about 50 feet above the sea at approximately 150 knots. Pilots would have to be trained to meet these exacting requirements, but with turbulence off the sea and the height of waterside buildings both in the practice areas and at Pearl Harbor, the requirements exacted by the torpedoes broke every safety regulation in the Imperial Navy's training manuals. After crossing the shoreline the bombers would have about three seconds to line up on their objectives and deliver their attack before having to bank steeply upward and to the right in order to prevent congestion over the objectives.

Over a period of months, however, the aircrew selected for this operation reached the required standard. It is no exaggeration to assert that the Japanese carrier pilots committed to the raid on Pearl Harbor represented the best-trained aircrew in the world at that time.

At an early stage in the planning Yamamoto selected Kagoshima Bay in southern Kyushu as the training area for aircrews. The bay, with its restricted waters, volcanic island and waterside buildings, bore a strong resemblance to Pearl Harbor. It was selected for precisely that reason.

The bomber crews exercised over Kagoshima Bay for weeks. The torpedo bombers,

perhaps the most vulnerable of the attacking aircraft, were subjected to approach runs through the buildings of Kagoshima before a flight at 50 to 70 feet above the waters of the bay. By the end of October the bombers were making up to four runs a day. The dive bombers, meanwhile, had their release point lowered from 2000 feet to 1500 feet to increase the prospect of securing a hit while the high-level bombers – whose accuracy record in China was low because of their poor quality bombsights – were intensively trained. To offset the weakness of equipment the Japanese had to rely on experience and instinct on the part of the aircrew. To try to achieve the best possible result the Japanese instituted 'pattern bombing.' This is the process by which a tight-flying formation drops its bombs on the signal of a lead aircraft which is manned by the best and most experienced crew available. In this way the Japanese could reasonably expect to achieve a very tight grouping and therefore a high rate of strikes. Against moving targets the pilots achieved an estimated 80 percent hit rate by the time their training was complete. When in September the aircrews were directed to train against anchored ships there was a general sense of anticlimax. Attacks on stationary targets as opposed to targets at sea were regarded as obviously less important, but when the purpose of their training change was revealed the aircrews responded. The final exercise of 6 November involved a 200-mile flight from the carriers to the targets in Kagoshima Bay, and it is evident that the results gave even Yamamoto cause for satisfaction.

The dictum 'Train Hard, Fight Easy' was to be fully borne out by the attack on Pearl Harbor, but much of the smooth running of the attack stemmed from Genda's care and attention to detail. All through the training phase the aircrew had to meet Genda's two basic demands. They had to be able to recognize enemy ships correctly and at a glance, and then line up on their objectives. They had to know exactly what they had to do and how it was to be achieved. There was no room for error; every bomb and every torpedo had to count. In the congested airspace over the objective pilots had to keep to very exact battle drills if they were not to mask the attacks of other types of aircraft. The attacks themselves had to be staggered in order to allow the different types of aircraft to mount their attacks under the most favorable conditions possible. The final problem Genda faced was the tricky one of devising a recovery program that would allow Japanese aircraft to regain their carriers without leading surviving American forces against the carrier task force.

There were many technical details to be settled when Genda presented his final proposals, but in all operational aspects the plan was complete. In November, the morning of Sunday 7 December (Hawaiian time) was selected for the attack. The best hope of favorable weather conditions, suitable for refuelling, came in the first half of December when moon conditions for the final night run to Pearl Harbor would be most favorable. A Sunday was selected because this was the time best to catch the Americans unprepared.

The final plan of attack involved two quite distinct operations. There was to be a strike by carrier aircraft and there was to be a major submarine effort off Hawaii. The first operation involved a task force of six fleet carriers, two battleships, two heavy cruisers and a light screen of one light cruiser and nine destroyers from the 1st Destroyer Flotilla. With this force sailed eight oilers. Two more destroyers were in company but these were detailed for the simultaneous bombardment of American installations on Midway. Three fleet submarines were detailed to scout the route of the task force. The second part of the attack involved no less than 27 submarines – 11 of which carried reconnaissance aircraft – with all but two detailed to take up their stations off Hawaii. The submarine force thus deployed represented nearly 42 percent of the entire submarine service. (For a full order of battle, and the fate of all the Japanese ships that took part in the attack see Appendix.)

The carrier task force was to sail from its remote anchorage at Tankan Bay in the Kuriles and make its way at 13 knots – the most economical cruising speed of the heaviest carriers *Akagi* and *Kaga* and the escorting destroyers – to a position some 500 miles north of Oahu by the evening of 6 December. Then, leaving the oilers to make for a preselected rendezvous, the force was to make a high-speed run through the night to be in its flying-off position about 260 miles north of Oahu by dawn. The task force was given strict instructions to abandon its mission if it was recalled or if it was compromised before 6 December. If the force was detected on the 6th the force commander, Vice-Admiral Chuichi Nagumo, was given discretion to continue or abandon the mission. British, American and Dutch merchantmen encountered en route were to be sunk. Other nationals were to be boarded and their radios rendered inoperative.

From its flying-off position the force would launch two strikes, one hour apart. Both strikes were to consist of slightly under 200 aircraft. Some 80 aircraft were to be held back for combat air patrol and as a reserve. The two attacking waves would attack the six air bases the Japanese believed were on Oahu – in fact there were seven – and the warships in the anchorage. If surprise was achieved the attack would be led by the torpedo bombers and followed by the high-level bombers and then the dive bombers. Fighters and dive bombers would spearhead the attack if surprise was lost. As there was a chance that major American units – either Admiral Pye's battle line or Admiral Halsey's mixed carrier-battleship force – might not be in harbor at the time of the attack, the bombers were to search up to 150 miles south of Oahu in an effort to gain contact. The recovery phase involved aircraft breaking off contact and flying south before reversing course and sweeping wide of Oahu to regain their carriers. This was ordered in an effort to mislead the Americans over the true whereabouts of the carriers. The carriers were to maintain radio silence at all times and were not to take any steps to help the aircrews regain their ships.

The submarines were to sail before the carrier force either from Japan via Kwajalein or directly from Kwajalein itself. Two submarines were detailed to scout the Aleutians and Samoa, but the remaining 25 were deployed off Oahu. From Yokosuka the 1st and 2nd Flotillas deployed four submarines to the north and seven submarines to the east of Oahu respectively. From Kwajalein nine submarines of the 3rd Flotilla took up station to the south of the island. The 1st Flotilla was to be joined on patrol by Nagumo's three submarines after they had led the way for the task force while the submarines lined up south of Pearl Harbor were to be joined by five submarines which were detailed to carry two-man midget submarines to Hawaii. These midget submarines, armed with two torpedoes, were to break into Pearl Harbor and rest on the bottom throughout the 7th. At dusk they were to carry out attacks on surviving American units. Their parent submarines were charged with recovering the midgets off Lanai, though there was little hope of this. These five fleet submarines, when they joined the 3rd Flotilla, were to undertake operational patrols designed to secure intelligence, rupture American lines of communication between the Hawaiian Islands and the United States and to deplete American strength by dealing with any warships that attempted to break out of Pearl Harbor during and after the attack. Many naval officers who were skeptical of the carrier part of the operation entertained great hopes of the submarines which would be operating in the orthodox fleet role for which they had been designed and

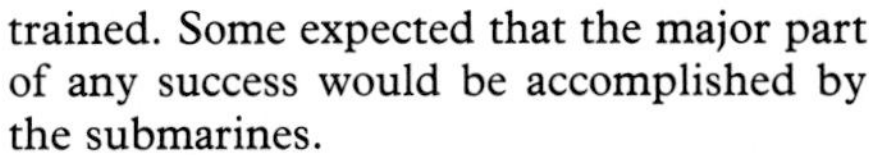

Left: The commander of the carrier task force which attacked Pearl Harbor was Vice Admiral Chuichi Nagumo, flying his flag in *Akagi*.
Below: Hostilities opened on 7 December when a midget submarine was sunk in the approaches to Pearl Harbor by the minesweeper USS *Condor*.

Bottom: A group photograph, showing senior officers of the US, Japanese, British, French and Italian navies, taken aboard a Japanese flagship in Chinese waters in 1932.

trained. Some expected that the major part of any success would be accomplished by the submarines.

When Yamamoto put forward his detailed proposals in May to the Naval General Staff he encountered a lukewarm reception. There was very little enthusiasm at all for a plan many regarded as a desperate and almost wild gamble.

Part of the resistance Yamamoto encountered was of an institutional or personal nature. He had made many enemies, and many felt that his plan was an attempt to arrogate the devising of strategy to himself. As the weeks slipped away – and American–Japanese relations deteriorated with alarming rapidity – opposition to the Pearl Harbor plan crystallized into five major objections, none of which could be lightly dismissed.

The whole *raison d'être* of the plan revolved around Yamamoto's belief that a war with the Americans was inevitable and that Japan had to launch a preemptive attack on American resources if she was to have any hope of success in the war. This was not fully accepted by many officers in the Imperial Navy, but this doubt was eroded gradually over a few months. After the Japanese occupation of southern Indo-China, the United States, closely followed by the British and Dutch, imposed an

embargo on Japanese trade in oil and steel in July 1941 and the possibility of war with the United States hardened into near certainty. Japan could only watch as her strength drained away, ebbing as each barrel of oil was used up out of her strategic reserve. At the very most Japan's reserves would be good for two years of war and her stockpiles of high-grade aviation fuel were sufficient for just six months of sustained operations. Unless Japan was able to find alternative supplies of oil very quickly or was able to get the three allied nations to lift their embargo, the Japanese knew that they would soon become too weak to do anything other than accept American terms for a resumption of trade between the two countries. The American terms involved the Japanese evacuation of Indo-China and China and their commitment to peaceful methods of adjusting relations between states. No Japanese government could accept such terms. Too much prestige, money and blood had been invested in the China venture. A lame acceptance of such terms would certainly have provoked mutiny and civil war inside Japan, and as her acid test Japan preferred to fight a foreign as opposed to a civil war. However, there were many officers in the Imperial Navy, such as Osami Nagano, who were appalled by the prospect of a war with the United States and who hoped that some means could be found to avoid it. People such as the Chief of the Naval General Staff were prepared to accept virtually any formula to avoid war, but in the last resort they were not prepared to accept the terms the Americans insisted on imposing.

Nagano fixed his argument on two major points. Firstly, every effort had to be made to find a peaceful means of resolving Japan's difficulties – but diplomacy in the autumn of 1941 merely served to show how irreconcilable were the differences between Japan and the United States. Secondly, he argued that there was no overwhelming or imperative need for the Japanese to attack the Americans at all; a war with the British and Dutch in Southeast Asia need not necessarily involve the Americans. There was much to be said for attacking the European empires and trusting that isolationist opinion inside the United States would be strong enough to prevent an American countermove. To Nagano it was inconceivable that President Roosevelt would be able to lead the Americans into a war over Malaya, the Indies or Siam; this was probably a correct analysis. In many ways the attack on Pearl Harbor came as a relief to the Roosevelt administration because it ended all kinds of problems for it. The issue of how to oppose Japanese aggression and the problem of securing public support for firm action were both resolved in their entirety.

Nagano's argument could be brushed aside with ease. If American hostility toward Japan was such as to ensure American participation in a war at some time or another, then an attack on Pearl Harbor was the best means of ensuring that American involvement came at a time of Japan's choosing and under the most favorable conditions possible for Japan. The Yamamoto formula was simplistic, but effective. The Americans alone were capable of resisting Japan's plans of expansion and their hostility was assured, therefore they had to be crippled at the outset of a war.

With this argument Yamamoto was able to disarm another major criticism of his proposals. It was argued that Japan should seize Southeast Asia before turning to face the Americans in the Marshalls–Carolines–Marianas war zone where the decisive battle to decide the fate of the Empire would be fought. This, of course,

Above: President Franklin D Roosevelt with members of his cabinet aboard the cruiser USS *Indianapolis* in New York Harbor, during a fleet review in May 1934.

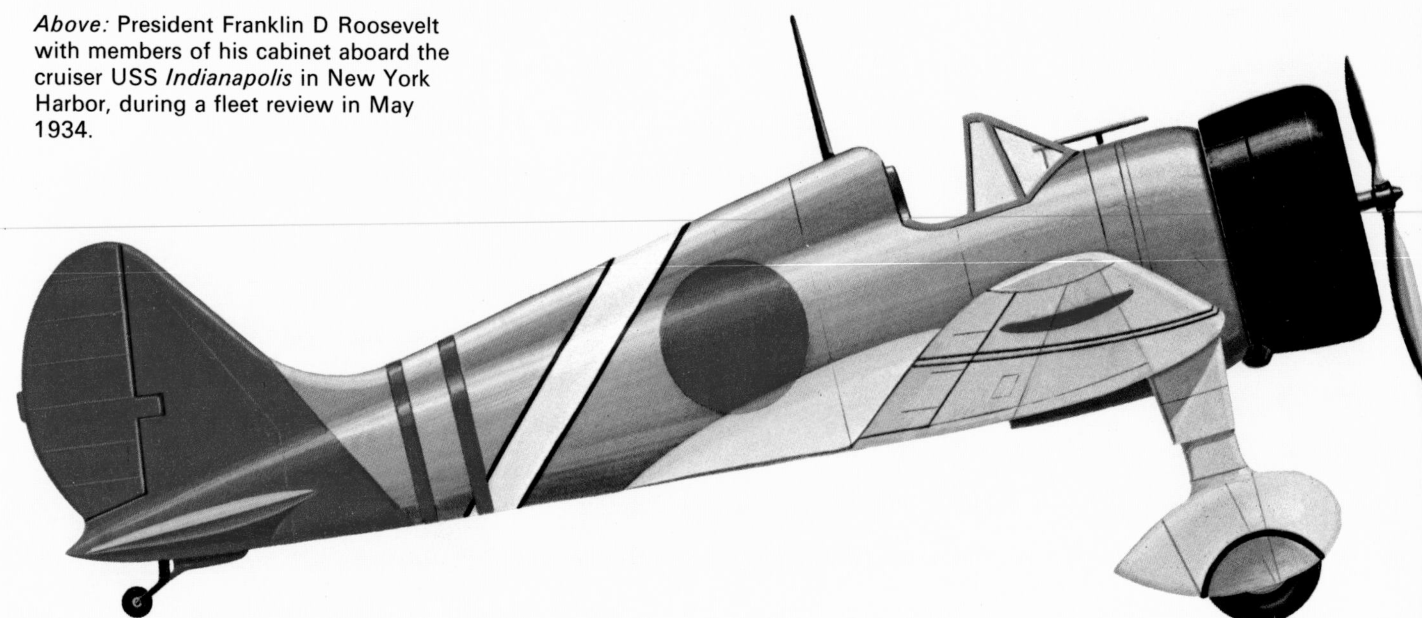

was thoroughly in keeping with Japan's prewar planning. Yamamoto's argument pointed to the prospect of shattering American power before such an eventuality arose – in effect Yamamoto was prescribing preventive rather than remedial medicine. If the Americans did sortie to the relief of the Philippines or attempt a reduction of the Marshalls, then an attack on Pearl Harbor would be a broken-back affair, made under crippling handicaps. With the certain knowledge of the implications of the Two-Ocean Act gnawing away at the backs of their minds, Japanese naval officers could not but be impressed by the possibilities opened up by the idea of a surprise attack on Pearl Harbor.

Nevertheless, even those who began to feel the hypnotic effect that all great operations cast over those involved in them had good reason to be apprehensive about various aspects of the planned operation. A carrier strike on Pearl Harbour would remove all the carriers from the crucial area of operations in Southeast Asia. This division of force in the face of an enemy was a dangerously rash policy. What was not realized by proponents of this argument – and what the Americans and British failed to appreciate – was the manner in which Yamamoto and his associates proposed to use long-range shore-based aircraft to make good the absence of the carriers. The Planning Bureau of the Naval General Staff accepted this, however, and devised its war plans in the summer of 1941 on the assumption that the carriers would not be available for operations in Southeast Asia – long before the plan of attack on Pearl Harbor was accepted by Nagano. Yamamoto could not argue this point rationally in defense of his plan. The use of land-based naval aircraft to provide air cover for major naval operations had never been tested. There was no answer to the doubts that arose on such matters as the desperately tight schedule of the carrier force, its possible refuelling problems, its vulnerability to detection and the possibility of heavy loss without commensurate gain. To these points Yamamoto had no effective answer. Detailed planning and intelligence could lessen the risks, but they could not eliminate the elements of chance altogether. Even such people as Onishi began to waver at this point. He had originally estimated a 60 percent chance of success for the proposed operation, but by September he had become decidedly more pessimistic. He came to accept the 40 percent chance assessed by Fukudome.

Indeed, the omens were not too good. In war games held in September to test the whole of the Pearl Harbor concept the first result was a 50 percent loss rate among the Japanese carriers. In the second game the loss rate was 33 percent. At Yamamoto's insistence the games were replayed until Yamamoto gained the result he wanted – decisive success for no loss – which seems a highly unsatisfactory manner of devising strategy. What clinched the argument for Yamamoto was not merely his own personal prestige and authority or his confidence in his plan or the merits of the plan itself – it was the nature of American demands. By October the negotiations between Japan and the United States were clearly floundering, and there seemed no way of avoiding an open break with the Americans. The Japanese came to believe that there was no option but to resort to arms; it naturally followed from this that the American fleet had to be eliminated.

Below left: The Mitsubishi A5M Claude carrier fighter had been largely superseded by the same manufacturer's A6M Zero at the outbreak of war in 1941.
Right: The Japanese navy's Aichi D3A Val dive bomber distinguished itself at Pearl Harbor.
Below right: The army's Nakajima Ki-49 Helen enjoyed little success.
Below: The army's Nakajima Ki-43 Oscar was a near-contemporary of the Mitsubishi A6M Zero.

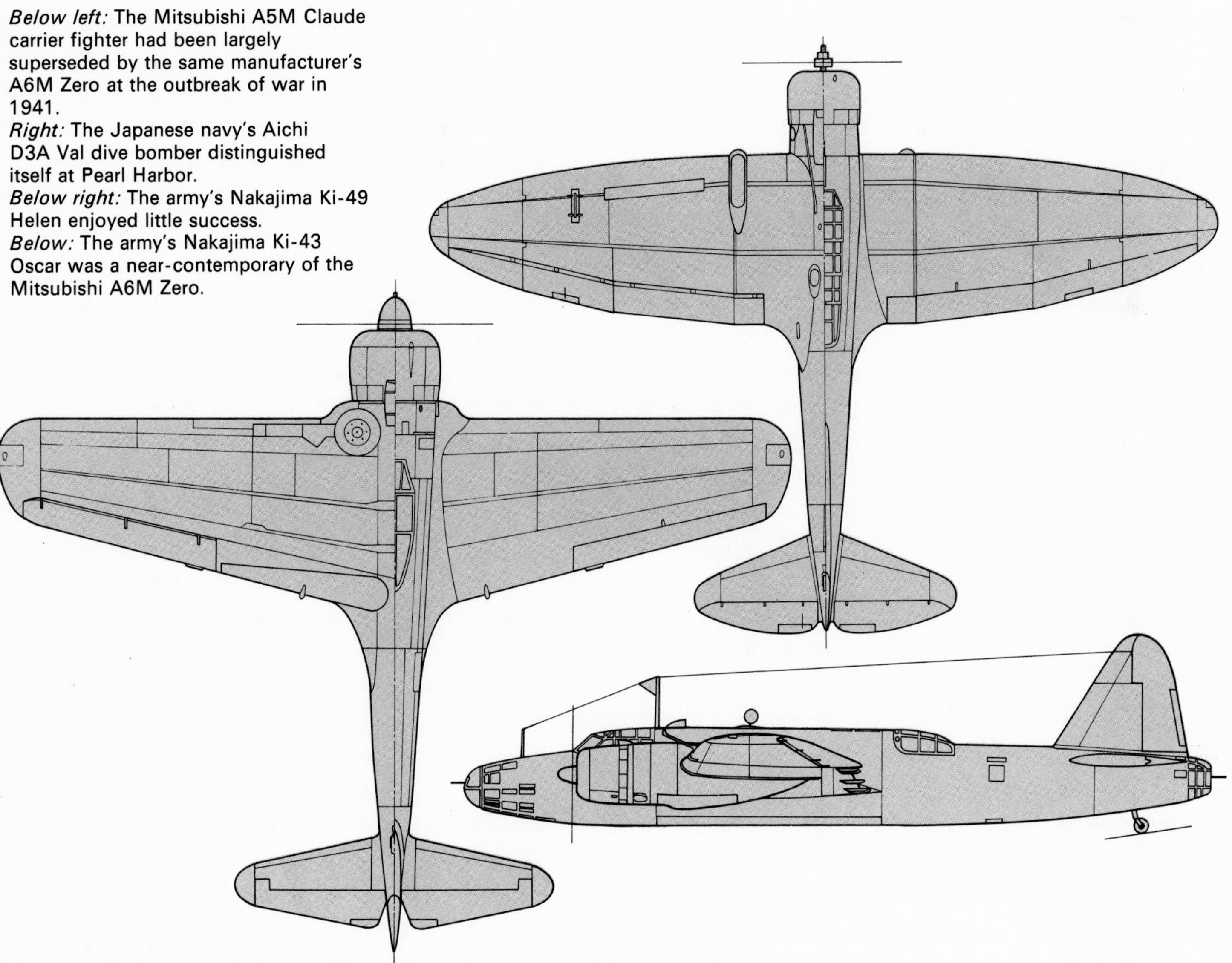

3. THE APPROACH OF WAR

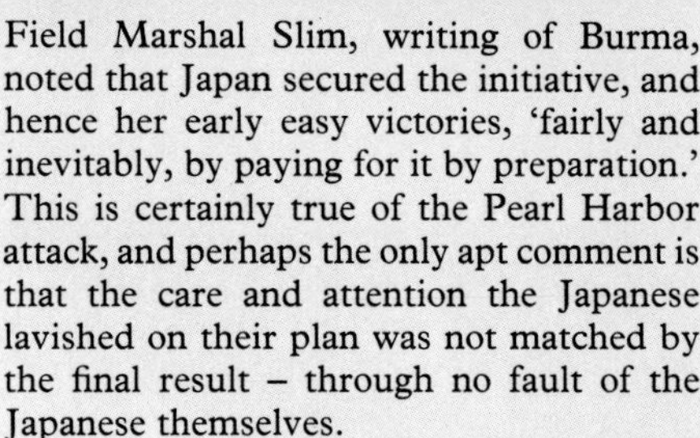

Left: General Hideki Tojo, Japan's war minister, leaves Tokyo by train. The dove of peace emblem is an ironic motif for the man who impelled Japan into the war.

Above: Aircraft parts are dispatched from store.
Above left: A Japanese assembly worker in an aircraft factory.

Field Marshal Slim, writing of Burma, noted that Japan secured the initiative, and hence her early easy victories, 'fairly and inevitably, by paying for it by preparation.' This is certainly true of the Pearl Harbor attack, and perhaps the only apt comment is that the care and attention the Japanese lavished on their plan was not matched by the final result – through no fault of the Japanese themselves.

Ironically, however, for all their efforts the Japanese attack might well have come to nought. The Americans could point to certain developments that clearly pointed to the critical state of American–Japanese relations, and they might well have taken certain measures that would have frustrated the attack. Throughout the summer of 1941 the tone of the Japanese press and radio was strident. The replacement of Prince Konoye by the militantly aggressive General Hideki Tojo as Prime Minister in October 1941 was correctly interpreted as a sign that the war party was in control in Tokyo. Moreover, on 1 December the Imperial Navy changed its codes and it was obvious that this was no routine security precaution. The codes had already been changed on 1 November. To change codes twice in a matter of a month could only point to a need for a very high level of security, far above normal requirements. It could only mean that the Imperial Navy was moving to its battle stations.

The Americans were aware of all these ominous developments, but they also had to hand a whole host of information, much of which served to confuse rather than enlighten. The most productive source of reliable information and intelligence came from Operation Magic. Magic was the name given to the most secret of all American clandestine operations at that time. The Americans had broken the most sensitive of the Japanese diplomatic and naval codes and as a result could read most of the signals between Tokyo and major Japanese embassies and consulates throughout the world.

From Magic the Americans obtained three important pieces of information. They knew that the Japanese had set a deadline of 25 November – later put back four days – for diplomacy to achieve results; if it failed to find a solution, then 'things will automatically begin to happen.' The Americans were also aware that the Japanese had prepared an elaborate series of weather reports – called the wind codes – to warn their people abroad of war or the severing of relations with certain countries. On 4 December the Americans became aware that the Japanese had used the codes relating to their relations with the United States. By then the US had discovered that the Japanese embassy in Washington had been ordered to present a major note to the Secretary of State, Cordell Hull, on 7 December. With a few hours to spare, Magic revealed the content of the note, and the Americans correctly regarded it as tantamount to a declaration of war. Yet with all these warnings they were still caught unprepared by the Japanese attack.

The manner in which the Americans were taken by surprise at Pearl Harbor is often regarded as amazing, but such a view is hardly fair. It is quite easy to see all the warning signs after the event, but it is not so easy to correctly evaluate and interpret – and then decisively act upon – hard intelligence in the midst of a deluge of ambiguous information. In the first week of December the United States knew that war was a matter of hours or days away, but they did not know who was to be attacked and where. They lacked the means to translate the warning, 'War Imminent,' into 'Planned Attack on Pearl Harbor.'

In the autumn of 1941 the Americans

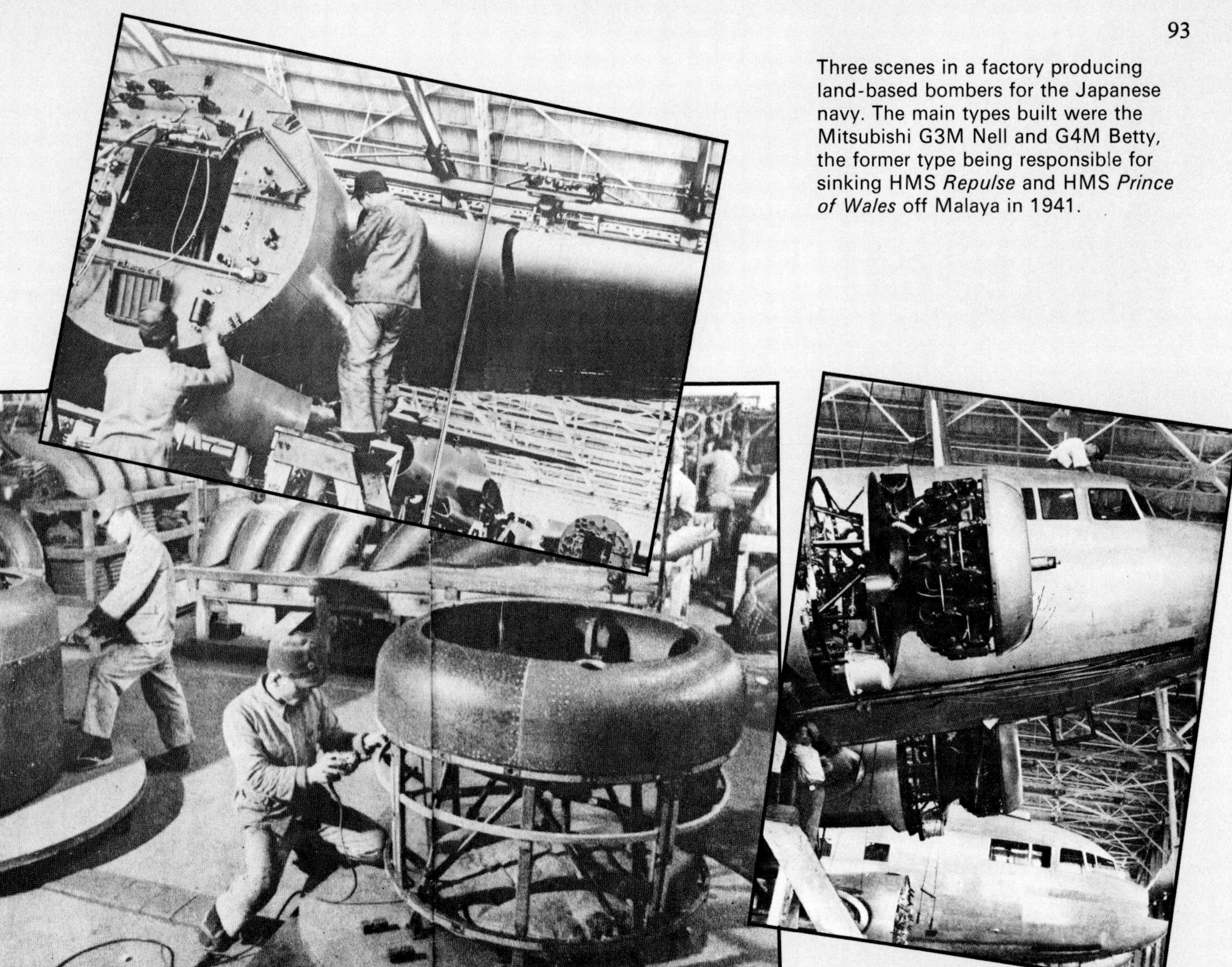

Three scenes in a factory producing land-based bombers for the Japanese navy. The main types built were the Mitsubishi G3M Nell and G4M Betty, the former type being responsible for sinking HMS *Repulse* and HMS *Prince of Wales* off Malaya in 1941.

seriously considered the likeliest target of any Japanese move to be the Maritime Provinces of the USSR. In the light of the German victories in the Soviet Union at this time and the known antagonism between the Japanese and Soviets, such an attack was a distinct possibility and the American assessment was not unreasonable. By November the Americans had revised their assessment, and correctly assumed that the main Japanese effort would be in Southeast Asia. They had no reason to assume that this effort would necessarily involve attacks on American possessions – just as Nagano had argued. If, however, the Japanese did move against the Americans then the likelihood was that they would attack the Philippines – yet even in this move there would be comfort of a kind for Pearl Harbor. American airfields in central Luzon were wrongly believed to be beyond the range of Japanese aircraft in Formosa. If the Japanese, therefore, were to move on the south and if they were to attack the Philippines then they had to use their carriers – hence there was no need to be concerned over the safety of Pearl Harbor. The carriers themselves were assumed to be in Japanese home waters. In fact the Americans by the beginning of December had no idea where the Japanese carriers were. This did not cause any real concern to the Americans; it had happened in the past and the Americans had always relocated the carriers in their home waters when the carriers switched from low frequencies, which the Americans could not find, to their normal high frequencies. This was almost a routine pattern; the Americans had lost and then found the Japanese carriers 12 times during the summer and autumn of 1941. The loss of contact with the Japanese carriers in November and December 1941 can be seen in retrospect to be absolutely crucial, but at the time it had no undue significance.

Unfortunately for the Americans the same was true of one Magic intercept that might have been taken as a clear sign that the Japanese had some move afoot with regard to Pearl Harbor. On 24 September the Japanese consulate in Honolulu was ordered by Tokyo to provide detailed information regarding American warships in Pearl Harbor. Up until that time the consulate had been instructed to give the strength and composition of American ships on the Oahu station, but after 24 September it was given detailed instructions to report arrivals and departures and the exact location of individual warships when they were at their moorings. The consulate was ordered to furnish information regarding ships moored together and it was given a grid pattern so that various stretches of water in Pearl Harbor could be married up to the warships with no possibility of misunderstanding between Honolulu and Tokyo. The signal, which was decoded by the Americans on 9 October, specifically mentioned just one type of warship in the Pacific Fleet, the carriers.

It is difficult to understand why this information was not properly appreciated. The information sought by Tokyo was necessary only if some form of offensive action against Pearl Harbor was being planned. The almost land-locked nature of the anchorage meant that the most likely form of attack was by carrier aircraft. This conclusion had already been reached by two high ranking American officers at Pearl Harbor. Rear Admiral Patrick Bellinger, the Navy's Air Defense Officer, and Major General Frederick Martin, the commander of USAAF on Oahu, had warned Washington that the Japanese might begin a war with an attack on Pearl Harbour. They estimated that such a raid would be made with six carriers approaching Oahu from

Left: US Navy enlisted men wheel an aircraft torpedo across the deck of USS *Lexington* (CV-2). Her gun armament mounted aft of the island was little used.
Below: USS *Yorktown* (CV-5) displaced 19,800 tons and could steam at 33 knots. Her aircraft complement was 81 machines.

the north. They had reached this joint conclusion from their knowledge of Japanese history, their awareness of their own commands' weaknesses and by the simple expedient of examining the options from Japan's point of view. The two commanders submitted their views to Washington in March 1941 – just at the time Genda was drawing up the plans for an attack – and urged that more radars and aircraft, particularly B-17 Flying Fortresses, should be made available for the defense of Pearl Harbor. Bellinger wanted to extend the search area around Pearl Harbor over a full 360 degrees.

Had these radars and aircraft been forthcoming then the Japanese would not have been able to launch their attack in the manner they did. However, they could not be supplied because the United States did not have the B-17s and radars, and their trained crews, in sufficient numbers to provide all-round defense for Pearl Harbor. Resources for the American services before Pearl Harbor, despite the 1940 measures, were desperately scarce and were being diverted on an ever-increasing scale to the Atlantic in an effort to stave off the defeat of Britain. What resources were available for the Pacific were being built up on the Philippines as part of a deterrent force. The corresponding neglect of Oahu was therefore inevitable, but the real point is that the Americans could not see any threat to Pearl Harbor.

Two factors blinded the Americans to Pearl Harbor's vulnerability. The first, paradoxically, was the presence of the US Pacific Fleet itself. The Americans saw their Pacific Fleet as a deterrent; they failed to see that it could act as a magnet. The Americans could see no reason to defend the fleet. One of the major reasons for this was the very isolation of Pearl Harbor. The generals and admirals on Oahu might feel dangerously exposed, but Pearl Harbor was over 3900 miles from Tokyo Bay. The Americans held similar views to the Japanese regarding distances, battle efficiency and fleet strengths. In 1941 the idea of an attack 4000 miles from a fleet base was simply inconceivable. No one really believed it to be politically or strategically possible.

The prevailing disbelief in such a possibility, the lack of proper means of sifting and evaluating information regarding Japanese intentions and capabilities, and the restricted access of Magic information were instrumental in the ignoring of the last warning the Americans received before 7 December. The warnings that came on the day of the attack were far too late to save a fleet that needed some four hours or more to get to sea. On 2 December the liner *Lurline* docked at Honolulu. In the course of her passage from California the liner picked up a series of radio transmissions that she could not identify. Unknowingly the *Lurline* had stumbled across the one security weakness in Japanese radio discipline. In November the Japanese had stepped up their radio traffic in order to confuse their opponents – though to an extent this was certain to be self-defeating – while at the same time ordering the carriers to observe strict radio silence. When the carrier task force was at sea the transmission equipment on the *Hiei*, the task force's communications center, was dismantled in order to prevent accidents, but in order to allow the destroyers to pick up transmissions from Tokyo the capital ships relayed signals from Tokyo on high frequencies simultaneously on low frequencies. US Intelligence missed this, but the *Lurline* accidentally picked it up. She detected and for some days tracked a force, obviously attempting to disguise its movements, closing on Pearl Harbor from the northwest. The liner reported this to the authorities on Oahu when she docked, but the significance of the information was missed – and with it the last chance of avoiding disaster.

Above: A Mitsubishi A6M Zero fitted with a center-line auxiliary fuel tank starts its takeoff run.
Below: An aerial view of the Pearl Harbor anchorage taken only weeks before the attack.

Right: Aircrew of the USAAF's Seventh Air Force relax on Hawaii's Waikiki beach.

4. TORA! TORA! TORA!

On 25 November Yamamoto, anticipating the failure of last-gasp diplomatic efforts to find a peaceful settlement with the Americans, ordered the carrier task force to sail on its mission the following day. Two weeks earlier some of the submarines in home waters that had been detailed for the attack had begun to sail for Kwajalein. There they refuelled between 18–20 November before continuing their mission, this time in the company of submarines already based on the atoll. In dense fog the carrier force slipped out of its desolate anchorage in the Kuriles on the 26th, the last of the carriers clearing Tankan Bay at about 0900 hours.

The task force steamed eastward, following the 43rd Parallel, into the stormy northern Pacific. It encountered only one merchantman – fortunately Japanese – during its entire mission. It steamed eastward at 13 knots with the six carriers, the *Akagi, Kaga, Hiryu, Soryu, Shokaku* and *Zuikaku*, deployed in two columns of three. The carriers were flanked by the heavy cruisers *Chikuma* and *Tone*, while the battleships *Hiei* and *Kirishima* brought up the rear. Nine destroyers, with the flagship the light cruiser *Abukuma*, were in the van. The oilers tended to straggle; their crews were unfamiliar with the exacting standards of station keeping demanded by the warships and every morning saw the escorts rounding up the scattered oilers.

All signals within the task force were by flag and lamp as the force ran into heavy seas. The price paid in storm damage and men washed overboard – particularly during an attempt to refuel on the 28th – was not small, but it had to be accepted. There was no time to search for drowning sailors. On 2 December the task force received the coded message, *Niitaka yama nobore*, which was the signal that Japan had finally decided upon war and that Nagumo was to proceed with the operation as planned. The next day the wind and sea moderated sufficiently to allow refuelling, and the force crossed the International Date Line, thereby gaining a day. The next day – the 4th by Tokyo time to which all Japanese warships worked irrespective of location, but the 3rd by local time – the force turned to the southeast to begin its approach to Pearl Harbor. For four successive days the warships topped up their fuel tanks before, on the evening of the 6th, they were in a position to drop the five remaining tankers and begin their high-speed run through the night in order to reach their flying-off position by dawn.

By the evening of the 6th the crews of the ships had been addressed by their captains, aboard the *Akagi* by Nagumo himself, and the Imperial Rescript announcing the start of the war was read. Yamamoto's personal message that the fate of the Empire rested upon the success of the operation was impressed upon all hands. To add to the gravity of the hour the most precious heirloom in Japanese naval history – the battle flag flown by the legendary Togo at the battle of Tsu-shima in 1905 – was broken out over the *Akagi*. While all the ceremonial of the occasion was being marked, the crisis of the operation was reached; as the task force neared Hawaii Tokyo informed Nagumo that intelligence reports from Oahu showed that no American carriers were in harbor.

When Nagumo's force sailed the Admiral believed that all six American fleet carriers were on the Pearl Harbor station. Japanese intelligence, however, was faulty. Five, not six, carriers had been in the Pacific, but two, the *Hornet* and *Yorktown*, had been transferred to the Atlantic while the *Saratoga* was off the west coast. The *Enterprise* and *Lexington* had been at Pearl Harbor, but as Nagumo closed on Hawaii both were at sea and their whereabouts were unknown to the Japanese. Following war warnings issued when the Americans believed that the Japanese might begin operations at the end of November – and later when Japanese moves against Southeast Asia were detected – the Americans had decided upon a reinforcement of the Pacific islands. Both the carriers had been ordered to ferry Marine Corps aircraft, the *Enterprise* to Wake and the *Lexington* to Midway.

The absence of the carriers opened up all kinds of possibilities for the Japanese task force, not least the prospect of being compromised and counterattacked. Intelligence reports were reassuring on this matter. There was no sign of any unusual American activity or precautions on Pearl Harbor. The warships were not protected by torpedo nets, which had been rejected on the grounds that they would unduly restrict the deep-water channels, and no barrage balloons were being flown. The commercial radio stations on Hawaii were broadcasting as normal. There was no sign that the Americans had any inkling that the Japanese had divided their forces to attack various targets separated by thousands of miles of ocean.

For Genda and those of similar persuasion the whole point of the attack would be lost if the American carriers escaped unscathed, but the rigidity of the timetable of the attack did not allow the Japanese to wait for them to return. Nagumo's Chief of Staff, Rear Admiral Ryunosuke Kusaka, was not unduly disturbed by the carriers' absence; he considered that the eight battleships at Pearl Harbor – the ninth, the *Colorado*, was undergoing dockyard work on the west coast – were more than equal in value to the absent carriers. Nagumo was not prepared to delay or abandon the plan of attack. It was inconceivable to him that he should hesitate on account of ships that were not at their moorings waiting to be attacked. He could reasonably hope that one carrier at least might return in time to be sunk. The heavy cruisers normally with the *Enterprise* had returned to their moorings, and it was not unreasonable to suppose that the carrier herself might be at her berth on the morning of the attack. To try to locate the missing carriers Nagumo ordered the two heavy cruisers to fly off their reconnaissance aircraft before dawn on the 7th to search Pearl Harbor and the Pacific Fleet's occasional alternative anchorage at Lahaina Roads, Maui. Both places were empty of carriers.

Soon after the cruisers flew off their aircraft and just before dawn on the 7th, the task force reached its flying-off position, 230 miles north and slightly to the east of Pearl Harbor. The carriers turned eastward into a fresh wind, but with a strong southerly sea running conditions for launching aircraft were tricky. Only two aircraft were lost as 183 took to the air in record time. Firstly, the 43 Mitsubishi A6M2 Zero-sen fighters rose to fly combat air patrols as 51 Achi D3A2 Val dive bombers and 89 Nakajima B5N2 Kate level-altitude bombers struggled into formation. Forty Kates, the cutting edge of the attack, carried torpedoes; the other Kates were armed with heavy armor-piercing bombs. As these aircraft rose from the decks of their carriers one thing was clear: the Americans at Pearl Harbor now lacked the time and the means to avoid anything other than a stunning defeat.

The last chance the Americans had of redeeming the situation came and went about 0400 hours when the minesweeper *Castor* made contact with one of the midget submarines as it approached the defenses of the anchorage. The encounter was only fleeting, and the duty destroyer *Ward* failed to obtain contact with the submarine when she came to the assistance of the *Castor*. An unconfirmed contact could not be used to alert the fleet, and when the *Ward* sank two midget submarines at 0645 and 0703 hours with guns and depth charges, it was too late for the American chain of command to appreciate and react to the situation. The destroyer *Helm* was ordered to assist the *Ward* and the *Monaghan* was ordered to stand by to give assistance if necessary, but little more could be done in a situation that seemed to lack urgency.

Similarly, there was a seeming lack of urgency concerning the last warning the Americans received before the first bombs fell. The last chance was provided by the radar station at Opana on the most northerly part of Oahu. The station obtained contact with incoming Japanese aircraft at 0702 and continued to track the first wave until 0739 when the aircraft entered a 'blind spot.' Privates Joseph Lockard and George Elliot reported contact with an extremely large number of aircraft closing Oahu from the north at 150 knots at 0706, but the Duty Officer at the Shafter Information Center, the tactical center for the radar stations on Oahu, misinterpreted the warning. A quite plausible explanation for the contact was possible. With the American carriers at sea the contact could be with aircraft flown home in advance of the carriers. Alternatively, the contact could be with a group of B-17s being flown in from California that morning. As a result of these considerations no precautions were taken – indeed the contact was not even reported to higher authorities. It would have made very little difference if they had been. None of the airfields was fully operational and the fleet could not have cleared harbor in the time that was available. All that could have been achieved was for some of the fighters to get into the air to meet the Japanese. Ammunition could have been broken out on ships and ashore. Japanese casualties would have been much higher than was to be the case, but the overall result could hardly have been changed by such actions.

As the Japanese aircraft came over Oahu the strike leader, Commander Mitsuo Fuchida, had to decide the form of attack. This was no easy task because he had to decide whether or not surprise had been

Above: Admiral Isoroku Yamamoto was Japan's greatest naval tactician and architect of the victory at Pearl Harbor.
Left: Warplanes crowd the flight deck of a Japanese carrier with engines running before takeoff. A6M Zeros are in the foreground, with Val dive bombers behind.
Below: A map of the Hawaiian island of Oahu and a plan of the Pearl Harbor naval base.

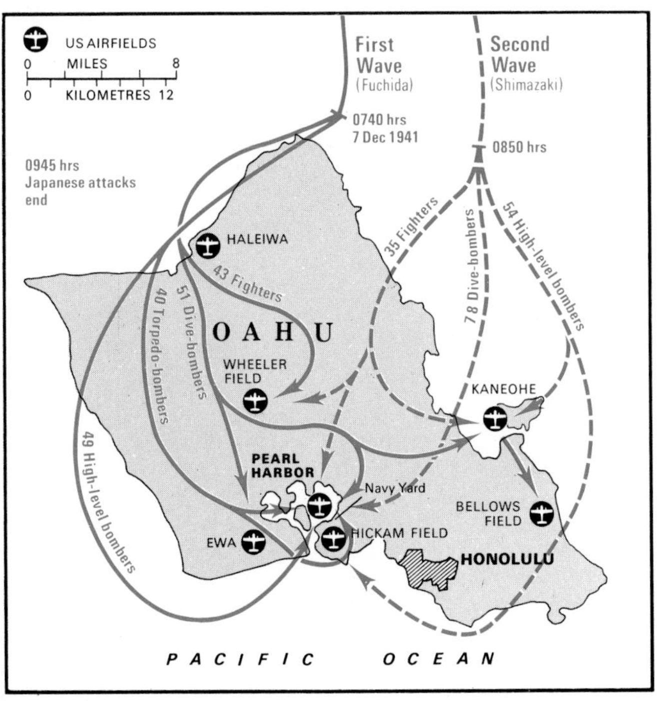

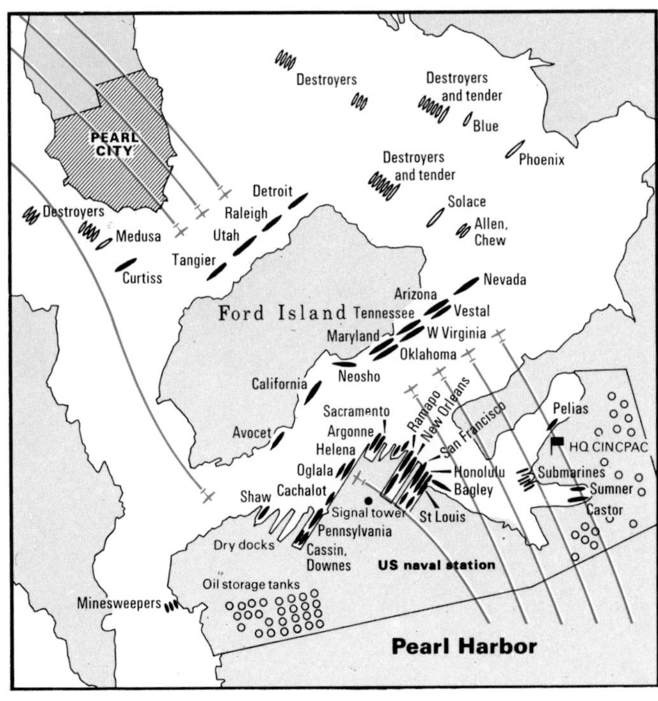

29

Left: Flight-deck crewmen position an A6M Zero for takeoff on 7 December 1941.
Below left: The Zero fighter won an enviable reputation during the early stages of the Pacific War.
Below right: B-17 Flying Fortress bombers parked on Hickam Field during the Japanese attack.
Right: Smoke and flames engulf the headquarters buildings at Hickam Field, the main USAAF airfield on Oahu.

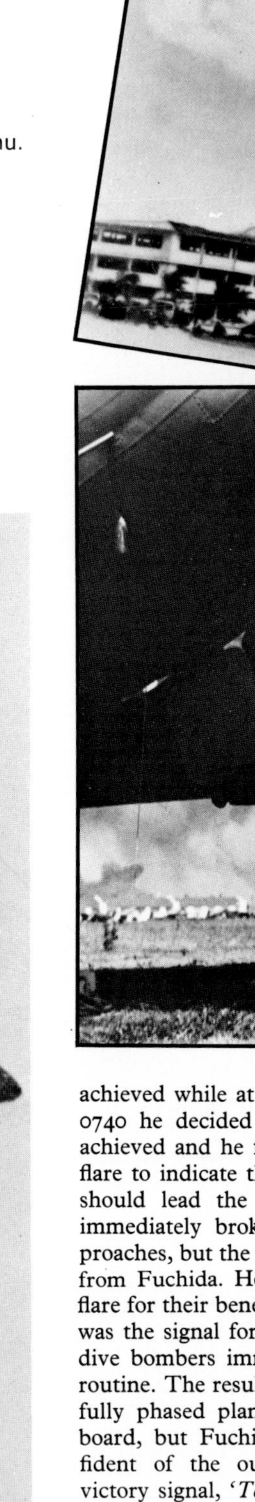

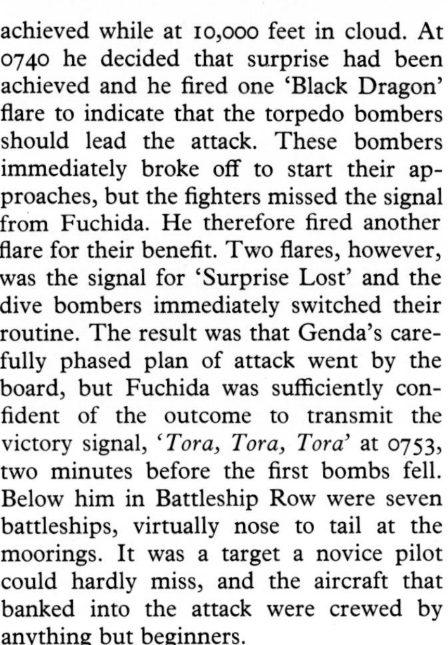

achieved while at 10,000 feet in cloud. At 0740 he decided that surprise had been achieved and he fired one 'Black Dragon' flare to indicate that the torpedo bombers should lead the attack. These bombers immediately broke off to start their approaches, but the fighters missed the signal from Fuchida. He therefore fired another flare for their benefit. Two flares, however, was the signal for 'Surprise Lost' and the dive bombers immediately switched their routine. The result was that Genda's carefully phased plan of attack went by the board, but Fuchida was sufficiently confident of the outcome to transmit the victory signal, '*Tora, Tora, Tora*' at 0753, two minutes before the first bombs fell. Below him in Battleship Row were seven battleships, virtually nose to tail at the moorings. It was a target a novice pilot could hardly miss, and the aircraft that banked into the attack were crewed by anything but beginners.

The first bombs fell on the Naval Air Station on Ford Island in the middle of Pearl Harbor, but in the opening wave Japanese fighters and dive bombers divided their attentions between this airfield and Hickam (US Army bombers), Wheeler and Bellows (US Army fighters), Ewa (US Marine Corps aircraft), Kaneohe Naval Air Station (reconnaissance aircraft) and Schofield Barracks (HQ of the 24th and 25th Infantry Divisions). Although all these airfields were subjected to attack at various times throughout the next two hours, the major part of the damage they sustained was inflicted in the first devastating minutes. Hardest hit were Kaneohe, which lost all 33 of its aircraft in the first assault, and Ewa, which lost 33 of its 49 aircraft in the opening attack. At the end of the day these two fields between them mustered one operational aircraft. At the time of the attack there were 394 aircraft on Oahu of which 139 army and 157 navy aircraft were operational. Of these only 88 were fighters, but such was the fury and violence

Below: The US Navy's shore-based aircraft did not escape the Japanese onslaught. A Catalina flying boat is in the left background, to its right lies a Kingfisher spotter floatplane.
Right: A burned out Curtiss P-40 fighter lies before No 3 hangar on the USAAF's Wheeler Field.
Far right: While the Japanese attack concentrated on the warships and naval installations in Pearl Harbor, airfield targets on Oahu were not neglected, as this blazing hangar attests.

Far right: The flame-scarred decks of the battleship USS *Pennsylvania* bear witness to the effectiveness of Japan's Aichi D3A dive bomber.
Right: USS *West Virginia* fell victim to the first attacking wave of Nakajima B5N Kate torpedo bombers.
Below: USS *California* was one of eight battleships sunk at their moorings, yet all but two were later raised and repaired.

Top left: A Japanese photo taken during the attack by Kate torpedo bombers on battleship row at about 0800 hours.
Above left: The result of the attack by the first wave of torpedo bombers can be seen in this Japanese photograph.
Left: Salvage tugs attempt to keep the cruiser *Raleigh* afloat. The capsized hull of USS *Utah* can be seen astern.

Above: The Mitsubishi Ki-21 Sally was one of the Japanese Army Air Force's chief bombers at the start of the Pacific War.
Below: This B-17 Flying Fortress force landed on Bellows Field to escape Japanese fighters. It had arrived on a ferry flight from the United States in the middle of the Japanese attack.

able to come into action. Eighteen aircraft were flown off the *Enterprise* and they arrived over Ford Island at about 0800 hours. The carrier herself had been due back at 0730 but she had been delayed by refuelling problems. At the time of the attack she was some 200 miles west of Oahu, but the sacrifice of her aircraft was not in vain. As her pilots ran into the Japanese attackers over Pearl Harbor warnings were sent to the carrier and the *Enterprise*, observing radio silence, vanished westward into the vastness of the ocean.

For the capital ships in harbor there could be no escape. As the torpedo bombers broke into the attack those on the inside of the turn reached their objectives slightly before their colleagues on the outside. The result was that the warships lined up on the northwest side of Ford Island took the first blows rather than the battleships to the southeast. Five aircraft came over Pearl City against the target battleship *Utah* and the cruisers *Detroit* and *Raleigh* which were anchored in the berths normally used by the carriers. The *Detroit* was missed by her lone assailant, but the *Raleigh* was struck by a single torpedo while the *Utah* took two. Immediately the *Utah*, because she had been decommissioned and lacked the armor protection needed to survive such damage, began to settle to port. One of the attacking Kates, however, held off, skimmed Ford Island and Battleship Row and let fly at the *Oglala* and *Helena*, moored together in the normal berth of the Pacific Fleet's flagship, the *Pennsylvania*. The torpedo passed under the *Oglala* and hit home on the cruiser at precisely 0757 hours. The *Helena* immediately settled but the *Oglala*, a minelayer, was effectively destroyed by concussion. She was 34 years old, and had not been designed as a warship. She was not compartmentalized and literally burst at the seams. It was later alleged that she died of fright, but this was no joke. Her lack of internal structural strength made her subsequent raising the most difficult of the salvage operations undertaken at Pearl Harbor.

It was then the turn of Battleship Row. At 0758 hours the first torpedoes hammered home against the *Oklahoma*, outboard of the *Maryland*, and the *West Virginia*, moored outside the *Tennessee*. The *Arizona*, inboard but unprotected by the repair ship *Vestal*, took two torpedoes in the first attack. In the next few minutes a series of torpedoes hit the hapless *Oklahoma* and *West Virginia*. The *West Virginia* was torn to pieces by perhaps as many as six torpedoes, but miraculously, with all power gone, counterflooding and the strength of the retaining wires held her list to 13 degrees and she settled more or less upright on the harbor bottom. The *Oklahoma* was not so fortunate. Five torpedoes gashed her port side wide open and she began to capsize. Two more torpedoes crashed into her as she began to keel over. By 0806 hours she had gone.

Above: The superstructure of the battleship USS *Arizona* is wreathed in flames and smoke. She later capsized, trapping 400 seamen in her hull. *Below:* Another view of *Arizona* showing the explosion of her forward magazine, which showered the harbor with blazing debris.

Left: West Virginia's ensign keeps flying after the attack.
Below left: Nevada was beached on Waipio Point to prevent her sinking at her moorings.

Bottom: USS *Oklahoma*, capsized astern of *Maryland*, could not be salvaged.
Below: The sky above Pearl Harbor was filled with AA bursts.

The *California* was anchored a little apart from the other battleships and made a poor target, but the torpedo bombers knew their business and finished her with just two torpedoes. In normal circumstances the *California* would perhaps have avoided sinking, but her double bottom had been opened up ready for inspection the following day. The sea water rushed unchecked through the ship and she began to settle rapidly. At the other end of the line the *Nevada* took a single torpedo that tore an enormous hole in her port bow, and soon afterward she was struck by two heavy bombs, one of which destroyed the starboard antiaircraft director. Within a matter of minutes of the start of the attack all the battleships in the Row, with the exception of the *Maryland* and *Tennessee*, had been crippled or severely damaged and the scene was set for the first of the three great moments of drama of the attack.

As the torpedo bombers completed their executions, the high-level bombers joined the attack. Not only was the *Nevada* hit but so too was the *West Virginia*. Two bomb hits on the *West Virginia* did massive damage. Her three armored decks forward of the bridge were telescoped together and most of the ship between the forecastle and forward turret was burned out. The two

Despite the devastation wrought by the Japanese, Pearl Harbor recovered from the attack with surprising speed. Six of the eight battleships were returned to service, as were many of the damaged smaller craft.

Left: Smoke billows from the burning USS *Arizona* at the end of the attack.
Below left: US Marines prepare to engage enemy aircraft with their rifles and a 0.5-caliber machine gun. In the background Douglas Devastator torpedo bombers are parked.
Below: USS *Arizona*'s exploding magazine caused such damage that, like *Oklahoma*, she was never salvaged.

battleships so far immune were also hit; both the *Maryland* and *Tennessee* were hit by two bombs apiece. One of the bombs that wrecked the forward areas of the *Tennessee* ripped out the bridge of the *West Virginia*, disembowelling her skipper, Captain Mervyn Bennion. Bennion was only one man, and a moment or two before he was fatally wounded nearly 1100 men had died when at about 0810 hours the *Arizona* was struck by a bomb on her forecastle. It penetrated through to the forward magazine and the battleship blew up in a sheet of flame that climbed hundreds of feet into the air. High above the stricken ship Fuchida's bomber was shaken by a massive shock wave which also swept men off the *Nevada*, *West Virginia* and *Vestal*. The repair ship, already struck by some of the bombs that had been aimed at the *Arizona*, was hurriedly pulled clear of the fiercely burning wreck by a tug.

By the time the *Arizona* had gone the first faltering barrage was being put up by the ships in harbor. Ten critical minutes passed between the first attacks and the first heavy antiaircraft fire, but gradually the barrage became intensive and more effective. The Americans were beginning to react, but at every turn they were fighting a losing battle. Ammunition lockers had to be smashed open, and even then some of the ammunition, dating from 1918, was found to be defective. The chains of the heavy machine-gun ammunition belts frequently broke, and many of the fuses and charges for the heavier antiaircraft ammunition failed to function. In ships where power was lost ammunition had to be passed by hand, often along crazily-tilting passageways. Gun crews, often lacking directional control, were frequently incomplete. Some ships, which were awaiting or undergoing repair, had no guns to fight with as their weapons had been either removed or partially dismantled. The American chain of command completely collapsed, but men fought as best they could, without much regard to the niceties of rank. By the time the American flak began to blacken the skies most of the damage to be inflicted by the Japanese had been incurred, but the Americans could ensure fierce resistance for the 170 aircraft of the second waves – 80 Vals, 54 high-level Kates and 36 Zeros – that were closing on their objectives.

There was a slight lull in the tempo of the attack on the warships between 0815 and 0830 hours, though at this time Bellows Field received some devastating treatment as nine Zero-sens followed a Flying Fortress coming in to land. In fact the second wave was late, but this did not matter much because many of the high-level bombers from the first wave had to make several runs over their smoke-shrouded objectives before they could drop their bombs. Yet even this small lull afforded the Americans little respite because during it they became conscious of the threat of the midget submarines. The *Helm*, which had steamed down the channel at 27 knots rather than the regulation 14 knots as the attack developed, obtained contact with a midget submarine outside the harbor entrance. The submarine survived the subsequent depth charging, but it was badly shaken and never under full control again. She later drifted ashore near Bellows Field and survived an attempt to scuttle her. Her commander, Ensign Sakamaki, survived to become the first prisoner of the Pacific War.

At 0830 hours, however, just as the second wave attack was beginning to develop, the destroyer-minelayer *Breese* sighted another midget submarine – but this time well into the harbor. The repair ship *Medusa* and the aircraft tender *Curtiss* also sighted the intruder, and with warning flags flying from the three ships' yards, the *Monaghan* turned to engage. All four American ships fired at the submarine, which in turn fired at, but missed, the anchored 508-foot long *Medusa* and the onrushing *Monaghan*, which caught the submarine a glancing blow. As the American warships passed over the Japanese boat, the *Monaghan* blew the submarine to pieces with a shallow-pattern depth-charge attack set at 30 feet. The destroyer escaped damage but ran ashore in the very restricted waters of the channel. However, she recovered and was able to reach the sea.

Further back in the harbor the second major incident was unfolding as at the end of Battleship Row the *Nevada* began to get under way. In normal circumstances it took about 3 hours 30 minutes for a battleship to raise steam and be maneuvered into the channel by tugs, but 45 minutes after the start of the attack the *Nevada*, without assistance, began to nose her way into deep water. Those who saw her agreed that one of the most magnificent and awesome sights of the day was the stricken battleship, against a black background of smoke and death, seeking the channel as the wind caught and unfurled the Stars and Stripes over her quarterdeck in a superb gesture of defiance.

As the *Nevada* moved down the channel, with no captain and only a handful of officers aboard, it seemed as if the entire second wave of attackers had the same thought of sinking her in the channel, thereby preventing any warship either

Left: Rescue teams attempt to save survivors from *West Virginia*.
Below left: This rusting hull served to remind American sailors of the 'day of infamy.'

Above: An Aichi D3A Val dive bomber noses over onto its target. Note that its underwing dive brakes are deployed.
Below: A Japanese midget submarine lies beached on a South Pacific island. Craft of this type opened the Pearl Harbor attack.

Above: Japanese bombs raise fountains of water around small craft in Pearl Harbor.

entering or leaving harbor. Dive bombers came at her from every direction, smothering her with a series of hits. Reeling under the impact of these blows and with fires spreading rapidly throughout her, the *Nevada* began to settle lower in the water. The danger of her sinking in the channel was appreciated and as she neared the floating drydock signal flags could be seen at the Naval District Headquarters ordering the *Nevada* to stay clear of the channel. With some reluctance the battleship was run aground at Hospital Point on the southern shore, where she was turned around by the tide to face the way she had come.

The *Nevada* perhaps achieved more than she realized by her abortive sortie. She began to get under way at about 0840 hours and immediately drew enemy aircraft against her. Japanese aircraft paid no attention to the aviation-fuel carrier *Neosho*, anchored between the *California* and *Maryland*, which began to get under way at 0835 hours. Japanese aircraft, intent on greater prey, let her get clear of Battleship Row unmolested. Had the Japanese attacked the *Neosho*, and had she exploded, it is distinctly possible that she would have destroyed three or four battleships. As it was, burning oil from the *Oklahoma* drifted down on the *California* and forced her abandonment at 1002 hours. Fortunately, however, the wind changed and blew the oil clear of the battleship which was quickly reboarded and her many fires, caused by both waves of attackers, were tackled.

With smoke covering so many targets, Japanese aircraft turned on the largest undamaged target remaining. This was the Fleet flagship *Pennsylvania* in Drydock 1010. She was berthed with the destroyers *Cassin* and *Downes*. During the first attack the drydock was flooded to prevent the battleship surging forward and crushing the destroyers if and when the dock gates were destroyed. This also had the effect of raising the battleship level to the dockside, thus allowing her antiaircraft guns to come into action. The flagship was only hit once but the destroyers were hit repeatedly. Even before the dock was flooded both the destoyers were in flames and at 0937 hours the *Cassin* was shaken by a massive blast and she keeled over to starboard and rolled on top of the *Downes*. Just along from the drydock was the destroyer *Shaw* in the floating drydock, and she was also badly hit. Her demise provided the third spectacular moment of the attack. A heavy fire, caused by a bomb hit at 0912 hours, reached her forward magazine at 0930 hours and the forecastle of the destroyers quite literally blew up. Debris, shells and bodies were thrown hundreds of feet into the sky in one awesome explosion.

By the time the *Shaw* exploded the full fury of the Japanese attack had passed, though a few more heavy blows were still to be struck. The *Curtiss* was hit by a bomb and a crashing bomber, and then shaken by a series of near misses. The 8325-ton destroyer-tender *Dobbin* was likewise badly jolted by a near miss that killed an entire gun crew while the *Raleigh* was struck by a bomb that passed through her and exploded in the bed of the harbor. This started a massive improvised operation to keep the cruiser afloat. The *Honolulu* was also caught by a near miss which damaged her oil tanks and warped her armor, but with that the raiders were gone. One last raking over the nearby airfields and it was all over, all except for Fuchida. The attack leader continued to circle for an hour assessing the damage before he, too, turned directly for the carriers. En route he picked up two fighter stragglers and returned them safely to their ships.

In order to help his aircraft return, Nagumo had moved his carriers to within 190 miles of Pearl Harbor, a desperately close distance but one which Nagumo felt was justified by the knowledge that those extra miles closer might make all the difference between recovery and loss of aircraft that were damaged or low on fuel. In all 324 of the attacking aircraft returned, the last being Fuchida at about 1300 hours. Fuchida went straight to Nagumo and Kusaka to report. With rearming and refuelling the aircraft well under way, Fuchida urged Nagumo to mount another assault. Fuchida argued that there were still many suitable targets for an attack and that the American defenses were negligible. He hoped that a second strike might catch one or more of the carriers.

Yamamoto, in the *Nagato* in Kure Harbor, anticipated the course of action that would be adopted. He predicted that Nagumo would withdraw and not renew the attack. Yamamoto knew of Nagumo's chronic doubts about the operation and that the Vice-Admiral had never had much confidence in the plan in the first place. Yamamoto knew that the responsibility of command of the carriers bore heavily on Nagumo and that Nagumo was well aware of the vulnerability of carriers to dive-bomb attacks. It was Nagumo who, in the argument before the attack, had pointed out that the carriers would be exposed along the whole length of their flight decks and vulnerable to attack. It was a fear that was to be realized at Midway in June. As Fuchida argued his case Nagumo hardened in his view that little could be expected from a renewal of the attack; the security of the carriers themselves was his first concern. Kusaka knew his Admiral's mind and at 1330 hours gave the order to begin the withdrawal.

5. THE DAY OF INFAMY

By confirming Kusaka's order Nagumo turned his back on the chance to secure total victory at Pearl Harbor. It was a chance that never came again to the Imperial Navy. Nagumo and Kusaka acted as commanders who had narrowly avoided defeat rather than as admirals who had a devastating strategic victory within their grasp. Admiral Chester W Nimitz, the commander of American naval forces in the Pacific for much of the war, was to comment that the weakness of the Pearl Harbor operation was that it was not sustained. The observation is accurate because it points to the fact that the Japanese were attempting to do too much in a single operational strike. Had the Japanese attempted a selective second and perhaps even a third strike then crippling damage might well have been inflicted. As it was, Nagumo's considered opinion was that despite his fears a major strategic success had been achieved, and that little more could have been attained that would have justified the risks.

Nagumo had good reason to be pleased with the success of the operation. At a cost of 29 aircraft – five Kates, 15 Vals and nine Zero-sens – and all five of the midget submarines, the Japanese sank or severely damaged 18 warships and auxiliaries, wiped out 80 percent of the aircraft on Oahu at the time of the attack, and killed and wounded 3681 American personnel. Nearly half of the 2403 Americans killed were lost in the *Arizona*. To a world that was accustomed to measuring naval power in terms of the number of battleships a nation possessed, Pearl Harbor was an unmitigated disaster. On 6 December 1941 the Americans possessed 17 battleships, nine of which were in the Pacific. By the end of the following day the Americans were left with a mere eight that were fit for operations. Eight had been lost or put out of commission at Pearl Harbor while the *Colorado* was in the naval dockyard at Bremerton, Washington. All that were left were the battleships of the Atlantic Fleet and some of these were rather elderly.

The debacle, however, was nowhere near as bad as first appearances suggest, and it was certainly less severe than it might have been. As the smoke from burning ships and installations billowed over Oahu what was not immediately obvious was the fact that the basic necessities for a successful counteroffensive remained unmolested. Losses were concentrated among the battleships. Grievous though the battleship losses were, with five sunk and three damaged, all

Below: Rescue teams work to release trapped seamen from the capsized hull of USS *Oklahoma*.

Right: The shocked reaction of Americans to the Japanese attack is reflected in the headlines of the *Honolulu Star-Bulletin*.
Below: The Japanese victory at Pearl Harbor was not entirely without cost. American sailors salvage an Aichi D3A shot down during the attack.

Honolulu Star-Bulletin 1st EXTRA

8 PAGES—HONOLULU, TERRITORY OF HAWAII, U. S. A., SUNDAY, DECEMBER 7, 1941—8 PAGES

PRICE FIVE CENTS

WAR!

(Associated Press by Transpacific Telephone)

SAN FRANCISCO, Dec. 7.—President Roosevelt announced this morning that Japanese planes had attacked Manila and Pearl Harbor.

OAHU BOMBED BY JAPANESE PLANES

SIX KNOWN DEAD, 21 INJURED, AT EMERGENCY HOSPITAL

Attack Made On Island's Defense Areas

CIVILIANS ORDERED OFF STREETS

ANTIAIRCRAFT GUNS IN ACTION

BOMB NEAR GOVERNOR'S MANSION

HOUR OF ATTACK—7:55 A. M.

CITY IN UPROAR

Hundreds See City Bombed

Names of Dead and Injured

Schools Closed

Editorial

HAWAII MEETS THE CRISIS

COURTESY: PACIFIC MERCANTILE LIMITED, H

Honolulu Star-Bulletin 2nd EXTRA

8 PAGES—HONOLULU, TERRITORY OF HAWAII, U. S. A., SUNDAY, DECEMBER 7, 1941—8 PAGES

PRICE FIVE CENTS

DEATHS OVER 400 ON OAHU, LATEST REPORT

TOKYO ANNOUNCES "STATE OF WAR" WITH U. S.

Japanese Raids On Guam, Panama Are Reported

Oahu Blackout Tonight; Fleet Here Moves Out to Sea

Four Waves, Start At 7:55, Oahu Hit In Many Places

Governor Proclaims National Emergency

Known Oahu Casualties

REPORTS GUAM, PANAMA ATTACKED

BULLETINS

Blackout For Oahu Ordered

Inter-Island Ships, Planes Are Held Up

Military Censorship On All Messages

Two Japanese Fliers Captured

Editorial

HAWAII MEETS THE CRISIS

these capital ships were old and slow. They were unable to give battle with the latest German and Japanese battleships on equal terms, and they were too slow to operate efficiently with the fleet carriers. Indeed, in a roundabout manner the loss of the battle line at Pearl Harbor was a blessing in disguise for the Americans, not least because it released survivors from the sunken ships for service in other warships at a time when trained manpower was desperately scarce in the US Navy.

In common with other major navies, the US Navy in the interwar period had been divided on the issue of the relative merits of battleships and aircraft carriers. There had been a three-way split between those who retained an undiminished confidence in the ability of a properly handled battleship to withstand air attack, those who regarded battleships as obsolete and a waste of resources and those who tried to balance the conflicting claims of the more partisan advocates of artillery and air power. The conventional wisdom of the day was that the battleship remained the arbiter of sea power and queen of the oceans. The gun was generally regarded as the prime weapon at sea and aircraft were subordinate to it. The role of aircraft was seen to be the provision of reconnaissance beyond the range of cruisers, defense of the battle line and the securing of air supremacy over the battle fleet, to spot for guns and to carry out attacks on the enemy battle line, particularly when it was out of the range of the guns or in flight. In this latter role aircraft attacks were seen as essential if the enemy line was to be engaged and destroyed in an artillery duel.

The experience of the first two years of war was inconclusive in that the results of combat could be interpreted in various ways. Only one capital ship – the *Hood* – was sunk in a straight artillery duel, but the example of the striking power of aircraft as shown at Taranto could be discounted by a world holding small regard for Italian martial prowess. Neither of the extremes could draw much comfort from battle experience. The battle of Cape Matapan in March 1941, however, showed that an enemy in flight could be brought to a gunnery engagement after crippling strikes by aircraft, and the end of the *Bismarck* in May 1941 seemed to confirm this. The *Bismarck* was destroyed by artillery and torpedoes after she had been crippled by attacks by carrier aircraft. The lesson that had it not been for the successful air strikes the *Bismarck* would have eluded the forces hunting her and made the safety of a friendly port was widely realized, but what was little appreciated at the time was the

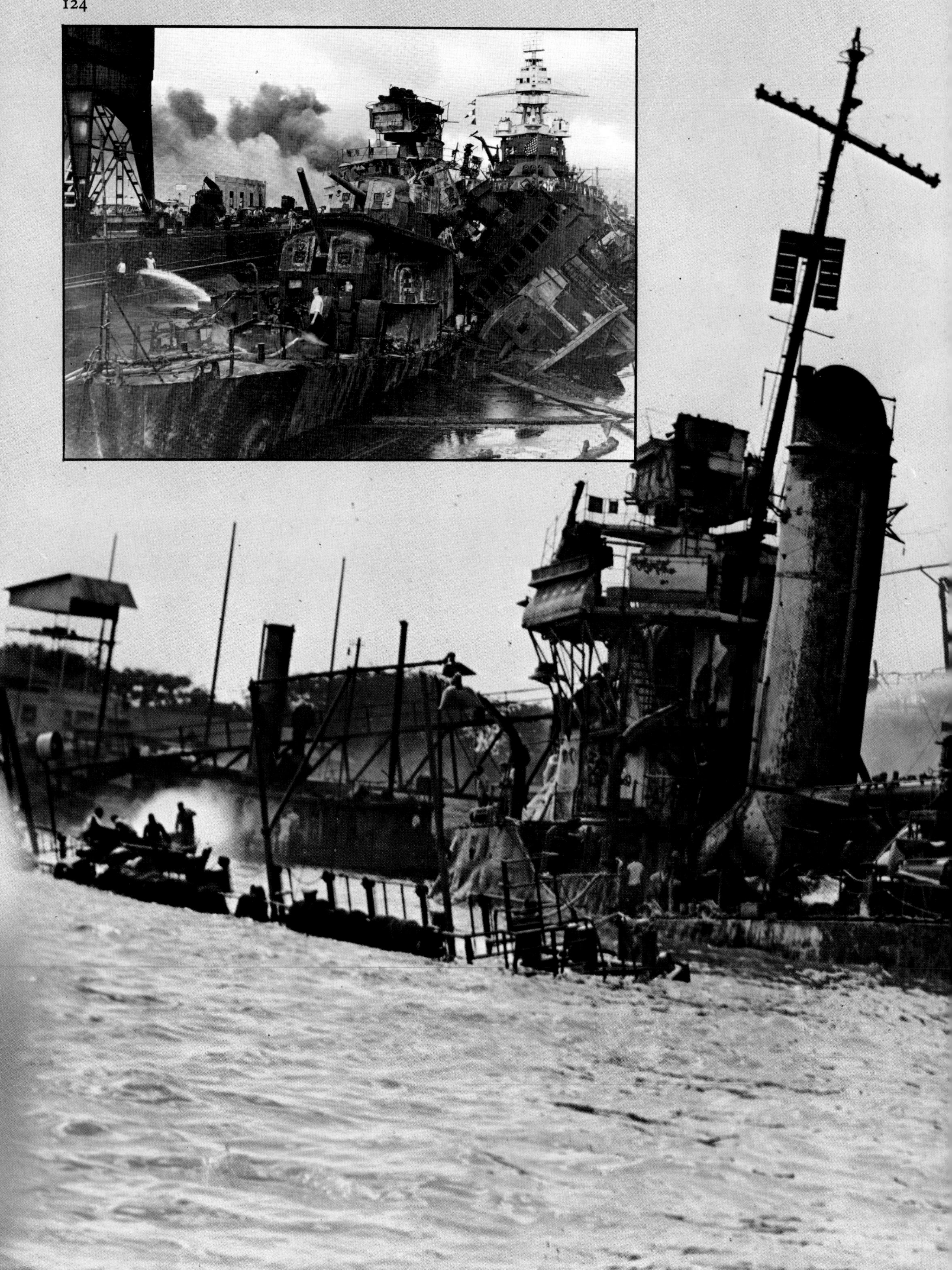

Left: The destroyers *Cassin* and *Downes* were wrecked in Drydock No 1.
Right: A floating crane salvages an Aichi D3A for analysis and evaluation by technical intelligence experts.
Below: USS *Shaw* rests on the bottom alongside the quay.

real lesson of the *Bismarck* chase. That was that the German battleship would have been caught and destroyed far more quickly and at far less cost had she been sought and engaged by strong, numerous and properly constituted carrier forces.

The Japanese attack at Pearl Harbor removed all these arguments within the United States Navy. Carrier aircraft had shown that at minimal cost to themselves they could destroy battleships far beyond the horizon range. As the Americans had no battle line left after the attack, they had to rebuild their tactical formations around the carriers. The war-winning Fast Carrier Task Group concept emerged directly from the Pearl Harbor disaster. The Americans had experimented with the idea in the inter-war period, but their exercises had proved inconclusive. Now, after Pearl Harbor, they had to make a virtue of necessity. Irreverently, the loss of the battle line at Pearl Harbor was almost welcomed in some quarters of the United States Navy. There were those who felt that what had been lost was only a collection of obsolescent scrap metal, of minimal fighting value. This was an overstatement, but it had more than an element of truth in it. Battleships still had a

major role to play, as time was to show, but they were now clearly subordinate to carrier aviation.

The concentration of losses among the battleships gave a distinctly misleading impression, because it served to disguise the simple fact that the overwhelming part of the US Pacific Fleet emerged unscathed from its ordeal. For the moment the Fleet had had its fangs drawn and was in disorder, but the major part of the US Pacific Fleet was intact and capable of action. The carriers, of course, were unscathed. The United States Navy possessed 18 heavy cruisers, 12 of them with the Pacific Fleet, but only three had been in Pearl Harbor at the time of the attack and none were damaged. Three light cruisers had been damaged, but these were only three of 18 such cruisers in the American fleets and their temporary loss did not lead to the withdrawal of any of the eight light cruisers in the Atlantic. Destroyers were in extremely short supply, but with 171 in service the loss of three could be absorbed. Not one of the submarines was damaged. With 112 already in service and another 65 on order, American submarine strength could only bode ill for a nation such as Japan so desperately dependent on sea communications for her very existence.

Left: The scarred bows of the battleship *Pennsylvania* in drydock during salvage operations.
Below left: A salvaged Val dive bomber is brought ashore.
Below: Only the superstructure and gun turrets of USS *Arizona* remained above water after her ordeal.

The attack on Pearl Harbor, therefore, can be seen as being at best no more than a moderately successful operation. Had the carriers as well as the battleships been caught and destroyed then the Japanese position would have been much stronger. The American position would have been correspondingly weaker than was the case, but in reality there was no means by which the Japanese could have destroyed or rendered ineffective the major part of the Pacific Fleet even by a series of strikes on the warships themselves. Yet this action was only the start of the war, and two consequences arose from this operation. Firstly, the strategic situation was such that, given Japanese resources, there was no point in the Pacific where the Japanese could reasonably hope to force the Americans to give battle under conditions favorable to Japan. There was no place that the Japanese could attack with reasonable hope of success and force the Americans to give battle against their will. Secondly, with the strategic initiative in the western and central Pacific denied them, the Americans for the moment could only react with tactical offensive action. This involved limited and peripheral carrier operations, snapping at the edges of Japanese main force undertakings, the commitment of the cruisers to action, and, most important of all, the unleashing of the submarines in an all-out unrestricted campaign against Japanese merchant shipping. The latter was to be critical in deciding the outcome of the Pacific war. Too much attention is focused on the great carrier battles. What ground the Imperial Navy down to defeat was the combination of the five great battles decided by naval aviation, a whole host of savagely fought actions – normally at night – between light forces and the unrelenting attrition of Japanese merchant shipping at the hands of American submariners. The submarine campaign was necessarily slow

to get into its stride, but in the end it accounted for more than half of Japan's total merchant shipping losses and brought the island empire to the brink of starvation. The submarines also accounted for many warships, including six of Nagumo's force. In 1941 the adoption of the submarine campaign by the Americans was a reflex action, forced upon the Americans by events, but it had devastating consequences for Japan.

There was, moreover, another aspect to the American campaign against Japanese shipping. What went largely unnoticed at the time was the hidden loss caused to Japan by her going to war. In 1941 Japan needed 10,000,000 tons of oceanic merchant shipping to sustain herself; she had only 6,000,000 tons under her own flag. The ships of other nations, mainly those nations with whom Japan went to war, made up the deficit. Thus, when she went to war, Japan lost 4,000,000 tons of shipping other than what she was able to capture or salve. In the event Japan was able to capture about 1,250,000 tons – at a time when her needs rose drastically. Among the losses at Pearl Harbor, therefore, must be counted some 2,750,000 tons of merchant shipping lost to Japan. It was an extremely high price to pay for eight battleships and 10 other warships and auxiliaries sunk or damaged.

The loss of this merchant shipping was catastrophic for Japan, but before the outbreak of the war the Imperial Navy never showed any awareness of the overwhelming importance of merchant shipping resources to Japan. The need for convoys and the general defense of merchantmen was neglected by a navy obsessed with the notion of battle with a numerically superior enemy. It was this obsession that blinded the Japanese to the critically important nature of the necessary back-up for a fleet – its fleet base complete with power stations, workshops, dockyards and oil dumps. Had the Japanese really sought to immobilize the Pacific Fleet by the most effective and simplest manner possible, they would have been well advised to have considered attacks not on the warships but on the dockyard facilities at Pearl Harbor. Without such facilities a fleet cannot operate, but the Japanese left them untouched. In 1940 and 1941 the United States Navy, working on a shoestring, had built up a reserve of 4,500,000 barrels of oil on Oahu. Most of it was stored above ground and was wide open to destruction from the air. Had the oil dumps and the other essential dockyard facilities – such as the power sources – been systematically attacked and destroyed, the Pacific Fleet would have been hard pressed to maintain even a minimal defensive stance in the central Pacific. The miraculous American recovery at Midway would have been impossible, and it is difficult to see how the Americans would have been able to make any strategically significant move for at least 18 months. The cost of rebuilding such resources – had they been de-

Left: A water-filled bomb crater on the apron at Hickam Field awaits attention, while repair work is started on the hangars.
Bottom: All that remains of this B-17 is the forward fuselage and the wings.
Below: President Roosevelt three months before Japan's surprise attack.

stroyed – might well have proved prohibitive in time and effort, but somehow given the vastness of American production, it is difficult to envisage how the ultimate outcome of the war could have been significantly affected.

Yet the material aspects of the Pearl Harbor operation pale into insignificance when set against the moral consequences of the attack. The Japanese believed that in attacking and destroying the Pacific Fleet they would leave the Americans frightened, confused and divided. They believed that the division between isolationists and interventionists in the United States was deep and a permanent feature of American political life. They could point to the fact that in the summer of 1941 the House of Representatives had come within two votes of abolishing the draft, thus doing away with the major part of American fighting strength. The forces of isolationism were indeed very strong in the United States but they were not so strong as to want peace at any price and they were not so strong that they could withstand the storm of righteous indignation that greeted the Japanese onslaught. Indeed, isolationist sentiment dissolved overnight as people who had been President Roosevelt's most bitter critics immediately pledged their loyalty and support to the Commander in Chief in the wake of the attack. The immediate reaction to the attack was not recrimination – though that was to follow – but to pledge all to total victory.

The Japanese plan of campaign envisaged a limited war. The Japanese idea was to fight a defensive war behind a firm defensive perimeter until the Americans, tiring of conflict and losses, would come to terms in a compromise peace. Pearl Harbor removed the very faint possibility that this might happen. If, as the Japanese believed, will is the most important element in war, then the war was already lost to Japan. After Pearl Harbor there was no possibility that the Americans would accept anything other than total victory or total defeat. The Japanese believed that their superior resolve would see them through against the odds, but when the President addressed the Congress on 8 December and asked for a declaration of war on Japan, he was speaking for a united roused democracy that could never be placated by half measures, that would not be satisfied with anything other than the total destruction of the enemy. As the President grasped the rostrum and denounced Japan, the lines of Longfellow – significantly from *The Building of The Ship* – which Churchill never tired of writing to Roosevelt, can hardly ever have seemed more appropriate:

Thou, too, sail on, O Ship of State!
Sail on, O Union, strong and great!
Humanity with all its fears
With all its hopes for future years
Is hanging breathless on thy fate!

Pearl Harbor was a victory for the Imperial Navy, but it was by such victories that Japan moved down the path of total defeat. Admiral Chuichi Hara commented after the war that Roosevelt should have pinned medals on the Japanese for the attack; nothing that the Japanese could have done could have proved more self-defeating. More than ships and men were lost that December Sunday at Pearl Harbor; what really perished was Japan's dreams of power and conquest. The tragedy was that it was to take 45 months to bring Japan to realize it – and it was only by a path through Hiroshima and Nagasaki.

6. EPILOGUE

Below left: Admiral Husband E Kimmel was C in C of the US fleet during the Pearl Harbor attack. He was held responsible for the poor defense of the base and dismissed on 17 December. *Below right:* American sailors recover the body of a Japanese airman. *Below:* America's recovery from the Pearl Harbor debacle was complete. Three cruisers are shown moored there in 1943.

Fortune was to reserve very different fates for the ships and indviduals involved in the Pearl Harbor operation. The US Pacific Fleet's Commander in Chief, Admiral Husband E Kimmel, was never given the chance to show his worth in war. He was removed from his command within two weeks of the attack and was replaced by Nimitz. Kimmel tried in the aftermath of the attack to retrieve something from the shattered ruins of his fleet and career by using his three fleet carriers to support the Wake garrison after it had repulsed a Japanese invasion attempt on 10 December. He was dismissed in the middle of the operation and Wake fell on 23 December with no attempt being made by the Pacific Fleet to prevent its loss. Kimmel, in effect, was made the scapegoat for the American disaster and was never employed again. The only comment that can be made upon his personal tragedy is to note that he was appointed to his command, the most prestigious command in the entire US Navy, over the heads of 32 more senior admirals, a recognition of talents he was never allowed to show in battle.

On the Japanese side personal fortunes were mixed. Fuchida and Genda both survived the war to become widely respected members of society in the new Japan. Fuchida became a protestant minister; Genda a Major General and Chief of Staff of the Japanese Air Self-Defense Force. Yamamoto was assassinated in April 1943 when a carefully planned American ambush caught his aircraft when he was on a tour of inspection of the upper Solomons. Yamamoto's aircraft was shot down in 1943. Nagumo, too, failed to survive the war. After the Midway disaster he was given command of the 1st Carrier Division – the *Shokaku* and *Zuikaku* – during the battles in the Solomons. After these battles had been lost he never again held a seagoing command and he ended his career and life as commander of Japanese forces on Saipan. He committed suicide when his forces were overrun.

The fate of the ships involved in the operations reflected the general outcome of the war. Only two of the battleships sunk at Pearl Harbor, the *Arizona* and *Oklahoma*, were destined to become total losses. The *Arizona*, along with the *Utah* which was also a total loss, still lies at Pearl Harbor. The *Oklahoma* was raised in 1944 in order to clear Battleship Row, but she was not taken in hand by the dockyards. By that stage of the war the US Navy had more than enough battleships to justify trying to recommission a ship 30 years old. She was sold for scrap, but sank while being towed to the West Coast.

The other three battleships that were lost, the *California*, *Nevada* and *West Virginia*, were all raised and entered the dockyards for reequipping and modernization. They emerged from the yards considerably better and more powerful than they had been before the attack. All three ships took part in operations off Iwo Jima and Okinawa. The *California* and *West Virginia* saw service at Leyte Gulf in the

company of the *Maryland, Pennsylvania* and *Tennessee*. The *Nevada* missed Leyte because of her service off Normandy and southern France. Thus all the battleships recovered at Pearl Harbor took their revenge in the final cornering of the Imperial Navy.

Of the carriers that were absent from Pearl Harbor two, the *Enterprise* and *Saratoga*, showed an instinct for survival that enabled them to survive much damage. Both saw the end of the war. The *Enterprise*, in winning 19 stars, gained more battle honors than any warship in American history. The *Lexington*, ferrying aircraft to Midway at the time of the attack, was lost to aircraft from the *Shokaku* and *Zuikaku* at the Battle of the Coral Sea in May 1942. The *Hornet* and *Yorktown*, in the Atlantic in December 1941, also succumbed in 1942, the *Yorktown* at Midway and the *Hornet* at the Battle of Santa Cruz in the Solomons in October. The *Hornet* was significant. Her career lasted a few days over a year. Within a year of her being sunk a new *Hornet* had been completed under the terms of the Two-Ocean Naval Expansion Act the Pearl Harbor operation had been designed to frustrate.

With the exceptions of the *Cassin* and *Downes* every other ship sunk or damaged at Pearl Harbor was brought back into commission. This included the *Shaw* and even the *Oglala*. The old minelayer showed powers of resistance to the salvage teams that she did not reveal on 7 December. She needed not one but two major operations to free her from the mud and get her afloat, and then she chose to sink again not once but twice. She then suffered a fire before she reached dry dock. Though the Americans might well have despaired of her at that stage, she was reconditioned and converted to serve out the rest of her time as a repair ship and PT-Boat tender. She was discarded in March 1947 when a venerable 40 years old.

The warships of the Japanese carrier force experienced fates that would have confirmed the very worst fears of Yamamoto and Nagumo had they been alive to witness them. The Imperial ships fought hard to the bitter end, but they could not withstand the overwhelming weight of firepower that the Americans were ultimately able to bring to bear. Nagumo's haunting nightmare of the vulnerability of carrier flight decks to bombing was brought home in the catastrophic battle of Midway when the *Kaga* and *Soryu* sank on 4 June and the *Hiryu* and *Akagi* sank the following day. All four carriers were lost to aircraft from the American carriers absent from Pearl Harbor on 7 December. The *Shokaku* and *Zuikaku* missed Midway because of the damage they had sustained at the Coral Sea; their absence was probably the difference between defeat and victory at Midway. The *Shokaku* was lost to submarine attack in the preliminary stages of the battle of the Philippine Sea,

the *Zuikaku* to carrier aircraft at the battle of Leyte.

Both the battleships involved in the operation, the *Hiei* and *Kirishima*, were lost at Guadalcanal. Both were gunned to destruction, the *Hiei* being given the *coup de grace* by aircraft from the *Enterprise*. Five of the destroyers, the *Akigumo, Arare, Asakaze, Tanikaze* and *Urakaze* were lost to submarines while the remainder, the *Hamakaze, Kagero, Kasumi* and *Shiranuhi* were lost to naval aircraft action, though the *Kagero* was first crippled by mines. Two of the destroyers, the *Hamakaze* and *Kasumi*, were lost during the last despairing sortie made by the Imperial Navy in defense of Okinawa. These destroyers shared the fate of the mighty 70,000-ton battleship *Yamato* which was overwhelmed by aircraft from nine of the carriers of Task Force 58.

What the *Yamato* could not survive mere cruisers could not hope to resist. The heavy cruiser *Chikuma* and the light cruiser *Abukuma* succumbed to air attack at Leyte Gulf, the heavy cruiser to naval aircraft, her lesser colleague to Army bombers. Thus in our list to date 19 of Nagumo's 20 ships have had their fate related, and 12 of them were destroyed either by air action alone or by air action in conjunction with another means of destruction. All but one

Left: American servicemen killed at Pearl Harbor are buried with full military honors.

of the 12 fell to carrier aircraft – a striking comment on the failure of Nagumo at least to search for the American carriers after the Pearl Harbor strike.

After the Okinawa action which saw the end of the Imperial Navy as a fighting force, just one of Nagumo's original ships remained, the heavy cruiser *Tone*. Perhaps her fate was the cruellest irony of all, coming as it did just three weeks before the end of hostilities. The last survivor of the ships that had steamed half way across the Pacific to strike the US Pacific Fleet in its lair was in turn sunk by aircraft from carriers while she rested at her moorings in the shallow waters of her base at Kure.

APPENDIX

Abbreviations

Standard American designations are given to all naval ships:

CV	Fleet Carrier
CVL	Light Fleet Carrier
BB	Battleship
CA	Heavy Cruiser
CL	Light Cruiser
DD	Destroyer
SS	Submarine

The use of an asterisk denotes a flagship.

Summary of Japanese Oiler, Submarine and Warship Losses by Year

	Oilers	Sub-marines	War-ships	Total
1941		1		1
1942		7	7	14
1943	3	10	1	14
1944	4	10	10	24
1945		1	3	4
Surrendered	1	1	1	3
	8	30	22	60

Summary of Japanese Surface Warship Losses by Location

The Battle of Midway	4
The Battle of the Philippine Sea	1
The Battle of Leyte Gulf	4
Okinawa	2
During the Solomons campaign[3]	3
In other theaters	7

Summary of Japanese Submarine and Warship Losses by Cause

	Japanese Losses of							
	CV	CVL	BB	CA	CL	DD	SS	Total
Sunk by aircraft[1]	3	2		2	1	4	2	14
Sunk by aircraft and mines						1		1
Sunk by aircraft and warships			1				3	4
Sunk by destroyers							11	11
Sunk by submarines	1					5	3	9
In surface engagements[2]			1				5	6
To unknown marine causes							5	5
Total	4	2	2	2	1	10	29	50
Surrendered at the end of the war						1	1	2
Grand total	4	2	2	2	1	11	30	52

[1] Carrier-based and land-based aircraft.
[2] Sunk by gunfire, ram and torpedo by any type of surface warship, including destroyers.
[3] Plus 10 submarines lost in the course of these operations.

Composition and Fate of Japanese Forces engaged in the Pearl Harbor Operation

1 Surface Warships and Auxiliaries

(a) The Pearl Harbor Strike Force: commander Vice-Admiral Nagumo.

(i) The Carrier Force. Vice-Admiral Nagumo.

1st Carrier Division				
CV	*Akagi**	Damaged by carrier aircraft, scuttled,	5 Jun 42	Midway
CV	*Kaga*	Sunk by carrier aircraft	4 Jun 42	Midway
2nd Carrier Division				
CVL	*Hiryu*	Damaged by carrier aircraft, scuttled	5 Jun 42	Midway
CVL	*Soryu*	Sunk by carrier aircraft	4 Jun 42	Midway
5th Carrier Division				
CV	*Shokaku*	Sunk by submarine attack	19 Jun 44	Philippine Sea
CV	*Zuikaku*	Sunk by carrier aircraft	25 Oct 44	Leyte Gulf

(ii) The Support Force: Vice-Admiral Mikawa

3rd Battle Division				
BB	*Hiei**	Sunk by gunfire and aircraft	13 Nov 42	Guadalcanal
BB	*Kirishima*	Sunk by gunfire	15 Nov 42	Guadalcanal
8th Cruiser Division				
CA	*Chikuma*	Damaged by carrier aircraft, scuttled	25 Oct 44	Leyte Gulf
CA	*Tone*	Sunk by carrier aircraft	24 Jul 45	Kure

(iii) The Screening Force: Rear Admiral Omori

1st Destroyer Flotilla				
CL	*Abukuma**	Sunk by land-based aircraft	26 Oct 44	Leyte Gulf
DD	*Akigumo*	Sunk by submarine attack	11 Apr 44	Philippines
DD	*Arare*	Sunk by submarine attack	5 Jul 42	Aleutians
DD	*Asakaze*	Sunk by submarine attack	23 Aug 44	Philippines
DD	*Hamakaze*	Sunk by carrier aircraft	7 Apr 45	Okinawa
DD	*Kagero*	Damaged by mines and sunk by aircraft	8 May 43	Solomons
DD	*Kasumi*	Damaged by carrier aircraft, scuttled	7 Apr 45	Okinawa
DD	*Shiranumi*	Sunk by carrier aircraft	27 Oct 44	Leyte Gulf
DD	*Tanikaze*	Sunk by submarine attack	9 Jun 44	Philippines
DD	*Urakaze*	Sunk by submarine attack	21 Nov 44	Formosa

(iv) The Supply Train

Kyokuto Maru	*Kenyo Maru*	*Kokuyo Maru*	*Kyokuyo Maru*
Shinkoku Maru	*Toho Maru*	*Toei Maru*	*Nippon Maru*

With the exception of the *Kyokuto Maru* all the ships in the Supply Train were lost.

(b) The Midway Assault Force: commander Captain Konishi

DD	*Sazanami*	Sunk by submarine attack	14 Jan 44	Yap
DD	*Ushio*	Surrendered		

Total Force: 22 warships and 8 oilers.

Below: Although seriously damaged and settling by the bows, USS *Nevada* was not abandoned. Repaired and returned to service, she participated in the assault on Iwo Jima in February 1945.

2 Submarines

(a) Reconnaissance Element, Pearl Harbor Strike Force: commander Captain Imaizumi

SS	*I-19*	Marine Loss	? Oct 43	Unknown
SS	*I-21*	Surrendered		
SS	*I-23*	Sunk in surface action	29 Aug 42	Guadalcanal

(b) General Reconnaissance Element

SS	*I-10*	Sunk by destroyers	4 Jul 44	Saipan
SS	*I-26*	Marine Loss	? Oct 44	Philippines

(c) The Special Naval Attack Unit

1st Submarine Flotilla: commander, Rear Admiral Sato
Based Yokosuka, deployment north of Oahu

SS	*I-9*	Sunk by destroyer	11 Jun 43	Aleutians
SS	*I-15*	Sunk by destroyer	2 Nov 42	Guadalcanal
SS	*I-17*	Sunk by surface warship and aircraft	19 Aug 43	Noumea
SS	*I-25*	Sunk by destroyer	3 Sep 43	New Hebrides

These submarines were joined on patrol by The Reconnaissance Element of the Strike Force

2nd Submarine Flotilla: commander, Rear Admiral Yamazuka
based Yokosuka, deployment east of Oahu

SS	*I-7*	Damaged in surface action, scuttled	5 Jul 43	Aleutians
SS	*I-1*	Sunk by destroyers	29 Jan 43	Guadalcanal
SS	*I-2*	Sunk by destroyer	7 Jul 44	Bismarcks
SS	*I-3*	Sunk in surface action	10 Dec 42	Guadalcanal
SS	*I-4*	Sunk by submarine attack	20 Dec 42	Guadalcanal
SS	*I-5*	Sunk in surface action	19 Jul 44	Guam
SS	*I-6*	Marine Loss	? Jun 44	Unknown

3rd Submarine Flotilla: commander, Rear Admiral Miwa
Based Kwajalein, deployment south of Oahu

SS	*I-8*	Sunk by destroyer	31 Mar 45	Okinawa
SS	*I-68*	Sunk by submarine attack	27 Jul 43	Bismarcks
SS	*I-69*	Sunk during air raid	4 Apr 44	Truk
SS	*I-70*	Sunk by carrier aircraft	10 Dec 41	Pearl Harbor
SS	*I-71*	Sunk by destroyer	1 Feb 44	Solomons
SS	*I-72*	Sunk in surface action	11 Nov 42	Guadalcanal
SS	*I-73*	Sunk by submarine attack	27 Jan 42	Midway
SS	*I-74*	Marine Loss	? Apr 44	Unknown
SS	*I-75*	Sunk by destroyer	1 Feb 44	Marshalls

The submarines of the 3rd Flotilla were joined on patrol by

SS	*I-16*	Sunk by destroyer	19 May 44	Solomons
SS	*I-18*	Sunk by surface warships and aircraft	11 Feb 43	Guadalcanal
SS	*I-20*	Sunk by surface warship and aircraft	16 Sep 43	New Hebrides
SS	*I-22*	Marine Loss	? Oct 42	Solomons
SS	*I-24*	Sunk in surface action	11 Jun 43	Aleutians

after these submarines had failed to recover their midget submarines following the attack on Pearl Harbor on 7 December 1941.

Total Force: 30 submarines: 5 for reconnaissance, 20 for general attack, 5 for parent craft to midget submarines.

MIDWAY

MIDWAY

LT. COL. A.J. BARKER

Page 136: The A6M Zero fighter of the Japanese Navy was dominant in the early stages of the war in the Pacific.
Page 137: A B-25 takes off from the *USS Hornet* for the Doolittle raid.
Pages 138/139: The *USS Enterprise* was one of the major participants in the Battle of Midway.
These pages: The *USS Atlanta* at sea in November 1942. The Atlanta class cruisers were armed with ten 5-inch guns.

1. PROLOGUE

Above: Admiral Chester Nimitz was C in C of the US Pacific Fleet during the Battle of Midway.

Japan's daring attack on Pearl Harbor on 7 December 1941 was a catastrophic surprise for the United States which compelled a radical change in both American and Japanese strategy. Admiral Kimmel was replaced as Commander in Chief of the Pacific Fleet by a keen-witted, blue-eyed Texan, Admiral Chester W Nimitz, and his primary task was defined as the holding of a line running between Hawaii and the vital American base at Midway Island, 1100 miles southwest of Pearl Harbor. He also was instructed to maintain communications with and between America and Australia. The United States was determined, at this point, to prevent a further Japanese advance toward the west, but not to attack.

Since Pearl Harbor the Japanese High Command had been so engrossed in the problem of acquiring oil that, with the exception of Admiral Isoruku Yamamoto, Commander in Chief of Japan's Combined Fleet, it had given little thought to a long-term strategic plan. However by March 1942 a brilliant run of success had given Japan all the oil she needed. The war, it seemed, was going well. Japan's initial objectives had been gained without a hitch and all that remained was to determine her future strategy. Should she concentrate on stabilizing what she had won, or should she allow the tide of victory to sweep her forward into new territories? And if so, where? Should she strike westward toward India and join hands with her Axis ally somewhere in the Middle East? Or should she concentrate her strength on a drive eastward against the United States? It was difficult to determine which course would be more effective and, if there was to be an offensive, which would be the most productive in terms of economic gain.

Following considerable and often heated deliberations the Japanese Supreme Command concluded that whatever strategy was adopted it would have to be implemented quickly. The Americans were known to be anxious to avenge Pearl Harbor and without some definite plan of action Japan might well be caught. Theoretically the planning of naval strategy was the responsibility of the Chief of the Naval Staff, Admiral Osami Nagano, who was senior to Yamamoto but Nagano's authority had declined after Pearl Harbor and by January 1942 the influence of Yamamoto and his staff was paramount and unquestioned. Thus it is not surprising that Yamamoto's headquarters should take the initiative and that the plan of action which emerged bore the stamp of the man responsible for the attack on Pearl Harbor.

At a series of conferences aboard Yamamoto's flagship, the giant battleship *Yamato*, various alternatives were considered. Seizure of the US Pacific Fleet base and of the Pacific Fleet itself would constitute the most damaging blow to the United States, claimed Rear Admiral Matome Ugaki, Yamamoto's zealous Chief of Staff. So an offensive should be directed against Hawaii. Such an operation, he maintained, would probably provoke a decisive clash with the US Pacific Fleet, in which Japan's superiority in aircraft carriers and battleships should weigh the outcome in her favor. Those who argued against this plan maintained it would be impossible to get a Japanese fleet within striking distance of Hawaii because it would have to pass within striking distance of the island of Midway, and Midway acted as a long-distance outpost to Hawaii. The garrison there would be sure to alert the US Pacific Fleet, so eliminating any hope of achieving surprise as at Pearl Harbor.

Another alternative that was considered was a 'go-west' plan, whose success depended on the destruction of the British Far Eastern Fleet and the capture of Ceylon. The Japanese army commanders opposed this on the grounds that an attack on Ceylon would necessitate moving troops from Burma and Malaya. The third alternative, proposed by Captain Sadatoshi Tomioka, head of the Naval General Staff's Plans Division, was that Australia should be Japan's next major objective. This was rejected by the army even more quickly than the proposed invasion of Ceylon. The Army High Command said such an operation against Australia would require a minimum force of 10 combat divisions and they could not be spared.

At this point Yamamoto decided to show his hand. Up to now he had refrained from voicing any opinion during the planning conferences. Now, reports of the increasing activity of US aircraft carriers and submarines were causing him considerable concern. Midway was an important forward fuelling point for US submarines. Its capture would limit their activities and the establishment of a Japanese air base there should also do much to curb the activities of American carrier-borne aircraft. A move against Midway was the first phase of Ugaki's plan for the invasion of Hawaii, but it was not this which interested Yamamoto. He knew that he must lure out and annihilate the US Pacific Fleet in 1942 or Japan would lose the war. Midway, he reasoned, provided ideal bait. Admiral Nimitz could not let Hawaii's sentry fall by default and whatever he chose to do about it would involve a move of the US Pacific Fleet westward to a point where the Combined Fleet could strike. Yamamoto was, in fact, merely pursuing his old dream. By destroying the American aircraft carriers, capturing Midway and threatening Hawaii he believed that America's will to fight would be undermined and the way for a negotiated peace would be opened up.

Thus it was that at the beginning of April Yamamoto's operations staff officer, Commander Yasuji Watanabe was sent to Tokyo to present the plan of Operation MI against Midway to the Naval General Staff. The admirals in Tokyo were bitterly opposed to it, but Yamamoto – the most important admiral in the Imperial Navy – was determined not to be put off, and the Naval

Below right: Vice-Admiral Chuichi Nagumo led the carriers of the Main Striking Force at Midway.
Below far right: Rear Admiral Aubrey Fitch commanded the Task Force 11 at the Battle of the Coral Sea.
Bottom: The Japanese battleship *Yamato* was the largest ship of its kind and was Yamamoto's flagship at Midway.
Below: Admiral Isoroku Yamamoto devised the Japanese assault on Midway Island.

General Staff reluctantly sanctioned the operation.

Meanwhile, as the detailed plan of Operation MI was being worked out, Vice-Admiral Nagumo, commanding the First Air Fleet, was engaged in operations around Ceylon which resulted in the sinking of two British heavy cruisers and the aircraft carrier HMS *Hermes*. In consequence neither he nor Vice-Admiral Kondo whose Second Fleet was similarly engaged in operations around Malaya were consulted regarding the battle plan. This proved to be a mistake because these two fleets were scheduled to play a leading role in the forthcoming operation. However, most of the wrangling over the plan was about when the operation would take place. Yamamoto favored an attack in the middle of May, while the Naval General Staff wanted it postponed until June in order to allow three more weeks' preparation.

It was now that two dramatic events occurred which affected both the timing and the probable outcome of the forthcoming battle of Midway. Of these the

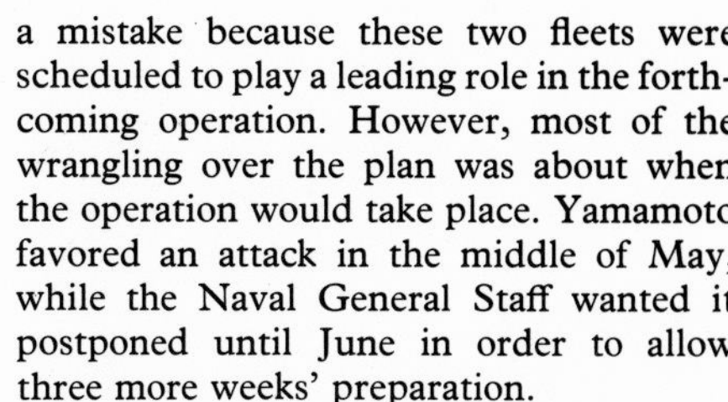

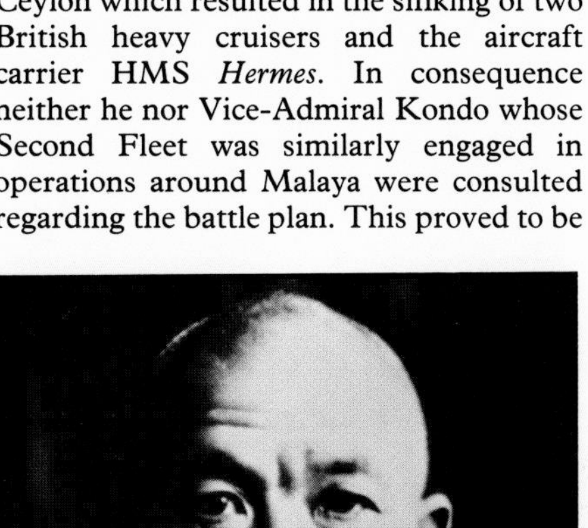

most important was the Americans' first defensive success in what is now known as the Battle of the Coral Sea – the first naval action in history fought almost entirely between aircraft carriers. The battle took place nearly 3000 miles from Midway on the northern approaches to Australia. Following Nagumo's sortie against Ceylon the Japanese had dispatched an invasion force to sail around the eastern end of New Guinea to take Port Moresby on the southern coast. Success of this venture would have meant that the Japanese would have secured the western approach to the Coral Sea. However, cryptographers in the US Navy had broken Japan's most secret code and the Americans had prior notice of the Coral Sea invasion, and guessed correctly that the main strike would be aimed at Port Moresby.

Above far left: A prewar shot of the carrier USS *Lexington* (CV-2), sunk during the Battle of the Coral Sea.
Above left: The Japanese *Shokaku* was damaged by US Navy dive bombers at Coral Sea, but managed to return to Japan for repairs.
Below: Shoho was not so fortunate, her sinking being marked by the famous signal 'Scratch one flattop.'

Left: Doolittle (fourth from left) led the audacious Tokyo raid by B-25 bombers flying from *Hornet*.
Below left: the Douglas SBD Dauntless dive bomber (foreground) and the TBD Devastator torpedo bomber provided American carriers with striking power at the Midway and Coral Sea battles.
Right: USS *Lexington* ablaze after receiving hits from two bombs and two torpedoes on 8 May 1942 in the Coral Sea.
Below: *Lexington* is abandoned by her crew as the fires aboard become uncontrollable. She was later sent to the bottom by torpedoes from US destroyers.

The Doolittle raid on the Japanese homeland on 18 April 1942 was important as a boost to American morale, rather than for its material effects. USAAF North American B-25 Mitchell bombers were launched from the carrier USS *Hornet* (CV-8) in one of the most remarkable feats of airmanship of World War II.

On 3 May the Japanese staged successful landings on Tulagi, but were bombed and strafed the next day by planes from the carrier USS *Yorktown*. The *Yorktown* then rendezvoused with the carrier *Lexington*, and a course was fixed for a surprise attack on the Japanese invasion forces now rounding the end of New Guinea. On 7 May a destroyer and an oiler, separated from the main US forces, were destroyed by Japanese carrier planes. The same day aircraft from *Lexington* and *Yorktown* caught the Japanese light carrier *Shoho*, and sank her. The next day, 8 May, aircraft from the two big Japanese carriers, *Shokaku* and *Zuikaku*, traded air attacks with the two US carriers. *Shokaku* was severely damaged and *Zuikaku* lost a number of first-class fighting planes and pilots. The *Lexington* sustained several bomb and torpedo hits. The damage seemed to have been brought under control, and it was not until some time later that fires and explosions broke out; a motor generator had been left running, igniting gasoline vapors released by an earlier torpedo hit. The condition of the ship worsened until, in the evening, the *Lexington* had to be abandoned. She was then torpedoed by one of her own escorting destroyers.

No clear-cut victory could be claimed by either side. However the Americans had forced the Japanese to turn back their invasion forces from Port Moresby, and two of the big Japanese carriers were damaged so badly they would not be on hand for the forthcoming battle of Midway – where they just might have turned the tide.

The other event which had a profound effect on the battle occurred before the Coral Sea action could take place. Indeed, although Midway was fought between 3 June and 6 June 1942, it was precipitated six weeks before, on 18 April. At 0800 that morning Vice-Admiral William F Halsey sent a signal from his flagship, the carrier *Enterprise*, then 650 miles off Tokyo, to Captain Marc Mitscher of the carrier *Hornet* nearby. The signal read, 'Launch planes. To Colonel Doolittle and his gallant command Good Luck and God bless you.'

As the Americans had hoped, Doolittle's raid on Tokyo deceived the Japanese into assuming that Doolittle's B-25 bombers – which had never flown from a carrier before – had taken off from a land base. President Roosevelt himself announced jocosely that the raiders had flown from 'Shangri-La.' Officers of the Imperial General Staff measured their charts. Except for the sterile and unlikely Aleutians, the American outpost nearest Tokyo was Midway Island, 2250 miles eastward. Not only must this be Shangri-La, the Japanese concluded, but it was additionally dangerous as 'a sentry for Hawaii,' 1140 miles farther. So it must be eliminated. Thus Yamamoto got his way and by the middle of May the ships chosen for Operation MI – Midway Island – were being mustered from the fringes of the empire.

2. PLANS AND PREPARATIONS

At the beginning of May the first draft of the plan for Operation MI was formally submitted to Admiral Nagano, Chief of the Imperial Naval Staff. It was approved and on 5 May an Imperial directive was issued ordering the Commander in Chief of the Combined Fleet to, 'carry out the occupation of Midway Island and key points in the western Aleutians, in cooperation with the Army.' The army was to provide an infantry regimental group for the assault landing on Midway. No specific date was set for the operation but the directive noted that operations would begin during 'the first 20 days of June.'

Thus it was that toward the end of the first week in May the largest fleet in the history of naval warfare began to assemble in Japanese waters. Its backbone was to be the Carrier Striking Force of four big carriers, *Akagi, Kaga, Hiryu* and *Soryu.* These were to be under command of Vice-Admiral Chuichi Nagumo, flying his flag in the *Akagi* and screened by the two fast battleships *Kirishima* and *Haruna*, two heavy and one light cruisers, and 11 destroyers. This was the force which was to track down and destroy the US Pacific Fleet. The remainder of the Combined Fleet was divided into four groups: the Submarine Advance Expeditionary Force which would take up positions before the other groups went into action; a Midway Occupation Force; a Northern Area Force; and the so-called 'Main Body' under the

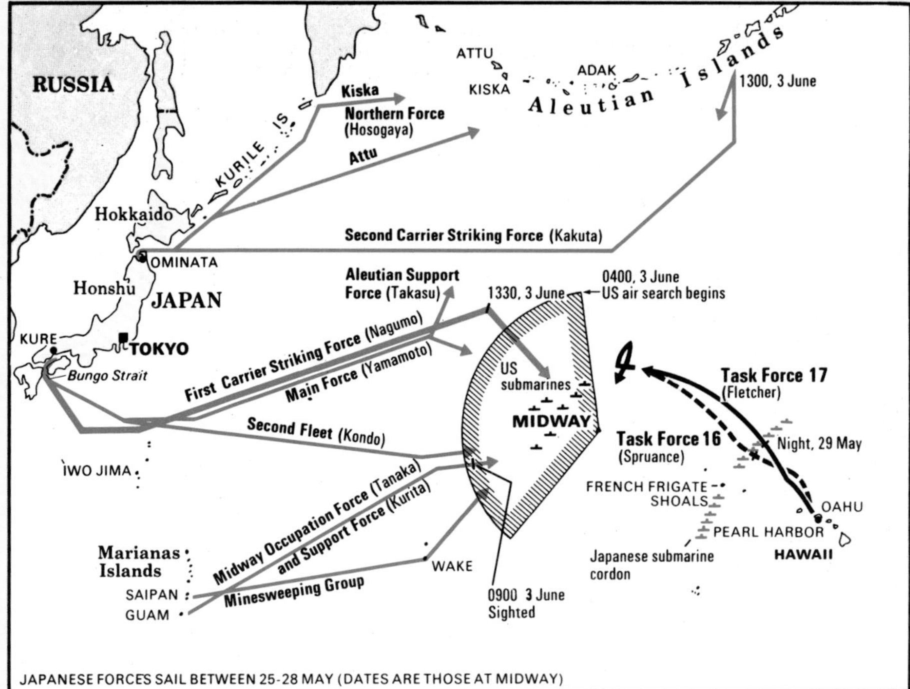

Above: A map showing Japan's moves against Midway and American dispositions for the defense of the island in May/June 1942.
Below right: The *Kongo* was with the Midway Occupation Force.
Below: Kaga sailed with the Japanese First Carrier Striking Force.

Above right: USAAF Boeing B-17 Flying Fortresses operated from Midway Island during the battle, a prewar formation being shown.
Right: Martin B-26 Marauder medium bombers were also based on Midway.

personal command of Admiral Yamamoto.

The submarines were an essential part of the plan. One of them was to reconnoiter ahead for the Midway Occupation Force, while four stationed themselves off the Aleutians and two others off America's west coast. Others were to cover Pearl Harbor – four taking up positions 500 miles west of Oahu and another seven across the route between Pearl and Midway. All were to be in position by 1 June. With these submarines in wait, west and north of Hawaii, Yamamoto presumed that in the absence of other sources of information he would have ample warning when ships of the Pacific Fleet were moving out to meet him. After radioing their reports the submarines could then attack and, hopefully, inflict the first losses in the 'one decisive action.'

Admiral Nobutake Kondo, who had played a leading part in the invasion of the Dutch East Indies, was nominated as commander of the Midway Occupation Force and he was to be responsible for the capture of the island. Under his command were two battleships, the light carrier *Zuiho*, eight cruisers and nine destroyers to escort the invasion force of 15 troopships carrying some 5000 soldiers. Vice-Admiral Moshiro Hosogaya was given command of the Northern Area Force, whose striking element rested on two carriers, the *Ryujo* and the new *Junyo*, under command of Rear-Admiral Kaukuji Kakuda. It was hoped that the Aleutian landings would divert American attention from Midway, and Hosogaya's Main Force was to station itself halfway between Midway and the Aleutians to intercept any American force coming from either direction.

The Main Body centered on seven giant battleships, including Yamamoto's flagship *Yamato*, from which he would direct the battle. The *Yamato* and her sister ship, the *Musashi*, both mounted 18 11-inch guns and were the most formidable warships in the world. Air cover for his force was provided by the old light carrier *Hosho*.

Altogether Yamamoto had 700 aircraft

and 200 ships – among them 11 battleships, eight carriers, 22 cruisers, 65 destroyers and 20 submarines. The total displacement of these ships exceeded 1,500,000 tons and they were manned by 100,000 officers and men, many of whom were veterans of actions in the Pacific and Indian Oceans. Yamamoto's main force of battleships was to be 600 miles northwest of Midway and screened by a large detachment under Vice-Admiral Takasu 500 miles north of Midway. Nagumo's carriers were to be stationed approximately 300 miles east of Yamamoto.

In terms of relative strength at the end of April Yamamoto had almost three times as many carriers as the Americans had. Against the four carriers currently believed to be available to Admiral Nimitz – *Yorktown, Saratoga, Hornet* and *Enterprise* – the Combined Fleet boasted seven large and four light carriers. The USS *Saratoga*, thought by the Japanese to be a threat, was in fact undergoing repairs in Puget Sound at the time of the battle. In view of this comfortable margin of superiority Yamamoto's main worry was that the Americans would refuse battle with such an invincible armada. Unlike the Americans he was limited by lack of information, for his Intelligence officers had no clue as to where the American carriers might be.

Yamamoto's overall plan was for the Northern Area Force to open the battle. Twenty-four hours before the Midway invasion Kakuta's two carriers, the *Ryujo* and *Junyo*, would deliver a paralyzing air bombardment on Dutch Harbor, and troops would then land on Adak, Attu and Kiska. This operation was intended to confuse Admiral Nimitz as to the Japanese intentions. The invasion was not intended to be a permanent affair, and Yamamoto wanted to withdraw his troops in mid-September, before winter set in.

At dawn the following day, Nagumo's big carriers would bomb Midway and, hopefully, destroy the American aircraft there. If the Pacific Fleet tried to interfere Nagumo would deliver the first blow against it. Meanwhile Yamamoto's main force would be moving to a position to the west for the finale. Simultaneously, after dusk on D-Day +1, the Midway Occupation Force would be put ashore by Admiral Kondo, and the first objective of the operation would have been attained.

By the end of April many of the ships that were to take part in the Midway operation had assembled in the Inland Sea; the focal point of all activity was the Hashirajima Anchorage in Hiroshima Bay. With the exception of the two giant carriers, *Zuikaku* and *Shokaku*, and their escorting vessels, Admiral Nagumo's Fleet had returned from its triumphant sweep round Ceylon two days after Doolittle's raid. It was not until 1 May that Nagumo, the Carrier Group commander, and Vice-Admiral Kondo, who was to escort the troopships, reported to Yamamoto aboard his bustling flagship. Only then did Nagumo, Kondo and the senior officers who had accompanied them for the briefing, learn about the proposed operation. Reactions were mixed. Nagumo was openly indifferent to the plan and the location of the operation. However Kondo had serious misgivings. He believed that the operation was doomed to failure because the Americans would employ substantial numbers of land-based aircraft against the Japanese forces as well as their whole carrier fleet. Yamamoto was in no mood to listen to Kondo and curtly dismissed his views.

Throughout May preparations were rushed forward for the coming operation. Dummy bombing and torpedo attacks were practiced on the hulk of the old 21,000-ton battleship *Settsu*, anchored at Iwakuni in the Inland Sea. Many of the pilots' practice attacks proved so disappointing that the staff officers supervising the training openly wondered how such poor aviators would ever equal the feats of their forerunners at Pearl Harbor. As they were not given enough time to practice, even their flying formations were ragged. Admiral Ugaki also staged a series of war games to test Yamamoto's command and control structure. The result was that at the end of the games Admiral Kondo, backed by most of the other admirals, urged that the invasion day be postponed to allow more time for the training of pilots and staff officers as well as for the battle preparations. Once again Yamamoto refused to listen. He insisted that early June was the only time when there would be enough moonlight for the night movements off the invasion beaches.

Another important matter that was raised was the problem of inadequate radio equipment aboard the carrier *Akagi*. The need to keep radio masts small and unobtrusive, so that they would not interfere with the landing and takeoff of the carrier's planes, meant that this problem was not peculiar to the *Akagi*. However, the *Akagi* was Nagumo's flagship and as Rear Admiral Kusaka, Nagumo's Chief of Staff, pointed out, it was vital that the *Akagi* should be able to intercept enemy radio messages. Two remedies were suggested. The first was that Yamamoto's flagship the *Yamato*, with its modern and powerful radio installations, should ignore the radio silence imposed on the rest of the fleet and relay all important intercepted messages to the *Akagi*. The second was that the *Yamato* should operate directly with the carriers, with Yamamoto assuming direct command of the Nagumo Force. Both suggestions were rejected.

This was but one of the important problems that were still left unanswered when the war games broke up. Many officers returned to their ships dissatisfied and uneasy. The only people, it seems, who were not unduly worried were Nagumo and his flying crews. They almost believed themselves capable of smashing the US Pacific Fleet on their own.

Shortly before the Coral Sea battle US Intelligence informed Admiral Nimitz that the Japanese offensive named Operation MI was about to be launched. The objective, according to intercepted signals, was somewhere labelled 'AF.' The intelligence officers who worked in the Intelligence Black Chamber at Pearl Harbor where Japanese secret messages were monitored and decoded, were not sure whether 'AF' was Midway or Oahu and whether D-Day would be at the end of May or in early June. Nimitz felt certain that it would be Midway and on 2 May he flew there from Pearl Harbor.

Midway is devoid of nearly all the attributes usually associated with South Sea Islands. The entire atoll is only six miles in diameter and very little of that is dry land. Of its two islets, Sand and Eastern, the first is less than two miles long and the other is little more than one. In the middle is a lagoon with a narrow ships channel leading into it, and on the western edge is an open harbor of sorts. All in all it is a miserable flyspeck of land, but since the attack on Pearl Harbor in December 1941 it was the most westerly American base in the Pacific.

On 2 May 1942 Admiral Nimitz inspected the installations on Sand and Eastern Islands accompanied by Lieutenant Colonel Harold Shannon, the Commanding officer of the 6th Marine Defense Battalion, and Commander Cyril Simard, who was in charge of the naval air station. Each island was self-contained, with its own barracks, power supply and support facilities. The chief difference between the two was that all the facilities needed for the airplanes, except the seaplane hangars, were located on Eastern Island. It was a hot day, but Nimitz thoroughly inspected the military installations, looking at gun sites, ammunition dumps, barbed wire and underground command posts. He told neither Shannon or Simard of his theories about the impending attack but before leaving he asked Shannon what equipment he needed to withstand 'a large-scale attack.' When Shannon had listed what was required, Nimitz reemphasized his point, 'If I get you all these things you say you need, can you hold Midway against a major amphibious assault?' Shannon assured Nimitz that he could.

Shortly after his return to Oahu, Nimitz wrote a joint letter to Shannon and Simard. He said he had confidence in them and was recommending their promotion. The

Above left: Japanese troops are ferried ashore at Lingayen Gulf during their invasion of the Philippines in December 1941.
Left: The Imperial Japanese Navy's 1st Destroyer Squadron deploys into attacking formation during prewar fleet exercises.

Japanese, he continued, were mounting a large-scale offensive against Midway, which was expected to be launched on 28 May. He informed them that he was rushing every man, gun and plane he could spare to Midway. He hoped it would be enough.

Following this letter everything that could be done to strengthen the atoll's defenses was put under way. Shannon's garrison now numbered 2138 Marines and Simand's fliers and ancillary troops totalled 1494. More antiaircraft guns were installed, the beaches had literally been covered with barbed wire and both the shore and sea approaches to it were heavily mined. Every position had been equipped with Molotov cocktails; arrangements had been completed for 11 torpedo boats to circle the reefs and patrol the lagoon; and finally, 19 submarines had been stationed to guard the approaches to the island from the southwest to the north, some at 100 miles, some at 150 miles and the rest at 200 miles.

By 3 June the ground defenses of Midway were as complete as they ever would be. Before the Japanese could establish a beachhead, they would have to smash those defenses. Nonetheless Simard and Shannon were worried. If Yamamoto's battleships and cruisers stood offshore, under an umbrella of Zeros provided by his aircraft carriers, and subjected Midway to an all-out bombardment it would take a lot of planes to beat them off. Nimitz had increased Midway's aircraft strength and by 3 June there 121 on the island. However 30 of them were reconnaissance aircraft, Catalina PBYs, slow, vulnerable and almost useless in combat and 37 of the other fighters and dive bombers were obsolete machines. Moreover most of the new pilots had only just completed their flying training and none of those who flew the dive bombers had had any practice in dive bombing. Worst perhaps was the fact that some of the pilots and crews were from the army, some from the navy and some were Marine. In those days interservice liaison was little more than wishful thinking.

Nimitz had done his best for Midway's land-based garrison. The US Commander in Chief knew full well that the islands' fate depended not on its troops and planes but on the Pacific Fleet which was desperately short of aircraft carriers. *Lexington* had been sunk and *Yorktown* severely damaged in the Coral Sea battle, and it did not look as if she could be repaired in time to help defend Midway. *Saratoga* was still at San Diego undergoing repairs from a torpedo attack by a Japanese submarine in January.

With *Lexington* definitely out of the running and *Yorktown* and *Saratoga* doubtful starters, Nimitz had only the *Hornet* and the *Enterprise*. Both were at sea patrolling the South Pacific between Pearl Harbor and the Coral Sea when they received orders to return to Pearl Harbor. The damaged *Yorktown* was also making for Pearl Harbor and on 27 May – the day after Nagumo's four carriers left the Inland Sea –

Above: Admiral William Halsey, one of the US Navy's leading exponents of carrier warfare, missed the Battle of Midway through ill health.
Below: Admiral Chester Nimitz visited Midway Island on a tour of inspection shortly after the battle ended.
Above right: Douglas TBD Devastators suffered heavy losses at Midway.
Above far right: Consolidated PBY Catalina flying boats performed a vital reconnaissance role.
Right: The carrier USS *Yorktown* survived the Battle of the Coral Sea to provide a much-needed contribution to the defense of Midway Island.

5-T-8

the *Yorktown* crept into dry dock there. (For the Japanese it was 28 May not 27 May, because the Japanese Navy used the East Longitude date, and set their clocks on Tokyo time.) At once a supply and requisitioning force, 1400 strong, swung into action on her. Her hull was patched, her compartments braced with timbers, and a few of the watertight doors were made to close. The repairs were rough-and-ready and three of the boilers damaged in the Coral Sea battle were not even touched. For this reason *Yorktown* could only reach a top speed of 27 knots.

Nimitz had had another problem to resolve during this period of preparation. Admiral 'Bull' Halsey, the US Pacific Fleet's most aggressive carrier admiral, fell ill. He was worn out with the strain of months of combat patrol after Pearl Harbor. Nimitz's choice of a replacement was Rear Admiral Raymond Spruance, a cruiser task force commander, who was exactly the opposite of the flamboyant Halsey. Quiet, courageous and cautious, Spruance's unassuming manner concealed a cool mind and sound judgment. In the days that were to come he was to justify Nimitz's confidence in him.

On the day that the giant *Yamato* sailed out of Hiroshima Bay with six other battleships behind her, Spruance sortied from Pearl Harbor, with *Hornet* and *Enterprise* screened by six cruisers and nine destroyers. This was Task Force 16. Twenty-four hours later *Yorktown* was pronounced ready for sea. Rear-Admiral 'Black Jack' Fletcher hoisted his flag in her again, and with two cruisers and five destroyers he too sailed from Pearl Harbor. This was Task Force 17, and like Task Force 16 it was on a course for Midway. On the island itself, the garrison watched and waited. Meanwhile, Yamamoto – unaware that his plans were known to the Americans – continued to believe that there would be little opposition to his invading force. According to his Intelligence there were 750 Marines, 24 flying boats, 12 bombers and 20 fighters on Midway, nothing much in the Aleutians, and little of military significance there apart from the US base installations at Dutch Harbor.

Yorktown and her escorts made contact with *Enterprise* and *Hornet* and their escorts shortly before noon on 2 June. Fletcher in *Yorktown* took command of the combined task forces and a course was then set for a point northeast of Midway.

Activity in and around Hiroshima Bay quickened as the cherry blossom faded during May 1942. Sixty-eight warships were anchored off Hashirajima. Among them were the seven great battleships *Yamato, Nagato, Mutsu, Ise, Hyuga, Fuso* and *Yamashiro* which the Navy Air Corps sarcastically referred to as 'The Hashira Fleet' because they had been at anchor since the beginning of the war, awaiting Yamamoto's 'one decisive surface battle.' Torpedo nets ringed these giants, for the

Far left: Rear Admiral Takeo Kurita commanded the Midway Occupation Force's Support Group.
Left: Vice-Admiral Raymond Spruance (right) took over direction of the battle when Fletcher's flagship was put out of action. He then became Chief of Staff to Nimitz (left).
Right: The Midway Occupation Force's Transport Group was under Rear Admiral Raizo Tanaka.
Below: Dauntless dive bombers crowd the after end of *Enterprise*'s flight deck. Astern are two oilers, two destroyers and USS *Hornet*.

Imperial Navy itself had demonstrated at Pearl Harbor what could happen to unprotected ships if they were attacked by torpedo bombers.

The harbor seethed with sea-borne traffic as ships plied between ships and shore, shuttling supplies. The weather was warm and summer was fast drawing on. The *Ryujo* and *Junyo*, the two carriers assigned to Vice-Admiral Hosogaya's Northern Force were loading heavy winter clothing. The Midway operation was still officially a secret, but it was not difficult for the sailors to guess that part of the huge armada would be operating in Arctic waters.

On 18 May Colonel Kiyinao Ichiki, who was to command the assault troops in the Midway landing, boarded the *Yamato* to be given the details of the operational plan. Ichiki was the last of the commanders to be briefed, and on 20 May the operation began to get under way. That day the transports carrying Ichiki's soldiers sailed from Yokosuka and Kure for Saipan. They arrived there four days later, to link up with Rear-Admiral Takeo Kurita's Support Force of heavy cruisers which arrived from Guam the same day. Part of Hosogaya's Northern Force also steamed out of the Inland Sea, heading for Ominato on northern Honshu, the staging point for the Aleutians invasion

The battleships and carriers which were to move directly to the battle area still had a week to wait, however, and Yamamoto decided to put the time to good use. On 21 May he led the Main Force, Kondo's Second Fleet and Nagumo's Carrier Strike Force out through the Bungo Strait into the open sea for two days fleet maneuvers – the biggest maneuvers since the outbreak of war, and the last ever to be staged in the open sea by the Japanese Imperial Navy.

When they arrived back in the Hashirajima Anchorage on 25 May, another rehearsal of the forthcoming operation was staged. Afterward Vice-Admiral Takagi, who had commanded the Japanese fleet in the Coral Sea battle, lectured the assembled officers on the forthcoming engagement. Lack of information and false reports led him to paint a much rosier picture of events than was actually true. He was certain that the *Yorktown* was so badly damaged – if not actually sunk – that she would be unable to take part in the operation. He could not know, of course, that emergency repairs would be effected at Pearl Harbor which would allow her to be ready in time.

The stage was now almost set for the battle, and on 27 May – Navy Day, when Japanese sailors celebrated Admiral Togo's victory over the Russians at Tsushima – Yamamoto invited all his senior officers to a farewell party aboard his flagship. The success of the operation was toasted in sake, drunk from cups presented to Yamamoto by the Emperor.

At 0800 hours next morning a signal flag was hoisted to the mast of Nagumo's flagship, the *Akagi*. As the *banzais* echoed round the harbor anchor chains rattled, and the unwieldy carriers and their escorting destroyers began to move. The order to sail had come at last, and the ships of Nagumo's Carrier Task Force were on their way to spearhead the Imperial Navy in its greatest battle ever.

When the carriers steamed out of anchorage it was a fine sunny day, and the crews of Yamamoto's battleships lined the rails to wave their caps and cheer as the ships of the Carrier Force passed. For their passage up the Bungo Channel the 21 ships formed a single column, with the light cruiser *Nagara* (Rear-Admiral Susumu Kimura) leading them. Behind the *Nagara* came Rear-Admiral Hiroaki's cruisers. With *Tone*, Hiroaki's flagship, and her sistership, the *Chikuma*, were the battleships *Haruna* and *Kirishima*. Behind *Kirishima* came the carriers *Akagi* and *Kaga* under Nagumo's direct command, with Rear-Admiral Yamaguchi's *Hiryu* and *Soryu* at the rear.

As they passed groups of fishing boats, their crews waved excitedly, and the sailors aboard the warships confidently returned their waves. All Japan was aware that this was the greatest armada ever seen in the Pacific and that its ships were about to take part in an enterprise which would change the history of Asia, if not of the world. The officers were less happy. Many of them were worried that news of the fleet's sailing might have leaked out. They felt that security had been slack, and people in Kure had guessed where they were making for. They would have been even more anxious if they had known that some of the ships had sent messages which had actually mentioned their destination. (One ship was asked where mail was to be directed, and confidently replied, 'Midway.')

Tension increased when the carriers entered the blue waters of the Pacific, where American submarines were known to be watching the progress of this formidable fleet. Nagumo knew his movements were being reported to Nimitz in Pearl Harbor because his radio operators were able to intercept the messages sent by US submarines. He was unable to stop the information getting through, but he himself was confident that Nimitz would not guess that the objective was Midway. The submarines did not attempt to attack the Japanese fleet; it was too powerful for them, and their first responsibility was simply to dog Nagumo and report his whereabouts. As the possibility of an attack always existed the Japanese armada adopted a circular formation when the shores of Japan became more distant. *Nagara* continued to lead the way, and behind her the four carriers were surrounded by two wide circles of screening ships, with 12 destroyers forming the outer circle. On board the ships, strict antisubmarine watches were maintained and planes patrolled overhead. As time passed and no submarines were sighted, tension gradually began to relax.

On 28 May, Hosagaya's Northern Force

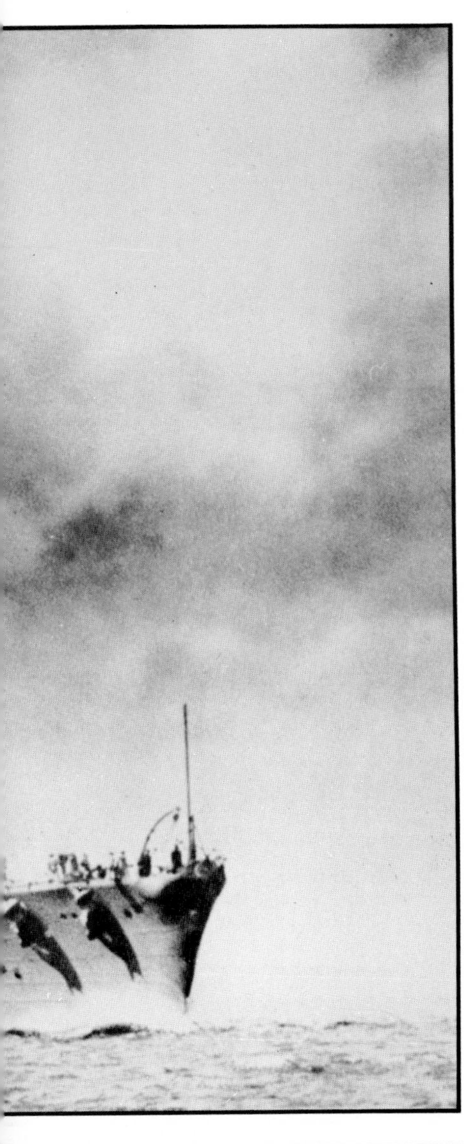

and the Attu and Kiska Invasion Forces sailed from Ominato. Further south the transports carrying the troops for Midway also sailed, escorted by the cruiser *Jintsu* and 12 destroyers. In order to deceive any US submarines which might be lurking in the area, the invasion convoy set off on a westerly course and skirted round Tinian before heading for the east. Meanwhile Kurita's Support Group of heavy cruisers sailed from Guam on a parallel course some 40 miles southwest of the invasion convoy. Last to leave anchorage were the cruisers and the destroyers, the light carrier *Zuiho* of Vice-Admiral Kondo's Second Fleet and, finally, Yamamoto's battleships. Kondo's ships accompanied Yamamoto for the first two days of their voyage, before sailing away to rendezvous with Ichiki's transports, plowing slowly toward Midway.

Five months had elapsed since the Japanese battleships had left home waters. Since the beginning of the war they had been kept back in the Inland Sea, training for what most of the officers hoped would be a major role in the anticipated battle against the US Pacific Fleet. The sailors were tired of training now; morale was high and they were anxious to show their mettle. Like Nagumo however, Yamamoto and Kondo were nervous about submarines, and when Intelligence reported six enemy submarines operating in Japanese waters along the path and four more near Wake Island, antisubmarine precautions were intensified. Once the open sea was reached, the battleships formed up in two parallel columns – *Yamato, Nagato* and *Mutsu* on the right, and *Ise, Hyuga, Fuso* and *Yamashiro* on the left – surrounded by a circular screen of cruisers and destroyers. The carrier *Hosho* steamed between the two columns of battleships, launching and recovering a constant sequence of antisubmarine patrol planes. Zigzagging erratically every five to 10 minutes, the fleet steamed steadily southeast at a speed of 18 knots along the planned route.

Nobody knew better than Yamamoto the potential consequences of his lack of knowledge of the Pacific Fleet's movements. Two days after the gigantic fleet had left the Inland Sea, Lieutenant Tomano – the survivor of an ill-fated earlier flight to Midway – was told to make a full-moon reconnaissance of Pearl Harbor. Before he launched his attack, Yamamoto wanted to know how many of Nimitz's ships were still in their base. For this long range reconnaissance Tomano was to fly one of the new 31-ton four-engined Kawanishi flying boats. Without a bomb load this aircraft could fly 5000 miles without refuelling at a cruising speed of 160 knots. For the flight to Oahu it was proposed that Tomano's aircraft should be refuelled off French Frigate Shoals near Midway by one of Yamamoto's I-Class submarines which was already making for the Shoals. From experience with a previous raid and their radio intercepts, the Americans knew that French Frigate Shoals were being used as a refuelling point, and when the Japanese submarine arrived there her lookout saw an American destroyer patrolling in the very area for which he was making. Her captain at once signalled that refuelling would be impossible, and, instead of telling the submarine to move to nearby Necker Island and refuel there, the Japanese Naval Staff in Tokyo cancelled Tomano's flight.

Above left: Mutsu was one of three battleships with the Main Body.
Left: The battleship *Hyuga* supported the diversionary Aleutians attack.

In the event, this was a stupid thing to do, for if Tomano had refuelled and flown on to Hawaii, he might well have sighted the *Yorktown* and *Lexington* Task Forces moving away from Pearl Harbor toward Midway. This at least would have given Yamamoto some prior warning as to the sort of opposition he was going to meet. As it was, Yamamoto sailed almost completely ignorant of the strength and position of the US carriers, and what little information the Japanese did glean was often lost through misunderstanding or inefficiency.

One signal from Tokyo tended to give weight to the theory that the US Pacific Fleet was in the South Pacific. The message said that there was a good deal of American fleet activity in the Solomons, suggesting the US carriers were still there. This seemed to indicate that Nimitz had not discovered the Japanese intentions, for Nagumo knew that were he aware of them, he would have recalled all his carriers to Pearl Harbor.

Nagumo's carriers did not have an easy voyage, and on 2 June they ran into a heavy sea mist which by dawn next morning had become an impenetrable blanket of fog. In his plotting room aboard the *Akagi* the commander of the Strike Force reviewed his plans. Despite the lack of information Nagumo felt reasonably confident that all was well, and he decided to go ahead with the attack on Midway as planned.

His carriers were still groping their way through the fog, and it was impossible to use visual signals – the only kind which could not possibly be intercepted. Owing to the full moon and the position of the troopships, Nagumo was tied to a strict schedule and consequently decided to risk using *Akagi*'s low-powered radio to send out an order to the fleet to change course toward Midway. If the Americans picked it up it would alert them and all surprise would be lost. He could only hope that such a low-powered transmission would be heard by his ships only. The flagship *Yamato* heard his message clearly and this was the only confirmation to reach Yamamoto that his carriers were going to attack as planned. Fortunately for Nagumo, the Americans on Midway did not pick up this vital message sent out just before the battle. Having taken the decision and made all his plans, Nagumo turned in to his bunk.

3. FIRST STRIKES

Far right: Vice-Admiral Frank Fletcher was the American tactical commander at the start of the Battle of Midway, but the disabling of his flagship *Yorktown* forced him to relinquish command to Spruance.
Left: A Japanese naval officer watches flight deck operations from the island of his carrier.
Below: American flight deck crews position a force of Dauntless dive bombers for takeoff.

The Battle of Midway opened at 0500 hours on 3 June 1942, more than 1000 miles north of the atoll itself, when aircraft from the carriers *Ryujo* and *Junyo* took off from a point south of Rat Island to strike at Dutch Harbor 250 miles east of the outermost edge of the Aleutian chain.

At Pearl Harbor Admiral Nimitz was not deceived by the reports of this attack. He knew that the main Japanese thrust was directed toward Midway, and he wanted to locate Yamamoto's armada as quickly as possible. The search for the Japanese ships began soon after 0400 hours on the morning of 3 June, when 23 Catalina flying boats rumbled down the runways at Midway. These slow and ugly parasol-winged amphibious reconnaissance aircraft were taking off on the mission for which Nimitz had intended them. The furthest limit of their searches was 700 miles, and with normal visibility of 25 miles, each could scan an eight-degree sector radiating from Midway. Thus the 23 PBYs were able to patrol a semicircle extending 700 miles from Midway. Any Japanese carrier which was going to attack at dawn must travel about that distance by nightfall. This would enable her to launch her planes before daylight next day – after steaming at top speed all night – at a point about 200 miles from the island.

Shortly after 0800 hours on the same morning, Ensign Jewell Reid of Kentucky was approaching the 700-mile limit of his patrol when he spotted something and immediately radioed back to Midway, 'Investigating suspicious vessels.' Half an hour later he reported sighting two cargo vessels, and soon afterward the 'main body, bearing 261, distance 700 miles from Midway. Six ships in column.' Below him Reid had seen Ichiki's invading force and Kondo's cruisers, but he was wrong in deducing this was Yamamoto's main body. The Main Force had not been spotted yet, nor had Nagumo's all-important carrier Task Force.

Reid continued to shadow Ichiki's transports and their escorts until 1100 hours, sending back a stream of radio reports. From there Nimitz deduced that there were 11 Japanese ships west of Midway, steaming toward the island at 19 knots. Nimitz decided that these ships were nothing to do with the carrier force he was hoping to find and he was right. It was not yet time to commit Fletcher's forces, but at 1230 hours nine B-17s took off from Midway to attack the convoy Reid had spotted. Four hours later they sighted a force of 'five battleships or heavy cruisers and about 40 others.' The Fortresses separated into three Vees and descended to 8000 feet. Extra fuel tanks in their bomb bays left room for only half a bomb load, four 600-pounders apiece but the bombardiers thought they hit a heavy cruiser and a transport. The Fortresses had not yet landed when four Catalinas with volunteer crews took off to make a night torpedo attack. Catalinas were not built to carry torpedoes, and their crews were not trained to drop them. Nevertheless three pilots managed to find the Japanese force. They approached from down-moon, so that the Japanese ships would be silhouetted, and one torpedo blew a hole in the tanker *Akebono Maru.* The weary crews then turned their airplanes back toward the dawn. They were almost home when they received messages that Midway was under attack.

Meanwhile, the two US Naval Task Forces had kept their position about 300 miles from Midway. Fletcher was certain that the carriers he was waiting for would approach Midway from the northwest, under cover of bad weather, and this was exactly what Nagumo's carriers were doing, as they sailed at top speed for Midway. As soon as the Japanese airplanes were committed to an attack on the island Fletcher hoped from his position on the flank to launch his own planes against their carriers. By 1930 hours on 3 June, with the Japanese attack on Midway expected to begin at dawn on 4 June, Nagumo's Carrier Strike Force had still not been located, and Nimitz was anxious. *Yorktown, Enterprise* and *Hornet*, together with their escorts, changed course to the southwest and headed toward Midway.

Aboard Nagumo's ships morale was rising as zero hour for their strike on Midway approached. According to Japanese intelligence the atoll was still guarded by only 750 troops and 60 planes. If this was the case Ichiki's force, 2800 strong and covered by 300 planes from the four carriers, ought to be able to overwhelm them easily.

At 1445 hours, when the Japanese carriers were about 250 miles northwest of Midway, the aircrews were ordered on deck. It was a dark, warm morning and as the pilots scrambled out of their bunks its silence was shattered by the roar of their planes' engines being warmed up. Nagumo himself briefed the *Akagi*'s pilots, ending his orders with the words, 'Although the enemy is lacking in fighting spirit, he will probably come out to attack during our invasion.' Despite this show of confidence, Nagumo was still inclined to be cautious. Only half his planes were sent to assault Midway and his best pilots had been held back to meet a possible American counterattack. He was still convinced that there were no American carriers in the immediate vicinity, but – just in case there were – he decided to put up an air search. Japanese air patrols were usually very meticulous, but on this occasion the patrol was very casual – with dire results. According to the air plan, a plane from the *Akagi* was to fly south for 300 miles, then turn and fly 60 miles east; a *Kaga* plane was to fly the same pattern southeast. Two planes from each of the heavy cruisers *Tone* and *Chikuma* were to fly 300 miles, turn left and fly 60 miles, and then return. The last plane, from *Haruna*, was to fly only 150 miles, then turn left and fly 40 miles before returning.

Had it worked as planned, this search would have produced vital information, but it did not. The carriers *Akagi* and *Kaga* launched their planes on schedule at 1630 hours, but *Tone*'s two planes were delayed for 30 minutes by catapult trouble, and one of the planes from *Chikuma* developed engine trouble and was forced to turn back at 1835 hours. Most of the others ran into bad weather and returned halfway through their search.

Above: Japanese aircrew parade before a mission.
Above right: Two American sailors relax during a lull in the action aboard USS *Yorktown*.
Above far right: The Nakajima B5N 'Kate' was the standard IJN carrier-based torpedo bomber in the early war years.
Below right: The Douglas SBD Dauntless proved to be a highly successful warplane at Midway.
Below: A Kate pictured during its takeoff run.

The luck of war was clearly against the Japanese at this moment. If the *Chikuma* plane which developed engine trouble had been able to continue its search it would have flown directly over the American carriers and Nagumo would have been warned. Similarly, the late takeoff of *Tone*'s two planes was also unfortunate. Had they taken off on time instead of half an hour late, they too might have found the American carriers and given an early alarm.

Dawn still had not broken when the floodlights on the *Akagi*'s deck were switched on and the first bomber sped down the flight deck and roared off into the night. Other planes followed and as they took off there were cries of *banzai*! from the flagship's crew who had assembled on deck to witness what was supposed to be an historic moment. Similar scenes were

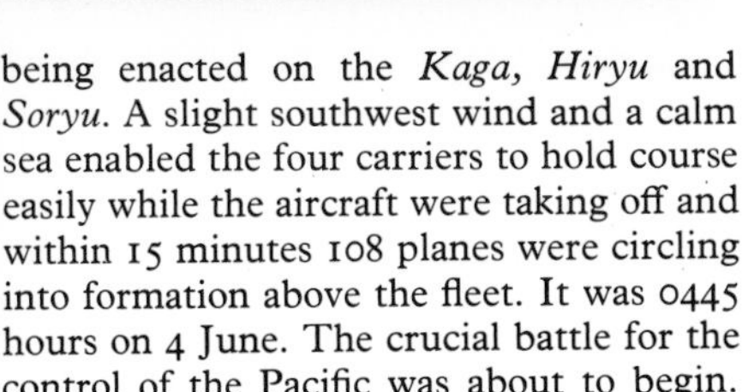

being enacted on the *Kaga, Hiryu* and *Soryu*. A slight southwest wind and a calm sea enabled the four carriers to hold course easily while the aircraft were taking off and within 15 minutes 108 planes were circling into formation above the fleet. It was 0445 hours on 4 June. The crucial battle for the control of the Pacific was about to begin.

At 0500 hours the Japanese planes were on course for Midway. Of the 108 planes, 36 were Zeros, 36 torpedo bombers (carrying bombs for the strike) and 36 were dive bombers. Lieutenant Joichi Tomonaga, the air ground commander from *Hiryu*, was their leader. This was his first battle in the Pacific, but he had flown operation missions in China as had Lieutenant Shoichi Ogawa commanding the dive bombers from *Akagi* and *Kaga*, and Lieutenant Masaharu Suganomai leading the Zeros.

Two hundred miles away from Nagumo's fleet, there was a great deal of activity. On board the *Yorktown*, 10 dive bombers were prepared for a search mission covering a 100-mile northern semicircle west to east. Almost at the same time 16 B-17s were taking off from Midway to look for and bomb the Japanese carriers, if they found them. The Catalinas had already taken off for their usual patrols. Thus, together with the reconnaissance planes, Tomonaga's strike force and the dive bombers for *Yorktown*, there were now 152 aircraft in the air from the two sides, and their pilots were all eager to begin the fight. This was the situation at 0520 hours when Nagumo signalled his ships to say that he would probably send a second assault wave against Midway soon after Tomonaga attacked.

Ten minutes later the *Akagi* was spotted by a Catalina which radioed back to Midway that it had a Japanese carrier in sight, bearing 320 degrees from the island, distance 150 miles. *Enterprise* intercepted the message and passed it to *Yorktown*. Nagumo's fleet was now speeding toward the island at 26 knots, but both Fletcher and Spruance knew approximately where he was. Minutes later a second Catalina radioed a message in clear, 'Many planes headed Midway, distance 150.' Tomonaga was halfway to the atoll. The alarm was sounded on Midway and every aircraft was ordered into the air, some to attack the Japanese carriers, some to intercept the incoming planes. By 0600 hours every airplane that could leave the ground was airborne.

Tomonaga's 36 Vals, 36 Kates and their escort of 36 Zeros hit Midway just before 0630 hours. They were met by 27 obsolescent Buffaloes, who had little hope of fending off the attack. They were not up against the famous Zero with its rounded wing tip which had proved such a success at the beginning of the Pacific war. This was a new, even more maneuverable aircraft with tapering wings – an improved version of the original Zero which was to become known by the Allies as the 'Hamp.' Not only were old Buffaloes inferior in performance, they were also outnumbered, and Lieutenant Suganomai easily prevented the inexperienced American pilots from reaching Tomonaga's bombers. Fifteen of the Buffaloes were shot down in the course of a brisk and lively action and of the 12 that survived, seven were so battered that they never flew again.

Meanwhile, Tomonaga's bombers were flying in to strike the sandy atoll. Commander Yahachi Tanabe, whose submarine, *I-168*, was prowling 10 miles south of Sand Island, had a first-class view of the bombing. 'The island,' he wrote after the war, 'turned into a mass of flames, with exploding fuel tanks and military buildings.

We saw it become covered with flames and thick, black smoke. I let my navigator, communications officer, gunnery officer and a few others take a turn looking through the periscope.' A cheer burst from the crew when Tanabe announced that a large fuel tank had exploded. In spite of heavy antiaircraft fire, bombs fell on the island's power station, as well as on the fuel tanks. However, the antiaircraft fire daunted the Japanese pilots and for the most part the bombing was erratic.

US gunners had shot down 10 Japanese planes and they swore that if visibility had not been reduced by the smoke from the burning oil tank they would have shot down 10 more. Tomonaga realizing that the damage his bombers had inflicted was far from effective, radioed at 0700 hours that a second strike was necessary, but at 0707 hours another report assured Nagumo that Sand Island had been bombed and 'great results obtained.'

A second strike had already been prepared and another 108 planes, manned by Nagumo's best pilots, were drawn up on his carriers' decks. Nagumo knew that if he gave the order to launch this attack he would have little left to send against American surface ships if his scouts spotted any. As he paced the flag bridge of *Akagi*, pondering the risk, US planes appeared on the horizon. These were 10 torpedo-carrying Avengers and Fortresses from Midway. The Avengers attacked first, dropping their torpedoes from a low altitude and pressed their attack home with great courage. Several torpedoes foamed toward *Akagi* but she nimbly dodged three of them and the other carriers dodged the rest. Zeros then shot down five of the Avengers and two of the B-17s and only three planes of the original 10 got back to Midway. It had been a valiant effort, but was piecemeal and ineffective. However, one important result was that it disturbed the Japanese at a critical moment and delayed the launching of the second strike against Midway.

Nagumo finally reached his decision to hit Midway again and eliminate the possibility of more land-based attacks on his fleet at about 0715 hours. By this time his search planes had been gone for over two hours and should have reached a point 200 miles distant. Yet there had been no reports of any US ships or carriers. In such circumstances, Nagumo felt it was safe to assume there were no carriers near him, and sent the fateful order, 'Planes in the second wave stand by to carry out attack.' Then he added, 'Reload with bombs.'

This second instruction threw the decks of *Kaga* and *Akagi* into confusion. Each of the 2 carriers had 18 planes loaded with torpedoes, ready for takeoff in case an enemy surface fleet was sighted. Now all 36 planes had to be taken below, their torpedoes removed and bombs slung in their places. The planes then had to be brought up to the flight decks.

In retrospect these orders may appear as a colossal blunder on Nagumo's part, yet in the context of events it was clearly a reasonable decision. Midway obviously had to be struck again and the airfield there put out of action. Nagumo's ships had been attacked by land-based aircraft and at the time the decision was taken there was no evidence of any enemy surface fleet in the area where they could be expected. So, Nagumo reasoned that to launch another attack on Midway would be no gamble. Also the first group of planes would soon be back to replace those he was now about to dispatch. As soon as they landed they could be refuelled and rearmed, ready for any surface engagement when his air patrols found a US fleet. Viewed objectively, it was a logical decision.

While the maintenance crews were lowering the torpedo bombers to refit them with bombs, an excited message came in from the *Tone*'s plane, 'Have sighted an estimated 10 ships, bearing 010 degrees, 240 miles from Midway, heading southwest at more than 20 knots.' If what the pilot had seen was a carrier task force, this was disastrous news and Nagumo's immediate response was to send back a curt signal ordering the pilot to, 'ascertain what types.' Half an hour passed before a coherent reply was received and during that time Nagumo's thoughts were again interrupted by another attack by American bombers. First came 16 Dauntless dive bombers from Midway. Of these, eight were knocked out and the other

Below left: A formation of Dauntlesses flies over Midway
Below: A Grumman TBF-1 Avenger carries out a practice torpedo drop in 1942.

eight driven off by Zeros almost as soon as they went into their attack dives. They were followed by the 15 Fortresses which had headed westward at dawn in search of the Invasion Force and which had turned north when they had picked up the radio report of the position of Nagumo's carriers. At 20,000 feet they dropped their bombs on the four carriers and Nagumo logged, 'Enemy bombs: *Soryu*. No hits. *Akagi* and *Hiryu* also subjected to bombing.' Pilots of B-17s, watching their 500-pound bombs splashing nearly four miles below, were certain they had hit the carriers. Returning to base with empty bomb racks, they claimed three hits on two carriers. In fact all they had scored was a near-miss on the *Akagi*.

A reply from the *Tone*'s reconnaissance plane came at 0800 hours, 'Enemy have five cruisers and five destroyers.' When Nagumo read the message he was greatly relieved. About half an hour later he was staggered when another message from *Tone*'s second plane reported, 'Enemy force accompanied by what appears to be an aircraft carrier.' Identification was not long coming, 'Two additional enemy ships apparently cruisers sighted. Carrier believed to be *Yorktown* with group.'

It was almost 0830 hours and Tomonaga's planes, returning from the first attack on Midway, were beginning to arrive overhead. Nagumo now knew that he was up against a big American fleet with at least one carrier. A quick decision was imperative. He could either attack the US ships before he launched another strike against Midway, or else he could recover and rearm the aircraft that were overhead before he did anything else. Most of the returning fighters were nearly out of fuel and some of the planes were obviously in distress. If he did not allow them to land at once, planes and pilots would be lost in the sea. On the other hand, if he recovered these planes and rearmed them he would be as strong as he had been when he launched the first wave. Other problems also had to be solved. He could send his dive bombers immediately against the American ships and he could launch his torpedo bombers even though they were now armed with bombs and even though they would also have to attack without fighter cover.

If he ordered the bombers on deck to circle out of danger until enough fighters could land, refuel and take off again to provide escort, the planes which had returned from Midway would have to be kept in the air until the bombers had cleared the deck. Damaged planes would have to take their chance. If they were not able to keep on flying they would have to crash-land in the sea.

Ultimately more was to rest on his decision than the Battle of Midway alone, but it is doubtful if Nagumo realized this at the time he ordered the flight decks to be cleared and the first wave of aircraft to be brought in.

4. DISASTER FOR NAGUMO

It was a clear, sunny morning with a few high clouds when Nagumo took stock of the situation at about 0900 hours on 4 June 1942. As he gazed out from the bridge of the *Akagi* everything seemed satisfactory. The survivors of the attack from Midway had flown off in their shrapnel-torn machines, and there was not an American plane in sight. His own mighty carriers were unscathed. Tomonaga's fliers had reported leaving a trail of destruction at Midway, and it was clear that the Americans had lost a large proportion of their Midway-based aircraft. Nagumo thought that the Americans had attacked with all their force, and so far their attacks had been easily driven off. As he looked at his four great carriers it seemed that he had every reason for confidence.

At 0834 hours the *Tone*'s scout radioed that he was returning to his ship. He had been in the air since 0500 hours and he was almost out of fuel. At that time the carriers were under attack and 20 minutes elapsed before Nagumo had time to reply. Then the scout was curtly instructed to postpone his return and to, 'maintain contact with enemy until arrival of four relief planes. Go on the air with your long-wave transmitter.'

Nagumo now felt ready to deal with the new menace, and he radioed Yamamoto, 'Enemy composed of one carrier, five cruisers, five destroyers sighted 240 miles from Midway. We are heading for it.' At the same time the blinker on the *Akagi* signalled his captains, 'After homing operations proceed northward. We plan to contact and destroy the enemy task force.' Ten minutes later, when the last Zero to return from Midway had landed on her deck, the *Akagi* turned and signalled for maximum battle speed. Soon the ships were shuddering as Nagumo's fleet speeded up to 30 knots. Aboard the four carriers the planes were being refuelled and rearmed; above them 18 fighters circled in a constant protective patrol.

By 0918 hours most of the Japanese torpedo planes had been rearmed and were ready for takeoff. On the lower decks the maintenance crews waited beside the heavy bombs they had changed for torpedoes. There had not been sufficient time to lower the bombs into the magazines, so they had been carelessly stacked around the carriers. On their flight decks *Akagi* and *Kaga* each had three fighters and 21 torpedo planes ready for takeoff, while *Hiryu* and *Soryu* each had three fighters and 18 torpedo planes ready.

The signal for them to take off was just about to be given, when there was a shout from the ship's lookout, who had spotted 15 American planes heading toward them low over the water. There was a frantic scurry as the Japanese fliers and deck crews tried to get their machines off the decks, and as the American attack started the Zeros swung into the air. Meanwhile the *Akagi*'s radio was buzzing with reports that more groups of American aircraft were heading toward the carriers. Both Nagumo and Captain Aoki on the bridge of the *Akagi* were perplexed and alarmed. There were more planes than could have been launched from a single carrier, and Nagumo ordered the *Soryu* to launch her scout plane to try to find out how many US carriers there actually were.

Dawn on 4 June had found the American fleet about 220 miles northeast of Midway. A four-knot breeze blew from the southeast, clouds were low and broken and visibility was about 12 miles. Fletcher's Task Force 17 with the carrier *Yorktown*, was steaming 10 miles to the north of Spruance's Task Force 16, with the carriers *Enterprise* and *Hornet*. Scout planes from the *Yorktown* had been in the air since before dawn, searching the sector northwest of Midway. It was not until 0603 hours that Fletcher got the message he had been waiting for, 'Two carriers and battleships,' together with their bearing, distance, course and speed. Reports that the Japanese were bombing the atoll flowed in while this data was being laid out and assessed on the plotting board.

The Japanese carriers were too far to be reached with an immediate strike. However, if Nagumo held his course – it was probable that he would be able to do so because a head wind would help the launching and recovering of his planes – an intercepting course would soon bring him within range of the Americans. At 0607 hours Fletcher ordered Spruance to, 'Proceed southwesterly and attack enemy carriers when definitely located. I will follow as soon as my planes are recovered.'

Spruance steamed ahead at 25 knots with *Enterprise* and *Hornet* and by 0700 hours the range had closed to within striking distance of his torpedo bombers. The two American carriers now separated, dividing the screening vessels between them. Finally, the carriers turned into the wind, and the first plane roared down the *Enterprise*'s deck. Nearly 150 miles away Midway's first Marine planes had begun their assault on the Japanese carriers, as 57 planes – 10 Wildcat fighters, 33 Dauntless dive bombers, and 14 Devastator torpedo bombers – from the *Enterprise* formed up. Nearby the *Hornet* had launched an almost identical group of planes, 10 Wildcats, 35 Dauntless dive bombers, and 15 Devastators. Each group was ordered to attack one of the carriers now estimated to be 155

Right: Aichi D3A 'Val' dive bombers, their engines running, await their turn to takeoff.
Below right: Douglas TBD Devastator torpedo bombers are pictured aboard USS *Enterprise.*

miles southwest. By 0806 hours the launch was completed, the carriers swung out of the wind and their squadrons sped away.

Meanwhile the *Yorktown* had recovered her planes from the morning search and had turned to steam after Spruance. Fletcher knew from his code intercepts that he could expect to meet four or five Japanese carriers and when the scout planes reported only two he hesitated to commit all his resources. By 0830 hours, however, he decided he could not afford to miss the target which had been offered to him. Half of *Yorktown*'s aircraft – six Wildcats, 17 Dauntlesses and 12 Devastators – were launched for a follow-up strike. The remainder of the *Yorktown*'s strength was kept in reserve, and more search planes were sent to look for the rest of Yamamoto's carriers.

Fifty minutes after *Yorktown*'s planes took off to join the battle, the first wave of aircraft from *Enterprise* and *Hornet* spotted two big columns of smoke just beyond the horizon. They had found Nagumo, and the first all-out clash between American and Japanese carrier fleets, for which the Coral Sea had been only a curtain-raiser, was about to begin.

The Japanese carrier force was a long way from its predicted position – it had maneuvered radically to dodge the planes from Midway, and had then turned north-east to attack Spruance. However, *Hornet*'s strike force Commander, Lieutenant Commander John Waldron, had flown a course straight for it. He had lost his fighters en route but was accompanied by his torpedo bombers. The *Hornet*'s fliers counted three carriers, six cruisers and 10 destroyers. He radioed back that the carriers' decks were loaded with planes, apparently being re-fuelled and rearmed, and that one of the carriers was definitely the *Soryu*. The message ended with the statement that he was going to attack. Apart from instructions to the squadron following him these were his last words.

To the lookouts on Nagumo's carriers, Waldron's torpedo bombers first appeared as tiny black specks on the horizon off *Akagi*'s starboard bow. When Waldron wiggled his wings as signal to start the attack, he was still eight miles from Nagumo's fleet. It was then that the Zeros circling high above plunged down on them and the rattle of the American rear gunners' machine-gun fire was punctuated by the louder, slower thump-thump of the Japanese fighters' cannon. As they came within range the antiaircraft guns aboard the cruisers and destroyers opened fire, and the carriers began to twist and turn in an effort to avoid the inevitable torpedoes. The antiaircraft fire was almost thick enough to screen the twisting ships. It gored huge holes in wings and fuselages, cut cables, smashed instruments and killed pilots and gunners. Plane after torn plane – 14 of them – plunged into the sea, burned briefly, and sank. A rear gunner in another squadron, miles away, overheard Waldron's last words, 'Watch those fighters! My two wingmen are going in the water.'

Except for the voice of the sole survivor, Ensign George Gay, nothing more was heard of the *Hornet*'s torpedo bombers. Gay heard Waldron and he heard his own gunner cry, 'They got me!' Then he was hit himself, twice, in the left hand and arm. His own target was the *Kaga*. He dropped his torpedo and flew down her flank, close to the bridge, where he could, 'see the little Jap captain jumping up and down and raising hell.'

A 20mm shell exploded on Gay's left rudder pedal, wounding him in the foot and smashing his controls, and his plane crashed between the *Kaga* and the *Akagi*. He swam back to get his gunner, but strafing Zeros made him dive and dive again and the gunner sank with the plane. A black cushion and a rubber raft floated to the surface. Gay was afraid to inflate the raft as it might draw the Zeros. So he put the cushion over his head and hid under it until twilight, with a hazardous grand-stand view of the great battle that raged all day. Gay, still alive, was picked up by a Catalina at 1430 hours the next day. Waldron had launched a suicidal attack. Yet if it had not been for the gallant action of these pilots Nagumo's planes would have had time to take off, and they could have reversed the tide of the battle.

Fifteen minutes after *Hornet*'s torpedo bombers, *Enterprise*'s torpedo planes arrived, followed by *Yorktown*'s. Like Waldron's squadron they were without fighter protection, which was still circling uselessly 20,000 feet above them.

Excitement was at its height on the Japanese carriers as the planes swooped down to launch their torpedoes. Waves of low-level Devastators lumbered in through the antiaircraft fire and as they battled to break through the curtain of shellfire, the Zeros followed them to within a few feet of the water, trying to shoot them down before they could reach the veering carriers. The second wave registered no hits on the fast and expertly-handled Japanese carriers. The mission was also virtually suicidal. Of the 41 torpedo planes that had taken off only six returned safely but the Devastators made a sacrifice more effective than they knew. When, in the heat of the battle, they drew the deadly Japanese fighters down to sea level the Japanese carriers were left wide open to attack. While fighting off the torpedo bombers, the Japanese forgot to look up. Hidden in the high clouds following the torpedo planes were the US dive bombers.

The *Hornet*'s torpedo bombers could not find Nagumo. An American scout plane had radioed accurately the Japanese position but, after this report was received, Nagumo changed course, and the Japanese were not where the Americans expected to find them. *Hornet*'s 35 dive bombers continued on a false course until their fuel ran low. Then 21 returned to the carrier, and the remaining fourteen headed for Midway, where three crashed. Their accompanying fighters, with their shorter range, crash-landed in the sea when their fuel was exhausted.

Enterprise's dive bombers also failed to find the Japanese in the position given to them. They searched the area but the ocean was calm – and deserted. There was not a Japanese ship in sight and the Squadron Leader, Lieutenant Commander Clarence McClusky, had to decide whether his information was incorrect or whether Nagumo had changed course. The narrow margin of luck by which great battles are decided now began to turn slightly toward the Americans. McClusky decided the Japanese carriers must have changed course and turned northward.

When McClusky gave the signal to turn north it was not only a lucky but a courageous decision, for his planes had already used up half their fuel. If they could not find the Japanese carriers quickly they would not be able to return. Just after 1000 hours – 25 minutes after he gave the change-course order – McClusky saw a faint white streak below him. It was the wake of a Japanese destroyer. Then three long vessels slid from under the broken cloud. Tiny flames and little dots all around them showed they were under attack. McClusky peered out of his cockpit and identified *Soryu* in the lead with *Kaga* and *Akagi* behind; he did not see *Hiryu* in the rear because she was still obscured by cloud.

Aboard the Japanese carriers the smoke was beginning to clear as the last torpedo plane staggered away, chased by Zeros, its crew exhausted by the fierce action. Nagumo had every reason to be pleased with the brisk morning's work. Wave after wave of American planes of all types had been beaten off without his carriers suffering any damage. All his aircraft were refuelled and equipped with armor-piercing bombs and torpedoes. He gave orders to launch them, and their engines began to roar as the four big Japanese carriers turned into the wind.

The first Zero was just leaving *Akagi*'s deck when a lookout shrieked a warning. With the guardian Zero still at wave-top height chasing off the last of the torpedo bombers, three of McClusky's planes screamed down on the *Akagi*. Other planes plunged down on the *Kaga*. This was the beginning of the end of Nagumo's carriers. With no radar to warn him of their approach and no fighters in a position to head them off, he was taken completely by surprise.

Only a couple of machine gunners recovered quickly enough to fire a few quick bursts at the Americans as the Japanese aircraft attempted to get clear of the carriers. It had little effect. As the American Dauntlesses pulled out of their whistling dives, their bombs were detached from their wings. Aboard the *Akagi* there was a blinding flash and two loud explosions. The guns stuttered into silence, their crews shocked or wounded, and when the thick black smoke cleared the American airplanes were nowhere in sight.

Peering through the smoke, Nagumo and his officers saw a fearful sight. The *Akagi* had received two direct hits. One had blown a huge hole in her flight deck and the other had wrenched and twisted the amidship elevator. The air was filled with burning splinters and the odour of petrol and hot metal. Charred, smoking corpses lay strewn over her deck. Then bombs that had been left lying on deck after the

Above, left and below left: The Mitsubishi A6M 'Zero' was the Imperial Japanese Navy's principal fighter aircraft, operating both from carriers and shore bases.
Below: The carrier *Kaga* takes violent evasive action to escape the bombs of Midway-based B-17s.

Left: *Hiryu* is straddled by the bombs of Boeing B-17s from the USAAF's 431st Bomb Squadron.
Right: A map traces the course of the Battle of Midway. At no time were the opposing ships in sight of each other.
Below: Captured Mitsubishi A6M Zero fighters are shipped to the United States for evaluation.

hasty reloading began to explode, shaking the bridge where Nagumo stood with his Chief of Staff, Admiral Kusaka, and Captain Aoki, *Akagi*'s commander.

Thick smoke made it difficult for them to see and the air was hot with yellow flames. As the fire licked along the flight deck more torpedoes and bombs began to explode and sailors fled from their fire-fighting apparatus half blinded. Spreading flames began to sear the bridge, their heat and smoke making it uninhabitable. Through the blackness Nagumo could see something worse – two glowing red smudges where *Kaga* and *Soryu* were supposed to be. He knew then that they too had been hit.

Kaga, *Akagi*'s sister ship, was hit by McClusky's planes almost at the same time as *Akagi*. On her flight deck she had 30 planes, all armed and fuelled awaiting the signal to take off when the American dive bombers shot out of the clouds. McClusky's planes were too busy diving in their quick attack and getaway to know what was happening aboard the other carriers. At the same time as they struck the *Kaga* and the *Akagi*, the dive bombers from the carrier *Yorktown* hit *Soryu*.

Yorktown's planes had been launched more than an hour later than those with McClusky. When they did take off the weather was clearing rapidly. This helped them to find Nagumo easily, and consequently their attack followed immediately after that of McClusky. When they came out of the cloud, McClusky's planes were diving on *Akagi* and *Kaga*, so *Yorktown*'s planes concentrated on the third undamaged carrier, *Soryu*.

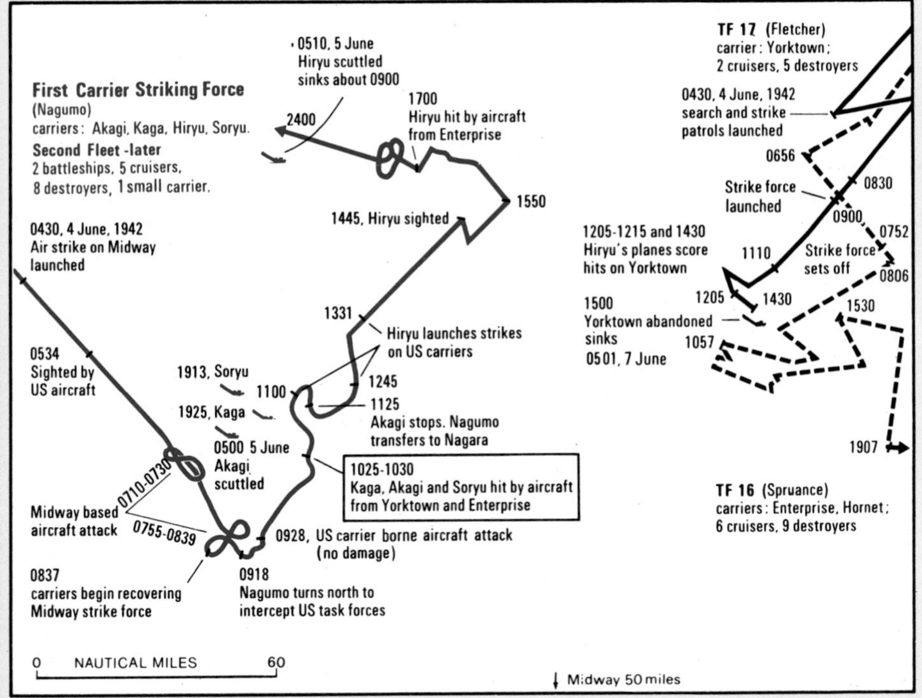

When she saw what had happened to her flagship, the destroyer *Nowake* came alongside to help with the fire fighting. Kusaka urged Nagumo to board her. The admiral, his face blackened with smoke, his eyes bloodshot, refused to leave his flagship. Captain Aoki pleaded with him, but as he spoke there were more explosions and the companionway to the bridge crashed in flames. Now the only means of escape was by rope from the bridge window.

Nagumo, realizing that the fires were out of control and that he could no longer direct the battle from the blazing carrier, climbed through the window. Helped by his flag lieutenant, Lieutenant Commander Nishibayashi, he swung down an already smoldering rope to one of *Nowake*'s boats alongside. The time was 1046 hours, only 22 minutes since McClusky's first bomber had come plummeting like a sparrow hawk out of the clouds. As Nagumo left, the blast of explosions reverberated every few seconds, the metal companionways between decks were red hot, and half-choked sailors were beginning to jump overboard.

By this time *Akagi* was not answering her rudder and there was no response from the engine room. Then the ship stopped, with her bows still pointing into the wind as though she was getting ready to launch the planes which were burning and exploding on her deck. The dynamos died and the lights went out and without electricity the fire pumps could no longer operate. Fire-fighting parties, wearing masks, rolled hoses down to the burning lower decks. As they staggered over the charred corpses of their comrades, explosions every few seconds wounded or killed more of them.

Doctors and medical orderlies worked in suffocating heat and blinding smoke. The clothing of wounded men began to smolder as they lay on deck. The lucky ones were strapped to bamboo stretchers and lowered over the side. Although fire had cut off the signal tubes to the bridge the engine rooms below were still undamaged, but the smoke filtering through the intakes made stokers gasp and clutch at their throats. Finally Commander Tampo, *Akagi*'s chief engineer, clambered up a red-hot ladder and staggered through flames and smoke to the bridge to tell Captain Aoki that his men were dying. Aoki gave the order for all engineroom crew to come on deck and an orderly slid down a burning rope and ran along the smoke blackened decks to tell them. He never returned, and no one escaped from the engine room.

By this time all of *Akagi*'s planes were either burning or had blown up, and the last of the aircrews were transferred to the destroyers. At 1615 hours Commander Tampo reported to the captain that there was no possibility of the ship steaming under her own power and as the last of the wounded were carried into the boats, the giant carrier was blazing from stem to stern. Finally Captain Aoki gave the order to abandon ship.

Aoki was the last man to leave the stricken vessel and it was 1920 hours when he was persuaded to board the launch from the destroyer *Nowake*. He had sent a message to Nagumo asking for permission to scuttle the *Akagi*. Nagumo never answered, but Yamamoto did, sending a brief order not to sink the ship. Yamamoto hated the idea of scuttling a vessel of the Imperial Navy, but his decision was determined also by his sentimental attachment to the ship. He had served many years on the *Akagi* and she was a great favorite of his. He was determined to tow her back if he could. When he received this message Aoki decided there was only one course open to him, and he lashed himself to one of *Akagi*'s anchors to await the end. Like most of the senior officers Aoki was intent on hari-kiri. Moreover he never got over the feeling that he ought to have stayed aboard and ultimately gone down with his ship. In the event he was persuaded by his silver-tongued navigator Commander Miura that he would be more useful alive than dead, and he was transferred to the destroyer *Nowake*.

The *Kaga* had suffered even more damage than the *Akagi* from four direct hits by 500-pound bombs. One which had landed near the bridge had killed everyone on it – including the ship's commander, Captain Jisaku Okada. The Flight Officer, Commander Takahisa Amagai, immediately took over the carrier, but the helmsman, blinded by a bomb flash, could not control her. Shattered glass on the bridge and smoke from bomb damage reduced visibility to zero, but the ship's position was far from hopeless, and Amagai ordered the crew to start clearing the decks and fighting the fires. Just as the fires were beginning to be brought under control, a small truck filled with gasoline for fuelling the planes blew up on the flight deck. Flames spread rapidly and when they began to lick the whole length of the carrier, Amagai was forced off the bridge. The damage-control crew whom he had organized fought desperately to halt the spreading flames. Realizing the end was near, Amagai ordered the Emperor's portrait to be lowered reverently down to the destroyer *Hagikaze*.

Some three-and-a-half hours after the dive-bombing attack, Amagai was still in command of the blazing *Kaga* when a new menace appeared. About half a mile from the carrier the telltale periscope of a submarine suddenly showed. The American submarine *Nautilus*, commanded by Lieutenant Commander William Brockman, which had been patiently stalking Nagumo's fleet, had seen an opportunity to strike a blow.

Minutes later, soon after 1400 hours, Lieutenant Commander Yoshio Kunisada, standing on the *Kaga*'s listing deck, saw three white torpedo wakes streaking toward the starboard side of the carrier. There was nothing anyone could do but wait for the explosion. Disabled as she was, the *Kaga* could not swerve to dodge the torpedoes. The destroyers *Hagikaze* and *Maikaze* raced up to where the *Nautilus* had been spotted, and there was a series of dull booms as a pattern of depth charges was dropped round the crash-diving submarine. Miraculously, two of the torpedoes missed, and although the third struck it failed to explode. Instead of blowing a hole in the side of the flame-wracked carrier it turned out to be a lifesaver. Several sailors who had jumped or been blown overboard grabbed a floating section of the torpedo and clung to it until they were picked up by the destroyers' boats.

Above: The *Ise* served with the Aleutian Support Force but after Midway became a carrier/battleship.

By the late afternoon it was clear that the blazing unmanageable hulk of the *Kaga* was doomed, and at 1640 hours Amagai gave the order to abandon ship. Two hours later it seemed that the fire had died down and, in the hope of saving his old ship, Amagai led a fire-fighting party back. When the men eventually got aboard they were driven back by the heat. No one could stand on the red-hot decks and Amagai was reluctantly compelled to order his party to return to the destroyer which had brought them. They got away just in time; soon afterward two mighty explosions ripped *Kaga*'s hull and she rolled over to sink in a hiss of steam. Eight hundred men, more than a third of her crew, died with her.

On board the *Soryu*, the third target of the American dive-bombing attack, the devastation had been almost as great as aboard *Kaga*. Thirteen US dive bombers had plummeted down on the *Soryu* while those on her bridge were watching bombs falling on the *Kaga*. Three bombs struck the ship in quick succession and in next to no time the whole of the flight deck was blazing. There may have been other hits too, but amid the noise and thump of exploding ammunition stacked on the deck it was hard to tell. Everything happened so quickly that most of those on the *Soryu* had little or no warning. Ten minutes afterward the engines stopped and the Soryu's rudder failed to answer. Then a tremendous explosion below decks blasted many of the crew into the water. Other sailors jumped overboard as flames began to scorch their clothes. The destroyers *Hamaka* and *Isokaze*, circling round the blazing carrier, picked up as many as they could.

Captain Ryusaku Yanagimoto, *Soryu*'s commander fought to get the *Soryu* under control. The whole ship was ablaze from stem to stern and with constant explosions wracking her, he saw that there was no hope of saving her. Reluctantly he gave the order to abandon ship. He himself was determined to comply with the tradition and go down with her, and he remained on the bridge. However, no officer in the Imperial Navy was more popular than Yanagimoto, and his men were determined that he should not commit hari-kiri.

Before they slid down the ropes to the waiting destroyers the biggest among them, a navy wrestling champion, Chief Petty Officer Abe, was sent to reason with him. Abe was to drag the captain to safety by force if necessary. When Abe climbed up to *Soryu*'s bridge, Yanagimoto was standing sword in hand, silhouetted against the roaring flames, and the sight unnerved the petty officer. Saluting, Abe said, 'Captain, I've come to take you to safety. The men are waiting, please come with me.' Yanagimoto did not reply. The stern look on his face was enough to deter Abe from laying hands on his skipper and he turned around and returned from the carrier in tears, and alone.

As the minutes ticked away the *Soryu* foundered lower and lower in the water. On the destroyer *Makigumo* standing by, someone began singing the Japanese national anthem *Kimigayo*. Others took it up and some say that they could hear Yanagimoto's voice singing it with them on the bridge of the dying carrier. At 1913 hours with the strains of the song still ringing out over the water, the *Soryu*'s stern dipped and her bow rose high. For a moment, the ship paused, then settled down and was gone.

5. THE END OF YORKTOWN & HIRYU

When Nagumo left the blazing *Akagi* he transferred his flag to the light cruiser *Nagara*. Three of his carriers were already burning, and only the *Hiryu* remained to him as a strike weapon. He was worried about his lack of information on the number of American carriers opposing him, for there had been no report from the *Soryu*'s scout plane. This was sheer bad luck, for the *Soryu*'s plane had located and identified the three US carriers but had been unable to report back because of a faulty radio. Fortunately for Nagumo *Hiryu* was the flagship of Rear Admiral Tamon Yamaguchi, who appreciated the vital need for information.

Yamaguchi was one of the most able of the Imperial Navy's senior officers – certainly a more resolute and clear-thinking commander than Nagumo. As soon as the extent of the disaster that had struck Nagumo's force became clear to Yamaguchi he assumed responsibility for the operations and wasted no time in launching an attack on Fletcher's fleet. He decided that the number of American carriers was immaterial, and at 1040 hours Lieutenant Michio Kobayashi – an experienced pilot who had taken part in the Pearl Harbor raid – was ordered to take off with 18 Val dive bombers and an escort of six Zeros.

At this time *Yorktown*'s planes which had sunk *Hiryu*'s sister carrier, *Soryu*, were winging their way home. At 1200 hours *Yorktown* was getting ready to recover the bombers and refuel her fighters when her radar picked up Kobayashi's planes, which were then 50 miles away. Refuelling was hastily abandoned, planes on the flight deck were quickly launched with orders to clear off out of trouble, and the returning bombers were waved away. A cruiser steamed up to either bow to add firepower

Below: Grumman F4F Wildcat fighters fly in echelon formation. Wildcats escorted the American carrier strike forces and performed defensive patrols.

Below: Yorktown, blazing amidships, lies dead in the water after the initial Japanese attack.

Above right: Naval antiaircraft guns took a toll of attacking aircraft.
Above: The scene on *Yorktown*'s flight deck after the attack.

Right: The second Japanese bomb to hit *Yorktown* struck between her funnel and mast, the blast extinguished the fires in five out of her six boilers.

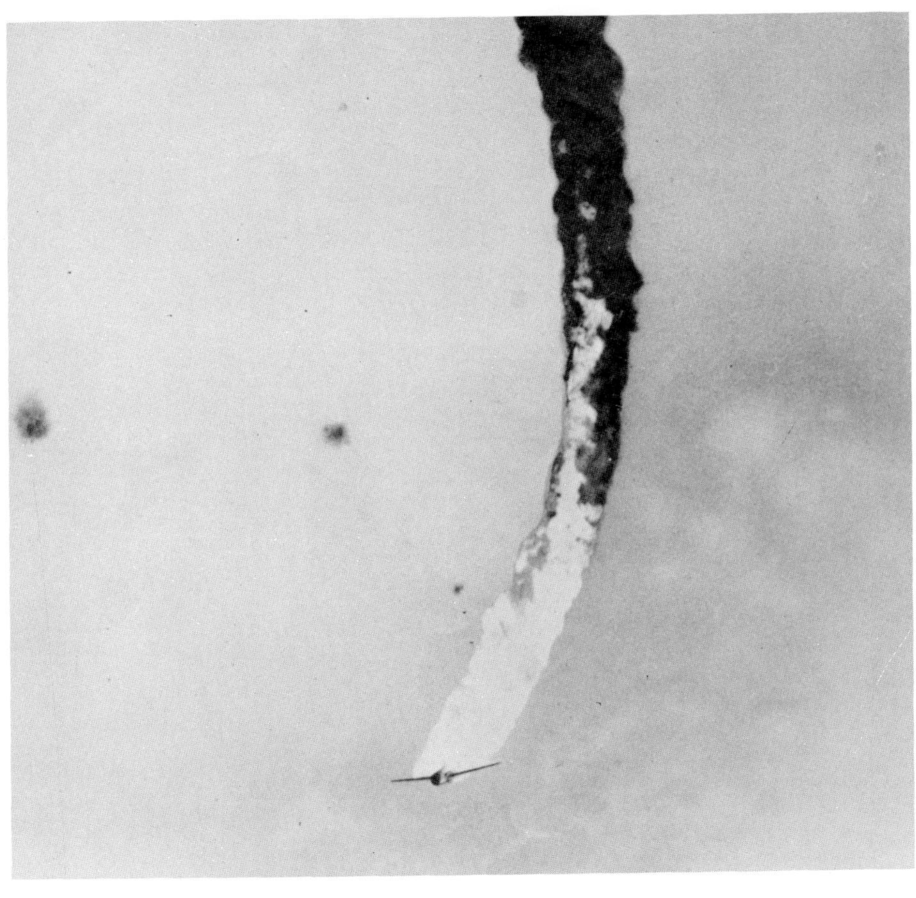

to *Yorktown*'s defenses, and fighters from the *Enterprise* and *Hornet* flew in to support her defensive umbrella – making a total of 28 Wildcats.

Kobayashi approached his target at 18,000 feet, and from about five miles distance he could see the American torpedo bombers, who were returning from their attack on his own fleet, circling to land on the US carrier. Clearly here was a bonus to his own strike and as he gave the signal to descend to 10,000 feet for the run in, he waved his Zero escort forward. They dived on the American bombers, chased by Wildcats, and in the fight which followed two Zeros were lost.

Other Wildcats now tore into the Japanese bombers in an effort to break up their formation, and the antiaircraft guns of the carrier and cruisers opened fire to put a curtain of steel above the *Yorktown*. Ten of Kobayashi's planes were shot down by the American Wildcats. There were not enough American fighters to stop some of the dive bombers getting through. Two more were disabled as they tried to pierce the shrapnel curtain, while another dropped his bomb harmlessly into the water and then crashed after it. Five of Kobayashi's original 18 planes survived and that was enough. Three bombs landed on *Yorktown*. One went straight down the smokestack into the engine room – knocking out all the boilers except one, and so effectively stopping the ship. The second exploded on the flight deck, blowing a big hole in it, and the third exploded near an ammunition magazine and a compartment of high-octane gasoline, which was hastily flooded with sea water to prevent fire.

Meanwhile *Soryu*'s scout plane had returned while Kobayashi's fliers were bombing *Yorktown* to find its home base blazing from end to end. So the pilot landed on *Hiryu* and reported to Rear Admiral Yamaguchi that the Americans actually had three carriers in action, *Enterprise*, *Hornet* and *Yorktown*.

This startling information forced Yamaguchi to make a quick reappraisal of the situation. *Hiryu* alone was now facing three enemy carriers, only one of which might have been knocked out in Kobayashi's attack. Clearly there was no time to be wasted, and he decided to strike quickly at the US carriers with every plane he could muster – a total of 10 torpedo bombers and six fighters.

Lieutenant Joichi Tomonaga, the officer who had led the assault on Midway, was chosen to lead the strike. There had not been enough time to repair his plane's fuel tank, damaged by gunfire over Midway, so he knew before he took off that he was flying a one-way mission.

At 1245 hours 16 planes took off from *Hiryu* and headed for the US carriers. En route they passed a forlorn little group of five Japanese planes flying in the reverse direction. They were all that was left of Kobayashi's strike.

When these five pilots landed on *Hiryu* they reported that six bombs had been dropped on an American carrier, that she could not move and was sending up great columns of smoke. Yamaguchi rightly concluded that this carrier must have been hit by at least two bombs and severely damaged. What he did not know was that damage-control parties in the *Yorktown* worked so effectively that in less than two hours – by 1400 hours – the carrier was again able to make 18 knots under her own power.

In consequence she was steaming along refuelling the rest of her fighters when at about 1430 hours her radar began tracking Tomonaga's torpedo group 40 miles away. Once more refuelling was suspended and the combat air patrol scrambled into the air. So speedily had *Yorktown*'s repairs been effected that when Tomonaga sighted an American carrier surrounded by escort ships he thought she was another undamaged carrier; he could not believe it was *Yorktown*.

As his orders were to attack undamaged carriers, he signalled the order to do so and the bomber formation bifurcated. Tomonaga led one line, his second-in-command, Toshio Hashimoto, led the other. When they went into their dive *Yorktown* was still trying to get the rest of her planes into the air.

As before, Wildcats managed to shoot down some of the Japanese planes before they got within range of the ship's guns, and the barrage deterred others. A few of the determined Japanese succeeded in getting through – one of whom was Tomonaga. Signalling his pilots to follow him, he dived his yellow-tailed plane straight through the antiaircraft fire to launch his torpedoes. Then, knowing he could never get back, he crashed his plane on *Yorktown*, where it blew up in a sheet of flame. A long, dark smudge of brown smoke on *Yorktown*'s deck marked his pyre.

Inspired by Tomonaga's example other pilots followed him through the barrage to launch their torpedoes. Two struck amidships, less than 60 feet apart on the port side. As Hashimoto turned from his attack thick yellow smoke belched from the carrier and her 20,000-ton hull gave a great shudder and stopped dead in the water. 'She seemed to leap out of the water,' said an American sailor, 'then she sank back, all life gone.' It was 1445 hours and Hashimoto radioed back to the *Hiryu*, 'Two torpedo hits on the carrier. Believed to be of the *Yorktown* Class.'

This second raid was the last Japanese attack against American ships in the Battle of Midway. Only five torpedo bombers and three fighters, half the number launched, got back to *Hiryu*. They landed at 1830 hours and gave Yamaguchi details of their attack, claiming one carrier severely damaged. This, with the previous attack on *Yorktown* made him think that two American carriers were mortally hurt. He had no

Above: A 'Kate' breaks away from USS *Yorktown* after making its torpedo run.
Right: An attacking aircraft plunges blazing into the sea.
Below right: Dauntlesses position themselves for the dive onto the target.
Below: A curtain of antiaircraft fire greets Japanese torpedo aircraft attacking the American carrier task forces.

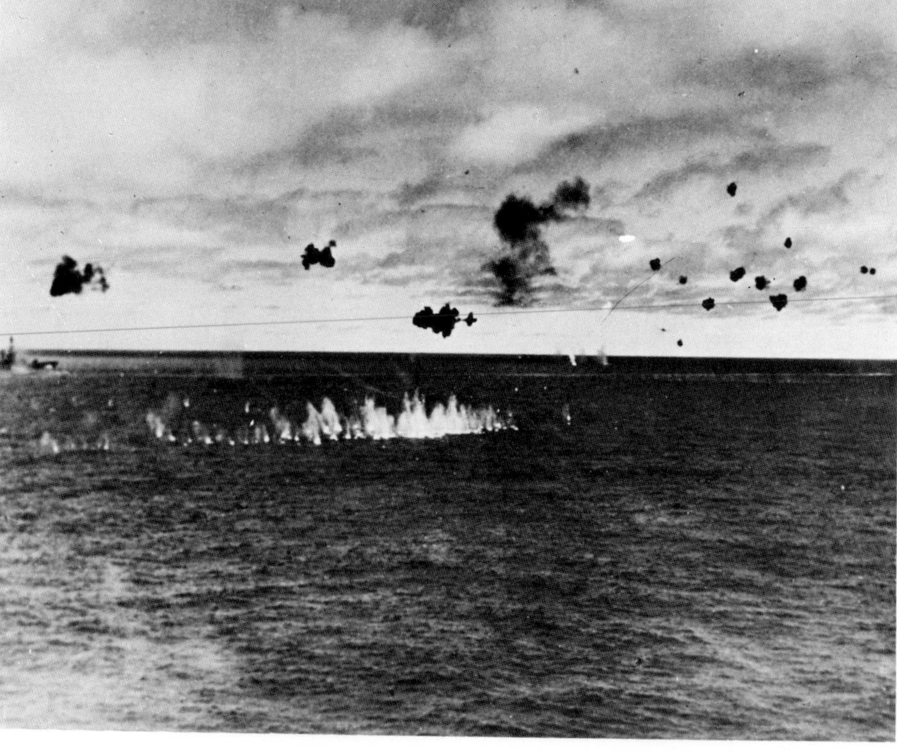

idea it was *Yorktown* his pilots had struck again. Even if he realized the situation there was nothing he could do to stave off the retribution that was now on its way.

At the same time as the survivors of Tomonaga's strike turned for home, the pilot of one of the *Yorktown*'s scout planes radioed to his own burning carrier. He had been searching the Pacific for three hours and had at last found Yamaguchi's *Hiryu*. His message gave its position as 100 miles away, and when Fletcher read it he decided that with dusk approaching an all-out strike was called for. At 1600 hours *Enterprise* began launching 24 Dauntless – 14 of which were refugees who had been unable to land on *Yorktown. Hornet* also launched 16 and the combined force set off without fighter escort because Fletcher, worried by the repeated attacks on his carriers, wanted his Wildcats to protect them against any more bombers. When the Dauntlesses had been flying for an hour they saw three curling towers of smoke silhouetted against the reddening sky. These marked the hulks of the *Kaga* and *Soryu* and the still burning *Akagi*. Swinging northward they now saw the rest of the Japanese fleet in a tight circle round their only surviving carrier, *Hiryu*.

Aircraft from *Hiryu* had made three attacks at dawn, including the one on Midway, and their number was sadly depleted. At 1630 hours, when the last of the ill-fated Tomonaga group was returning from *Yorktown*, they had been reduced to six fighters, five dive bombers and four torpedo bombers. Aircrew and sailors alike were exhausted, for in addition to their own attacks, 79 planes had attacked *Hiryu* since sunrise, and she had been kept busy dodging 26 torpedoes, and 70 bombs.

Yamaguchi, aggressive and desperate, was determined to salvage Yamamoto's operation, destroy the American carriers, and pluck victory from the jaws of defeat. He had decided to make a last attempt at dusk, when the uncertain light would give his few remaining planes a better chance to make a surprise attack on the Americans. This tactic had been tried without success in the Battle of the Coral Sea but Yamaguchi decided that he had no alternative but to risk it again.

At five o'clock – half an hour after Tomonaga's last plane landed – sweet rice-balls were served to the hungry, exhausted crew of the *Hiryu*. A handful of them had just finished refuelling the pitifully few planes for Yamaguchi's twilight attack, and the rest were hastily eating the rice as the carrier was turned into the wind to begin launching. Suddenly *Enterprise*'s bombers dived out of the sun. *Hiryu* had no radar, and once again there had been no long-range warning of their approach. Her commander, Captain Tomeo Kaku, swung the ship to starboard as the bombers came down and the Americans lost three planes to antiaircraft fire and Zeros. *Hiryu* twisted like a giant eel, but more American planes dived through the barrage, and four bombs exploded simultaneously on her deck.

One, bursting in front of the bridge, put the navigator out of action and the others burst among the planes, waiting to take off. One after another they began to explode, starting enormous fires. Men staggered, blinded, round the decks, falling over bodies, scorched by flames, suffocating from heat and smoke. Columns of black smoke rose as the carrier lost speed and finally stopped. Within minutes, Yamaguchi's flagship was a helpless hulk, torn apart by the explosions. So great was the apparent damage that the remainder of *Enterprise*'s pilots turned away to bomb one of the Japanese escorting battleships, the *Haruna*.

When what was left of Tomonaga's squadron returned from their attack on *Yorktown* to land on the *Hiryu* she was burning furiously, and they were compelled to circle like fledglings over a burning nest. The fighters attacked the second half of the US strike force – the sixteen Dauntlesses from *Hornet* – which arrived shortly afterward, but shortage of fuel cut short their efforts and one by one all the remaining Japanese planes plunged into the sea. Meanwhile the *Hornet*'s Dauntlesses went on to bomb the battleship *Haruna* and the cruiser *Chikuma*.

For some time it seemed as if the fire in the *Hiryu* might be brought under control, but she was doomed. By midnight she lay helpless on the water, with a list of 15 degrees. Her steering had gone and most of the fire pumps were out of action. Several desperate attempts to fight a way through the smoke and flames to the engine rooms had failed. Like her adversary, *Yorktown*, she was dying.

A brilliant moon provided the backcloth to leaping flames and black smoke when at 0230 hours Admiral Yamaguchi ordered Captain Kaku to summon all hands. Etched against the flames, he addressed the crew from the bridge, 'As officer commanding this carrier division,' he said, 'I am solely responsible for the loss of *Hiryu* and *Soryu*. I shall remain on board to the end. But I command all of you to leave the ship and continue your loyal service to His Majesty the Emperor.' Yamaguchi then took off his black admiral's cap and gave it to his Flag Lieutenant, Commander Ito, as a memento. In return Ito gave him a piece of cloth with which to lash himself to the bridge and make sure he would go down with the ship. Then to the accompaniment of a few desultory *banzais*, *Hiryu*'s flag and the Admiral's were ceremoniously lowered. Some of Yamaguchi's officers asked for permission to die with him, but he ordered them aboard the destroyer *Kazaguma* standing alongside. Only Captain Kaku refused to board the destroyer, insisting that it was his duty as well as his right to stay aboard the blazing carrier with his admiral.

When everyone else had left the ship, the two men lashed themselves to the helm and waited for her to sink. It seemed that the *Hiryu* was as stubborn about sinking as the *Yorktown*, and at 0510 hours Captain Abe, commander of the escorting destroyer division, gave the order for a *coupe de grâce* to be administered. At 0510 hours two torpedoes found their mark and a couple of deafening explosions followed. The *Hiryu* began to settle down and Abe, satisfied that he had seen the last of the carrier, ordered the destroyers to return. At 0540 hours he reported by radio to Yamamoto that the *Hiryu* had been scuttled. An hour and 20 minutes later, however, a scout plane from the light carrier *Hosho*, which had been sent to locate the Nagumo Force, radioed that the smoldering wreck of the *Hiryu* was still afloat and that men could be seen on board. Yamamoto's reaction was to pass the information to Nagumo, ordering him to verify that the *Hiryu* had gone down and to make every effort to rescue any survivors. Nagumo sent a destroyer and the *Nagara*'s seaplane to do this, but the *Hiryu* was never seen again. It was learned afterward that the *Hiryu* had actually remained afloat until about 0820 hours. The men who had been seen on deck were survivors of the engine-room crew, who had miraculously escaped when Abe's torpedoes blasted an exit from where they were trapped below decks. Subsequently, after the carrier sank, they were picked up by an American ship, and spent the rest of the war in captivity.

Above: The fires aboard the Japanese carrier *Hiryu* led to her being abandoned.

Right and below right: After second torpedo attack, the listing *Yorktown* was abandoned.

About 150 miles away *Yorktown* was also dying. At 1458 hours on 4 June – following Tomonaga's attack – her ebullient commander, Captain Elliot Buckmaster, had given the fateful order 'Abandon ship.' All the available evidence had suggested that *Yorktown* was in danger of sinking, and the decision was undoubtedly correct. Fletcher, who had already transferred his flag to the cruiser *Astoria* confirmed the order, and Buckmaster was the last to leave the ship – or so everyone believed at the time. More than 2000 men were taken off the doomed carrier and at 1800 hours the ships that had been standing by moved off to the east. The carrier was now alone, except for the destroyer *Hughes*, which had orders to sink her if she started to burn. (Fire would have given her position away and made possible her capture by the Japanese.) She was still alone, but the list she had taken on earlier seemed to be correcting itself, and Buckmaster, who had never given up hope of saving his vessel, had now concluded that a salvage operation was feasible. That night, while he studied ways and means, key men were sought out for a salvage party.

Above: The Japanese submarine *I- 68* sank the damaged *Yorktown.*

Above right: Destroyers stand by the stricken *Yorktown.*

Right: Yorktown survivors parade aboard a rescuing cruiser.

First, it was decided, the flight decks and hangar decks would have to be cleared of debris, in order to lighten the ship. Next, the four 5-inch guns on the port side would have to be cut away. Then, with power furnished by escorting ships, water and oil could be pumped from *Yorktown*'s port tanks to the starboard. This, it was reasoned, would bring the carrier back to an almost even keel. Finally, water tenders would light off the boilers, and *Yorktown* could limp to port on her own power. All this might be speeded up because the fleet tug *Vireo,* moored at French Frigate Shoal, between Midway and Oahu, was already on her way to take *Yorktown* in tow while the work progressed.

With luck all might have gone well, but at 0626 hours on 5 June, the *Hughes* picked up a Japanese scout plane on her radar. It had come from the cruiser *Chikuma* and at 0652 hours its pilot radioed that he had sighted 'an enemy aircraft carrier of the *Yorktown* Class.' This message sealed the *Yorktown*'s fate. As soon as Yamamoto received it he radioed another message to Lieutenant Commander Yahachi Tanabe in the submarine *I-168* off Midway. *I-168* was to 'locate and destroy the American carrier.' Tanabe had just been waiting submerged after bombarding Midway. Now he set a course for *Yorktown*'s estimated position.

A short time later the fleet tug, *Vireo,* arrived and began to make preparations to take *Yorktown* in tow. Sailors from *Hughes,* after making their trip to *Yorktown,* reported that the carrier seemed to be holding her own, and that although the fire had flared up again, it did not seem to pose serious danger. Almost simultaneously, 20 miles to the east, Captain Buckmaster and his salvage party set off in the destroyer *Hamman.*

By 1200 hours *Yorktown*'s salvage operations were in full swing. The *Vireo* had taken the carrier in tow and was pulling her back toward Hawaii. It was a slow tedious business, and the huge hulk was really more than the little *Vireo* could manage – even at three knots. However, the men working aboard *Yorktown* were making considerable progress, pumping out flooded compartments and cutting away the guns to lighten her. The *Hamman* was then secured along her starboard side, supplying power for the pumps, and five other destroyers circled her to guard against submarine attacks.

Tanabe arrived on the scene at about 1300 hours and the brief action that followed can be counted one of the great submarine exploits of the war. After threading his way under the US destroyer cordon, Tanabe came up to periscope depth. He waited his opportunity, fired four torpedoes, and dived. Aboard the *Yorktown* the salvage party had paused for a lunch of sandwiches and warm Coca-Cola when one of them, standing on the starboard side of the hangar deck, commented, 'Hey, look! There's some black fish.'

Two of the torpedoes hit the *Yorktown,* and when her battered hulk had absorbed the two shocks Buckmaster knew there was no longer any hope for her. *Hamman* had no time to pull clear and one torpedo cut her in two. She sank almost at once, and as she went down her depth charges exploded under water, killing many of the men who had been thrown overboard or who had dived into the water.

While Buckmaster was again getting his men off his stricken vessels, six US destroyers tried to sink the *I-168.* Tanabe recorded later that he and his men counted 60 near misses by depth charges, and at the end of the attack the *I-168* was crippled – unable to move, with no lights, no pumps working, batteries damaged and chlorine escaping from them. This deadly gas was the submariner's greatest fear. Tanabe watched as a mouse 'staggered drunkenly across my foot.' Then, unexpectedly, the American destroyers broke off the attack. They had been ordered back to *Yorktown* to investigate sonar contacts picked up by two other destroyers. Tanabe, puzzled but relieved, took *I-168* to the surface, using up most of his remaining compressed air. 'When I got to the bridge,' he wrote later, 'there was no sign of the enemy carrier. But between myself and the eastern horizon I could see three American destroyers.' One of them, *Hughes,* saw *I-168* surface and all three destroyers – *Hughes, Gwin* and *Monagham* – came about and started pursuit. Tanabe, taking advantage of every second, continued to charge his batteries and refill his air tanks, even as *Hughes* came within range and opened up with her forward 5-inch gun. At the last moment Tanabe submerged, turned 180 degrees, and ran directly under the American destroyers. The trick worked, *I-168* escaped and Tanabe eventually got back to Kure.

Tanabe's victim, *Yorktown,* remained afloat until the following morning (6 June Japanese time, 7 June US time). Then she simply turned over and sank.

6. YAMAMOTO'S REACTION

Not until it was too late did Admiral Yamamoto take any part in the battle which he had wanted to turn into a decisive fleet engagement. At dawn on 4 June his flagship, the *Yamato*, was 800 miles northwest of Midway, and some 300 miles from Nagumo's carriers. Because he had insisted on radio silence it was some hours before the Commander in Chief appreciated the extent of Nagumo's defeat.

At first, everything had seemed to be going well. *Akagi*'s radio silence only seemed to confirm that events were shaping as he had expected. So too did Tomonaga's message reporting the completion of his mission against Midway. To Yamamoto it was quite logical for Tomonaga to suggest a second strike against the atoll as American air strength on Midway had to be eliminated before the Japanese invasion. Surprise, it seemed, had been achieved, and the Commander in Chief and his staff awaited the next message with confidence.

At 0740 hours, the terse flash from the *Tone*'s scout plane saying 'Have sighted 10 ships, apparently enemy,' caused a few speculative frowns. While Yamamoto pondered this message no one spoke. Soon afterward another message from *Tone*'s plane reported, 'American fleet has five cruisers, five destroyers – and one carrier.' Yamamoto glanced at the bridge clock. The timing was perfect. Nagumo's second wave of planes on the deck of the carriers would now be ready to take off and they would soon make short work of the lone American carrier.

Half an hour later, however, came the first indication that all might not be as well as it seemed. From the scout plane came the report, '100 carrier-borne enemy planes heading for the Nagumo Force.' This meant that there must be more than one American carrier, yet Yamamoto still felt confident about the outcome of the forthcoming battle.

For two long hours nothing more was heard from Nagumo's carriers. Then at 1050 hours the chief signals officer, Commander Yoshio Wada, silently handed Admiral Yamamoto a radio message. It was from Rear Admiral Abe in the cruiser *Tone* informing the Commander in Chief of the fate of Nagumo's carriers. Abe's message ran, 'Fires raging aboard *Kaga, Soryu* and *Akagi* resulting from attacks by enemy carrier and land-based planes. We plan to have *Hiryu* engage enemy carriers. We are temporarily withdrawing to the north to assemble our forces.'

The news that three of his carriers were out of action broke Yamamoto's imperturbability. There was only one course open to him now: he must take over the direction of the battle and his battleships must steam toward Midway. This was a decision he should perhaps have taken at the outset of the operation; now it was going to prove too late. No sooner had he decided to steam full ahead to join Nagumo than fog came down. Speed was vital, but it took Yamamoto more than an hour to get his gigantic fleet under way and as it began to steam toward Midway at 20 knots the fog was thickening. The ships followed a zigzag course to avoid the American submarines – a hazardous maneuver in heavy fog, but one which Yamamoto decided he must take if he was to push ahead to help Nagumo.

En route there was an anxious planning conference in the operations cabin of the *Yamato*. While the merits and drawbacks of the proposed operation were being debated Yamamoto said nothing. Then, pale and tight-lipped, he signified that he had decided on a night action.

The destruction of Midway was necessary in order to eliminate it as an American aircraft base. To get things moving, orders were sent to Tanabe in the submarine *I-168* – still patrolling off the atoll – to close in on the island and start shelling the airfield with her 4-inch deck gun. This bombardment was to be kept up until Tanabe was joined by the four heavy cruisers from Kondo's invasion group, *Mikuma, Mogami, Suzuya* and *Kumano*. The battleship *Hiei* would also join the action as soon as she arrived.

At 1220 hours Yamamoto signalled a general order of the day, 'All forces will attack the enemy in the Midway area.' Half an hour later a more detailed instruction was transmitted, 'Commander (Midway Forces) will dispatch part of his strength to bombard and destroy air bases on Midway. All combat forces from both Midway and Aleutian area will engage the enemy fleet in decisive battle.' Yamamoto was still looking for his one decisive engagement.

How soon Vice-Admiral Kakuda's two carriers *Ryujo* and *Junyo* would reach the battle area was the crucial issue, for if they arrived in time the Japanese would still have a superiority in carriers. At 1630 hours a signal was received from *Kakuda*. It was not encouraging. Despite dense fog, he had carried out his strike on Dutch Harbor, as planned, but his ships could not be expected to join the Midway battle before the afternoon of 6 June – 48 hours later. Then at 1615 hours Admiral Yamaguchi radioed from *Hiryu*, 'Pilots report enemy force is apparently composed of three carriers, five large cruisers and 15 destroyers. Our attacks succeeded in damaging two carriers.'

At 1736 hours the scout plane from *Chikuma* radioed that the Americans were

Right: Admiral Yamamoto, sailing with the battleships of the Main Body, took little part in the Battle of Midway, but the final decision to disengage was his.
Below: The battleship *Mutsu*, here firing her broadside, was one of Yamamoto's battleships.

only 90 miles from Nagumo's fleet – and were withdrawing eastward. Yamamoto had already sent Kondo and his fast battleships racing toward them at top speed. A night action might turn the battle in Japan's favor because the Imperial Navy was better trained for night actions than the Americans. The Americans' superiority in aircraft carriers would not count at night as they were not trained for night-flying operations. The Japanese superiority in numbers might save the day. Sunset was at 1823 hours, and at 1755 hours came the worst news of all, '*Hiryu* hit by bombs and set on fire at 1730 hours': Yamamoto's last remaining carrier had gone.

Soon after this Yamamoto received Nagumo's message saying that he had left his burning flagship and transferred to the *Nagara*. 'There are still four enemy aircraft carriers,' the signal continued, 'possibly including light aircraft carriers, six cruisers and 16 destroyers. They are steaming westward. None of our aircraft carriers is operational. We plan to contact the enemy with scout aircraft tomorrow morning.' 'Tomorrow morning' was too late for Yamamoto. Earlier he had radioed Tokyo that the American fleet was nearly destroyed and that what was left of it was retreating eastward. It was more a hopeful prophecy than a statement of fact. To make it a reality, Yamamoto had ordered his two carriers in the Aleutians, *Ryujo* and *Junyo*, to join him and they were on their way. The carrier *Zuiho*, with the troop convoy, was moving up from the southwest. Within sight of the flagship *Yamato* was the ancient *Hosho*, the world's first carrier built from the keel up. Yamamoto knew he was inferior to the Americans in aircraft strength, even with these reinforcements, but he had overwhelming superiority in total number of ships and guns.

At this point Yamamoto was still determined that the Midway operation should continue. Temporarily, as he saw it, the Japanese had lost control of the air, but the situation was not yet hopeless, and his reinforcements were on their way. Hashimoto's message that *Yorktown* was burning encouraged Yamamoto to cling to the original plan, and so at 1915 hours – an hour and 20 minutes after *Hiryu*'s loss – he sent a message to his command, 'The enemy fleet which has practically been destroyed is retiring. Combined Fleet units in the vicinity are preparing to pursue the remnants and at the same time occupy Midway.' This directive was neither true nor practical with the forces Yamamoto could muster at the moment. The Japanese Commander in Chief must have known this when he dictated the signal, and it must therefore be concluded that it was intended only to boost flagging morale.

As the US fleet withdrew toward the east, hopes of night engagement were failing. Yamamoto persisted. Not only did he want to continue the fight, he also wanted to pick up his burning carriers which yet might be saved. He also had hopes of capturing *Yorktown* – for he knew he could easily deal with the destroyers standing by her – and towing her back to the Inland Sea.

Aboard the *Nagara* there was not the same resolute determination to see the operation through to the bitter end as there was on the *Yamato*. Nagumo's officers had witnessed the destruction of all their carriers and their morale was low. Some were abjectly depressed, but one or two were possessed by a sort of do-or-die hysteria, which centered round a wild plan to throw the destroyers guarding the strike carriers into Yamamoto's night engagement.

Then came a blinker message from *Chikuma*, 'Scout plane sighted five enemy carriers, six cruisers and 15 destroyers 30 miles east of the burning carriers.' The pilot had seen the *Yorktown* adrift, and had then spotted the *Enterprise* and *Hornet*. To evade American fighters he had then been forced to take cover in the clouds and when he came out of them he found the two American carriers a second time. Somehow he must have lost his bearings; everyone by that time was weary and confused. Whatever the reason, he reported finding five carriers. Nagumo, whose heart was no longer in the battle, was now thoroughly confused. He was certain that his pilots had knocked out two carriers. Yet there was a scout reporting five more – all of them operational.

Meanwhile in Tokyo the Naval General Staff were tensely following the progress of the battle. When the report came in that *Hiryu* had suffered the same fate as *Akagi, Kaga* and *Soryu*, they realized the operation was doomed. But did Yamamoto realize it? Like Yamamoto, Admiral Nagano, the Chief of Naval Staff, was not too deeply concerned about Japan's four finest carriers. Even after this disaster, the Imperial Navy still had more warships of every category in the Pacific than the United States. What worried him more was what Admiral Yamamoto, smarting under Nagumo's terrible defeat, might do next. American strength on Midway was not destroyed. Moreover they still had at least one undamaged carrier, if not two. If Yamamoto continued to press home his attack on Midway he might lose the whole Japanese fleet. Yet no orders, no advice, were given by Tokyo. Nagano had decided that it was Admiral Yamamoto's battle and he must fight it as he wished without interference. Nagano simply waited, picking up signals and reading them in silence. It was defeat; he knew it; everyone knew it; no one was willing to be the first to admit it or to call off the operation. That was Yamamoto's decision – and his alone.

At 2130 hours there was a panic-stricken signal from Nagumo, based on the false report of *Chikuma*'s scout plane. 'The total strength of the enemy,' he said, 'is five carriers, six cruisers and 15 destroyers. We are retiring to the northwest escorting *Hiryu* at 15 knots.' Admiral Ugaki, Yamamoto's Chief of Staff, put everyone's thoughts into words when he threw down the second signal and muttered savagely, 'The Nagumo force has no stomach for a night engagement.' Yamamoto silently agreed with him and it was at this point that he decided to relieve Nagumo and put Admiral Kondo in charge of the whole attack force. Kondo, who had shown both good judgment and initiative in the crisis, was already on his way to join the battered remnants of Nagumo's fleet and to attempt to provoke a night battle. With him was a formidable fleet of four fast battleships, nine cruisers and 19 destroyers, all geared for a night surface action.

'Commander in Chief Second Fleet Kondo will take command of Nagumo forces, excepting *Hiryu, Akagi* and the ships escorting them,' Yamamoto ordered. This left Nagumo in command of the two blazing half sunken hulks of his remaining carriers, but as far as the battle was concerned, he was relieved from duty.

At midnight the radio transmitter on the flagship *Yamato* was still busily signalling orders to Kakuda to rendezvous as soon as possible with remnants of Nagumo's fleet. It was also ordering Kondo to prepare for a decisive surface action. Yet even as the signal went out it was becoming increasingly evident that there was little hope of contacting the American fleet before dawn.

In spite of their victory against the Japanese carriers it was a nervous night for both American admirals as they tried to assess the results of the day's battle. Fletcher's task force, maimed by the loss of *Yorktown*, sheltered behind *Hornet* and *Enterprise*. Although the Japanese carriers had gone, Spruance still feared the appearance of Yamamoto's big battleships. He was fully aware that Yamamoto might yet restore the balance by bringing them in for a surface engagement. Now that he was in tactical command of the Pacific fleet, he was determined not to fall into a trap, and so he decided to sail east during the night. Later he said, 'I did not feel justified in risking a night encounter with possibly superior enemy forces. Nor did I wish to be too far from Midway next morning. I wanted to be in a position from which to either follow up the retreating enemy or break up a landing attack on Midway.'

Admiral Spruance did not believe it was likely that the Japanese would try to land on Midway after losing their four carriers, but it was a possibility which could not be disregarded, and Midway had to be protected. Having pulled back to a position which would allow him sea room to maneuver if Yamamoto decided to commit his battleships, he kept his task force in the same approximate area about 250 miles northwest of the atoll.

On Midway itself Tomonaga's mission and a series of confusing messages and radio intercepts had made it a trying and anxious day. Tomonaga's attack was seen at first as the foretaste of disaster, and seven of the atoll's Flying Fortresses were ordered back to Oahu. There, it was presumed, they would be needed in the battle for Hawaii, which would surely follow the fall of Midway. Midway's air strength was now down to two fighters, 12 dive bombers, 18 Catalinas and four serviceable Fortresses.

Above: B-17 defensive armament had to be increased after combat experience. *Left:* A Dauntless with its fuel exhausted ditches alongside a cruiser.

Below: Despite its high performance, the Zero failed to protect the Japanese carriers at Midway.

In the afternoon Midway learned of the crippling of the four Japanese carriers and the four Fortresses were sent on a strike against Nagumo's battered fleet. Their pilots returned claiming that their bombs had struck some of the Japanese ships. They also returned with some alarming news: they had been attacked by Zeros on their mission. If four carriers had indeed been sunk, the fact that Zeros were still flying suggested that there was a fifth somewhere around. The possibility that the Japanese fighters were from the doomed *Hiryu*, using up their last drop of fuel before ditching, was never considered.

At dusk 11 American Marine dive bombers took off to find the fifth carrier, but heavy squalls and a moonless sky defeated their search. Getting back to base was also a problem. Only the blue blur from their exhausts kept them together and only the fires on Midway started by Tomonaga's raid guided them home.

Both the Midway Command and Spruance were alarmed by the possibility of a fifth carrier in the vicinity, and tension which had begun to relax rapidly built up again. Unconfirmed alarmist reports at once

Above: Midway saw the operational debut of the Grumman TBF Avenger.

began to circulate. At 2100 hours one of the patrol boats reported a landing on the small island of Kure, 60 miles to the west. This suggested that the invasion was imminent. Back at Pearl Harbor, the Pacific Fleet submarine commander, Rear Admiral Robert English also believed this and pulled his boats back to a five-mile radius round Midway. At midnight two Catalinas took off armed with torpedoes in readiness to attack the approaching ships while the garrison prepared itself. Eighty-five 500-pound bombs were loaded by hand and 45,000 gallons of gasoline were hand pumped into the planes.

The tension reached its climax at around 0100 hours, when Tanabe's submarine – acting in accordance with the orders he had received from Yamamoto's alert at 2030 hours – surfaced in the lagoon, and a shell winged its way toward Midway. Five more followed in quick succession before two searchlights pinpointed the submarine. Shore batteries began firing back and their aim was effective. Shells bracketed *I-168* almost at once and the disappointed Tanabe had no choice but to beat a hasty retreat. He headed south, away from the island, shaking off surface pursuers. Angry and disappointed, Tanabe assumed that *I-168* has finished its job for this battle. (He had not yet been told to find and sink the crippled *Yorktown*.)

On Midway the garrison was waiting for the attack which they believed to be imminent. Two hundred miles away Spruance also thought that the shelling was the prelude to invasion, and his view was confirmed when the US submarine *Tambor* reported 'many unidentified ships' only 90 miles from Midway. There were the heavy cruisers *Mogami* and *Mikuma* and their escorts – part of the vanguard of the occupation force, now on their way under Yamamoto's orders to relieve the *I-168* and shell the atoll. Spruance thought this might be a landing force and he gave orders for his fleet to steam toward Midway at 25 knots.

Spruance began sailing toward the atoll at full speed, Yamamoto was sitting in his operations room on his flagship reassessing the situation. He now knew that the Americans had at least two carriers still operational and that by sailing east they had managed to dodge a night action. Yamamoto had also received more depressing news. His fleet was sailing 19 degrees off course. This meant all hope of a night battle was lost. *Yorktown*, too, was obviously sinking, so he gave up the idea of capturing her. If he continued on his present course his own ships would almost certainly be attacked by planes at dawn.

A madcap attempt to snatch victory from disaster was now proposed by the Chief Operations Officer, Rear Admiral Kuroshima. The *Yamato*, he suggested, should lead the battleship flotilla to Midway in broad daylight and shell the shore installations. The invasion would then go on. Rear Admiral Ugaki, the officer who had 'bent' the Midway war games in favor of the assault, was appalled. 'Engaging shore installations with only surface craft is stupid,' he said. 'A large number of American planes are still based on Midway. Some of the enemy carriers are still intact. Our battleships will be destroyed by enemy air and submarine attacks before we could even get close enough to use our big guns.'

Ugaki had, perhaps, indulged in fantasies during the war games, but basically he was a sane and level-headed man, prepared to take a realistic point of view. The Imperial Navy, he argued, must accept that it has been defeated at Midway. This did not mean that Japan had lost the war. Nor was the sinking of the four carriers so much of a calamity; including those nearly completed, the Navy still had eight carriers. However if Yamamoto acted rashly now a minor setback could turn into a catastrophic defeat. 'In battle,' he added, 'as in chess, it is a fool who lets himself be led into a reckless move through desperation.'

Ugaki's intervention scotched Kuroshima's scheme. Not all Yamamoto's staff officers were satisfied. To some, the need to 'save face' was paramount and they were prepared to gamble everything for a chance to do so. Eventually one individual voiced his worries. 'How can we apologize to His Majesty for this defeat?' he asked.

Yamamoto had not spoken during the discussion, but his sternly set features broke as he replied abruptly, 'Leave that to me, I am the only one who must apologize to His Majesty.' From this brief comment it is evident that Yamamoto – the shrewd, aggressive cardplayer – had all but decided to abandon the Midway operation.

7. RETREAT

It was after midnight on 5 June when Yamamoto figuratively folded his hands and cancelled Operation Midway. Admiral Kondo's fleet, still racing toward a night attack on the US carriers and the bombardment of the atoll, was ordered to withdraw and join him at a rendezvous where all the ships would refuel for the long voyage home. Some two and a half hours later (at 0255 hours on 6 June) he ordered Ichiki's troopships to make their way back to Japan. The operation was definitely over, all that remained now was the humiliating and hazardous task of rounding up the scattered elements of the Combined Fleet and getting them out of the battle area without being discovered by US scout planes or submarines.

When the four heavy cruisers assigned by Kondo to the task of shelling Midway received a message to say the operation was cancelled, they turned about. This was the force of unidentified ships picked up earlier by the US submarine *Tambor*, and when the Japanese ships changed course, the *Tambor* followed. In the race eastward toward Midway, the Japanese cruisers had been unable to keep pace with the destroyers so that when the order cancelling their mission was received they were unprotected. Suddenly a lookout on Vice-Admiral Takeo

Below: Mikuma sank at Midway.

Right: The Japanese destroyer *Yukikaze* escorted the Transport Group of the Midway Occupation Force. Her main armament comprised 5-inch guns and torpedo tubes firing the famous 'long lance.'
Below: A US Navy gun crew member updates his scoreboard.

Left: The Dauntless dive bomber emerged from the Battle of Midway with an enviable reputation as a warplane. It was to remain in front-line service until 1944.
Right: The US Marine Corps defenders of Midway produced this suitably bellicose view of the battle.
Below: Four heavy cruisers of the *Takao* Class, *Takao, Maya, Atago* and *Chokai*, served in the Midway operation. Their main armament was 10 8-inch guns.

Above: Vought SB2U Vindicators of the 2nd Marine Air Wing were based on Midway Island.

Left: Mikuma was sunk by Dauntlesses from USS *Enterprise* on 6 June.

Kurita's flagship, *Kumano*, spotted the *Tambor* which had just surfaced for better observation. Panic ensued as the *Kumaro* flashed orders for an immediate 45 degree turn to port. The signal, 'Red! Red!' was blinked to the *Suzuya* next astern and the *Kumaro* swung left. *Suzuya*, in turn, relayed the signal and also turned left, as did the third ship *Mikuma*. It was two hours before sunrise, and it was dark and foggy. Tension had relaxed when the cruisers turned away from Midway and this may account for the lack of vigilance. Whatever the cause, *Mogami*, the last ship in line, failed to get the emergency turn signal in time and collided with *Mikuma*. Although the cruisers had reduced their speed since they had turned about, they were still making about 28 knots and consequently the *Mogami*'s bow was damaged and one of *Mikuma*'s oil tanks was holed.

When he was told of the accident, Admiral Kurita turned back to see what help he could give. When *Mogami*'s skipper, Captain Akira Soyi, reported that he could make 12 knots, Kurita decided to push on to the rendezvous, leaving the *Mikuma* and two destroyers, the *Arashio* and the *Asashio*, as escort for the *Mogami*. Dawn was breaking by this time and men in the four ships were gazing apprehensively at the sky in anticipation of an attack by American aircraft. They did not have long to wait.

Morale in Yamamoto's fleet was now at a low ebb. During the night some of Nagumo's destroyers had ferried casualties from the four carriers to Yamamoto's battleships where better medical facilities were available. The sea was rough, making it impossible for the destroyers to get alongside the battleships, so the transferring the wounded was a slow process. All through the pitch-dark night the casualties were pulled aboard by ropes attached to bamboo stretchers. By dawn the sick bays and crew quarters of the four battleships were jammed with wounded, most of them burn victims. Witnessing this scene, every sailor in the battleships became aware that the Imperial Navy had just suffered a great and crushing defeat. Few could console themselves for the loss of the four great carriers by the fact that their main battleship strength remained intact. After what had happened to them, they knew better than anyone that big guns were as useless as bows and arrows in the Pacific.

Throughout the hours of darkness Yamamoto's battleships headed east to link up with Nagumo and Kondo withdrawing west. The sun rose at 0440 hours and the sky was clear and cloudless. Visibility was about 40 miles and as the morning progressed it seemed that this was the best weather they had had since the Japanese had left home waters. It was ideal weather for aircraft, and sentries stared warily at the open sky, watching for signs of US planes.

Kondo's main force linked up with Yamamoto at about 0700 hours, when both fleets were then 320 miles northwest of Midway. Five hours later Nagumo's battered ships appeared on the horizon. Standing on the bridge under the hot Pacific sun, Yamamoto silently watched them approach. The returning ships bore little resemblance to the proud fleet that had sailed so confidently out of the Inland Sea only 10 days before. The carriers were gone and many of the destroyers were missing; some of them were still picking up survivors of the battle clinging to oil-slippery wreckage.

By dawn on 6 June Spruance had realized that the Japanese were pulling back. Between then and 0800 hours Midway planes reported that all Japanese vessels within their range were withdrawing, and he was now convinced that Yamamoto was retreating. The submarine *Tambor*, which was still doggedly trailing the twin cruisers, now identified them as *Mogami* and *Mikuma*, steaming fast 175 miles away. There were several other ships over 250 miles away, but there was no sign of Nagumo's carriers. The only evidence that they had ever existed was the shape of the oil patches on the water.

Now that the Japanese were leaving the battle area Spruance sent every available plane to harry and destroy them. The 12 Marine bombers left on Midway – six Vindicators led by Captain Richard Fleming and six Dauntlesses led by Captain Marshall Tyler – took off to follow *Mikuma*'s clearly visible oil trail. At 0805 hours

Mikuma's captain reported 'waves of dive bombers,' as the Dauntlesses dived on her sister ship the *Mogami*. Then the Vindicators swooped down on *Mikuma*. Fleming's engine was hit by a shell but he held his course and dropped his bomb. Pilots coming behind him watched his plane smash into *Mikuma*'s after turret.

Meanwhile Spruance's carriers were steaming up to close the gap, and it was not long before planes from the *Enterprise* discovered the *Mogami* and the *Mikuma*, limping along 150 miles away. Three successive attacks were made and repeated hits were scored on the two damaged cruisers. Although her captain tried hard to head for the nearest Japanese base at Wake Island, the *Mikuma* was sinking fast.

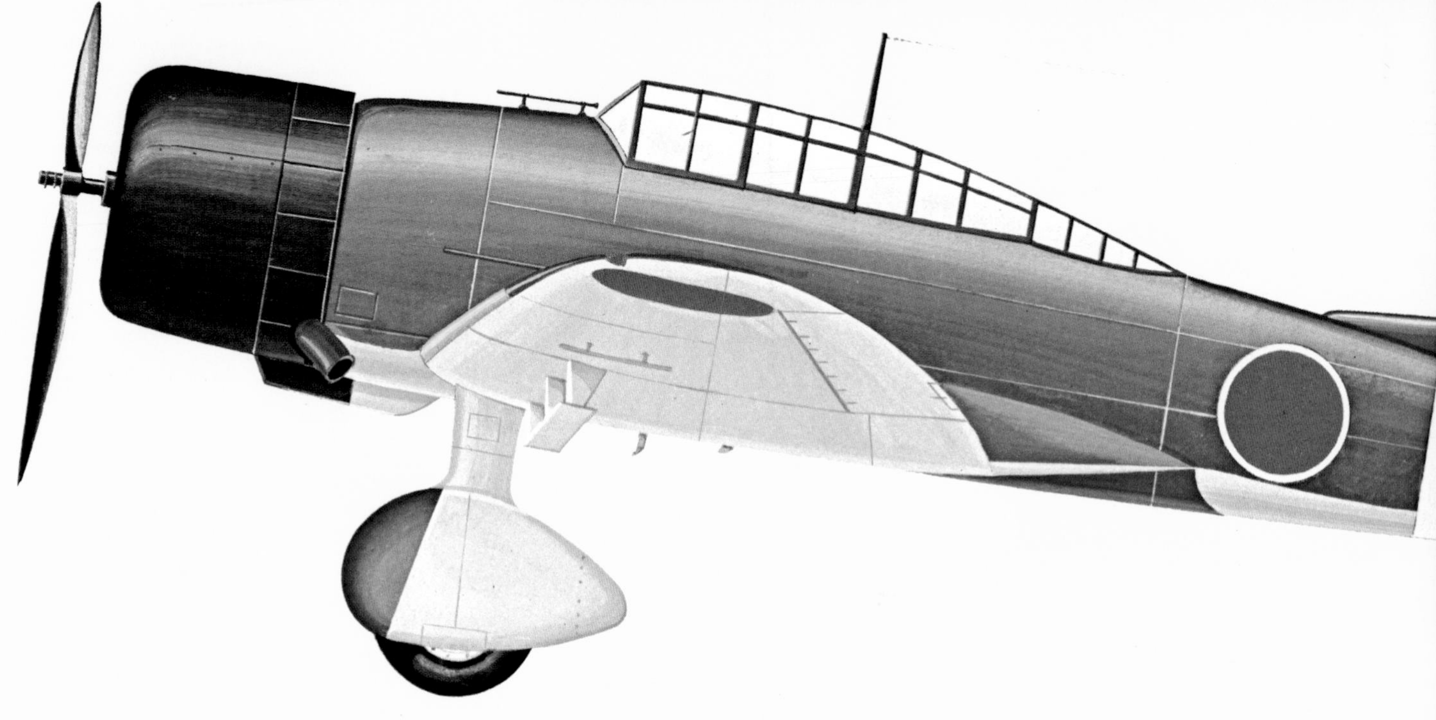

Above: The Aichi D3A 'Val' dive bombers suffered heavily at Midway and thereafter gradually disappeared from front-line units.
Top: The Grumman F4F-4 Wildcat was the standard fighter in the US Navy in 1942–43 and was credited with over 900 victories in air combat.

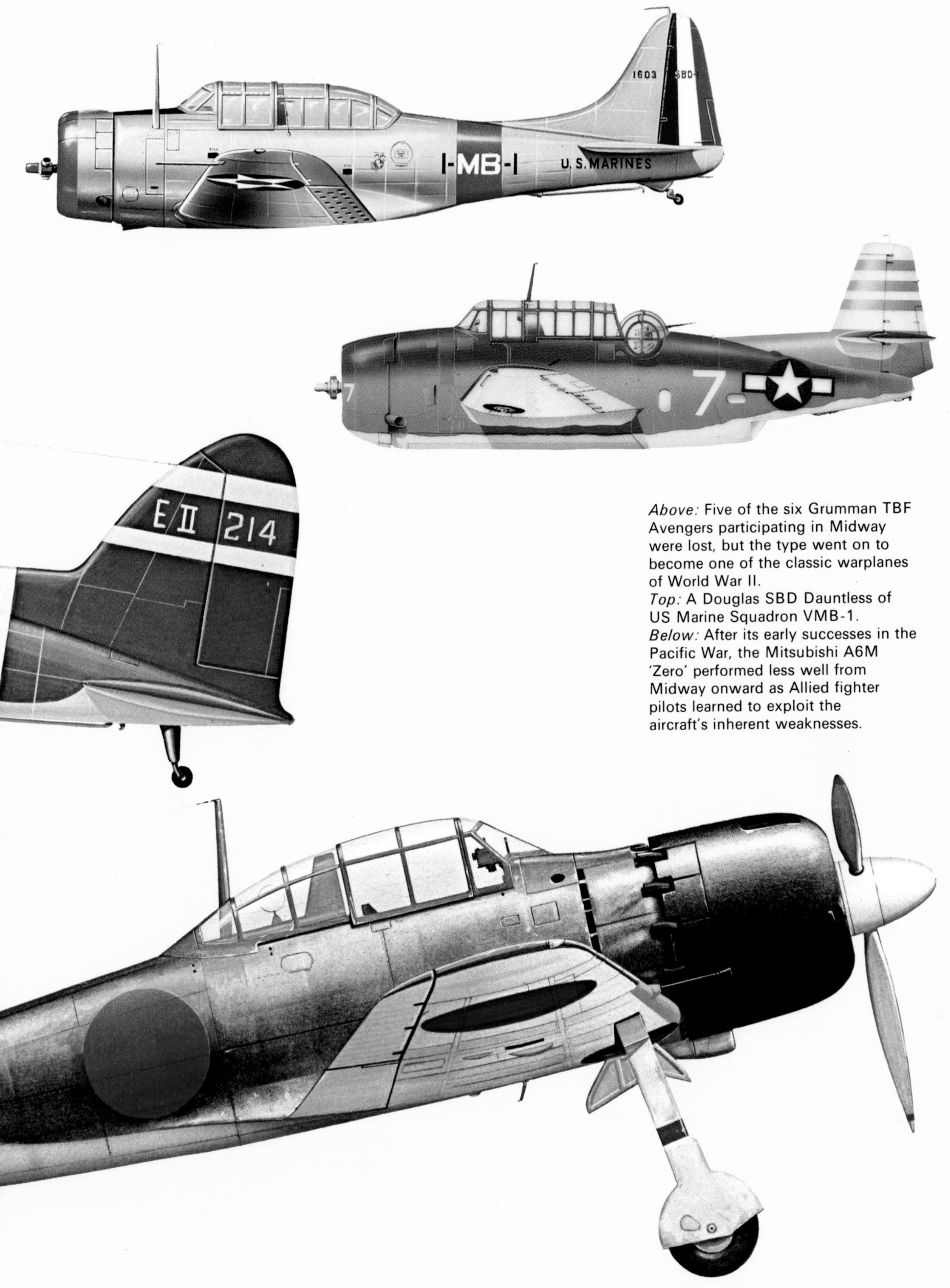

Above: Five of the six Grumman TBF Avengers participating in Midway were lost, but the type went on to become one of the classic warplanes of World War II.
Top: A Douglas SBD Dauntless of US Marine Squadron VMB-1.
Below: After its early successes in the Pacific War, the Mitsubishi A6M 'Zero' performed less well from Midway onward as Allied fighter pilots learned to exploit the aircraft's inherent weaknesses.

At 1200 hours, as the third attack force flew away, she suddenly turned over and went down – taking 1000 men with her. Apart from carriers, the *Mikuma* was the largest Japanese surface warship to be sunk since the beginning of the war. She had always fought with her sister ship *Mogami*, and she perished in *Mogami*'s defense when she deliberately drew down bombers upon herself.

The *Mogami*, also fighting fiercely to protect herself and her sister ship, received heavy bomb damage and lost her bow, but although listing heavily she was still able to steam along at 20 knots. She was the last Japanese warship to get clear of the American planes in the Midway battle. Escorted by destroyers she managed to creep back to Truk, but she was out of the war for more than a year.

Next on Spruance's list was the burning Japanese carrier *Hiryu* which he thought was still afloat. In fact she had sunk hours before. In the early afternoon 12 B-17s took off from Midway to locate her. All they found was the destroyer *Tanikaze* which Nagumo had sent to rescue survivors from *Hiryu* if she were still afloat. *Tanikaze* was steaming back to report *Hiryu*'s fate when the Fortresses swooped on her. They made two attacks, dropping 80 bombs, but the fast-moving destroyer was too quick for them and they achieved only a few near-misses.

The two American carriers *Hornet* and *Enterprise* were now about 130 miles from Midway and the gap between them and the fleeing Japanese was widening. So that they could carry maximum fuel, Spruance ordered the bombers to take off armed only with a single 500-pound bomb each. In his anxiety to achieve the biggest kill possible, he held the attack back until 1500 hours while his two carriers steamed at full speed to close the range. This late takeoff meant that his planes could not return before dark and the carriers would have to light up their flight decks to recover them. Spruance, who still believed he was pursuing the fourth Japanese carrier, *Hiryu*, accepted the risk. Again his planes found only the much-harried *Tanikaze* and they attacked her with no more success than the B-17s. Darkness descended as

they flew back and *Enterprise* and *Hornet* switched on deck and searchlights to guide them in. This was a risk because the lights made them a sitting target for any Japanese submarine lurking in the area. Spruance was more concerned about his pilots, as most of them had never before landed on a carrier at night. They all came in safely on the illuminated deck, except one who landed in the sea and was rescued later.

Now that it was dark and the American carriers were approaching the bad weather area, Spruance decided to call it a day. His fuel was running low and his pilots were exhausted from two days of almost continuous operations. He had been informed that there were no Japanese warships for more than 250 miles ahead, but he was not going to risk running into any of Yamamoto's big battleships in the dark where they would pound him to pieces. In addition he was approaching the 700-mile flying range of Wake Island, where he believed the Japanese had flown a large number of planes in readiness for a landing on Midway after its capture. So Spruance changed course west to rendezvous with a tanker Admiral Nimitz had sent out for his ships.

Above: Shokaku missed the Midway battle but was sunk in the Philippine Sea in June 1944.

Left: Dauntlesses of Scouting Squadron 64 over the Solomons in April 1943.

It was a wise decision for Yamamoto was again spoiling for a fight. His ships were over 600 miles from Midway on the day they were to have invaded it, and he was still looking for an opportunity to convert defeat into victory. The attacks on *Tanikaze, Mogami* and *Mikuma* had given him a plain indication that the American carriers were not far away, and he correctly judged that if he turned south he would meet them. At 1200 hours on 6 June he ordered seven cruisers and eight destroyers to make their way toward the crippled *Mogami*. Surrounded by his other battleships, he ordered the *Yamato* to head in the same direction.

At this juncture Yamamoto believed that he was opposed by one carrier, two other ships which had been converted to carriers, and several cruisers and destroyers. If this fleet were lured on westward by the stricken *Mogami* an opportunity might yet occur for the Japanese to strike a decisive blow. With any luck, Kondo's cruisers would be able to engage the Americans during the night, or Yamamoto's battleships take them the following morning. Control of the air was vital if the battle was to turn in Yamamoto's favor, but as the Japanese could muster a total of about 100 planes – including those of the carriers *Hosho* and *Zuiho* and the seaplanes of the battleships, cruisers and tenders – this was just feasible. To make it certain, however, it was desirable to lure the American fleet to within range of the 50 medium bombers based on Wake Island. (These planes could already reach to within a few miles of where the *Mikuma* had sunk.)

Had Spruance not changed course that evening and called off the chase the Americans would have fallen into Yamamoto's trap. It was not to be. A combination of factors – the need to refuel and refit his carriers, the tiredness of his crews, bad weather and above all a canny suspicion that caution was needed caused Spruance to turn back. Yamamoto pursued his grandiose scheme until the morning of 7 June. Then, with no enemy in sight and his ships in need of fuel, the plan was finally abandoned and he turned for home.

Further attempts were made by the Americans to hit the retreating Japanese fleet by the Midway-bound Fortresses. No contacts were made and when the pilots of the Fortresses returned to Midway the greatest sea battle since Trafalgar was over. It had lasted 48 hours and had been won in the five minutes when American dive bombers caught Nagumo's carriers with their flight decks lined with planes.

APPENDIX

US and Japanese Losses in the Battle of Midway

US losses

Japanese claims about the losses and damage inflicted at the Battle of Midway were grossly exaggerated. Actual losses, quoted in American sources, are given. The unamended Japanese figures are also included for comparison.

Actual losses

Ships
Sunk: carrier *Yorktown*,
destroyer *Hammann*

Aircraft

Shot down or destroyed in Midway air strike	45
US carriers	15
Shot down by combat air patrol	90
Shot down by antiaircraft fire of Japanese ships	29
Total	179

Damage to ground installations
Eastern Island
1 hangar damaged by fire, 3 buildings damaged by fire, airstrip damaged

Sand Island
1 seaplane hangar damaged by fire, seaplane platform destroyed, 2 fuel storage tanks damaged by fire, 2 antiaircraft emplacements destroyed

Japanese claims

Ships
Sunk: 2 *Enterprise* Class carriers
1 *San Francisco* Class heavy cruiser
1 destroyer

Aircraft

US carrier-borne aircraft lost		109
US shore-based aircraft lost		
Marine	28	
Navy	6	
Army	4	
Total shore based		38
Total		147

Damage to ground installations
Eastern Island
Marine command post and mess hall destroyed, powerhouse damaged, airstrip damaged but still usable
Sand Island
Seaplane hangar destroyed, fuel storage tanks destroyed, aviation fueling system damaged, hospital and storehouses set on fire

Below: USS *Yorktown* during the first attack at the Battle of Midway.

Japanese Losses
Ships
Sunk: 4 carriers (*Akagi, Kaga, Hiryu, Soryu*), 1 heavy cruiser (*Mikuma*)
Severely damaged: 1 heavy cruiser (*Mogami*)
Moderately damaged: 2 destroyers (*Arashio, Asashio*)
Slightly damaged: 1 battleship (*Haruna*), 1 destroyer (*Tanikaze*) 1 tanker (oiler) (*Akebono Maru*)
Aircraft

Lost in Midway air strike	6	
Fighters of combat air patrol failed to return	12	
Lost in attacks on US carriers	24	
Lost with carriers when they sank	280	(approximate)
Seaplanes lost	10	(approximate)
Total	332*	

*US sources quote a figure of approximately 250 planes lost, and this figure of 332, taken from Japanese sources, exceeds the actual operational complement of Nagumo's four carriers (262 planes). The difference partially accounted for by the fact that the Japanese losses include fighter aircraft of the Midway Expeditionary Forces which was being ferried to Midway in these carriers.

Summary of Opposing Forces in the Battle of Midway

The Composition of the Japanese Task Force for 'Operation MI' against Midway
The task force proper was composed of five major tactical groups, some of them subdivided into two or more subgroups. There was also a land-based air force group which is shown as group 6.
Overall command was vested in Admiral Yamamoto aboard the *Yamato*; Rear Admiral Matome Ugaki, his Chief of Staff, travelled with him. All groups moved to the operational area independently.

1. The Advance Expeditionary Force

Vice-Admiral Teruhisa Konatsu in the light cruiser *Katori* (flagship of the sixth Fleet) at Kwajalein

Submarine Squadron 3
Rear Admiral Chimaki Kono, submarines *I-168, I-171, I-175* deployed between latitude 20°N, longitude 166°20′W, and latitude 23°30′N, and longitude 166°20′W.

Submarine Squadron 5
Rear Admiral Tadashige Daigo, submarines *I-156, I-157, I-158, I-159, I-162, I-164, I-165, I-166*, deployed between latitude 28°20′N, longitude 162°20′W, and latitude 26°N, longitude 165°W.

Submarine Squadron 13
Captain Takeharu Miyazaki, submarines *I-121, I-122, I-123* for transporting fuel and oil to French Frigate Shoals and other islands en route to Pearl Harbor.

2. The First Carrier Striking Force: Vice-Admiral Chuichi Nagumo
Carrier Division 1
Admiral Nagumo carriers *Akagi* (flagship), *Kaga*; 42 fighters, 42 dive bombers, 51 torpedo bombers

Carrier Division 2
Rear Admiral Tamon Yamaguchi, carriers *Hiryu* (flagship), *Soryu*; 42 fighters, 42 dive bombers, 42 torpedo bombers

Support Group
Rear Admiral Hiroaki Abe, battleships *Haruna, Kirishima*; heavy cruisers *Tone* (flagship), *Chikuma*

Screening Group
Rear Admiral Susumu Kimura, light cruiser *Nagara* (flagship); destroyers, *Kazagumo, Yugumo, Makigumo, Akigumo, Isokaze, Urakaze, Hamakaze, Tanikaze, Arashi, Nowaki, Hagikaze, Maikaze*; supply ships *Kyokuto Maru, Shinkoku Maru, Toho Maru, Nippon Maru, Kokuyo Maru*

3. Midway Occupation Force: Vice-Admiral Nobutake Kondo

Covering Group
Admiral Kondo, battleships *Kongo, Hiei*; heavy cruisers *Atago* (flagship) *Chokai, Myoku, Haguro*; light cruiser *Yara*; light carrier *Zuiho* (12 fighters, 12 torpedo bombers); destroyers *Murasame, Harusame, Yudachi, Samidare, Asagumo, Miegumo, Natsugumo, Miyazuki*; supply ships *Genyo Maru, Kenyo Maru, Sata, Tsurumi*; repair ship *Akami*

Support Group
Rear Admiral Takeo Kurita, heavy cruisers *Kumano* (flagship), *Suzuya, Mikuma, Mogami*; destroyers *Asashio, Arashio*; supply ship *Nichiei Maru*

Transport Group
Rear Admiral Raizo Tanaka, light cruiser *Jintsu* (flagship); 12 transports and freighters carrying 'Kure' and 'Yokosuka,' 5th Special Naval Landing Forces and Army Ichiki Detachment; two construction battalions 'Survey Group,' weather group, etc (about 5000 officers and men); oiler *Akebono Maru*; patrol boats 1, 2, 3, 4, carrying assault detachments; SNLF; destroyers *Kuroshio, Oyashio, Hatsukaze, Yukikaze, Amatsukaze, Tokitsukaze, Kasumi, Arare, Kagero, Shiranuhi*

Seaplane Tender Group
Rear Admiral Ruitero Fujita, seaplane carriers *Chitose* (16 seaplanes [floats], 4 scout planes), *Kamikawa Maru* (8 seaplanes, 2 scout planes), these 30 planes were to be established at a base on Kure Island; destroyer *Hayashio*, patrol boat No 35

4. The Main Body (First Fleet)
Admiral Yamamoto, battleships *Yamato* (Combined Fleet flagship); *Nagato, Mutsu*; light carrier *Hosho* (8 Type-96 bombers); light cruiser *Sendai*; destroyers *Fubuki, Shirayuki, Hatsuyuki, Murakumo, Isonami, Uranami, Shikinami, Ayanami, Amagiri, Asagiri, Yugiri, Shirakumo*; seaplane carriers *Chiyoda, Nigshin* (carrying 2 motor torpedo boats and 6 midget submarines

Aleutian Support Force Department
Vice-Admiral Shiro Takasu, battleships *Hyugu* (flagship), *Ise, Fuso, Yamashiro*; light cruisers *Oi, Kikama*; supply ships *Toli Maru, Naruto, San Clemte Maru, Toa Maru*

5. The Northern (Aleutians) Force: Vice-Admiral Moshiro Hosogaya
Main Body of Northern Force
Heavy cruiser *Nachi* (flagship), 2 destroyers

Second Carrier Striking Force
Rear Admiral Kakuji Kakuta, light carrier *Ryujo* (flagship, 16 fighters, 21 torpedo bombers); carrier *Junyo* (24 fighters, 21 dive bombers); heavy cruisers *Maya, Takao*; 3 destroyers.

Attu Invasion Force
Rear Admiral Sentaro Omori, light cruiser *Abukuma* (flagship); 4 destroyers; 1 minelayer; 1 transport carrying Army Landing Force (1200 troops)

6. Land-based Air Force: Vice-Admiral Nishizo Tsukahara
Midway Expeditionary Force
Captain Chisato Morita, 36 fighters (transported by carriers); 10 land bombers (at Wake); 6 flying boats (at Jaluit)

24th Air Flotilla
Rear Admiral Minoru Maeda

Chitose Air Group
Captain Fujiro Ohashi, 26 fighters; 36 torpedo bombers (at Kwajalein and Wake)

1st Air Group
Captain Samaji Inouye, 36 fighters; 36 torpedo bombers (at Aur and Wotje)

14th Air Group
18 flying boats (at Jaluit and Wotje)

Commander in Chief, Admiral Chester W Nimitz

Deployment and Composition of the United States Pacific Fleet during the Coral Sea and Midway battles

1. **Carrier Striking Force:** Rear Admiral Frank J Fletcher

Task Force 17: Admiral Fletcher
carrier *Yorktown* (25 fighters, 19 scout planes, 18 bombers, 13 torpedo bombers); cruisers *Astoria, Portland*; destroyers *Hammann, Hughes, Morris, Anderson, Russell, Gwin*

Task Force 16: Rear Admiral Raymond A Spruance
carriers *Enterprise* (27 fighters, 19 scout planes, 19 bombers, 14 torpedo bombers), *Hornet* (27 fighters, 18 scout planes, 19 bombers, 15 torpedo bombers); cruisers *New Orleans, Minneapolis, Vincennes, Northampton, Pensacola, Atlanta*; destroyers *Phelps, Worden, Monaghan, Aylwin, Balch, Coryngham, Benham, Ellet, Maury*: supply ships (oilers) *Cimarron, Platte, Dewey, Monssen*

2. Submarines: under operational control of Rear Admiral Robert H English at Pearl Harbor

Midway Patrol Group
Cachalot, Flying Fish, Tambour, Trout, Grayling, Nautilus, Grouper, Dolphin, Gato, Cuttlefish, Gudgeon, Grenadier

'Roving Short-Stop' Group
Narwhal, Plunger, Trigger

North of Oahu Patrol
Tarpon, Pike, Finback, Growler.

3. Land-based aircraft, Midway 4 June 1942 – Captain Cyril T Simard
32 Catalina seaplanes and 6 torpedo bombers from 1 and 2 US Northern Patrol
27 fighters and 27 dive bombers for the Marine Aircraft Group 22 (2nd Marine Air Wing)
4 B-26 and 19 B-17 bombers of Seventh Army Air Force

4. Local Defenses Midway – Captain Simard
6th Marine Defense Battalion, 8PT (Motor Torpedo) Boats and 4 small patrol craft
The following were also deployed among the islands in the Hawaiian Group:
tenders *Thornton, Ballard*, French Frigate Shoals, destroyer *Clark*, French Frigate Shoals, oiler *Kaloli*, Pearl and Hermes Reef, Cvt yacht *Crystal*, Pearl and Hermes Reef, sweeper *Vireo*, Pearl and Hermes Reef. 4 Patrol Vessels.
There was also a Midway Relief Fuelling Unit (which left Pearl Harbor on 3 June and arrived at Midway three days later) comprising the following:
oiler *Guadaloupe*; destroyers *Blue* and *Ralph Talbot.*

E7

D-DAY

D-DAY

BRIGADIER PETER YOUNG

Page 200: Sherman tanks pass through the village of Reviers in Normandy shortly after the landings in June 1944.
Page 201: Troops practice disembarking during a training exercise for D-Day 'somewhere in England'.
Pages 202/203: One of the German coastal batteries makes a practice shoot.
These pages: A scene on Omaha Beach following the first landings.

US
PROCESSED
DEGASSED

1. PREPARING FOR INVASION

On 6 June 1944, in the greatest combined operation of all time, the Allies assaulted the strongly fortified coast of France, broke through the defenses and secured a lodgment. This, with the battle for Normandy that followed, must rank among the decisive battles of the world.

The assault was made at a time when the Germans were already fighting for their lives on the Eastern Front and when the Allies had already won mastery of both air and sea. Even so the result was far from being a foregone conclusion. The Allied troops who took part, though fairly well trained, were not for the most part very experienced. If the Allied leaders had proved their skill in former campaigns, the same must also be said of the German leaders, von Rundstedt and Rommel. However, the Allies had built up a remarkable partnership. Cooperation between the Americans and the British was close and efficient, and if this account emphasizes the part played by the two main Allies, it must be remembered that the Canadians, French, Poles, Belgians, Dutch, Czechs and the Yugoslavs all played a valiant part in the ultimate victory.

The Allies owed their success in large measure to the skills they had developed in the techniques of amphibious warfare. The British Combined Operations Headquarters had set new standards in interservice cooperation, masterminded by Lord Louis Mountbatten.

Allied industrial capacity ensured that their forces went into battle well armed and well equipped. Wars are won by fighting men; morale is even more important than weaponry. The campaigns in Sicily and Italy in 1943, allowed the Germans to demonstrate the skill and determination which had won them their great victories of the 1939–41 period. How would the young Allied warrior measure up to the German soldier of 1944? That was the question.

Top left: Field Marshal Erwin Rommel during a tour of inspection of the Atlantic Wall defenses in spring 1944.
Top right: Rommel's immediate superior in 1944 was Field Marshal von Rundstedt.
Left: A German machine-gun section covers a potential landing beach on the invasion coast.

The Allies had made no secret of their intention to invade Europe, and as early as 1942 there had been a great deal of ill-informed pressure for a 'Second Front Now!' Sympathy for the Soviets and sheer ignorance of the Allies' unpreparedness contributed to this clamor. It has been argued that the invasion should have been launched in the summer of 1943, but few if any of those who held responsible positions on the Allied side were of that opinion at the time. When the blow eventually fell, the Germans had been preparing their defenses for the better part of four years.

The task of repelling the invasion fell to Field Marshal Karl Rudolf Gerd von Rundstedt, who in March 1942 was recalled from retirement for the second time and appointed Commander in Chief, West. His responsibilities included the defense of France, Belgium and Holland, the countries where the Allies were expected to launch their assault. He was answerable only to the Führer himself.

On 23 March 1942, in Directive No 40, Hitler laid down the defensive policy by which he intended to foil any Allied attack. Fortified areas were to be prepared in coastal sectors exposed to a landing, and reserves were to be held ready for a counterattack. It was laid down that 'enemy forces which have landed must be destroyed or thrown back into the sea by immediate counterattack.'

Von Rundstedt had scarcely assumed command when, on 28 March, the British carried out a fierce raid on the naval base of St Nazaire. The great dock was put out of action, and Hitler, greatly displeased, ordered the construction of yet more formidable defenses. The results of the British and Canadian raid on Dieppe on 19 August confirmed the Führer's good opinion of the value of coastal fortfications. Von Rundstedt, for his part, believed in the more conventional strategy of a strong *masse de manoeuvre*, held well back, but capable of launching a massive counterattack against an Allied beachhead.

Von Rundstedt was the supreme example of the orthodox general of the Prussian school. A little old fashioned perhaps, he was nonetheless the man given the credit for having struck down France in the Blitzkrieg of 1940. From there he had gone on to the Soviet Union, but blunt criticism of the Führer's strategy had led to his replacement. He was greatly respected by the German officer corps, which helped him in his dealings with Hitler. He had a low opinion of his master – though he had the wit to conceal it. His new job had its consolations; he enjoyed a civilized life at his headquarters in the Château de St Germain-en-Laye, overlooking the Seine. He needed something to make up for a task which he himself was to describe thus:

'I had over 3000 miles of coastline to cover from the Italian frontier in the south to the German frontier in the north, and only 60 divisions with which to defend it. Most of them were low-grade divisions and some of them were skeletons.'

Well versed in military history, von Rundstedt was familiar with Frederick the Great's dictum, 'Little minds want to defend everything; sensible men concentrate on the essential.' What were the essentials and if he should succeed in selecting them, would Hitler let him develop his strategy unhindered? During 1943 it became evident that the answer to this last question was an emphatic no. Hitler was growing more nervous. General Gunther Blumentritt commented:

'He was constantly on the jump – at one moment he expected an invasion in Norway, at another in Holland, then near the Somme, or Normandy or Brittany, in Portugal, in Spain, in the Adriatic.'

At the tactical level the task of defending the Channel coast fell to Field Marshal Erwin Rommel, an officer of outstanding tactical skill. Rommel felt that 'the war will be won or lost on the beaches. The first 24 hours will be decisive.' Unfortunately for the Germans his ideas did not entirely coincide with those of von Rundstedt, upon whom the ultimate responsibility rested.

Rommel, unlike so many of the German generals, could boast no aristocratic origins. He was the son of a Bavarian schoolmaster. Commissioned in 1912 he had distinguished himself greatly in World War I, at platoon, company and battle group level. He had fought in turn against the French, the Rumanians and the Italians, always with outstanding success. Skill, courage, vigor and initiative were the hallmarks of his operations. His decorations included the highest, the Pour le Mérite. Rommel was fortunate in that his battle experience was not confined to the trench warfare of the Western Front. He did not belong to the school of thought which believed in limited advances following a barrage. His exploits in Rumania and Italy had shown him the value of speed and surprise to achieve deep penetration of an enemy position.

Rommel stayed on in the small army allowed to Germany by the Treaty of Versailles, rising to the rank of colonel, and commanding the Führer's bodyguard in the Sudetenland and in Poland in 1939. Convinced of the value of the tank in modern warfare, he asked for the command of an armored division, and was given 7th Panzer, which he led with notable élan in the Blitzkrieg of 1940. Thereafter his advancement was rapid for although Rommel was not a fanatical Nazi Hitler preferred him to the Prussian aristocrats, who had such a firm grip on the German General Staff.

In February 1941 Rommel, now a Lieutenant General, was sent to Libya, where the Italians had been roughly handled in the so-called Wavell Offensive. During the next 18 months he built up a tremendous reputation as a tank commander in desert warfare. His capture of Tobruk on 21 June 1942 won him the field marshal's baton, and a reputation for invincibility. However, Auchinleck held him at El Alamein, and Rommel found himself far from his base, starved of supplies and suffering from a stomach ailment. On 23 October, when Rommel was in hospital in Germany, a new British general, Montgomery, fell upon his army and broke it in the long and bitter battle of El Alamein.

Rommel's reputation survived the loss of North Africa, and, after a spell in Italy, he was sent to inspect the defenses of northern France in November 1943. At first Rommel had no direct responsibility, and he felt that this made him ineffectual. He complained to Berlin and was given command of Army Group B under von Rundstedt. Although this clarified the chain of command it also revealed the fundamental difference in outlook of the two field marshals.

Von Rundstedt believed in a powerful, mobile armored reserve, a *masse de manoeuvre*, which would move against the invaders wherever they might choose to land. This was, of course, excellent theory. The lack of such a reserve had paralyzed Gamelin in 1940. Rommel, the great exponent of mobile warfare, had a far greater practical knowledge of handling tanks than von Rundstedt. Even so one might have supposed that his commander in chief's solution would have appealed to him. In fact Rommel had no faith in von Rundstedt's plan. It was not that he was abandoning the principles that had won him his desert successes. Practical tactician that he was, he simply appreciated that Allied air superiority would delay the armored reserve so much that it would rob it of its mobility. It would not be able to move quickly enough to prevent the Allies securing a foothold, building up a bridgehead and eventually achieving a breakout. Under all the circumstances Rommel felt that the only hope was to prevent the Allies landing at all; to stop them on the beaches. This meant that a thin gray line, supported by armor spread out close to the coastline, must be organized so as to hurl back the Allies on D-Day, as had been done at Dieppe in 1942.

In fact the plans of the two field marshals were never really reconciled. Von Rundstedt continued to sit on his mobile reserves, while Rommel sped up and down the coast, inspecting units and fortresses, siting guns, inventing obstacles and gingering up the defenders with his considerable powers of leadership. With the benefit of hindsight one must concede that, given Allied domination of the skies above Normandy, Rommel's plan was more realistic than von Rundstedt's, however correct that may have been in theory.

During the period of rather more than two years between von Rundstedt's appointment and D-Day the forces at his command suffered considerable erosion. Every time the Germans suffered a setback elsewhere Hitler nibbled away at von Rundstedt's armies until their quality became decidedly uneven. That is not to say that von Rundstedt did not still have formations of superb military value. No soldier worth the name would underrate the 10 Panzer divisions which formed the solid core of his forces.

One way of measuring the strength of Germany at the beginning of 1944 is simply to examine the layout of divisions in the field:

Eastern Front	179
France and the Low Countries	53
Balkan States	26
Italy	22
Scandinavia	16
Finland	8
	304

Of these, 24, stationed in the occupied countries, were still in the process of formation. Worse still, there was no general reserve in Germany. Hitler had a tremendous army at his command, but it was already committed. Only by robbing other fronts could he reinforce the West. Even

so, the occupation forces were formidable. In wartime the ration strength of an army tends to be a good deal higher than its real strength. Not *all* quartermasters are honest. However that may be, on 1 March 1944 there were in France:

Army	806,927
SS and Police	85,230
Volunteers (foreigners)	61,439
Allies	13,631
Air Force	337,140
Navy	96,084
Total	1,400,451
Armed Force Auxiliaries	145,611

Of the Air Force personnel over 100,000 were in Flak formations, and more than 30,000 were 'paratroops.' The Luftwaffe in the West under Field Marshal Hugo Sperrle had about 890 aircraft available for operations. Of these about 150 were reconnaissance and transport aircraft.

Vice-Admiral Krancke commanded Naval Group, West. Naval personnel manned a number of the key coastal batteries with radar equipment – thus complicating defense policy. The ships and craft available included a weak destroyer flotilla, some torpedo boats, a number of patrol craft and minelayers. There were U-Boats based at Brest, and other Atlantic coast ports, but they were not under Krancke. These, in broad terms were the forces the Allies had to reckon with.

At the last meeting of the Cairo Conference, on 6 December 1943, President Roosevelt nominated General Dwight

Above: A Freya early-warning radar sited to cover the approaches to Brest on the Channel coast.
Above right: Churchill and Roosevelt met at Quebec in August 1943 to discuss plans for the invasion of Western France.
Right: At Casablanca in January 1943 the British Prime Minister came under strong pressure from the Americans to launch a cross-Channel invasion in the near future.

David Eisenhower as Supreme Allied Commander for Operation Overlord. Before he took up his new appointment, as he generously conceded later, Lieutenant General Frederick E Morgan had already 'made D-Day possible.'

At the Casablanca Conference in January 1943 the Allies had decided to set up a Combined Allied Staff to plan Overlord. The Chief of Staff to the Supreme Allied Commander (designate), Morgan, was British, and his deputy, Major General Ray W Baker, was a United States army officer. The organization became known as COSSAC.

Morgan received his directive on 26 April 1943. This stated, 'our object is to defeat the German fighting forces in Northwest Europe.' It instructed COSSAC to prepare plans for a full-scale assault against the Continent as early as possible in 1944, with 'an elaborate camouflage and deception scheme' extending over the summer of 1943 designed to pin the Germans in the west by keeping alive their expectation of an invasion that year. In the event of the Germans collapsing there was to be a plan ready so that whatever forces were available in the United Kingdom could immediately be sent to the Continent. At the Trident Conference, held in Washington in May 1943, the target date for Overlord was set for 1 May 1944. COSSAC was given a list of the forces which, it was thought, would be available:

5 infantry divisions in assault vessels
2 follow-up infantry divisions
2 airborne divisions
20 divisions for movement into the lodgment area.

The capture and development of ports would permit the landing of divisions direct from America, or elsewhere, at a rate of from three to five a month.

The assault of ships and landing craft would amount to some 3300. It seems a huge figure, but in fact shortage of landing craft was to plague the Allies until the end of the war in Europe. About 11,400 aircraft, including 632 transport planes for airborne operations, would be available.

In the first week of June General Morgan was told to submit his outline plan by 1 August 1943. That he was able to do so was due to Winston Churchill's aggressive policy, which, even before Dunkirk, had called for raids on the enemy-held coast, and plans for an eventual return to France. The small organization under General A G B Bourne, Royal Marines, which in 1940 was charged with this task, had expanded under Admiral of the Fleet, Sir Roger Keyes. Later it expanded far more significantly under Vice-Admiral Mountbatten, whose Combined Operations Headquarters, though affiliated to the Admiralty, the War Office and the Air Ministry, was separate from them. Mountbatten, who held equivalent rank in all three services, sat as a member of the Chiefs of Staff

Committee. He was the recognized authority on the planning and mounting of seaborne assaults, whether commando raids or full-scale invasions. The zeal and originality which Mountbatten brought to Combined Operations Headquarters permeated through to the staff of all three services in the planning of Overlord.

At the Quadrant meeting in Quebec in August 1943 the COSSAC plan, after being considered in turn by the British Chiefs of Staff and the American Joint Chiefs of Staff was finally submitted to Churchill and Roosevelt by their Combined Chiefs of Staff. It was accepted, with some useful modifications. Churchill urged that the force should be increased by at least 25 percent and that the assault front should be extended to include the eastern coast of the Cherbourg peninsula. The Combined Chiefs, although they agreed that the force should be strengthened if possible, did not increase the allocation of ships and craft.

General Morgan was now given authority 'for taking the necessary executive action to implement those plans approved by the Combined Chiefs of Staff.' Since nearly four months were to pass before Eisenhower's appointment Morgan was working as Chief of Staff to an unknown Supreme Commander. All that was known was that, at Churchill's suggestion, he was to be an American, since the United States would eventually be providing a larger proportion of the Allied force.

Eisenhower was an admirable choice for Supreme Commander, not by virtue of battle experience in World War I – he had none – nor outstanding strategic skill, but because his lack of personal ambition, his sincere, warm and friendly personality fitted him to run a team which included such idiosyncratic characters as Patton and Montgomery. Son of a Texan railroad

Above: General Dwight D Eisenhower was appointed Supreme Commander of the Allied Expeditionary Force in December 1943.
Below: German coastal artillery was sited in concrete emplacements overlooking potential landing beaches.

worker, he was brought up in poverty, but won his way to West Point, and was commissioned in 1913. He served under the great General Douglas MacArthur in the Philippines, and later attracted the attention of General George C Marshall, who was Roosevelt's principal military adviser throughout the war. Eisenhower was hardly of the caliber of either of these giants, but he was an excellent chairman, and enjoyed great popularity with the British.

As Deputy Supreme Commander a British Air Chief Marshal, Sir Arthur Tedder, was chosen. He had already worked harmoniously with Eisenhower in 1943 when he had been Commander in Chief, Mediterranean Allied Air Forces. His success in planning and executing operations over Tunisia, Sicily and Italy made him an excellent choice, for it was evident that the air arm would be of paramount importance in the campaign ahead. Eisenhower considered him 'one of the few great military leaders of our time.' A Luftwaffe comment of the time is flattering:

'Tedder is on good terms with Eisenhower to whom he is superior in both intelligence and energy. The coming operations will be conducted by him to a very large extent. . . . Obviously we are dealing here with one of the most eminent personalities among the invasion leaders.'

Not unnaturally Eisenhower wished to retain his trusted Chief of Staff, Lieutenant General W Bedell Smith, who had been with him in North Africa, Sicily and Italy. Although he was Eisenhower's hatchet man, he could be diplomatic as well as tough. Morgan, whose knowledge of how the COSSAC plan had developed was invaluable, became a deputy chief of staff.

The naval commander was Admiral Sir Bertram Ramsay, the man who brought the British Expeditionary Force (BEF) home from the beaches of Dunkirk. He had helped to plan the landings in North Africa in 1942, and had commanded the Eastern Naval Task Force in the assault on Sicily. He was a punctilious man who believed in attention to detail – there are enough hazards at sea without leaving things to chance when you do not have to. Nevertheless some of the American admirals were to be critical of the amount of detail in his orders. Ramsay remained calm and urbane.

Command of the Allied Tactical Air Forces was given to Air Chief Marshal Sir Trafford Leigh-Mallory who, like Ramsay, had special qualifications for his role. After commanding 12 Group in the Battle of Britain, he had been the Air Force commander of the Royal Air Force School of Army Cooperation, and Air Officer Commanding in Chief, Fighter Command. He

Left: A German sentry keeps watch from a camouflaged observation post. Allied measures against German radar were so successful that these lookouts provided the first warning of invasion.

was prepared to stand up to 'the bomber barons.'

Command of the Allied Armies, 21st Army Group, was given to General Sir Bernard Montgomery. Eisenhower wanted to have General Sir Harold Alexander, but the British government knew that the victor of El Alamein could not be lightly set aside. In any case Alexander had all the qualities required to run the very mixed team of Allies then slogging their way up Italy. So it fell to Montgomery to command the land forces in Overlord. He was a strange man, not really very likeable, though he had sufficient sense of humor to be amused by his own peculiarities, which, besides a brusque manner, included a direct line to the Almighty. Although he got on badly with some colleagues – Patton for one detested him – he had an almost magical influence on the British soldier. When Montgomery was in command the men thought they could not be beaten. Though a strong-minded, efficient, sound and relentless commander, it cannot be said that he was especially gifted as a strategist. However, in the spring of 1944 his chief reverse, at Arnhem, still lay in the future. Thus far his road had been strewn with laurels. Had he not routed the great Rommel himself?

Command of the American First Army, which was one of the two assault armies, was in the safe hands of Lieutenant General Omar N Bradley. Commissioned in 1915, Bradley was made Lieutenant Colonel only in 1936, when he was already 43. During World War II promotion came rapidly, and in Tunisia and Sicily he had been a corps commander. He and Eisenhower had been friends since their West Point days, and the latter wrote of Bradley's 'ability and reputation as a sound, painstaking, and broadly educated soldier.' The newspapermen, led by Ernie Pyle, took a liking to him, and he became 'the GIs' general.'

The follow-up army of this group, the 12th Army Group, was the United States Third Army, under the dynamic and talented Lieutenant General George S Patton. His army took no part in the D-Day landing but its very existence was another worry for von Rundstedt.

The assault army of the 21st Army Group was the British Second Army, whose commander, Lieutenant General Sir Miles Dempsey, had commanded a corps in Sicily and Italy. He was an exceptionally fine commander, but unlike most of his contemporaries he left no memoirs and is therefore comparatively little-known today. He was good-tempered, steady, confident and considerate, and was tremendously respected by all who knew him. He had a perfect understanding of the army he handled, and had the knack of giving clear and precise verbal orders. Above all he had the ability to work with Montgomery, apparently without the least friction. Taken all round Dempsey was just about the ideal commander for the Second Army. Many a British general of far less worth has ended his career with a field marshal's baton in his hand!

The First Canadian Army, under Lieutenant General Henry D G Crerar was the follow-up army of the 21st Army Group. It did not become operational until 23 July, but nevertheless its very existence had to be taken into account by the Germans.

In a sense the Allies already had an army in Europe before D-Day, the Resistance. In theory the constitutional government was the Vichy regime under old Marshal Pétain. His authority had been greatly reduced and Pierre Laval, who secured the collaboration which the Germans demanded, governed only by their consent. By 1944 it was clear that the true voice of France was that of General Charles de Gaulle, whose Headquarters was, of course, in London.

The French Resistance has been called 'a blend of courage and patriotism, ambition, faction and treachery.' It comprised numerous groups, whose political background varied from Communist and *Front Populaire* to Catholic. By 1944 the Maquis consisted of perhaps 100,000 people, many of whom had made their way to the mountains rather than be sent to Germany to work as conscript labor. They were the raw material for guerrilla war.

The Belgian Resistance, the 'Secret Army,' was some 45,000 strong. In the second quarter of 1944 55 air operations supplied it with arms. However, the *Abwehr* (German secret service) had been extremely successful in capturing Allied agents dropped into Holland, and the Dutch Resistance was still poorly equipped.

A complicated organization in England endeavored to control and to arm these Resistance movements. In this work the British Broadcasting Corporation and the Special Operations Executive (SOE) played an indispensable part.

The Allied planners, while agreeing that the flames of resistance must be fanned by every possible means, placed no reliance upon its activities. Any sabotage, or any armed rising, was simply to be regarded as a bonus. It is not easy to quantify the achievements of these patriotic men and women, but it is evident that they tied up thousands of enemy soldiers by their very existence. By ambush and sabotage they inflicted serious delays on the German reserves as they moved up to battle during the summer of 1944.

Besides armies that actually existed the Allies made good use of others that did not. It was essential to the success of Overlord that the Germans, who still enjoyed a great numerical advantage in land forces, should be led to make faulty dispositions. It was recognized, of course, that the German commanders were aware of Allied preparations for an assault. At the same time it was thought that, given good security, they might be deceived as to where and

when the landing was to take place. For this reason it was essential that the preliminary bombing did not point to Normandy as the chosen beachhead. Therefore, for every target attacked in the actual assault area, two were bombed elsewhere, especially in the Pas de Calais. This cover plan greatly increased the number of sorties which had to be flown by the Allied air forces, and therefore their casualties, but its strategic success cannot be doubted.

In order to misrepresent their overall strategy the Allies devised a deception plan (code named Bodyguard). This was supplemented by Fortitude which was the cover plan for Normandy. The story that the Allies tried to sell was that the campaign of 1944 would open with the invasion of southern Norway. Then, in about the third week of July, the main attack would be launched against the Pas de Calais. Dummy landing craft were assembled in southeastern ports and harbors; radio traffic, training exercises and so on built up the desired impression. Even after D-Day the belief was encouraged that the attack on Normandy was a diversionary one.

The fictitious invasion of Norway was entrusted to Lieutenant General Sir A F A N Thorne, Commander in Chief, Northern Command. His 'Fourth Army,' consisting of three imaginary corps, was assembled in Scotland. There were *some* troops in Scotland, but for the most part the Fourth was a phantom army, conjured out of the air by radio traffic from a skeleton headquarters consisting largely of signals staff. Troop movements and exercises, and some well-calculated leaks pointed to landings on the Norwegian coast. This deception was to be maintained until July. Hitler was sensitive to any threat to Norway. Infuriated by the commando raid which wiped out the garrison of Vaagso on 27 December 1941, he had built up the garrison of Norway to some 300,000 men. It was essential to the Allies that they should not be moved to France, where only 100,000 of them would have added greatly to the defensive power of Army Group West. The Fourth Army was by no means the least effective of the armies that 'fought' on the Allied side in World War II.

The imaginary invasion of the Pas de Calais was scheduled for mid-July. A mythical assault force of 12 divisions was to be built up to 50 divisions. There were, of course, many real formations in east and southeast England. These made themselves

Top left: General Bernard Montgomery commanded all land forces on D-Day.
Far left: Omar Bradley (center) commanded the Americans.
Left and below: Allied troops assemble and train for D-Day.

appear even more formidable than they were by increasing the volume of radio traffic. Nothing was neglected that might add to the desired impression. Inspired leaks through the press, as well as through diplomatic and underground channels built up the picture. In the southeastern counties, forces – real and imaginary – were assembled openly, while in the southwest no effort of concealment was spared. German situation maps showing Allied dispositions in Britain prove the extent to which these deceptions worked.

Their success was helped by the fact that Hitler had been convinced at the outset that the Allies' main assault would come against the Pas de Calais. Indeed all the German leaders were convinced that it should be strongly guarded. This view was not unreasonable. It was the shortest sea route from England to France, and the shortest route for an Allied thrust at the industrial Ruhr. The German leaders thought it probable that the Allies would attack in several places, but opinions differed as to where the subsidiary assaults would land. Norway, the Atlantic coast, Portugal and the Mediterranean coast of France all came under discussion. In October 1943 von Rundstedt pointed out that 'Normandy with Cherbourg, and Brittany with Brest are additional important

Left: A German infantryman mans his defensive position.
Below: A heavy gun pokes from its massive concrete emplacement.
Right: The text of General Eisenhower's message announcing the invasion.
Below right: The Allied commanders, from top left, Bradley, Ramsay, Leigh-Mallory, Bedell-Smith, Tedder, Eisenhower, Montgomery.

THE FOLLOWING IS FOR YOUR INFORMATION AND NOT FOR BROADCAST OR PUBLICATION
GREEN PRIORITY STAND-BY FOR PRIORITY TRAFFIC RESUME TRAFFIC

BLUE

WAR V JBJB
FROM JBJB
TO COMBINED CHIEFS OF STAFF WASHINGTON D C
COMMUNIQUE NUMBER ONE IS ABOUT TO BE RELEASED.

RED URGENT URGENT - JUNE, 6, 1944 9:15 AM

WAR JDJD V JBJB
FROM JBJB

TO OFFICE OF WAR INFORMATION FOREIGN NEWS BUREAU WASHINGTON D.C.

COMMUNIQUE NUMBER ONE SUPREME HEADQUARTERS ALLIED EXPEDITIONARY FORCE

UNDER THE COMMAND OF GENERAL EISENHOWER, ALLIED NAVAL FORCES,

SUPPORTED BY STRONG AIR FORCES, BEGAN LANDING ALLIED ARMIES THIS

MORNING ON THE NORTHERN COAST OF FRANCE.

END COMMUNIQUE

areas on the Channel front,' and, though it took him some time, it seems that Hitler came to think there was something in this. By 4 March 1944 he was describing them as 'particularly threatened' and two days later General Alfred Jodl, his personal Chief of Staff, told von Rundstedt that the Führer attached 'particular importance to Normandy,' and especially Cherbourg. This led to the reinforcement of the Cotentin peninsula by the 91st Airlanding Division, 6th Parachute Regiment and other units. In April the 21st Panzer Division was moved from Brittany to Caen and the Panzer *Lehr* Division from Hungary to Chartres.

Von Rundstedt's forecasts of Allied intentions were pretty sound. In his situation report of 15 May he emphasized the Allies' need to capture big harbors:

'Le Havre and Cherbourg are primarily to be considered for this purpose, Boulogne and the Cotentin peninsula in the first phase would therefore seem very natural. . . .'

On 29 May he concluded that the air attacks on the Seine bridges 'may indicate enemy designs on Normandy (formation of a bridgehead).'

The Allies, in fact, intended to land three airborne and five seaborne divisions between the River Dives and the Cherbourg Peninsula, and to form a beachhead, which would include the towns of Caen, Bayeux and St Lô. The role of the airborne divisions was to secure the flanks of the beachhead, while the seaborne divisions pushed inland.

On the eve of the invasion there were three German infantry divisions guarding the beaches where the five Allied seaborne divisions were to land. Of these, the 709th and 716th Divisions were static and the 352nd Division was a field division. In support south of Caen was the 21st Panzer Division, a powerful armored formation under Major General Edgar Feuchtinger.

The HQ of the German LXXXIV Corps was near St Lô. It was commanded by General Erich Marcks, a tall, scholarly looking man, who had lost a leg in Russia.

It may be doubted whether the German forces in the area selected for the Allied landing were in themselves sufficient to hurl the invaders into the sea. It cannot be said that either the 709th or 716th Divisions were particularly formidable formations. Much would depend on the handling of the 21st Panzer. Much more would depend on the speed with which these divisions could be reinforced. Some help might be expected fairly soon from the 711st Division, static though it was, and from the 77th Field Division. Although these might help to hold the ring, they were not likely to turn the tide of battle. However, the Germans had three more armored divisions disposed where they might intervene in Normandy. These were the 116th Panzer, just east of the Seine, the 12th SS Panzer and Panzer

Below: Part of the massive invasion fleet off the English south coast.

Top left: Rear Admiral Alan G Kirk (foreground) commanded the US Western Task Force.

Far left: The battleships USS *Nevada* and USS *Texas* in line astern.

Lehr. Much would depend on the speed with which the Germans could get all, or some, of these into the battle.

In May German air reconnaissance seldom reached even the south coast of England. Nevertheless, on 4 June Admiral Krancke expressed doubts as to 'whether the enemy has yet assembled his invasion fleet in the required strength.' Next day, Army Group B, with no fresh intelligence at hand but noting the concentration of Allied bombing between Dieppe and Dunkirk considered that it pointed to 'the previously assumed focal point of the major landing' (the Pas de Calais). 'As yet,' wrote von Rundstedt that same day, 'there is no immediate prospect of the invasion.' Rommel left his headquarters to stay with his family for a night, on his way to visit Hitler.

So, on the eve of D-Day the Germans were off their guard, the weather was foul in the channel, and the eight Allied divisions were yearning to go. Why should 150,000 or so young men be so keen to stick their necks out? How did they come to be so well motivated? Every unit had been visited by the King or Ike, Monty, Dempsey, Bradley, or various other leaders, who had stressed the importance of the operation which was about to be launched. The British soldier is not lacking in cynicism, and this may well apply to the GI as well. The reason why the men were so eager to get cracking was that in the interests of security they had been assembled in tented camps, surrounded by barbed wire, where they had spent no less than a week. They had been allowed out only in formed groups, and had little to do but watch old films – *Claudia* springs to mind – and listen to a few more pep talks. The terrors of the West Wall were as nothing compared to a few more days in the Allied version of the Concentration Camp.

At 0415 hours on Sunday 4 June the Allied Commanders in Chief were told that the weather forecast for the 5th heralded poor visibility and low cloud over the beaches with rising seas in a mounting gale. Eisenhower had no alternative but to postpone the invasion for 24 hours. The bombarding warships on their way from Scotland had to turn back. The parts of Rear Admiral Kirk's convoy that were already on their way to the Utah assault area had to be recalled. Not until 0900 hours on Sunday 5 June was Admiral Ramsay certain that all units were on their way back to shelter.

At 2130 hours the Commanders in Chief met once more in the library at Southwick House. They were told that a break in the weather was coming. The rain in the assault area was going to clear up for 48 hours. The wind would drop, though the sea would still be rough and choppy. Heavy bombing would be possible on Monday night, 5 June. Another postponement would mean that D-Day would have to be put off for two weeks, with all the ill effects that would bring to the assault troops who were keyed up for action.

Eisenhower asked each senior commander for his opinion. Leigh-Mallory and Tedder thought it would be 'chancy.' Ramsay – whose opinion in such a matter must have held great weight – thought that the assault should go ahead, and Montgomery agreed with him.

Eisenhower reflected for a while, and then made his decision:

'I am quite positive we must give the order. . . . I don't like it, but there it is. . . . I don't see how we can possibly do anything else.'

2. THE AIRBORNE ASSAULT

The airborne assault was a vital part of Operation Overlord. The Allies sent in three airborne divisions (see appendix for breakdown), two American and one British, to prepare for the main assault by taking certain strategic points and by disrupting German communications.

The task of the British 6th Airborne Division was to hold the eastern flank of the beachhead. This called for the seizure of the bridges over the River Orne, between Caen and the sea, and the capture of the Merville battery, which could enfilade the lodgment area, posing a dangerous threat to the left flank of the seaborne landings. In general it was intended to deny the Germans the rather rough tract of wooded and flooded country between the rivers Orne and Dives. It was a tall order for a single division, even though it was to be reinforced by 1st Commando Brigade, which was to land from the sea.

Experience, especially in Sicily, had shown that landing parachutists and gliders on a windy night is a hazardous business. A large proportion of the troops engaged are certain to be dropped in the wrong place. Commanders who find themselves in the right place too often find themselves with no more than a handful of the troops allotted to their task. Lest this should seem too gloomy a picture it must be appreciated that the enemy commander, studying his map and marking every report of a hostile landing, will be doubly confused if some of the attackers have landed in the wrong place. The problem of where and when to launch the defenders' reserves – and there are never enough of these – becomes more intractable. So if some pilots lose their way, and if others release their gliders at the first burst of flak, some good may still come of it so long as the airborne troops do *something* on landing. The men of the 6th Airborne Division, as the Germans soon learned, would make a nuisance of themselves wherever they landed!

Top right: Eisenhower talks with paratroops before D-Day.
Right: British Horsa gliders on their landing zone near Caen.
Opposite: American gliders landed on the Cherbourg Peninsula, west of the main seaborne landings.

Below: Horsa gliders of the British 6th Airborne Division lie in a field north of Ranville. The tail sections have been removed to unload equipment.
Bottom: Many gliders landed in the wrong place, two which fell into German hands being shown.
Opposite: A tank crew supporting infantry near Bénouville.

Major R J Howard was charged with the surprise capture of the Bénouville and Ranville bridges. His party comprised five platoons of the 2nd Oxfordshire and Buckinghamshire Light Infantry and 30 officers and men of the 249th Field Company, Royal Engineers. They crossed the French coast just after midnight, and six Horsa gliders were released. The first stuck its nose into the German wire surrounding the Bénouville bridge, and two others touched down within 100 yards. Two of the other gliders landed within 150 yards of the Ranville bridge. Both bridges were rushed and within 15 minutes had been taken, intact. Casualties were light, though the leading platoon commander was killed. The sappers found that the bridges had not been prepared for demolition. German prisoners from the 736th Grenadier Regiment of the 716th Infantry Division were taken.

To have taken the bridges was a great exploit, but unless they could be held there would be no communication with the troops who landed east of the Orne. Howard took up a defensive position about the bridges. There was a good deal of desultory firing for there were German troops in the nearby villages of Bénouville and Ranville. A troop of three tanks approached, but was discouraged when the leader was hit by a PIAT (Projector Infantry Anti-Tank). The PIAT weighed 34.5 pounds and was a short-range weapon. It hurled a 2.5-pound bomb and was supposed to be effective at 100 yards, but it is thought that its successes were, generally speaking, scored at point-blank range.

A little later the German officer in command of the bridge defenses drove up in his car and was captured. This classic *coup de main* had been pulled off without one of the six gliders, which, released too far east, had landed eight miles from the target.

The task of 3rd Parachute Brigade was to cut the bridges over the River Dives, so as to delay German troops advancing to attack the British left flank. It was to occupy the high ground commanding these approaches, and to capture the Merville battery. The task of the 5th Parachute Brigade was to capture and hold the Orne crossings.

Every operation of war, however successful, has its share of *friction de guerre* (grit in the works). A typical example of this complicated operations for the 3rd Brigade. A path-finder party which was to land on dropping zone K was dropped in error on zone N where, in all innocence, it began to send out the code letter K and to call in more troops of the 3rd Brigade. It was some time before this mistake could be put right.

The 5th Brigade was carried in 129 aircraft. All but five dropped their troops, but they were greatly dispersed and much

time was lost while searching for equipment containers in the dark, and while trying to find the rendezvous.

It was 0130 hours before half the 7th Battalion and 591st Parachute Squadron, Royal Engineers, found their way to the rendezvous, without many of their machine guns, mortars and radios. They were sent to reinforce Major Howard. There was confused fighting in the villages of Bénouville and le Port, and the Germans actually overran the Regimental Aid Post, killing the chaplain! When dawn came the fighting was still going on, but the vital bridges were still in British hands.

The task of 12th Battalion was to hold the eastern approaches to the Ranville bridge. Fifteen of its 32 aircraft dropped their passengers accurately. Seven others were less than a mile out. The other 10 were wildly adrift. By 0400 hours the Battalion had occupied Le Bas de Ranville and taken prisoners from 736th Grenadier Regiment.

Meanwhile 13th Battalion, whose task was to take Ranville and, with some sapper units, to clear and improve Drop Zone N, had taken its objective. They had also captured some men of 125th Panzer Grenadier Regiment, which belonged to 21st Panzer Division, stationed southeast of Caen.

At about 0330 hours the 68 Horsas of the third flight crossed the coast. Fifty – 25 of them somewhat damaged by flak – landed with few casualties. Low cloud now obscured the coast and some of the 18 missing gliders were simply lost. In other cases, no doubt, the towropes had parted. This wave brought in nine 6-pounder and two 17-pounder antitank guns, heavy engineer stores and equipment, and Major General Richard Nelson Gale. One may imagine his relief when he learned that the *coup de main* had been successful, and that the bridgehead was holding out.

Meanwhile 3rd Brigade, though widely dispersed, had been carrying out a variety of tasks. The commander of 8th Battalion, with 160 men who had landed correctly on zone K, had taken up a position on the high ground southwest of the Bois de Bavent, so as to cover a party which was demolishing the Bures bridge. Troops that had landed by mistake in Zone N also made for the high ground west of the Bois de Bavent. Most of 3rd Parachute Squadron was sent to blow the Bures bridge, but Major J C A Roseveare, with an officer and seven sappers crowded into a jeep and trailer full of explosives and made for Troarn. At the entrance to the village they ran into a barbed-wire knife-rest. In the dark it took them 20 minutes to clear this obstacle out of the way. They sent out a scout, who shot a German cyclist. The garrison stood to arms. The jeep dashed through the village with 'a Boche in every doorway shooting like mad.' Firing back, they hurtled down the slope to the river and, astonishingly, they only lost one man on their reckless ride. Working as fast as they could they blew a wide gap in the center span of the bridge. Abandoning the jeep they made their way across country and rejoined their party, who had blown the Bures bridge, swimming several small streams on the way.

The Canadian Battalion had a stiff fight at Varaville and captured the château there, though a pillbox held out. A valiant Frenchman, putting on a red beret, armed himself with a rifle and is credited with slaying three snipers in the nearby woods. Here, as at Amfreville and the other villages of this area, the civilians came out to tend the wounded.

By far the worst task that fell to 3rd Brigade was the destruction of the Merville battery. It was thought that it had four guns. If it was not destroyed before daylight it would command the beaches on which 3rd Infantry Division and 1st Commando Brigade were to land. L F Ellis in Volume I of *Victory in the West* describes the position:

'The guns were in steel-doored concrete emplacements six feet thick, two of which were also covered by twelve feet of earth. They were in a fenced area of seven hundred by five hundred yards within which was a belt of barbed wire, double in places, fifteen feet thick and five feet high. An anti-tank ditch was incomplete but mines had been sown profusely and there were a dual-purpose gun position and about fifteen weapon pits. Outside the main position was a wired in strong-point with five machine-gun emplacements and several other anti-aircraft gun positions.'

(It so happens that the author was in this position two days later. Believe me it was a stinker.) The task of destroying the position fell to Lieutenant Colonel Terence Otway

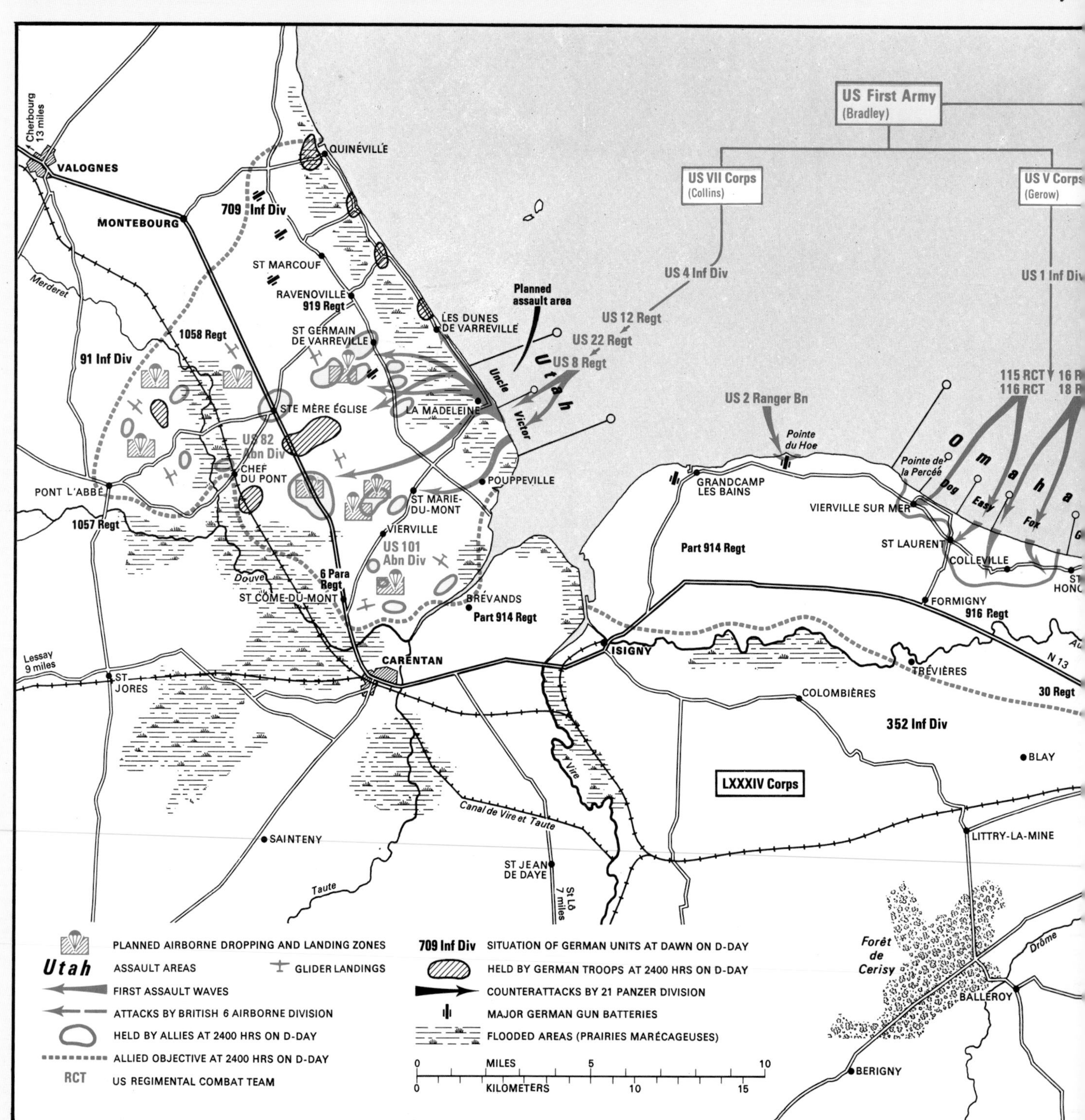

and the 9th Parachute Battalion. It would have been difficult enough had the whole operation gone according to plan. The intention was to use a small reconnaissance party and three companies. One, which was to be a firm base on which to rally, was to make a diversion against the main entrance. A second was to breach the defenses. A third was to make the assault. As a sort of bonus a party, carried in three gliders, was to crash land on the battery just as the assault went in. All this was to be accomplished in four and a half hours of darkness. It was not an easy task.

The reconnaissance party dropped as planned and set off for the battery. That was just about all that *did* go according to plan. Much equipment was lost in the flooded area round Varaville, and only half the Battalion dropped within a mile of the rendezvous. At 0255 hours Otway set off with 150 men. He arrived to find that his reconnaissance party had done rather well They had cut the outer wire, marked paths through the minefield *with their feet*, and dealt with a number of booby traps.

Otway reorganized his men into seven parties. Two were to breach the main wire, four were to deal with the four guns and one was to make a diversion at the main entrance. At this juncture two of the Albemarles appeared, and flew around looking for the place to crash land. It had not been possible to put out lights to guide them, but eventually the gliders were released, landing 200 yards away. Their troops engaged the Germans in the perimeter defenses.

Otway's seven parties went into action; the wire was breached and the main gate stormed. The garrison was overwhelmed in a brief and bloody assault. The 75mm guns were put out of action. Then the Battalion's signal officer took 'a somewhat ruffled pigeon' from his pocket and sent it

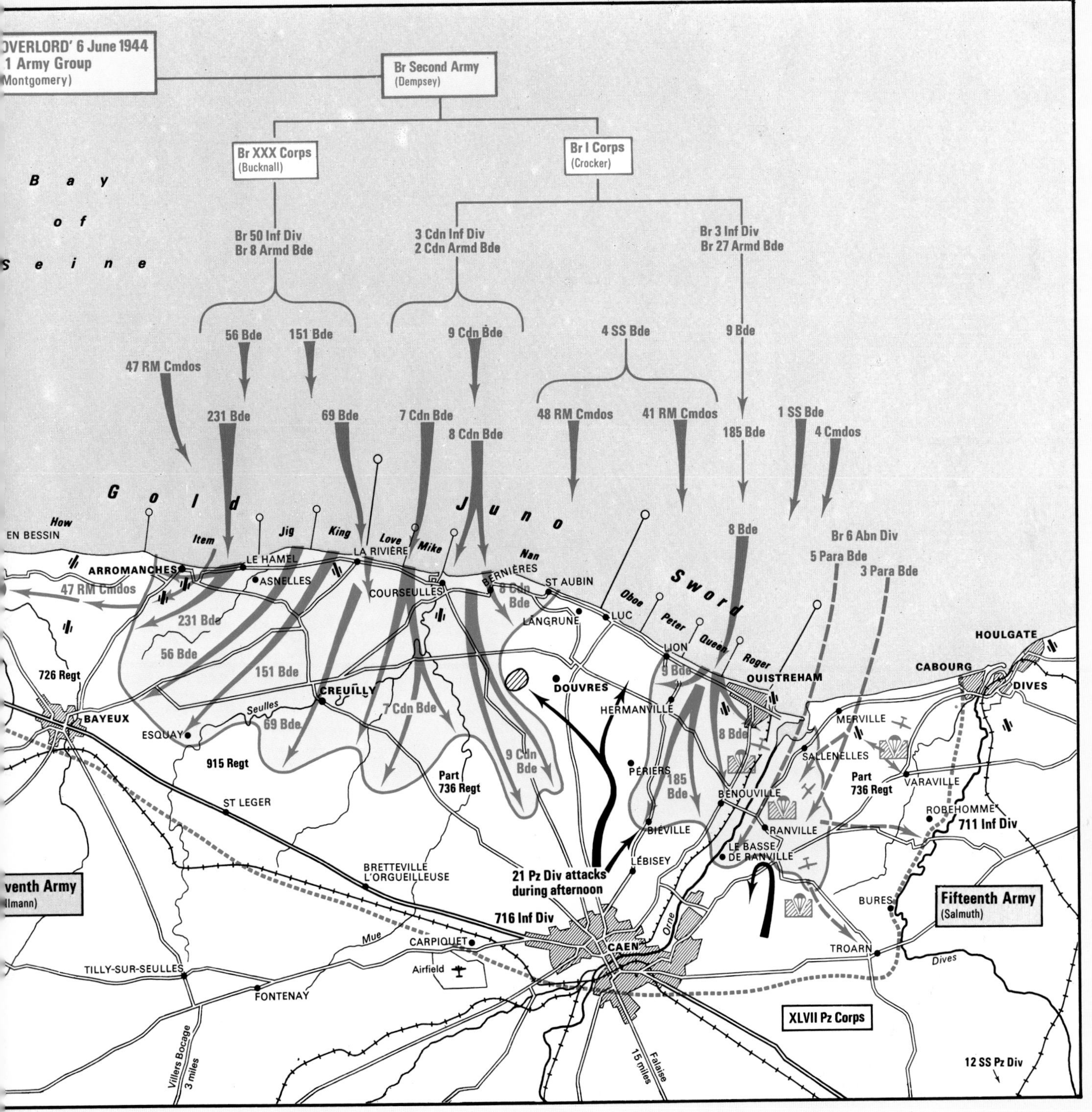

off to England to report the success. The bird was probably glad to leave.

This assault cost Otway's party 70 casualties. With the 80 survivors he made for his next objective, the high ground at Le Plein. In German hands this would have given their gunners wonderful observation posts, overlooking 3rd Infantry Division's area.

So, when dawn came 6th Airborne Division could claim that, despite every sort of accident, it had carried out all its main tasks. The Orne bridges were held. Three of the bridges over the Dives – Troarn, Bures, and Robehomme – had been blown, as well as another over a tributary at Varaville. The Merville battery was out of action. The beginnings of a defensive position was being formed on the high ground that runs from Le Plein to Troarn; vital ground. If the Germans could reconquer the area between Dives and the Orne they could render the beachhead untenable, and drive the Allies back into the sea.

At 0840 hours the 1st Commando Brigade under Brigadier Lord Lovat, DSO, MC, began to land west of Ouistreham. By midday the leading commando, 6, had reached the Bénouville bridge. It was deployed to strengthen the line on the high ground at Le Plein. This brigade, some 2000 strong, consisted of 3, 4, 6 and 45 (Royal Marine) Commandos.

Meanwhile two American Airborne Divisions, 82nd and 101st, had been dropped all over the Cotentin peninsula. Their task was to aid the assault of the United States First Army and facilitate the capture of the vital Cotentin peninsula. It was an ambitious plan. Some 18,000 men were to be dropped by night into an area of Normandy bocage and floods. The German defenders were more numerous than in the tract of country between the Orne and the Dives. The German troops were mostly from 91st Division. This unit had been specially trained to combat airborne attacks.

In order to avoid the antiaircraft defenses of Cherbourg the American IX Troop Carrier Command made an indirect approach via the Channel Islands. They were protected by Mosquitos of Air Defence of Great Britain, while Stirlings of Bomber Command dropped 'window' so as to deceive the German radar. The bombers went on further south to simulate diversionary landings.

As soon as the airborne forces turned east and crossed the coast of the Cotentin peninsula they ran into heavy flak and small-arms fire. There was thick cloud and formations tended to break up; even the pathfinders found it difficult to identify their targets. In consequence the drops were widely scattered. In *Cross-Channel Attack* G A Harrison describes the scene:

'The first actions of all airborne units in the Cotentin on D-Day were attempts by

Left and right: Groups of paratroops, who had been dropped wide of their assigned landing zones, soon fell into German hands.
Below left: Two privates of the US 101st Airborne Division don Indian warpaint before their drop.
Below: An American reconnaissance aircraft took this photograph of Horsa and Hadrian gliders within hours of their landing.

small groups of men to carry out in the fog of the battlefield their own portion of the assigned plan. There could be little overall direction from above.'

The accounts of what they achieved, especially those of 101st Airborne, are thin indeed. *Time* magazine supplements the official records. An officer told of seeing German tracer ripping through men's parachutes as they descended. In *D-Day* Warren Tute relates that:

'In one plane, a soldier laden with his 90 pounds of equipment got momentarily stuck in the door. A 20mm shell hit him in the belly. Fuse-caps in his pockets began to go off. Part of the wounded man's load was TNT. Before this human bomb could explode, his mates behind him pushed him out. The last they saw of him, his parachute had opened and he was drifting to earth in a shroud of bursting flame.'

General Matthew B Ridgway, the commander of 82nd Airborne Division, parachuted to earth and, collecting 11 officers and men, set up his HQ in an orchard. He wrote:

'The Germans were all around us, of course, sometimes within 500 yards of my command post, but in the fierce and confused fighting that was going on all about they did not launch the strong attack that could have wiped out our eggshell perimeter defenses.'

The 82nd Airborne was meant to be dropped astride the Merderet, to capture Ste Mère Eglise and to facilitate the advance into the Cotentin. Only one regiment was dropped at all accurately and in a brilliant action a party from this unit quickly seized and held the village. The other troops of the division were scattered up to 25 miles away; many were left struggling in the marshy ground on either side of the Merderet.

The 101st Division was also widely dispersed but senior officers were able to collect parties and move toward the causeways inland from Utah which were their main objectives. Other groups managed to take bridgeheads over the Douve which would later be important in allowing a link with the Omaha forces. Although at dawn perhaps only 1000 of the division's men were under command they did manage to give valuable aid to the forces moving inland from Utah.

Chaos reigned in the Cotentin that night. Everywhere the paratroops – their efforts supplemented by French saboteurs – were cutting the telephone lines. Even so news of the first landings got through to LXXXIV Corps HQ at St Lô:

'At 0111 hours – unforgettable moment – the field telephone rang. Something important was coming through; while listen-

Below: The crew of an RAF Bomber Command Short Stirling bomber pose with their aircraft. Stirlings were also used as transports and glider tugs by the airborne forces.

ing to it, the General [Marcks] stood up stiffly, his hand gripping the edge of the table. With a nod, he beckoned his Chief of Staff to listen in. "Enemy parachute troops dropped east of the Orne estuary. Main area Breville–Ranville and the north edge of the Bavent Forest. Countermeasures are in progress." '

This message, which came from 716th Division (Lieutenant General W Richter) galvanized Marcks' HQ. 'The Corps Command post resembled a disturbed beehive,' wrote one of its staff officers, 'Priority messages were sent in all directions.' Marcks, in no doubt that this was the invasion, sent out the signal 'Alarm coast,' and between 0111 hours and dawn the warning went by field telephones to his units and formations. The information was passed to OKW (Armed Forces High Command) and to von Rundstedt's GHQ.

At OKW Field Marshal Wilhelm Keitel thought that the landing in Normandy must be a diversion. The real invasion would come at Calais. He was not going to wake the Führer for a false alarm. A better general than he, von Rundstedt, also believed this was a diversion and that the real blow was still to come – in the Pas de Calais.

In the prevailing confusion it was not strange that some of the generals on both sides simply did not know what was going on. Falley of the 91st Airborne Division went to find out for himself and was ambushed by American paratroops. This was reported to Ridgway whose comment was:

'Well, in our present situation, killing Divisional Commanders does not strike me as being particularly hilarious.'

Below left: Dead American soldiers await burial at Ste Mère Eglise. Total Allied casualties by the end of August were 209,672.
Bottom: Allied troops mopping up at Breville after a night assault against the village on 12 June.
Below: German dead collected for burial at Ste Mère Eglise on 7 June were among the 80,783 casualties suffered by Army Group B that month.

3. BREACHING THE ATLANTIC WALL

As the assault fleet butted its way through the gale in the Channel, and the airborne divisions flew into France, the heavy bombers of Bomber Command set off to attack the 10 most dangerous coast-defense batteries. Three of them had to be attacked early on, for Allied airborne troops would be landing near them soon after midnight. These were the Merville battery and those at Fontenay and St Martin de Varreville in the Cotentin. The other seven were to be bombed between 0315–0500 hours, so that they would scarcely have time to recover before dawn, when the naval bombardment would begin. These were the batteries at La Pernelle, Maisy, Pointe du Hoe, Longues, Mont Fleury, Ouistreham and Houlgate.

On average each battery received 500 tons of bombs delivered by about 100 aircraft. Of 1056 Lancaster, Halifax and Mosquito aircraft 11 did not return and 70 crew were lost.

Right: The British battleship HMS *Rodney* bombards the German defenses near Caen. Her main armament comprised nine 16-inch guns, supplemented by 12 6-inch guns.

Above: Armorers of the USAAF Eighth Air Force with 0.5-inch machine guns and belts of ammunition in front of a North American P-51D Mustang fighter.
Right: Boeing B-17 Flying Fortresses fly in formation over England.

L

L
297059
S

Right: The bridge over the Seine at Mantes was badly damaged by Allied bombers in a campaign aimed at isolating the invasion beachhead from reinforcements.
Far right: French refugees hastily evacuated the invasion area to escape Allied bombardment.
Below: Supermarine Spitfires were used to spot the fall of naval shells. This aircraft was flown by US Navy Squadron VCS-7.

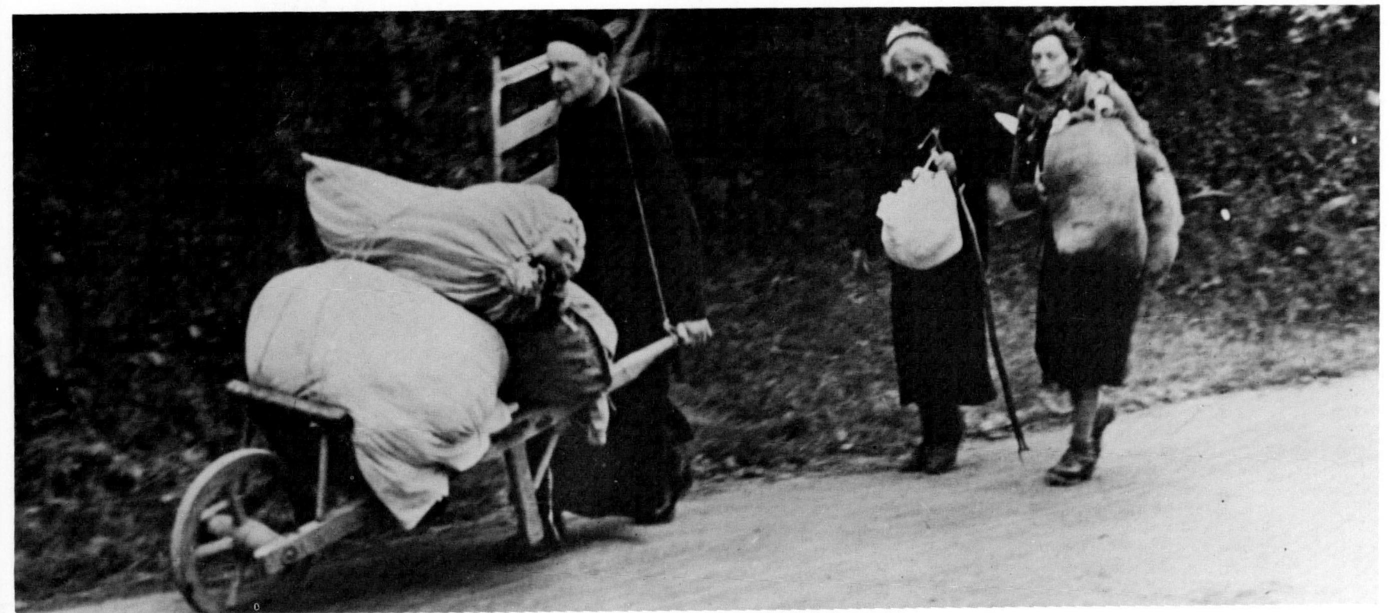

Meanwhile in the ships and landing craft the invaders were spending a truly horrible night, thrown about by the violence of the gale, and for the most part seasick. As their craft pitched and rolled veterans of Sicily took what comfort they could from the thought that rough weather tended to put the Germans off their guard. Indeed, both at sea and in the air the Germans remained totally inactive. No aircraft seems to have spotted the assault fleet streaming into the Channel as darkness fell. No watcher on the coast of Normandy seems to have observed the Allied minesweepers at work.

Meanwhile two bomber squadrons, fitted with radar-jamming equipment, were masking the Germans' warning system. To add to the confusion dummy airborne landings were being made at Mattot, Marigny and Yvetot, the last being intended to suggest that an attack north of the Seine was planned. Feints by motor launches and aircraft were made near Boulogne and in the Dieppe and le Havre area, but there seems to have been little enemy reaction.

Soon after 0500 hours the British bombarding squadrons, guided in by the midget submarines *X20* and *X23* which were flashing green lights to seaward, began to take up their positions, and at about 0530 hours the fleet opened fire. Fifty miles of the Normandy coast rocked as salvo after salvo of heavy shells tore into the fortifications of the West Wall, and as ton after ton of bombs hailed down from the sky. One can imagine the Germans, many of them alerted soon after midnight by messages from LXXXIV Corps, peering through the loopholes of their fortifications and trying, despite smoke and debris, to make out the ships and craft bearing down upon the beaches.

The bombardment fell upon the German defenders and the French inhabitants alike. The French, for the most part, stayed in their homes, even when these overlooked the beaches. At Ver sur Mer an elderly couple was found dead in bed, without a scratch on either of them. On 6 June 1944 an enormous weight of bombs and shells was delivered in the space of a few hours. It was a crucial phase of the operation and, of course, a tremendous encouragement to the men in the landing craft as they ran in, head-on, to sample whatever the West Wall might have in store for them.

With the dawn, wave after wave of day fighters began to come over, spreading out across the whole battlefield, ready to engage enemy aircraft or army reinforcements. A ceaseless patrol by four squadrons of Lightnings was kept up over the mine-free lanes which had been swept across the Channel. Thirty-six squadrons of Spitfires ensured that there were always six squadrons giving low cover over the assault area. Above the clouds, at about 8000 feet, three out of 16 squadrons of American Thunderbolts maintained a constant patrol. There were 30 reserve squadrons, which had six ready at all times as an immediate striking force. This mass of aircraft flew overhead unchallenged. Not a single German plane intervened during the first hours of the invasion. There were Dunkirk veterans in the invasion force – not very many perhaps, but some. To them the air situation was a pleasant change.

Under this unparalleled air cover the warships came in to bombard. On the exposed eastern flank HMS *Warspite, Ramillies* and *Roberts* opened fire, at about 0530 hours, with their 15-inch guns upon the batteries east of the Orne, at Villerville, Bénerville and Houlgate. It was an unforgettable sight. Battleships, cruisers, destroyers and support landing craft were engaging targets all along the British front. Admiral Krancke complained in his war diary that 'it was only to be expected that no effective blow could be struck at such a superior enemy force,' but in fact the German Navy did strike back. Allied aircraft had laid a smoke screen to shield the anchorage from the heavy batteries at Le Havre. Three enterprising German torpedo boats dashed through the screen and sank the Norwegian warship *Svenner* before disappearing into the smoke. This startling attack was the only maritime riposte the enemy made that morning.

For the most part the fire of the German Coast Defense batteries was desultory and ineffective. However, the four-gun battery at Longues, though engaged by *Ajax* at 0530 hours, opened up on the headquarters ship, *Bulolo*, at about 0600 hours. It was silenced by 0620 but it reopened fire later and compelled *Bulolo* to move seaward. The cruisers *Ajax* and *Argonaut* then took on the battery. It received 179 shells, and two of its guns were put out of action by direct hits through the embrasures. By 0845 hours the battery was silenced. The Bénerville battery, though silenced at the outset by *Ramillies*, opened up later and compelled *Warspite* to move her berth. To their credit it must be said that there were some determined German fighters at Longues and Bénerville.

By this time a fantastic regatta had begun. All along the front the assault craft were manned and lowered into the choppy sea for the final run in. In the American sector 269 medium bombers, Marauders of the Ninth Air Force, flew over to blast the defenses of Utah and silenced most of them. Bad visibility over the other beaches precluded pinpoint visual attacks on batteries and strong points. Instead wave after wave of aircraft flew in, in line abreast, releasing their bombs on the orders of pathfinders aiming by instruments.

About five minutes before H-hour some 38,000 five-inch explosive rockets deluged the beaches. They were fired electrically from assault craft, each of which was capable of launching 1000 rockets in 90 seconds. As their salvoes finished exploding the first seaborne soldiers of the invading armies set foot on shore.

4. OMAHA AND UTAH

The American landings were made on Utah and Omaha. Utah proved to be the easiest landing, and Omaha the most difficult of the whole Allied assault. The Utah beaches, on the east coast of the Cotentin, were assailed by VII Corps under Lieutenant General J L Collins. The Omaha beaches, between Vire and Port en Bessin were attacked by V Corps under Lieutenant General L T Gerow.

The Americans had decided to go in at 0630 hours, about an hour earlier than the British owing to the difference in tides. At low tide it would be easier to clear the obstacles. The naval bombardment was not to open until 0550, 20 minutes later than on the British front. The defenses on the beaches where the British landed suffered two hours bombardment before H-Hour, as opposed to only 40 minutes on the American front. With the benefit of hindsight Admiral Kirk, commanding the Western Task Force commented that:

'the period of bombardment was extremely heavy but was of too short duration to silence or neutralize all the defenses, particularly in the Omaha area.'

Rear Admiral Hall was of the same opinion:

'the time available for the prelanding bombardment was not sufficient for the destruction of beach defense targets.'

Another major difference between the American and British plans was the choice of the lowering positions ('transport areas'), where the troops transferred from ships into landing craft. The American lowering position was 11 miles from the coast, the British only seven. The American soldiers running in to Utah and Omaha had to put

Below: US infantrymen wade ashore from their landing craft, which has grounded on Utah Beach.
Below right: Survivors from a landing craft sunk off Utah Beach are helped ashore.

up with three hours in small craft in rougher conditions than any they had met with during training. For those approaching Utah this was not so bad for their run in was sheltered under the lee of the Cotentin peninsula. Force U had one piece of bad luck. It ran into an undetected minefield, and lost the navigational leader of the left-hand assault group, which had four DD (amphibious) tanks aboard, and the destroyer *Corry*.

The US 4th Infantry Division made the opening attacks on Utah. By mistake the landings all took place on the southern part of the beach which happened to be less well defended. The landing began punctually at 0630 hours against slight opposition, which was quickly overcome. The 28 DD tanks still available swam in 3000 yards and landed safely some minutes behind the infantry. The engineers and naval demolition parties set to work to destroy the beach obstacles, and cleared them within an hour, giving landing craft a clear run in. This was an achievement which could not be paralleled anywhere else on the whole front.

Above: The forward 14-inch guns of USS *Nevada* in action.
Left: Minesweepers clearing the approaches to Utah.

Above: A German soldier lies dead before the pillbox that he defended on Utah Beach. Preliminary bombardment left these defenses largely undamaged.
Above right: By the evening of D-day the beaches had become crowded with men and equipment.
Right: Wounded American troops are evacuated from the beaches by an LCM (Landing Craft, Mechanized).

The infantry now pushed inland with the object of capturing the causeway roads leading to Pouppeville, Ste Marie du Mont and Audouville la Hubert. Meanwhile, follow-up troops, vehicles and equipment were coming in unopposed, their movement inland was delayed only by the lack of beach exits and the need to breach the sea wall separating the land from the shore.

The first contact between American seaborne and airborne troops took place near Pouppeville, which was attacked at about 0800 hours by a small party of parachutists. Some of the garrison held out until noon.

By 1000 hours there were six battalions ashore and progress inland was delayed by flooding rather than German opposition. This is not to say that there was no resistance. Still, by a combination of accidents some of the leading assault craft missed the stronger German defenses. The mining of the vessel guiding them in and the strong current sweeping down the shoreline brought them in several miles south of of their planned landing place. Brigadier General Theodore Roosevelt Jr, a veteran aged 57 who had persuaded his Divisional Commander to let him go ashore 'to steady the boys,' took the vital decision to push inland, deepening the beachhead for the follow-up troops. Ably supported by Commodore James Arnold, the naval officer in charge of the beachhead, he solved the traffic problem, bringing in

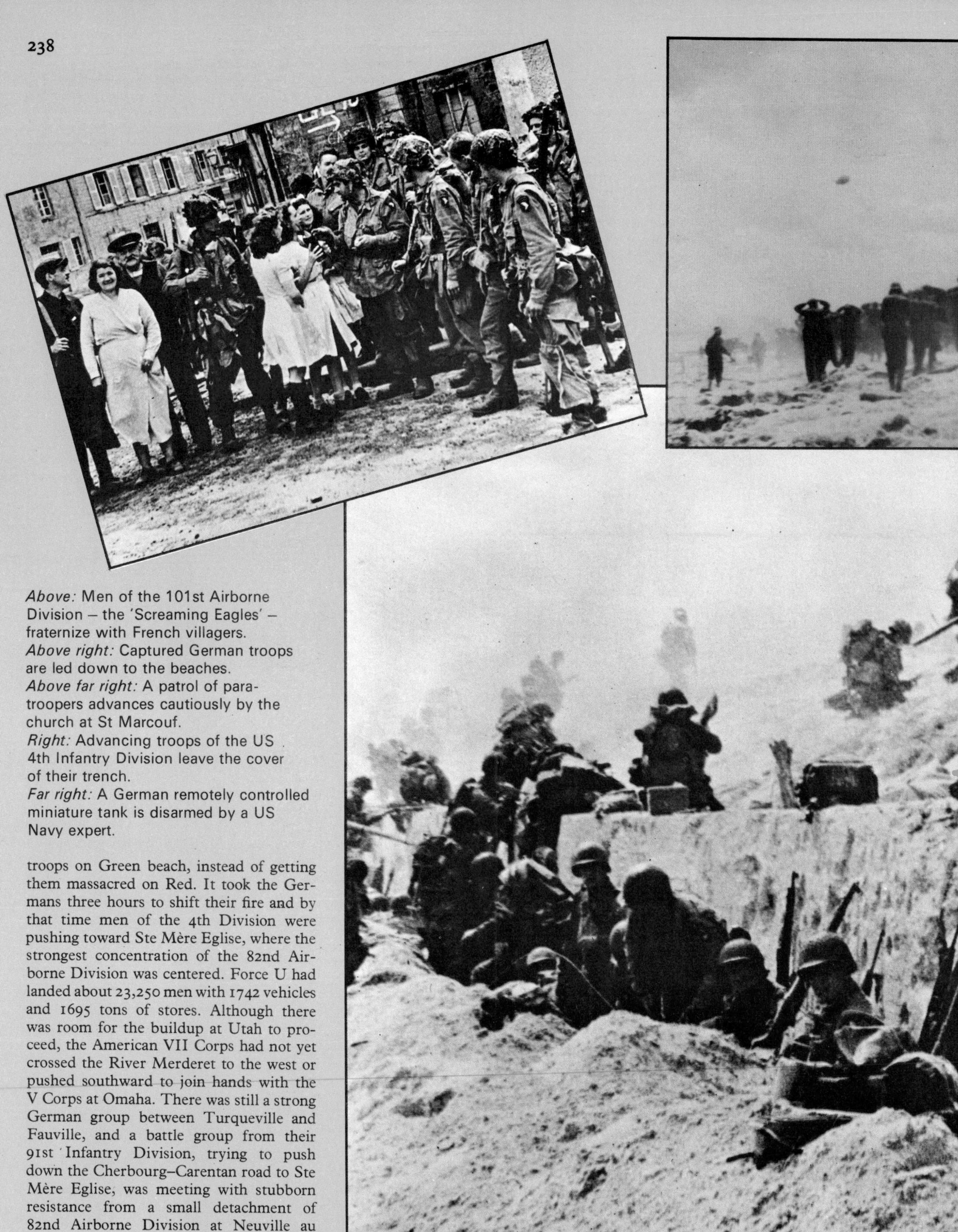

Above: Men of the 101st Airborne Division – the 'Screaming Eagles' – fraternize with French villagers.
Above right: Captured German troops are led down to the beaches.
Above far right: A patrol of paratroopers advances cautiously by the church at St Marcouf.
Right: Advancing troops of the US 4th Infantry Division leave the cover of their trench.
Far right: A German remotely controlled miniature tank is disarmed by a US Navy expert.

troops on Green beach, instead of getting them massacred on Red. It took the Germans three hours to shift their fire and by that time men of the 4th Division were pushing toward Ste Mère Eglise, where the strongest concentration of the 82nd Airborne Division was centered. Force U had landed about 23,250 men with 1742 vehicles and 1695 tons of stores. Although there was room for the buildup at Utah to proceed, the American VII Corps had not yet crossed the River Merderet to the west or pushed southward to join hands with the V Corps at Omaha. There was still a strong German group between Turqueville and Fauville, and a battle group from their 91st Infantry Division, trying to push down the Cherbourg–Carentan road to Ste Mère Eglise, was meeting with stubborn resistance from a small detachment of 82nd Airborne Division at Neuville au Plain.

The 101st Airborne Division was having a difficult time. Of 32 gliders bringing reinforcements, 11 landed in or near Hiesville as planned, but many crashed or fell into the hands of the Germans. Although

detachments covered the bridges at La Barquette and near Brévands, between the sea and Carentan, two battalions of the German 6th Parachute Division, counter-attacking from that town, had infiltrated between them and the rest of the 101st Division.

The landing craft plowing toward Omaha were buffeted by a stronger wind and rougher seas than Force U had encountered off Utah. The land behind the sand dunes at Utah is only a few feet above sea level, but the Omaha beaches are overlooked by bluffs which rise in places to 150 feet and command the beaches. Whereas the Utah defenses had been well and truly battered from air and sea, those at Omaha had been missed by the bombers. They were protected from seaward and the 40-minute naval bombardment had been unable to silence the guns. To make matters worse the German troops at Omaha, the 352nd Infantry Division, were not only more numerous than those of the static 709th Division defending Utah, they were also better soldiers. Moreover, their defensive position, naturally strong, had been skillfully fortified. There were eight big guns in concrete bunkers, 35 antitank guns in pillboxes, and 85 machine guns, sited to cover three rows of obstacles on the beach below the high-water mark. The four exits from the beach and a belt of shingle, in itself a tank obstacle, had been made more difficult to cross by mines and wire. Within a mile to the rear lay three strongpoints, the fortified villages of Colleville sur Mer, St Laurent sur Mer and Vierville sur Mer, giving depth to the position. Beyond them was the flooded valley of the River Aure.

The 12-mile run in to Omaha began in darkness and there was no little confusion in the transport area. Landing craft straggled before they crossed the line of departure. Two, carrying artillery, had actually foundered before reaching the transport areas. Of the 32 DD tanks, launched 6000 yards offshore, 27 foundered in the rough seas. Landing craft carried 51 to the shore, but

Right: Troops huddle on the deck of a LCVP heading for Omaha Beach. This craft could carry 36 troops, plus a vehicle.
Far right: The last moments of LCI-85, a US Coast Guard craft sunk by German shell fire.
Bottom: The battleship USS *Arkansas* was part of Bombarding Force C, assigned to Omaha Beach.
Below: Troops file down the ramp of a Landing Craft Infantry (LCI).

eight of these were knocked out by gunfire. Not less than 10 of the craft carrying infantry were swamped on the run in, and 22 howitzers and an infantry cannon company were lost. The weather was too much for the DUKWs (amphibious trucks), which carried them, and so the infantry struggled ashore without most of the artillery which was supposed to support it, and without tanks.

The Germans held their fire as the assault craft came in. As soon as the first reached the shore, the defenders opened up with a tremendous fire of guns, mortars and machine guns. A landing craft carrying 35 men was hit by four mortar bombs and simply vanished. Men from another craft, which foundered 1000 yards offshore, were dragged down by the weight of their equipment. The scattered troops, wading ashore, not always with the units to which they belonged, ran into a hail of bullets and sought such cover as they could find. Some tried to conceal themselves behind the German beach obstacles. Others lay in the water and crept in with the rising tide. Nine companies went into the assault. Two bunched in front of Les Moulins, and elements of four got ashore in the Colleville sector. One company was carried far to the east and landed an hour and a half late. The demolition teams had particularly

great many other vehicles burning. The defensive fire of his men had been excellent. He could see the dead and wounded lying in the sand. Even so, at about 0730 hours little parties of determined men had begun to struggle through the barbed wire and were working their way inland through the minefields. Eight United States and three British destroyers gave invaluable fire support at this dangerous period. The tide of battle was turning.

By 0900 hours small groups of American soldiers, which had infiltrated the German posts along the crest, were gradually wiping them out and making their way toward St Laurent and Vierville. Units from 29th and 1st Divisions gathered by Colleville, and with covering fire from a destroyer, had made a gap in the wire and were storming an enemy strongpoint. They had got going again because the officers and non-commissioned officers knew that 'leadership is done from in front.' One, who is deservedly remembered, was Colonel Canham, 'They're murdering us here,' he said to men cowering on the beach, 'Let's move inland and get murdered.'

At about 1000 hours Major General C R Huebner, the assault commander, intervened decisively. He held back the waves of vehicles, whose arrival on the beaches could only add to the confusion, and sent in more combat troops. In response to his call for naval gunfire support, destroyers ran in to within 1000 yards of the shore.

A battalion of the 1st Division, veterans of Sicily and Salerno, fought their way through the minefields to attack Colleville. The 29th Division, which was having a very rough time, infiltrated as far as Vierville and St Laurent. About noon the German gunners began to run out of ammunition and, because of the Allied command of the air, convoys could not get through to replenish it.

Meanwhile three companies of US Rangers were carrying out a bold and unusual exploit against the battery at Pointe du Hoe. They scaled the cliffs with ropes and ladders and, with covering fire from two destroyers, *Satterlee* (US) and *Talybont* (British), stormed the position only to find that the guns had been removed and concealed inland.

There was a time during that morning when a determined counterattack might have driven US V Corps into the sea. In view of the 352nd Division's optimistic reports, General Marcks sent his reserves elsewhere. By nightfall the Americans had possession of a patch of French soil some six miles long, and in places two miles deep. Reinforcements came in during the night until, with over 34,000 men ashore, the beachhead was secure.

The day's fighting had cost V Corps 3000 casualties, 50 tanks, and 26 guns. In addition 50 landing craft and 10 larger vessels were lost.

The plan for the Omaha landing left much to be desired. However, it was the infantrymen who, despite their top brass, fought and won this vital foothold.

Above left: A victim of the first assault wave, a US infantryman, lies dead beside a beach obstacle.
Above far left: Wounded troops of the US 1st Infantry Division find shelter.
Below: Landing Ships Tank (LST) discharge supplies onto Omaha Beach.

5. THE BRITISH LANDINGS

The British Sector was divided into three assault areas and 10 landing beaches, but the troops went in over only five of them. There were five Assault Brigades, or rather brigade groups, an intermediate brigade, and four follow-up brigades. In addition there was 1st SS Brigade (Commandos) and 4th SS Brigade (less 46 [RM] Commando).

The 1st Commando Brigade went in on Queen Beach, with the object of joining the 6th Airborne Division as soon as possible, although 4 Commando was first to take Ouistreham.

The 4th Commando Brigade was split up as each unit had a separate task.

	Beach	*Task*
41 (RM) Cdo	Queen	Capture Lion-sur-Mer
46 (RM) Cdo	—	Capture Houlgate Battery
47 (RM) Cdo	Jig	Take Port en Bessin
Bde HQ and 48 (RM) Cdo	Nan	Attack Langrune-sur-Mer

Between Omaha and Gold there was a 10-mile gap. The British sector, between Port en Bessin and the River Orne, stretched for 24 miles.

At midnight on 6 June many of the D-Day objectives, notably Caen, were not as yet in British hands. On the other hand the Germans were far from achieving Rommel's aim of driving the invaders straight back into the sea.

Generally speaking, the seaborne landings were successful, which is not to say that everything went according to plan. However, one way and another, and despite the worst a determined enemy could do, every group managed sooner or later to carry out its task.

The most westerly objective of any British unit was Port en Bessin, the inter-Allied boundary. This was to be attacked by 47 (RM) Commando. They had a rough landing on Gold beach near St Côme de Fresne as the majority of their 16 landing craft were hit. As the first wave waded ashore they came under such heavy machine-gun fire that one marine is said to have remarked, 'Perhaps we're intruding. This seems to be a private beach.' The Commando suffered 43 casualties in the

Above: The gunshield of a US LST, manned by the Coast Guard, is repaired before the landings.
Left: Troopers of 13th/18th Hussars come ashore on 6th June.
Top: The minesweeper USS *Tide* sank on 7 June after hitting a mine off Omaha Beach.
Top right: American assault troops shelter beneath the cliffs at Colleville-Sur-Mer.
Right: A convoy of LCIs en route to the beachhead, protected by barrage balloons.

Left: Royal Marine commandos disembark from LCIs.
Right: The Mulberry artificial harbor at Arromanches provided a much-needed sheltered anchorage for supply ships.
Bottom right: The aftermath of the D-Day assault was a litter of broken vehicles and equipment and a row of corpses.
Below: A British casualty-clearing station positioned in the shelter of a sea wall.

landing. The rest concentrated at the back of the beach, and then set off westward across country. It had a sharp fight at La Rosière in the evening, but eventually reached Point 72, a prominent hill 1.5 miles south of their objective, where they dug in for the night. They attacked the little town of Port en Bessin next day, and with some fire support from HMS *Emerald* and three squadrons of rocket-firing Typhoons gradually overcame the opposition, though with heavy casualties. Eventually, at 0400 hours on 8 June, the garrison, still 300 strong, surrendered. The little harbor was put into immediate use, and proved of great value.

The 231st Brigade, veterans of the invasion of Sicily, landed on a two-battalion front. On their front the fortified village of Le Hamel was the main German strongpoint. This was still holding out when the second wave went in at about 0815 hours, and began to press toward Arromanches les Bains. The 1st Hampshire, the right assault battalion, lost its senior officers and progress was slow and costly. However the 1st Dorset swiftly took Les Roquettes and pushed inland. Flail tanks of the Westminster Dragoons and other Funnies landed punctually and set to work clearing mines and obstacles.

The 6th Battahon Green Howards of 69th Brigade made short work of a strongpoint at Hable de Heurtot and a battery position at Mont Fleury, whose gunners had been discouraged by bombing and by 12 direct hits from HMS *Orion*. In this fighting Sergeant Major S E Hollis won the Victoria Cross.

At La Rivière the 5th Battalion East Yorks was cornered by the sea wall, but naval gunfire and a flail from the Westminster Dragoons solved the problem. The tank knocked out an 88mm gun in its bunker and 45 prisoners were taken. There followed a long, hard fight for the village, which cost 90 casualties. Two guns and 30 prisoners were taken in the strongpoint at the lighthouse near Mont Fleury. The battalion then pushed on inland toward Ver sur Mer. The 7th Battalion Green Howards passed through the assault battalions and took a battery beyond that village. It had been softened up by bombing and by HMS *Belfast*, and yielded 50 gunners, who had fired 87 rounds from their four 10cm gun howitzers, before losing heart.

The two assault brigade groups of the 50th Division, supported by DD tanks of the 4/7 Dragoon Guards and the Nottinghamshire Yeomanry were now pushing inland, and at about 1100 hours the 151st Brigade began to land over the beaches taken by the 69th Brigade. Le Hamel was still holding out, but by the early afternoon all four brigades of 50 Division were ashore. Since the oft-rehearsed counterattack of the 915th German Infantry Regiment did not come to pass, progress was fairly satisfactory, although the 56th Brigade met with opposition outside Bayeux, which, however, fell next day.

The 3rd Canadian Division Group, who had not been in action before, landed a little late due to the rough weather. Most of their DD tanks got ashore, some of them ahead of the infantry. Effective covering fire from destroyers and support craft kept the Germans quiet until the landing craft touched down. The crews behaved with great resolution and valor, driving the larger landing craft on to the shore, and worming the smaller ones through the numerous obstacles as best they could. Ninety out of 306 landing craft employed by Force J were lost or damaged.

Courseulles, one of the main German positions on the Canadian front, held out stubbornly against the Regina Rifles, and there was fierce street fighting until well into the afternoon.

The Winnipeg Rifles, the reserve battalion of the 7th Canadian Brigade, avoided Courseulles and made good progress. They took Vaux and Ste Croix sur Mer.

Bernières, like Courseulles, was a hard nut to crack. The sea wall was 12 feet high in places, and behind it there were many fortified houses. Some had been demolished by naval gunfire, but the strongpoint was still a formidable one. Its infantry garrison had the support of two 50mm antitank guns, two heavy mortars and eight machine guns. The Queen's Own Rifles were enfiladed as they dashed across the beach, and suffered heavy losses. However, once they had outflanked the position by storming the sea wall, the defenders gave up. St Aubin sur Mer held out for three hours against the North Shore Regiment and assault engineers' tanks, and sniping went on until night fell.

By 1400 hours the whole Canadian Division was ashore: infantry, artillery and armor. The narrow strip of beach, uncovered by the rising tide, was choked with troops and vehicles, while damaged landing craft littered the water's edge. Congestion on the beaches, and in Bernières, delayed the Canadians. When they tried to debouch into the open, undulating country beyond they were met by the fire of 88s and machine guns. Between Rivière and Bernières there were 11 antitank guns, belonging to the 716th Division, disposed across the path of the Canadians within a mile of the coast. Even so the 7th Canadian Brigade made good progress, taking Banville and Ste Croix sur Mer, and 'hordes of prisoners.' By 1600 hours they were across the Seulles. Three companies of the 726th Infantry Regiment had departed in disorder at their approach.

Near Fontaine-Henry the Regina Rifles, supported by tanks, came under heavy fire from 88s, but pushed on and took Le Fresne-Camilly.

The 8th Canadian Brigade took a battery 1000 yards west of Tailleville, bypassing another with 80 rockets, whose cables had been cut by the bombing so that they could not be fired. By 1430 hours, Bény sur Mer had fallen with 50 prisoners and a battery of the 1716th Artillery Regiment (4 10cm guns) which had received more than 200 5.25-inch shells from HMS *Diadem*. At Tailleville a battalion HQ with a company of the 736th Grenadier Regiment held out in fortified houses connected by tunnels. It was late in the afternoon before the place was in the hands of the North Shore Regiment.

Thus the two leading Canadian brigades had advanced four or five miles inland. By 1430 hours the reserve brigade (9th) had made its way through Bernières and assembled south of the town. Its objective was Carpiquet, 10 miles away. It was not until after 1900 hours that the brigade reached Bèny sur Mer, though some of the North Nova Scotia Highlanders, lifted on tanks of the 27th Canadian Armored Regiment, arrived in the dusk at Villons les Buissons, after capturing some mortars and antitank guns. There was German armor, from 21st Panzer, between this force and the British 3rd Division. The Canadians were ordered to form a 'fortress' round the crossroads, where the road from Anisy to

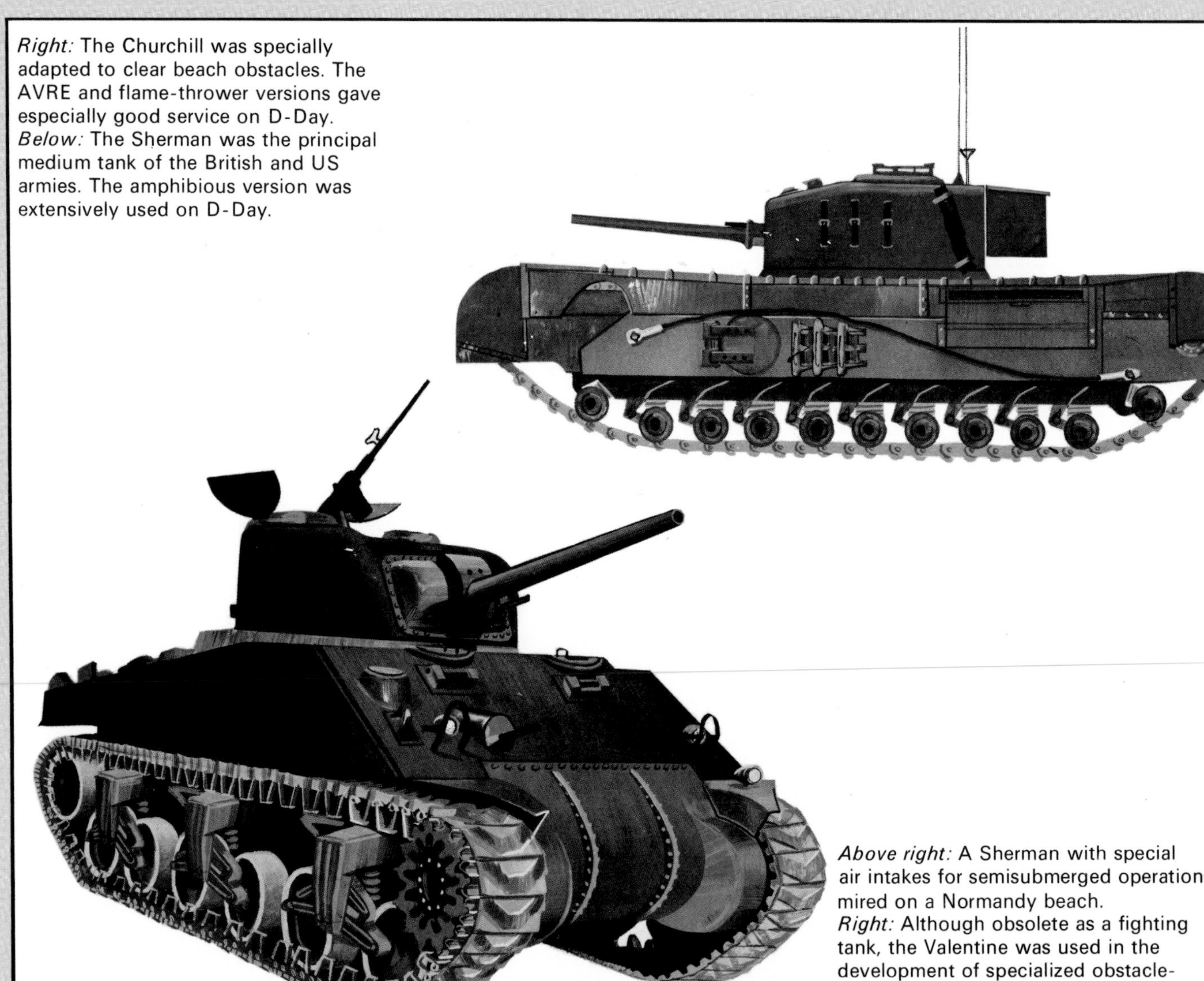

Right: The Churchill was specially adapted to clear beach obstacles. The AVRE and flame-thrower versions gave especially good service on D-Day.
Below: The Sherman was the principal medium tank of the British and US armies. The amphibious version was extensively used on D-Day.

Above right: A Sherman with special air intakes for semisubmerged operations mired on a Normandy beach.
Right: Although obsolete as a fighting tank, the Valentine was used in the development of specialized obstacle-clearing AFVs.

Villons les Buissons crosses that from Courseulles to Caen.

Considering the congestion at Bernières the inexperienced but hardy Canadians did rather well on D-Day, though it is true that they were not counterattacked. Their armor had been particularly successful, knocking out a dozen or more of the dreaded 88s. Two troops of the 1st Hussars had actually reached the objective, the Bayeux–Caen road. However, they lacked infantry support and were compelled to fall back to their squadron.

The HQ of the 4th SS Brigade and 48 Commando encountered difficulties landing on Nan Beach (Juno) at about 0900 hours. Five of their six landing craft struck mines and one was hit by shellfire; two of them sank. A 'heavy swell and a vicious tidal stream . . . carried away and drowned men attempting to swim.' The beach defenses had survived the preliminary bombardment, but with the cover of a smoke screen the Commandos reached the cover of a low cliff and the sea wall, to find themselves among:

'a jumble of men from other units, including many wounded and dead; the beach was congested with tanks, heavy propelled guns and other vehicles . . . Tank landing craft were arriving all the time and attempting to land their loads, added to the general confusion.'

Y Troop, whose officers had become casualties, was taken back to England by a tank landing craft which had picked it up when its own craft had sunk. It was unable to rejoin its unit until two weeks later. Z Troop, some 40 strong, landed thanks to a stout-hearted leading seaman, who ferried men ashore in two lifts.

No 48 Commando, now only some 200 strong, took Langrune but was then held by a strongpoint near the shore. With the aid of a Sherman tank this was taken at about 1600 hours on 7 June. Two officers and 33 men of the 736th Grenadier Regiment laid down their arms. They had made a very creditable defense.

The 3rd Division, which Montgomery had commanded in the Dunkirk campaign, was the one with which he had first made his name. He never concealed his view that it was much better trained than the others in the BEF, and it had certainly proved itself a very useful formation. It must be said, however, that it was not really any better than other divisions, for example 1st and 4th, whose commanders were disinclined to publicize their exploits.

Since 1940 the 3rd Division had spent four years training in England, without any taste of active service. That it was thoroughly trained will be obvious. It may be that it had reached, and indeed passed, the point when it was overtrained. It is possible, though this is not a criticism which can be applied to *all* the units of the division, that it was a bit 'stale.'

The British 3rd Division, under Major General T G Rennie, was to attack on a front of one brigade. It landed on Queen Beach and spread out to cover the 2.5 miles between Lion sur Mer and Ouistreham. Both places were well fortified and about halfway between them was a strongpoint at La Brèche, bristling with wire,

Above: A German flak ship sunk in Port-en-Bessin harbor.
Right: A bulldozer demolishes defense works at Port-en-Bessin.

machine guns, mortars and the usual guns in casemates. The countryside was flat. On the north side of the coast road was a fairly high ridge of sand crowned with a more or less continuous row of houses.

The 8th Brigade landed on time and in the right place. Fire support was effective, but as the craft neared the shore the Germans opened up. Most of the DD tanks of the 13th/18th Hussars were launched at sea, and though 10 were knocked out in the surf, or soon after, 28 were left to support the infantry. The armored vehicles of the assault engineers landed with the leading wave and were the only supporting troops available from the very outset.

Here as elsewhere the crews of the landing craft showed the utmost determination. Of 18 craft that carried the self-propelled guns of the 7th, 33rd and 76th Field Regiments Royal Artillery, 14 became total wrecks; five from the effects of obstacles, three from mines and six from enemy fire. Miraculous though it may seem the 20 landing craft carrying the first infantry wave of 8th Brigade all got ashore without a casualty at 0730 hours. The leading companies of 1st South Lancashire and 2nd East Yorkshire Regiments began to attack the La Brèche strongpoint and to clear the houses along the dunes. 41 (RM) Commando (4th SS Brigade), which suffered heavy casualties on the beach, set off to attack Lion sur Mer. It made some progress, but the place was not finally subdued until next day, when a battalion of the Lincolnshire Regiment attacked it.

Along with two French troops of 10 (Inter-Allied) Commando, 4 Commando landed at 0820 hours on the heels of 8th Brigade, which they found 'pinned to the beach by intense fire.' The Commando passed through them, and took a pillbox which had been causing casualties. Then, led by the French troops under Commandant Kieffer, they moved against the defenses of Ouistreham. A French gendarme, who met them, rendered invaluable service by pointing out the various German positions. After severe hand-to-hand fighting 4 Commando, with the support of four Centaur tanks from the Royal Marine Armored Support Regiment, took the Riva Bella battery, though not without heavy casualties.

A superb unit, 6 Commando, set off to blaze a trail inland and join hands with the 6th Airborne at the Bénouville bridge. 3 and 45 (RM) Commandos were to go in at H+90 and to follow 6 Commando. With the exception of 45 Commando, which was going into action for the first time, the 1st Commando Brigade was rather more experienced than most of the Allied troops who landed on D-Day. 4 Commando had stormed the Varengeville battery at Dieppe, 6 Commando had fought with great distinction in North Africa, and 3 had been at Vaagso, Dieppe, and the landings in Sicily and Italy.

Neither the La Brèche strongpoint nor Ouistreham had been subdued when at about 0900 hours the five landing craft infantry (LCI) carrying 3 Commando arrived 1000 yards from the beach and hove to within easy range of quite a number of German guns. They formed a line abreast with the precision worthy of a ceremonial parade.

Above: French sailors from the invasion fleet in Port-en-Bessin.
Left: The Tricolor flies over Port-en-Bessin again.
Below: Commandos push inland from the beaches.
Bottom: 6th Royal Scots Fusiliers during the breakout from the beachhead.

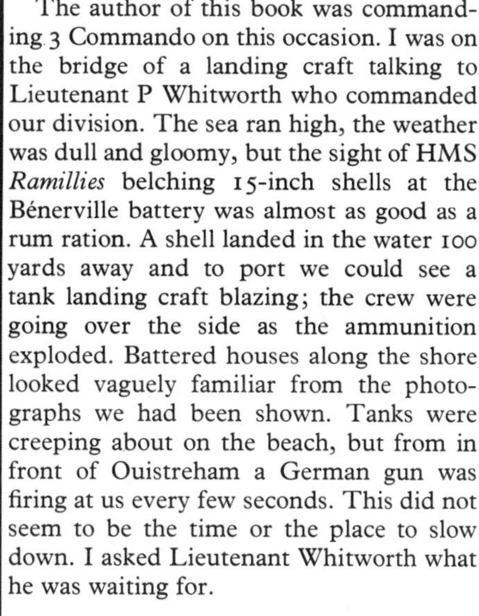

The author of this book was commanding 3 Commando on this occasion. I was on the bridge of a landing craft talking to Lieutenant P Whitworth who commanded our division. The sea ran high, the weather was dull and gloomy, but the sight of HMS *Ramillies* belching 15-inch shells at the Bénerville battery was almost as good as a rum ration. A shell landed in the water 100 yards away and to port we could see a tank landing craft blazing; the crew were going over the side as the ammunition exploded. Battered houses along the shore looked vaguely familiar from the photographs we had been shown. Tanks were creeping about on the beach, but from in front of Ouistreham a German gun was firing at us every few seconds. This did not seem to be the time or the place to slow down. I asked Lieutenant Whitworth what he was waiting for.

'There are still five minutes to go before H+90,' he said with admirable sang froid.

'I don't think anyone will mind,' I replied, 'if we're five minutes *early* on D-Day.'

'Then in we go.'

We set off in a beautiful line, and not a moment too soon. Another shell. An air-burst just ahead; the bits that reached us had lost all force. Then the next craft to starboard was hit, and seemed to shy like a horse. As we beached the gun at Ouistreham hit us and many of my men were up to their necks in water before they could struggle out of the hold.

The 4th division got all its five craft ashore, though three were hit and two completely wrecked. Such was the spirit of the RNVR, who put us ashore on D-Day. The commando lost about 30 men, mostly from the explosion of our own mortar bombs in one of the stricken craft. The first man ashore was Major J E Martin, our veteran administrative officer, who, as a trooper in the 9th Lancers, had had his baptism of fire on the Western Front in the year that I was born. He went right through – from Normandy to the Baltic.

There were quite a lot of infantry sitting about on the beach, and one cried out, 'Don't touch the bloody wire, it's mined.' We sorted ourselves out among the houses on the dunes, undisturbed except for a little indiscriminate mortar fire. Ahead lay 1000 yards of flat marshy meadow without a vestige of cover.

This, the first stage of our journey to the Bénouville bridges, was covered by a German quick-firing gun, but we survived its attentions more or less unscathed and pushed on to our forming-up place. Nearby we found a company commander of the assault brigade. He had his CSM (Company Sergeant Major) and two men with him. The rest, I rather thought, might be the men we had seen sitting on the beach.

Below: King George VI shakes the hand of Lt Col Peter Young, who commanded No 3 Commando during the Normandy invasion.

La Brèche fell at about 1000 hours, after causing the assault brigade heavy casualties. The beaches were still under fire from guns inland, some of them beyond the Orne, but the 185th and 9th Brigades were able to come ashore during the morning and early afternoon. During the morning the 8th Brigade took Hermanville and Colleville and attacked two strongpoints, Morris and Hillman, a mile beyond. The first, which had suffered from air and naval bombardment, surrendered with 67 men and four field guns as soon as the attack began. The second, which was the well-sited HQ of 736th Regiment, held out until 2000 hours.

By about 1100 hours the infantry of 185th Brigade Group had assembled in woods about half a mile inland. Its vehicles, and heavy weapons, however, were held up by congestion on the beaches and by minefields. So at about 1230 hours the foot soldiers set off without them, reaching Périers ridge at about 1400 hours. Here they were joined by the leading tanks of the Staffordshire Yeomanry. There were German guns in the woods to their right, and these knocked out five tanks. They had to be ejected. The Staffordshire occupied a feature called Point 61, as a flank guard and base of fire, and the rest of the column moved on in the direction of Caen. It was some hours before the main body of the brigade got going. At 1500 hours 1st Battalion Royal Norfolk was ordered to secure high ground on the left of 2nd Battalion King's Shropshire Light Infantry. They thought St Aubin d'Arquenay was still in German hands, though in fact the Commando Brigade – including the present writer – went through it at about noon, making for Bénouville. Under this misapprehension the Norfolks moved through a large field, where, sadly, they soon lost 150 casualties to the machine guns of Hillman. It was not until 1900 hours that Beauville and Biéville were in British hands. The 2nd Battalion Royal Warwickshire, ordered to advance late in the afternoon, occupied St Aubin d'Arquenay at about 1800 hours – at least six hours after the Commandos had passed through. Opinions will differ as to whether this lack of urgency should be attributed to brigade or battalion.

Hesitation, at the highest level, afflicted the opposition. At 1432 hours Army Group B at last received permission – 12 hours after it had been requested – to move up 12th SS Panzer in support of Seventh Army. At 1507 hours authority was received to move Waffen SS 1 Panzer Corps and Panzer *Lehr* Division. General Dollmann (Seventh Army) ordered Lieutenant General Bayerlein (Panzer *Lehr*) to move on Caen at 1700 hours. The latter, with memories of the RAF in the Western Desert, urged that it was foolish to move before nightfall, but Dollmann, determined to attack at dawn on 7 July, would have none of this. Before Bayerlein and his HQ had passed Beaumont sur Sarthe the bombs began to fall. A nightmare move followed, with Allied aircraft striking at every bottleneck on the five routes by which the long columns of vehicles were struggling to advance. Bayerlein wrote:

'At 2300 we drove through Sées. The place was lit up by flares hanging above it like candles on a Christmas tree, and heavy bombs were crashing down on the houses which were already burning. But we managed to get through.'

Meanwhile Feuchtinger had made his counterattack against 3rd Division. Under the continuous air attack requested by Dempsey, the 21st Panzer had crossed the Orne. By this time the 8th Brigade at Hermanville, Colleville sur Orne and Ouistreham was fairly well set, though 2nd Battalion East Yorkshire was occupied with a battery (Daimler) south of Ouistreham, and 1st Battalion Suffolk with the Hillman strongpoint. The 9th Brigade was assembling just inland of the beach, but was not yet ready to advance into the gap between the Canadians and Hermanville. The main body of 185th Brigade was moving on Caen. The 2nd Battalion King's Shropshire Light Infantry (KSLI) with a squadron of tanks (Staffordshire Yeomanry) and some antitank guns, were at Beuville and Biéville. It must be said that KSLI seem to have had a real sense of the need to thrust forward on D-Day.

Soon after 1600 hours German tanks were reported moving up from Caen. A squadron supporting 1st Battalion Suffolk at Hillman was immediately moved to Biéville. No sooner had it taken up its position than 40 German tanks, moving very fast, came in from the west. The Staffordshire Yeomanry knocked out two with their 6-pounders. The rest sheared off into the woods. When they reappeared they suffered more casualties. Veering off once more, they were reinforced, and working round the right (western) flank approached the Périers ridge. They ran into the squadron, which had been positioned at Point 61 for just such an eventuality. The Germans lost three more tanks, and once again retired. They were now known by the British to have lost 13 tanks at a cost of one

Above: This baby was born during the Allied bombardment of Caen.
Top left: A stretcher bearer of the Durham Light Infantry tends a wounded German soldier.
Left: A British sniper takes cover by the roadside at Tilly-sur-Seulles.
Top right: An Allied motor convoy winds through the narrow streets of Bayeux on its way to the front.
Right: The ruins of Caen after its capture on 9 July.

self-propelled gun. In fact Feuchtinger's losses were much heavier. According to him he began the day with 124 tanks, of which 54 were knocked out by nightfall. Eight Typhoons of the Second Tactical Air Force had accounted for six by dive bombing them on the outskirts of Caen. The division was nearly out of gasoline.

The repulse of 21st Panzer is very much to the credit of 3rd Division, and if they may be criticized for slowness, they deserve credit for their staunch conduct in the face of this dangerous counterattack.

The Commando Brigade joined hands with the 6th Airborne Division at about midday, the first commandos arriving on folding bicycles. Lovat sent them with all speed to relieve 9th Parachute Battalion and secure the Amfreville–Le Plein ridge, which overlooked the 3rd Division's area.

'We reached the bridges to find that they were under a desultory fire from a building perhaps 800 yards to the south. A group belonging to my bicycle troop were taking cover under the low bank to the left of the road.

I told them to get on their bikes and go across flat out. One was shot clean through the head. The rest got through. Now it was our turn, and we showed a very pretty turn of speed.

Lord Lovat came up, and told me that our planned move to Cabourg was off. We were to occupy Le Bas de Ranville so as to protect the HQ of the 6th Airborne Division and to block the German armor coming from the south. As we have seen the 21st Panzer did not turn up, which was just as well for we had not much in the way of antitank weapons. So we passed a peaceful afternoon in the June sunshine.'

At about 2100 hours some 240 gliders, towed by transport aircraft, came flying in low over the coast to land at Bénouville and Ranville. It was an astonishing sight. At a stroke the effective strength of the 6th Airborne Division was doubled. The reinforcements included two strong battalions and the reconnaissance regiment as well as some artillery. The effect on the morale of both sides was marked.

The telephone log of the German Seventh Army records, 'Attack by the 21st Panzer Division rendered useless by heavily concentrated airborne troops.' Rommel's HQ was told that the 21st Panzer had 'been halted by renewed air landings.' The sight of this massed air landing taking place in their rear was naturally very discouraging to the Germans and led them to call off their counterattack. The Panzers fell back to a position between the KSLI and Caen. At midnight Seventh Army's signals diary summed up the situation in the Caen area:

'2400 hours. 716st Infantry Division is still defending itself at strongpoints. Communications between division, regimental and battalion headquarters, however, no longer exist, so that nothing is known as to the number of strongpoints still holding out or of those liquidated. . . . The Chief of Staff of Seventh Army gives the order that the counterattack of 7 June must reach the coast without fail, since the strongpoint defenders expect it of us.'

They were due for a disappointment.

6. A FATEFUL DAY

Why did the Allies win the battle of D-Day? Was Montgomery a greater general than von Rundstedt? Why did the Germans, with some 40 divisions at their disposal, get so many of them in the wrong places that the Allies were able to fight their way ashore, and stay there?

It must be remembered that in the first place the Allies had complete command in the air. In the second they had absolute command at sea. In the third, though Montgomery was not without fault he was probably a much better general than von Rundstedt, besides being more than a match for Rommel. He was, moreover, nobly supported by Bradley and Dempsey.

If the Allies had the advantage in the air and at sea, the Germans should have had a tremendous advantage on land, for they had far more divisions and, especially, many more Panzer divisions. Moreover their men were, on the whole, much more experienced than the Allies'. They were well led at every level.

The key point is that for one reason and another the German commanders were in two minds as to the significance of the reports that reached their headquarters. At 0215 hours Major General Pemsel reported to Rommel's Chief of Staff, General Speidel, 'the sound of engines can be heard coming from the sea on the eastern Cotentin coast . . . ,' and that Admiral, Channel Coast, reported the presence of ships in the sea area Cherbourg. To Pemsel all this activity indicated a major operation. Speidel did not agree and, more to the point, nor did von Rundstedt, who remained convinced that the main attack must come at Calais, and that therefore it had not yet begun.

Von Rundstedt was the key figure in the crisis, for Rommel was away. Keitel's opinion was neither here nor there, for had von Rundstedt been convinced that the genuine D-Day had arrived, one may suppose that the old Prussian warrior would have used his initiative and moved his reserves to where he thought Montgomery would least like to see them.

The most effective place to attack was Caen. A strong counterattack against the British left flank was the Germans' best chance of doing real damage on D-Day. As the campaign developed Montgomery expressed himself as being very well content to hold the mass of the German armor on the British front. However that may have been later on, a mass of German armor round Caen was the last thing the British wanted to meet on D-Day. Thanks to von Rundstedt's initial misapprehension there was only one Panzer division near enough to make itself felt early in the day. This was 21st Panzer under Lieutenant General Edgar Feuchtinger, an officer by no means lacking in initiative. His division was stationed at St Pierre sur Dives, only 15 miles from the coast. He had some 170 armored vehicles and tanks at his command. He has described the frustrations he suffered during the early hours of 6 June:

'I waited impatiently all night for some instructions. But not a single order from a higher formation was received by me. Realizing that my armored division was closest to the scene of operations, I finally decided at 0630 hours that I had to take some action. I ordered my tanks to attack the 6th Airborne Division which had entrenched itself in a bridgehead over the Orne. To me this constituted the most immediate threat to the German position.'

This was a shrewd and correct judgment, the more so as the 6th Airborne was very far from being entrenched by 0630, nor had it yet been reinforced by the commandos. Feuchtinger continues:

'Hardly had I made this decision when at 0700 hours I received my first intimation that a higher command did still exist. I was told by Army Group B that I was now under command of Seventh Army. But I received no further orders as to my role. At 0900 hours I was informed that I would receive any future orders from LXXXIV Infantry Corps (Marcks), and finally at 1000 hours I was given my first operational instructions. I was ordered to stop the move of my tanks against the Allied airborne troops, and to turn west and aid the forces protecting Caen.'

This was the crucial decision. Feuchtinger's armor, which had already been moving toward the coast 90 minutes before the first man of the British 3rd Division set foot ashore, was now condemned to spend the vital hours of D-Day in recrossing the single surviving bridge over the Orne at Caen. Had it carried out its original plan the 21st Panzer must have advanced via Le Bas de Ranville, which was held that afternoon by 3 Commando under the present author. An unpleasant situation would have occurred.

Another German commander who reacted quickly was General F Dollman, the commander of the Seventh Army. In the early hours of 6 June he gave orders for a three-pronged attack which, coming in from north, south and west, would crush

Above: Beachhead trenches were abandoned once the fighting moved inland.
Opposite: General George Patton, wearing his famous pearl-handled revolver, discusses the tactical situation with Bradley and Montgomery in early July.
Top left: The crew of a German 88mm gun in action. This famous weapon could be used against both tanks and aircraft.
Top right: The crew of a PzKpfw IV lie buried in front of their shattered tank in Normandy.
Above left: Axis troops manning this field gun include renegades from the Indian army enlisted by Germany from prisoners of war.
Left: Machine gunners of the Waffen SS keep watch for aircraft.

the American Airborne Divisions. Unfortunately for him, his divisional commanders had not got back from Rennes, where they had been attending an anti-invasion exercise. American soldiers and Resistance fighters alike had been busy cutting telephone lines, and several German commanders were simply unable to communicate with their Headquarters. Chaos and darkness was their lot, and that of their subordinates.

One of the best units in the Cotentin was the 6th German Parachute Regiment. It was decided to use it for the attack on the Americans between Carentan and Ste Mère Eglise, which has already been mentioned. Major Friedrich-August Freiherr von der Heydte collected his men, and then surveyed the scene from the tower of St Côme church. Six miles away he could see Utah, and found the sight 'overwhelming.' There, in the middle of the morning of D-Day, scores of landing craft were peacefully unloading in the sunshine. It was like 'Berlin Wannsee on a summer's afternoon.' The American airborne troops were nowhere to be seen.

Von der Heydte's first battalion broke through the scattered units of 101st Division without any difficulty, but his unit was cut in two by a follow-up landing of gliders and paratroops. The advance of US 8th Infantry Division from Utah spelled disaster for the 6th German Parachute Regiment, but they were not to know that until next day, 7 June.

At Omaha General Dietrich Kraiss, as we have seen, was convinced that his 352nd Division had stopped the Americans in their tracks. Reports from 716th Division were not so encouraging. The British were pressing toward Bayeux, where LXXXIV Corp's reserve, 915th Regiment, was stationed. This unit had practiced the counterattack toward the coast not once but many times. Now was the time to

carry it out in earnest. Imagine Kraiss' wrath when, at 0400 hours, he discovered that the 915th Regiment had been sent to Carentan to mop up the airborne landing! The General's reaction was to send a counterorder, which took an hour to get through. The troops – one may imagine their comments – turned about and moving on foot, on bicycles and in old French *camions* moved toward Omaha. However, one way and another they never managed to reinforce the defenders, who were gradually being winkled out of their bunkers. A veritable curtain of naval gunfire did much to prevent the replenishment of ammunition, which was essential if the Germans in the front line were to hold out. The counterattack of 915th Regiment came to nothing. A rather more dangerous onslaught was made by the 21st Panzer which, hampered by refugees, had made its way through Caen. The Allies were already in sight of the city with its tall cathedral when, late in the afternoon General Feuchtinger sent his armor in. He wrote:

'Once over the Orne river I drove north toward the coast. By this time the enemy . . . had made astonishing progress and had already occupied a strip of high ground about 10 kilometers from the sea. From here, the excellent antitank gunfire of the Allies knocked out 11 of my tanks before I had barely started. However, one battle group did manage to bypass these guns and actually reached the coast at Lion sur Mer, at about 1900 hours.'

Above: Assault troops of the US 4th Infantry Division come ashore in full equipment.
Top left: LCVPs, pictured off the Normandy coast, were unarmored assault landing craft.
Top: A US Navy beach party takes over German-built trenches.
Left: LCTs were specially built as tank landing craft, but they carried many other vehicles.

This force, half a dozen tanks and a handful of infantry, was insufficient to turn the tide of battle. Indeed about three hours earlier the British had come up against the last tanks of the 21st Panzer counterattacking to save Caen. Before the Germans went into the attack General Marcks, with all the gravity he could muster, told their battalion commander, Colonel von Oppeln-Bronowski:

'Oppeln, the future of Germany may very well rest on your shoulders. If you don't push the British back we've lost the war.'

Nobody, who has not fought with and beaten the Germans, need trouble to boast of his soldiership! Yet for once these warwise warriors were taken by surprise. Rommel, for one, had been on leave. The storm in the Channel put the Germans off their guard. None of these things would have mattered had von Rundstedt's initial dispositions been correct. The Germans had a long tradition of expertise in land operations but von Rundstedt proved incapable of countering an amphibious operation. He should have seen that there were only two areas where the Allies could make their initial landfall. The obvious one was the Pas de Calais; the other was the one actually chosen, the area between the Orne and the Cotentin. A combination of

Below: The Mulberries enabled the speedy unloading of supplies for the front.

Bottom: Access to the beaches after D-Day was controlled and regulated by beachmasters.
Below: Without the shelter of artificial harbors, vessels were at the mercy of the elements, as these barges bear witness.

the two, though unlikely, was possible. It follows that the infantry in each of these areas should have been good quality, mobile divisions. Low grade static divisions were simply not good enough. In addition each of these two vital areas needed at least *two* Panzer divisions, one on each flank, and a Corps reserve of at least one more infantry division.

Field Marshal von Rundstedt, for all his service and experience, was baffled by the complexities of amphibious warfare. Even so it should not have been beyond his wit to work out that some parts of the coast were simply not going to be included in the Allies' beachhead area. One was the stretch of coast on either side of Dieppe, with its steep chalk cliffs and shingle beaches – especially after the fiasco of 1942. It follows that in this area the 84th Field Division could have been replaced by a low-category static formation.

Another area which was held with unnecessary strength was Brittany. There was no need for the 77th Division at St Malo, which could have been replaced by a static garrison. The same applies to the 353th Division as an Allied landing in Brittany was highly improbable. Not only was it much further from the ports of the south of England, it was too far from Paris, Antwerp and the other main objectives of any Allied campaign. Had von Rundstedt analyzed the situation more astutely and made a sounder allocation of his best divisions, it is possible that the Allies would have been repulsed on D-Day.

The D-Day battle fell naturally into three phases. The first was the breaking of the Atlantic Wall, the second was the thrust inland, and the third was the consolidation in order to repel the inevitable counterattack.

The first phase, despite initial setbacks at Omaha, was everywhere remarkably successful. The Atlantic Wall, for all the skill that had gone into its construction, proved a great deal less formidable than expected. Or, to put it another way, the Allied troops, and particularly the British and Canadians, came trained and equipped to deal with every sort of obstacle. This is perhaps the place to pay tribute to Major General Sir Percy Hobart, whose 'funny' tanks loaded the dice in favor of the British infantryman.

Progress made in the second phase of the D-Day fighting was disappointing, in that Caen, Bayeux and St Lô were still in German hands when night fell. It must be remembered that the planners were bound to be optimistic in selecting their objectives for D-Day. Complete success was not perhaps to be looked for from troops who, after a night spent being seasick in ships and landing craft, had already stormed the West Wall. Credit must go to those, including 6th Airborne and the commandos, who actually attained most of their objectives.

In any big amphibious operation it is essential at the outset to capture enough ground to give the force room to maneuver. Experience shows that one can capture terrain on D-Day which thereafter can only be taken at heavy cost, because the enemy has had time to organize defenses. It therefore behooves the advancing troops to take risks on D-Day, to get a move on. It cannot be said that all the Allied troops engaged bore this in mind. Some, it must be said, were decidedly cautious. It was rather unfortunate for the British that the 21st Panzer appeared on the front of a division which had been trained to plod forward at 100 yards in three minutes, covered by massive artillery fire. Tactics appropriate enough for a set-piece battle were not necessarily the best answer for the fluid situation met with on D-Day.

The consolidation phase was something which the Allied commanders at every level thoroughly understood. They were quick to dig in and secure the ground they had gained. Thanks to such imaginative devices as the Mulberry harbor and PLUTO (Pipeline Under The Ocean) the administrative buildup put the Army Group on a sound footing in good time before, on 19 June, the worst storm in the Channel for more than 40 years struck the Assault Area.

Many years have passed since the Allies won this astonishing victory. It is not likely that the world will see such another, for a single nuclear weapon in the assault area might suffice to bring the whole amphibious machine to a disastrous halt. It is a solemn thought.

Yet, if it is no longer possible to contemplate an operation of this kind, it is worth pausing for a moment to recall the magnitude of the effort which the Allies put forth on 6 June 1944. Allied aircraft flew 14,000 sorties during the night of 5 June and on D-Day. In these operations 127 aircraft were lost and 63 damaged.

More than 195,000 men were engaged in the ships and craft taking part in the naval operations. Over 23,000 airborne troops, about 8000 British and 15,500 American, were landed from the air. Total American casualties were 6000.

In the British Sector the airborne troops and commandos had about 1300 casualties, including 100 glider pilots. Casualties among the seaborne troops were some 3000, of whom about 1000 were Canadians. Thus 156,215 troops were landed, from sea and air, in Normandy, and at a cost of some 10,300 casualties, broke Hitler's Atlantic Wall in a single day.

To one who had fought at Dunkirk and Dieppe it did seem that – at long last – our side had managed to get itself organized. In four years we had invented and mastered the intricate techniques of amphibious warfare. The road from the beaches of Normandy to the shores of the Baltic was a long one, and few indeed were to go the whole way. Still, they had got off to a good start.

APPENDIX

US D-Day Assault Divisions

OMAHA BEACH

1st US Division
116 Infantry
16 Infantry
18 Infantry
26 Infantry
115 Infantry
2nd Rangers
5th Rangers
741 Tank Battalion
111 Field Artillery Battalion
7 Field Artillery Battalion
81 Chemical Battalion

UTAH BEACH

4th US Division
8 Infantry
22 Infantry
12 Infantry
359 Infantry (attached from 90th Division)
70 Tank Battalion

British D-Day Assault Divisions

SWORD BEACH

3rd British Division
8th Brigade
1st Battalion The Suffolk Regiment
2nd Battalion The East Yorkshire Regiment
1st Battalion The South Lancashire Regiment
9th Brigade
2nd Battalion The Lincolnshire Regiment
1st Battalion The King's Own Scottish Borders
2nd Battalion The Royal Ulster Rifles
185th Brigade
2nd Battalion The Royal Warwickshire Regiment
1st Battalion The Royal Norfolk Regiment
2nd Battalion The King's Shropshire Light Infantry
Divisional Troops
3rd Reconnaissance Regiment RAC
3rd Divisional Engineers
3rd Divisional Signals
7th, 33rd and 76th Field, 20th Antitank and 92nd Light Antiaircraft Regiments RA
2nd Battalion The Middlesex Regiment (Machine Gun)

JUNO BEACH

3rd Canadian Division
7th Brigade
The Royal Winnipeg Rifles
The Regina Rifle Regiment
1st Battalion The Canadian Scottish Regiment
8th Brigade
The Queen's Own Rifles of Canada
Le Régiment de la Chaudière
The North Shore (New Brunswick) Regiment
9th Brigade
The Highland Light Infantry of Canada
The Stormont, Dundas and Glengarry Highlanders
The North Nova Scotia Highlanders
Divisional Troops
7th Reconnaissance Regiment (17th Duke of York's Royal Canadian Hussars)
3rd Canadian Divisional Engineers
3rd Canadian Divisional Signals
12th, 13th and 14th Field, 3rd Artillery and 4th Light Antiaircraft Regiments, RCA
The Cameron Highlanders of Ottawa (Machine Gun)

GOLD BEACH

50th British (Northumbrian) Division
69th Brigade
5th Battalion The East Yorkshire Regiment
6th and 7th Battalion The Green Howards
151st Brigade
6th, 8th and 9th Battalions The Durham Light Infantry
231st Brigade
2nd Battalion The Devonshire Regiment
1st Battalion The Hampshire Regiment
1st Battalion The Dorsetshire Regiment
Divisional Troops
61st Reconnaissance Regiment RAC
50th Divisional Engineers
50th Divisional Signals
74th, 90th and 124th Field, 102nd Antitank and 25th Light Antiaircraft Regiments, RA
2nd Battaltion The Cheshire Regiment (Machine Gun)

Other Formations

79th Armored Division
30th Armored Brigade
22nd Dragoons
1st Lothians and Border Horse
2nd County of London Yeomanry (Westminster Dragoons)
141st Regiment RAC
1st Tank Brigade
11th, 42nd and 49th Battalions RTR
1st Assault Brigade RE
5th, 6th and 42nd Assault Regiments RE
79th Armored Division Signals
1st Canadian Armored Personnel Carrier Regiment
1st Special Service Brigade
Nos 3, 4 and 6 Commandos
No 45 (Royal Marine) Commando
4th Special Service Brigade
Nos 41, 46, 47 and 48 (Royal Marine) Commandos
Royal Marine
Armored Support Group: 1st and 2nd Royal Marine Armored Support Regiments
Units of the Royal Artillery and Royal Engineers

Airborne Forces

6th Airborne Division
3rd Parachute Brigade
8th and 9th Battalions The Parachute Regiment
1st Canadian Parachute Battalion
5th Parachute Brigade
7th, 12th and 13th Battalions The Parachute Regiment
6th Airlanding Brigade
12th Battalion The Devonshire Regiment
2nd Battaltion The Oxfordshire and Buckinghamshire Light Infantry
1st Battalion The Royal Ulster Rifles
Divisional Troops
6th Airborne Armored Reconnaissance Regiment RAC
6th Airborne Divisional Engineers
53rd Airlanding Light Regiment RA
6th Airborne Division Signals

US 101st Airborne Divisions
501st Parachute Infantry
502nd Parachute Infantry Regiment
506th Parachute Infantry
377th Parachute Field Artillery Battalion

US 82nd Airborne Division
505th Parachute Infantry
507th Parachute Infantry
508th Parachute Infantry

BATTLE OF THE BULGE

BATTLE OF THE BULGE

JOHN PIMLOTT

Page 264: German prisoners march to the rear after being captured by elements of the US 82nd Airborne Division near St Vith.
Page 265: US troops pass the Siegfried line 'dragon's teeth' at Roetgen, Germany in September 1944.
Pages 266/267: M-4 Sherman tanks lined up in a snow-covered field near St Vith, Belgium.
These pages: US tanks group to attack the Germans in Houffalize, Belgium.

1. THE ROAD TO THE ARDENNES

At exactly 0530 hours on Saturday, 16 December 1944, the quiet of the fog-enshrouded hills of the Ardennes region in Belgium and Luxembourg was shattered by the crash of a synchronized artillery bombardment. On a front stretching some 85 miles, from Monschau in the north to Echternach in the south, a total of 25 German divisions, 10 of which were armored, stood poised to smash their way through a weak American defensive screen. It was an attempt to repeat the victories of 1940, when German armored formations had advanced with stunning success through exactly the same area. In both cases the aims were the same: to cross the Meuse River, sweep through to the coast and split the Allied armies in two, so causing their collapse.

In 1940 the Allies had been France and Britain, fielding unprepared and antiquated armies which stood little chance against the new, highly mobile technique of Blitzkrieg. Four years later, with amassed experience and more sophisticated weapons, the British had been joined by the Americans, and together they should have been a harder match. However, the Allies were overstretched, a state of affairs epitomized by the fact that the Ardennes region was defended by a mere six divisions, with little armored content. The Allies were somewhat complacent about the imminent defeat of Germany. Strategic and tactical surprise were therefore complete on 16 December and the German gamble seemed, for a time, to have been worth the risk. The bitter and confused fighting, under appalling weather conditions, imposed enormous strains on the Allied forces. Although in retrospect it may be seen that eventual Allied victory was never put seriously in doubt, German tanks did penetrate to within a few miles of the Meuse, Anglo-American strategic differences were once more aired in public and, to Hitler and his staff, collapse must have seemed a possibility. After all, it had happened in 1940.

To understand how this situation arose it is necessary to go back six months, to the Allied invasion of Europe. This operation, code named Overlord and executed on 6 June, was a risky enterprise. At best the Allied forces, under the supreme command of General Dwight David Eisenhower, could only hope to put five divisions ashore in the first 24 hours. Their method of arrival, over a narrow and congested stretch of sea, was precarious. Support from naval vessels, air fleets and parachute units was vulnerable, and resupply and reinforcement impossible to guarantee. In the event, through a combination of deception, surprise and German hesitation, the assault was successful, although not to the extent envisaged by the Allied planners.

At 0200 hours on 6 June American and British airborne forces dropped on the right and left flanks respectively of the proposed landing area and consolidated temporary positions. Four and a half hours later, after air and naval bombardments, the first wave of ground forces, commanded in this initial phase by General Sir Bernard Montgomery, went ashore on five beaches. Anglo-Canadian units, using specialized armor to overcome defensive obstacles, enjoyed the most success on the Allied left. They managed to link up and advance inland by the end of the day. However, they failed to take one of their main objectives, the important communications center of Caen, and a dangerous gap existed between them and their airborne flank support. The situation was no better on the right. Although American forces had penetrated inland from the westernmost beach (Utah) and made contact with 82nd Airborne Division, they were out on a limb, unconnected to the units on their left which had experienced enormous problems just getting ashore on Omaha beach. By the end of 6 June, the beachhead area was precarious.

However, with Hitler firmly convinced that this was merely a feint, designed to draw German units away from the Pas de Calais, counterattacks were piecemeal and a rapid buildup of Allied forces and supplies was allowed to take place. Even so, the envisaged rate of advance soon fell behind schedule and the breakout, essential if success was to be ensured, became a long and painful process of attrition in the close and difficult Normandy countryside. As German reinforcements arrived they were concentrated chiefly around Caen and it was here that some of the hardest fighting took place. By late June it was clear to Montgomery that the Germans were building up their forces, particularly their armor, preparatory to a counterattack against the Anglo-Canadian forces. In an attempt to prevent this, he initiated two operations, code named Epsom and Goodwood. Epsom, mounted between 26–30 June, was a failure in terms of territory gained as the maximum advance, west of Caen, was only three miles. However, it did cause irreplaceable casualties to the enemy. This process of holding down the German armor continued with Goodwood, initiated on 18 July. Caen itself was at last taken, but the opposition was still considerable. All that the Allies could do was to hold on their left, to the south of Caen, tying down German armor and enabling the Americans on the right to break out, free from solid opposition.

Fortunately by late July the US First Army, under General Omar Bradley, was in a good position. After linking up its

Left: Paratroops descend from C-47 transport aircraft over Arnhem. This bold attempt to speed up the Allied advance ended in failure.
Below left: An American patrol moves cautiously through Thimister in Belgium, September 1944. The sign points to Aachen in Germany.
Below: British paratroops advance through Arnhem, where they met fierce opposition from the 9th SS Panzer Division.
Bottom: American engineers inspect the antitank defenses of the Siegfried Line.

Ruhr and racing for Berlin. Eisenhower was aware of problems which his front-line commanders tended to ignore, particularly the problem of supply. Although the important port of Antwerp had been captured the Germans had destroyed much of it before withdrawing and its seaward approaches through the Scheldt estuary were still controlled by the enemy. All supplies still had to be carried from the Normandy lodgment area. As the Allies advanced, this supply line, maintained by a constantly moving convoy of trucks which in fact used more supplies than it delivered, became increasingly tenuous. Eisenhower therefore favored a broad, controlled advance by all the Allied armies together, geared to the supplies available, at least until the area west of the Rhine had been cleared. 21st Army Group found and exploited a weakness in German defenses through Belgium and so received priority of supply (much to Patton's chagrin), but neither Bradley nor Devers was expected to hold back. The advance was to be a steady, plodding affair.

Unfortunately, this slowness, combined with the onset of harsher autumn weather, gave the Germans time to recover. In mid-September Montgomery tried to exploit his advantage by using airborne forces to take key bridges in the path of his advance but he was only partially successful. The parachute drops at Eindhoven, Nijmegen and Arnhem (Operation Market) went in on 17 September and the British Second Army, spearheaded by Lieutenant General Sir Brian Horrocks' XXX Corps, immediately pushed forward to link up (Operation Garden). The bridges at Eindhoven and Nijmegen, held by men of the US 101st and 82nd Airborne Divisions respectively, were quickly taken. However, German resistance at Arnhem, occupied by the British 1st Airborne Division, proved to be too strong. As the ground forces came to a halt south of the Neder Rijn, the airborne survivors were withdrawn and the northward thrust petered out. Montgomery shifted his emphasis to the Scheldt estuary in the west, intent on clearing Antwerp preparatory to a new drive to the Rhine, the Ruhr and beyond. However, with deteriorating weather and shorter winter days, it was obvious that this could not begin much before the spring.

Between late September and mid-December the situation was similar along much of the Allied line. The exhausted troops, operating at the end of an over-extended supply chain and in steadily worsening conditions, found the going hard. Viewing the front from north to south on the eve of the Ardennes assault, 21st Army Group, with the Canadians on the left and the British on the right, was stuck on the river Maas, with a small salient jutting up to just south of Arnhem. It had achieved only minor advances in the east, toward Venlo and Roermond. Supporting 21st Army Group on its right

Left: General 'Sepp' Dietrich commanded the Sixth SS Panzer Army in the Battle of the Bulge.
Above: The slogan 'victory at any cost' sounded increasingly hollow as the Allies advanced.
Below: Hitler on an inspection.

Above: Troops consult a map during exercises. German manpower resources were strained by 1944.
Below right: Hitler remained the final arbiter on matters of strategy.
Below: The apparently invulnerable Siegfried Line was a failure.

was the newly-activated US Ninth Army under Lieutenant General William H Simpson – a part of Bradley's enlarged 12th Army Group – which was pressing toward the Roer river against tough opposition. To its right was Hodges' First Army, exhausted after a hard advance against Aachen (taken on 21st October) which had developed into one of the bloodiest battles of the European war, as division after division was decimated in the difficult terrain of the Hurtgen Forest. The losses involved in this battle – 33,000 American casualties in two months – together with the need to mount a fresh offensive against the Roer Dams before the Germans breached them and flooded the countryside, had led to a concentration of forces on Hodges' left. This was one of the reasons why VIII Corps, commanded by Major General Troy Middleton, was spread out so thinly in the Ardennes, an area where action was neither expected nor desired. Only to the south had any deep penetrations been made, with Patton's Third Army advancing through Metz and into the Saar, protecting the left flank of 6th Army Group which had actually reached the Rhine at Strasbourg. Even then, however, a dangerous enemy salient – the Colmar Pocket, containing the German Nineteenth Army – remained in the Vosges mountains. It was an uneven front line, reflecting the inevitable results of Eisenhower's broad-advance strategy and, with the majority of forces concentrated in the north and the south, was dangerously weak in the center. It was a weakness which the Germans were ready to exploit.

General Alfred Jodl, Chief of the German Operations Staff, began to study the feasibility of a counteroffensive in the west as early as the first week in September. Under strict instructions from Hitler, whose grip on the strategic direction of German armed forces had become even stronger in the aftermath of the 20 July bomb plot, Jodl concentrated upon certain basic prerequisites. In a special briefing to the Führer, given at OKW (Armed Forces High Command) HQ at Rastenburg in East Prussia on 6 September, he isolated three main problems which would have to be solved; Allied air power, the German supply situation and secrecy of preparation. He went on to postulate that the first could be negated by mounting the offensive during a period of bad flying weather, the second could be eased by increasing industrial production and a careful allocation of resources, and the third could be solved by restricting information to a select number of relevant planners only, at least in the early stages. Taking all these points into account, he concluded that 1 November would be the earliest possible date for the assault.

The guarded optimism inherent within these findings probably reflected Hitler's known desire for some sort of 'master stroke' in the west, but whether genuinely felt or not, it set the wheels in motion. During the next three weeks Hitler and Jodl analyzed the Allied advance, trying to discern its strategic shape and find an area of potential weakness. By mid-September, as a definite front line began to emerge, they concluded: that the Allies lacked a strategic reserve capable of being used to plug any gap made by a counteroffensive; that Anglo-American cooperation was little more than a veneer, implying that Allied reaction to a German attack would be slow and disjointed; and that the Allied center was thinly held. The last mentioned discovery suited Hitler's strategic instinct. By 20 September he was convinced that the Ardennes was the key to success, as it had been in 1940, not only because of the scarcity of Allied forces in the area but also because the heavily-wooded, almost mountainous country of the Eifel to the east was ideal for a secret concentration of attack formations.

Five days later selected members of Jodl's staff were given their first indication of the plan when Hitler, in a monologue reminiscent of the heady days of 1940, painted a picture of extraordinary detail to them. He began by outlining the broad concept of the offensive – a breakthrough on the Ardennes front which would enable armored units to cross the Meuse between Liège and Namur preparatory to a rapid advance on Antwerp which would split the Allied armies in two and lead to their collapse. He went on to discuss in some depth how this was to be achieved. He estimated that a minimum of 30 divisions would be needed, 10 of which would have to be armored. These would be organized into four armies. Those on the north and south of the assault area – around Monschau and Echternach respectively – would be composed almost entirely of infantry, with the task of pressing forward to protect the main assault from flank attack. For the main assault, two Panzer armies, containing a mixture of tank and infantry formations, would be used. After a short, sharp artillery bombardment designed to confuse the defenders, infantry units would advance on a 50-mile front to isolate or take out the forward American positions. This would open the way for the armor which would, in the Blitzkrieg pattern of 1940, find and exploit lines of least resistance, by-passing defensive locations and leaving them to be mopped up by the following infantry. The aim at all times was to be Antwerp, with no deviations whatsoever. The tanks were to force the Meuse on the second day, swing northeastward around Brussels and reach the coast before the Allied High Command could react. If the old magic could be regained, the Allied front would crack wide open and, after an initial period of shock, would quickly degenerate into panic and collapse. At this point, according to Hitler, the Anglo-American alliance would fall apart, the war-weary British would surrender and the demoralized Americans would withdraw to concentrate on their war in the Pacific. With the west thus

Below: Lieutenant General Hasso von Manteuffel led the Fifth Panzer Army in the Ardennes.
Right: French machine gunners clear the road to Belfort.
Bottom: The occupiers of Flushing.

secure, all German forces could turn against the menace from the east, saving European culture from the Bolshevik hordes and, like the Prussian hero Frederick the Great in 1762, snatch victory from the jaws of defeat. It was an ambitious, almost insane, plan, but Hitler's charisma was still strong enough to fire the enthusiasm of his close advisers. He called for a draft operation plan to be drawn up immediately, based on a projected date of attack in late November.

In retrospect, it may be seen that the entire concept contained within it the seeds of its own destruction. From the outset the idea of a counteroffensive, the choice of ground, the allocation of forces, the tactics and timings all emanated from Hitler alone and owed more to his strategic 'insight' than to any deep General Staff analysis of the true situation. This was guaranteed to cause problems with the professional army officers involved in the attack, for not only were they not consulted in the initial planning stage but they were also to be allowed little initiative or freedom of maneuver once the attack began. The plan was too rigid, reflecting perhaps the development of Blitzkrieg over the previous four years. In 1940 the technique had been one of flexibility and improvisation but by 1944 it had become a 'theory,' with preconceptions about its effectiveness. Thus for Hitler to call for speed and no deviation from the main objective was restrictive and, given the geography of the Ardennes, shortsighted. His choice of area for the attack may be understandable, but his presumption that big, heavy tanks could advance quickly and easily through forests and hills, down steep-sided narrow roads and across a myriad of streams and rivers in atrocious winter conditions was leaving too much to chance. A determined defense of key crossroads, junctions or communication centers, or the destruction of selected bridges, could wreck the careful timings completely.

These were all 'intangibles,' glossed over in the euphoria engendered by Hitler's enthusiasm, and in late September OKW staff officers had other, more immediate concerns. Chief among these was the collection and organization of the forces required for the assault. As early as 25 September Field Marshal Gerd von Rundstedt, Commander in Chief, West, was ordered to withdraw I and II SS Panzer Corps from the front line, ostensibly for rest and reorganization. In reality, however, they were to constitute the backbone of a newly activated SS Panzer Army – the Sixth, under the trusted Nazi SS Oberstgruppenführer Josef 'Sepp' Dietrich – which was to form the main assault force on the German right, responsible for the thrust between Monschau and St Vith. Its infantry component, together with the bulk of those for the other three armies, was to be provided from the *Volksgrenadier* Divisions currently being put together in

Germany from among the latest batch of conscripts, men from broken formations and even personnel from disbanded air force and naval units. It was estimated that 10 of these divisions could be made available by 20 November, a further three by 30 November and a total of 20 by 10 December. They would be joined by the more conventional infantry divisions already holding the Ardennes sector, under Fifteenth Army in the north and Seventh Army in the south. The second of the assault tank formations, responsible for the sector between St Vith and Wiltz, was to be Fifth Panzer Army, commanded by General Hasso von Manteuffel, currently fighting in the south but to be withdrawn for reorganization in late October. All units would be part of Army Group B, under Field Marshal Walther Model, theoretically subject to orders from Rundstedt but, for the purposes of the attack, answerable directly to Hitler at OKW. All this was agreed to at another of Jodl's briefings, on 11 October, and a code name for the plan – *Wacht am Rhein* – was assigned.

Secrecy was still a major consideration. OKW announced to all commanders on the Western Front that it was not possible to stage a counteroffensive in the foreseeable future. However, as the plans became more specific the circle of those in the know had to be widened. On 21 October Hitler personally briefed SS Obersturmbannführer Otto Skorzeny, a renowned commando leader, on the part he was to play. He was ordered to recruit English-speaking soldiers from throughout the armed forces, organize them into the so-called 150th Panzer Brigade and, in an operation code named *Greif*, infiltrate them through American lines, in American uniforms, to create maximum disruption in rear areas as the main assault went in. It was a minor part of the overall plan, but one which was to enjoy considerable success.

The following day, 22 October, was devoted to briefing Generals Siegfried Westphal and Hans Krebs, Chiefs of Staff to Rundstedt and Model respectively, and here the problems began. Neither officer was impressed with the broad sweep of the *Wacht am Rhein* concept, fearing not only that it was too optimistic but also that too little time had been allowed for its preparation. They went back to their superiors full of doubts and questions, and these were reflected in papers submitted to Hitler by both Rundstedt and Model in late October, offering scaled-down alternatives. Rundstedt favored a breakthrough just to the Meuse with the aim of trapping the Allied divisions facing the Siegfried Line. Model suggested a pincer attack, to be carried out by Fifth Panzer Army from the Ardennes and Fifteenth Army from Aachen, again with the aim of trapping American front-line formations rather than winning the war at a stroke. Such reservations were inevitable from men who had been fighting for over five years, who had seen defeat and

Right: German infantrymen file through forest country.
Center right: A German engineer lays a minefield.
Below right and far right: The German army, with its wealth of experience on the Eastern Front, fought better in severe winter weather than the less acclimated Allied forces.

Above: An American armored recce patrol advances in eastern France.

had come to distrust Hitler's 'grand slam' strategic solutions. Their views were anathema to the Führer, by now convinced that all professional army officers were defeatists and plotters. Two concessions were made, caused more by the Allied attacks against Fifteenth Army around Aachen and the Hurtgen Forest than by the misgivings of the field commanders. Fifteenth Army, fighting for its existence, was deleted from the *Wacht am Rhein* plan and the assault date was postponed, initially to 10 December and finally to 16 December. Neither date satisfied the Field Marshals. As late as 2 December, in a special meeting in Berlin, Model, ably supported by Manteuffel, tried desperately to persuade Hitler to accept his 'little slam' alternative, but to no avail. Rundstedt, virtually squeezed out of the command chain by this time, disassociated himself from the whole affair. The die was cast, but those responsible for the plan's execution had strong reservations.

Final orders were issued on 11 December and three days later the attack formations moved quietly up to the front line from their concentration areas in the Eifel. Their arrival boosted the strength of the Ardennes sector to 23 divisions, with a further two in reserve, and of this total 10 were armored. Running from north to south, Dietrich had under his command four Panzer Divisions (1st SS, 2nd SS, 9th SS and 12th SS), one Parachute Division (3rd, in an infantry role) and four *Volksgrenadier* Divisions (12th, 246th, 277th and 326th). He fielded a total of 450 tanks and self-propelled guns. To his left, Manteuffel also had nine divisions, but fewer AFVs (about 350), for although he commanded four Panzer Divisions (2nd, 9th, Panzer *Lehr* and 116th) as well as the 15th Panzer Grenadier Division, none was up to full strength. They varied between 60–80 percent effective. They were supported by the 18th, 26th, 62nd and 560th *Volksgrenadier* Divisions. To Manteuffel's left, in the deep south of the assault area, Seventh Army under General Erich Brandenberger contributed five divisions (5th Parachute, 79th Infantry, 212th, 276th and 352nd *Volksgrenadier*), but had no armor at all. OKW held a reserve of two full-strength divisions (3rd Panzer Grenadier and 9th *Volksgrenadier*) and two elite brigades (*Führer Begleit* and *Führer Grenadier*), to be released on the express orders of Hitler alone. Taken overall, this was less than Jodl had originally promised, but with 275,000 men, 1900 heavy artillery pieces and 950 AFVs available, a formidable force had been gathered together.

Facing this force in mid-December were six American divisions, totalling little more than 75,000 men, and theoretically in no condition to withstand an assault. In the north, opposite Dietrich's right, were the 2nd and 99th Infantry Divisions, part of Major General Leonard Gerow's V Corps. The 99th had been in the line about a month and was not battle hardened; indeed the 2nd was in the process of attacking *through* them as part of the advance toward the Roer Dams. Even the veteran status of the 2nd – it had been in the thick of the fighting since Normandy – was of little immediate value because of this complex maneuver, while its concentration for the assault had left a defensive gap to the south. This region, stretching for two miles in the area of the strategically important Losheim gap, was ostensibly covered by 14th Cavalry Group – a portion of 2nd Division not needed in the Roer Dams attack – but it was overstretched and poorly deployed. It was also still under command of Middleton's VIII Corps (whence 2nd Division had recently come) in an arrangement guaranteed to cause chaos and confusion. It held the Corps interface, responsible for tying together Gerow's forces with those of Middleton and was neither briefed nor deployed to carry out its task. It was a dangerous gap in an area earmarked by Dietrich for his armored advance.

The northernmost of Middleton's units was the newly arrived 106th Infantry Division, recently moved into what was known as the Schnee Eifel region to replace 2nd Division. Its area of responsibility was in fact a part of Germany, jutting out in a salient of small villages, hills and steep-sided valleys which begged to be bitten off – a process high on the list of priorities facing troops of Manteuffel's right wing. Major General Alan Jones, commanding the 106th, considered his position to be exposed and overextended, opinions shared by Major General Norman D 'Dutch' Cota, commanding the veteran 28th Infantry Division to his south. The 28th, sent to the Ardennes to recover from horrific casualties suffered in the Hurtgen Forest, was responsible for 23 miles of front, facing the Our river, a fast-flowing waterway which the bulk of Manteuffel's armor had to cross. An adequate defense was little short of impossible. To the right of the 28th was part of another new division, 9th Armored (later to achieve fame as the captor of the intact Remagen bridge over the Rhine in March 1945) which, although responsible for only six miles of front, was overstretched since two of its three Combat Commands were being held back as Middleton's mobile reserve. They faced attacks from Brandenberger's forces, although the bulk of these were arrayed against the last of the US divisions in the line, the 4th Infantry, another veteran division recovering from the Hurtgen Forest battle. All in all, American defenses were in poor condition. Lulled into a false sense of security by the quiet of the Ardennes sector, taken in by German deceptions and secrecy, and composed of a dangerous mixture of combat-weary and 'green' troops, the troops were about to face an absolutely overwhelming assault.

2. THE WINTER OFFENSIVE

The initial artillery bombardment, in the predawn dark and cold of 16 December, lasted approximately three-quarters of an hour. Its aim appears not to have been the destruction of front-line American units – because of the need for secrecy and the lack of time available few German commanders had plotted such locations accurately – but the severing of communications as a preliminary move in the policy of creating confusion. In this, the artillery succeeded. All along the front line small American outposts – the sharp end of divisional deployments – suddenly found themselves isolated from higher command elements, a state of affairs which left them unsure about what to do and confused about what was happening. The first day of the battle is therefore extremely difficult to describe in generalized terms for it quickly and inevitably dissolved into a series of small-unit actions. Furthermore, as each of these small units, unaware of what was going on to its right or left, imagined that it alone was being attacked, the overall picture which gradually seeped through to Divisional, Army and Army Group commanders was fragmentary and impossible to analyze. The chaos which Hitler saw as a vital prerequisite to success was therefore well-advanced by the end of the first 24 hours. The shape of the future battle could also be discerned. The German assault divisions could not break through and destroy American defenses with ease. A significant number of small units, in a remarkable display of initiative and stubborness, stood firm, holding the enemy advance for vital hours or even days. As the Germans should have learned from their experiences on the Eastern Front, Blitzkrieg could be countered by defense in depth. In many cases, without realizing it, the small units in action on 16 December were helping to

Below: 155mm Long Tom field guns in action.

Left: An infantryman hitches a ride on a tank.
Right: Troops take cover during house-to-house fighting.
Below: A medium tank of the US Sixth Army, fitted with a mine roller, clears the way for the advance over the River Moselle.

form such a defense and contributing significantly to the eventual failure of *Wacht am Rhein*.

This may be seen to good effect in the north, where Dietrich planned to push aside the 99th Division, take the important Elsenborn Ridge and break through the Losheim gap. For the frontal assault he deployed three divisions, 3rd Panzer Grenadier, 12th and 277th *Volksgrenadier* on his right against the main American locations and 3rd Parachute on his left to open up the Losheim gap. In addition he had ordered Colonel Friedrich-August von der Heydte to organize a parachute landing into the Baraque Michel mountain area, a few miles north of Malmédy, with the aim of securing the important road junction at Baraque Michel through which the armored spearheads of 12th SS Panzer Division would move in their advance on Liège. It was classic Blitzkrieg, reminiscent of the attacks on Holland and Belgium in 1940, but it did not go smoothly. As early as 0400 hours on 16 December von der Heydte, impatiently awaiting the arrival of nearly half his force at Lippspringe airfield, was forced to postpone the operation as trucks to carry the men from their billets had not turned up.

Responsibility for the northern breakthrough therefore rested with the ground forces alone and, in this first 24 hours, results were mixed. The attack upon 99th Division began well enough, with infantry and assault pioneer units moving deep into American lines under cover of fog and howling winds, but the expected collapse did not materialize. Under the impression that this was merely a spoiling attack, designed to upset the advance on the Roer Dams, and steadied significantly by the presence of the battle-hardened 2nd Division, the greenhorns of the 99th acquitted themselves well. An attack upon Buchholz Station in the south, near the Corps divide, was beaten off by noon; heavy fighting in the twin towns of Rocherath and Krinkelt in the center did not produce an American withdrawal; and the area of Monschau-Höfen in the far north was successfully defended. Indeed, by the end of the day the bulk of 99th Division had not been shifted from its original positions. Hodges, unaware of the true nature of the German offensive, had refused permission to cancel 2nd Division's attack toward the northeast.

Not all of the 99th survived the day. One platoon, stationed at the road junction of Lanzerath, had borne the full weight of 3rd Parachute Division and, not surprisingly, succumbed. It did succeed in delaying the German advance until dusk, however, regardless of the fact that its neighboring unit in the Losheim gap, a squadron of 14th Cavalry Group at Manderfeld, had withdrawn southward during the morning after heavy fighting. In fact the 14th Cavalry was all but destroyed, losing most of its equipment and seeing many of its subunits surrounded, annihilated or dis-

persed, and this opened the Losheim gap completely. Even so, 3rd Parachute Division had suffered heavy casualties and had been forced to divert valuable resources to take out isolated American outposts. Dietrich had been obliged to commit 12th SS Panzer earlier than intended in an effort to maintain momentum and this had caused further problems. With deep snow obscuring the roads and a lack of bridging equipment with which to cross the Our, a massive traffic jam had quickly built up on the east bank of that river. Sixth SS Panzer Army, far from racing easily to the Meuse, was getting dangerously bogged down.

By comparison, Fifth Panzer Army achieved far more, partly because Manteuffel's area of attack included easier ground and partly because of the weaknesses in the strength and deployment of the American divisions facing him. He had three major aims. On his left, south of Dasburg, General Heinrich Freiherr von Lüttwitz's XLVII Panzer Corps, comprising three divisions (2nd Panzer, Panzer *Lehr* and 26th *Volksgrenadier*) was to cross the Our river, seize Clervaux (Clerf) and the important road junction at Bastogne, and cross the Meuse south of Namur. Further north, General Walter Krüger's LVIII Panzer Corps, containing two divisions (116th Panzer and 560th *Volksgrenadier*) was to cross the Our near Lutzkampen, take the town of Houffalize, skirt the Ourthe river to its right and cross the Meuse between Namur and Andenne. Finally, in almost a subsidiary action on the extreme right, elements of General Walter Lucht's LXVI Infantry Corps were to nip out the Schnee Eifel salient preparatory to capturing St Vith and protecting the northern flank of Fifth Panzer Army. Thus the entire assault was concentrated against 28th and 106th US Infantry Divisions, strung out in a series of isolated and vulnerable outposts and unprepared for battle. The outcome was inevitable.

The 106th Division, concentrated in the Schnee Eifel, was in trouble even before Lucht's attack, spearheaded by 18th *Volksgrenadier*, began. Once 14th Cavalry Group to their north withdrew under heavy pressure, the Losheim gap opened up, enabling German troops to infiltrate to the rear. These troops spent much of the day locating and attacking artillery units, forcing them to withdraw and effectively cutting off the three regiments of the 106th from their fire support. Thus, although German frontal assaults were held at Bleialf in the center and Winterspelt in the south, a deep penetration had been made in the north, in the Losheim gap, and the 106th was effectively isolated. In the absence of clear information, Major General Jones, in his headquarters at St Vith, was paralyzed, although becoming acutely aware that the entire Schnee Eifel region, containing the bulk of his division, was in very great danger of being taken out. He was perhaps fortunate not to realize that virtu-

Left: A German passes a blazing American half-track on 17 December, the second day of the German Ardennes offensive.
Below Left: A German machine gunner shelters behind a wrecked armored vehicle.

Above: An American armored car lies abandoned in the path of the German advance.
Below: Derelict American vehicles bear mute testimony to the shock of the German counteroffensive.

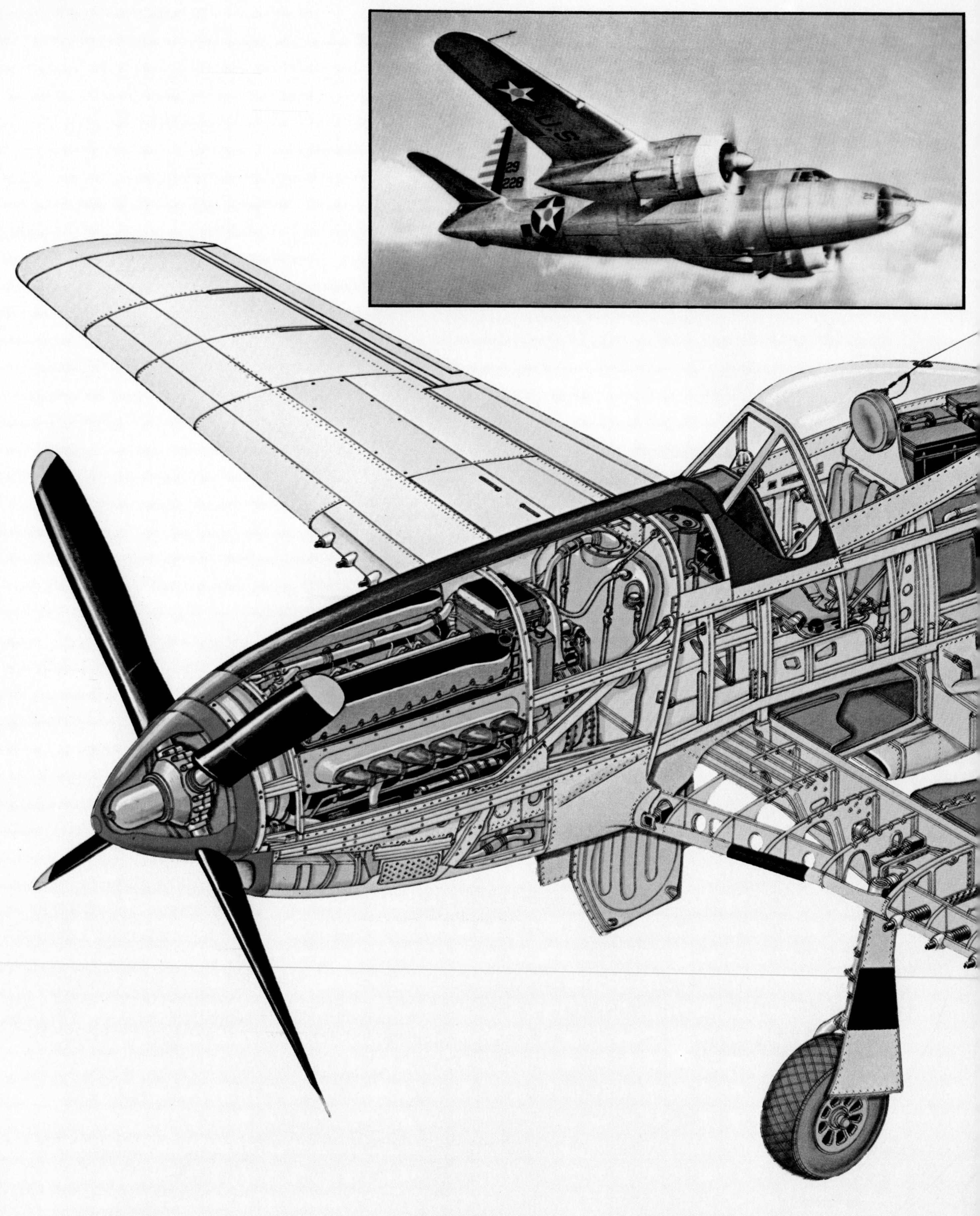

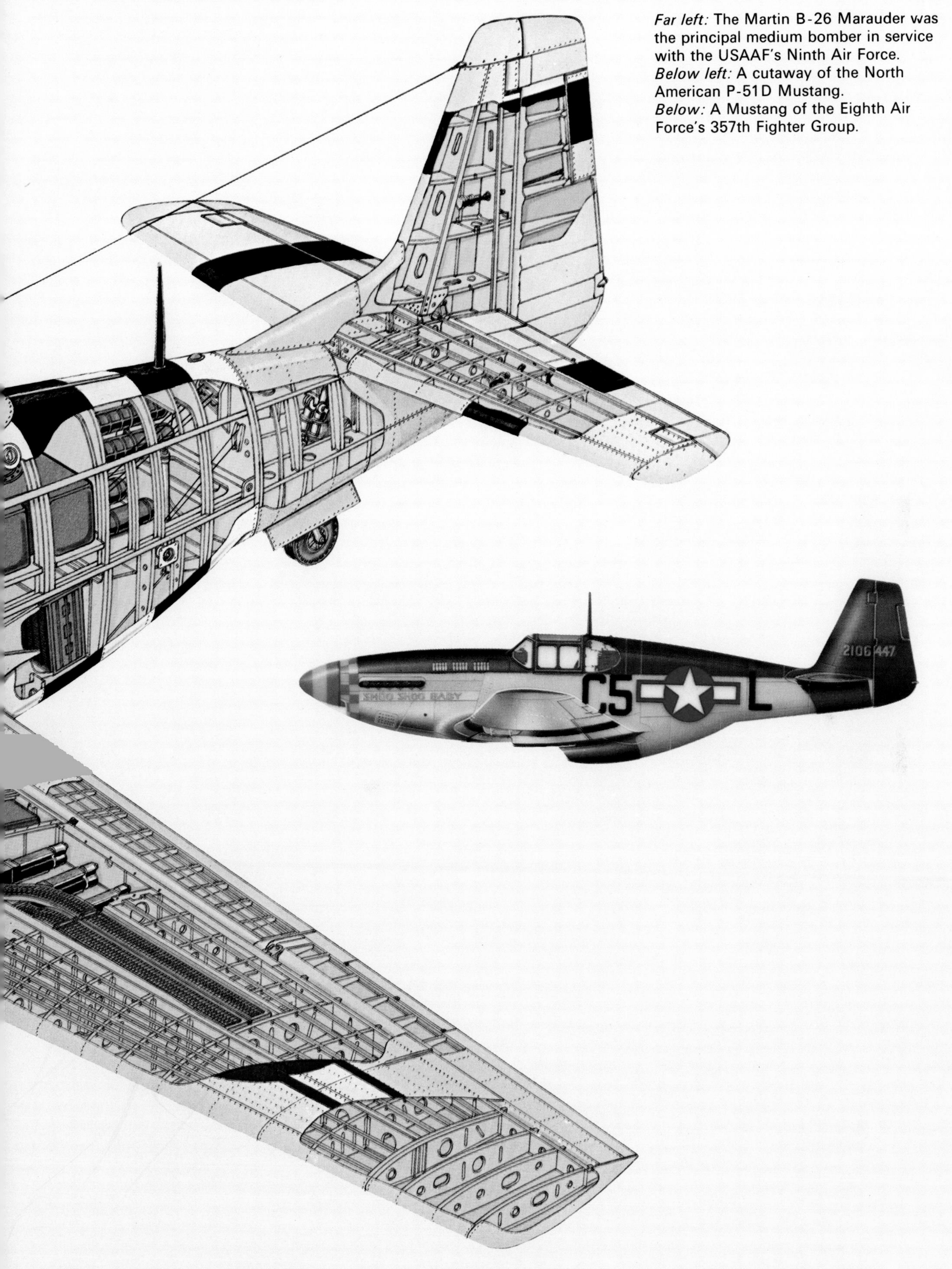

Far left: The Martin B-26 Marauder was the principal medium bomber in service with the USAAF's Ninth Air Force.
Below left: A cutaway of the North American P-51D Mustang.
Below: A Mustang of the Eighth Air Force's 357th Fighter Group.

Left: German troops regroup in a newly recaptured village.
Below: Men of the 82nd Airborne Division bring in a captured trooper of the Waffen SS.

Below: Lieutenant General Courtney Hodges' First US Army bore the brunt of the initial German onslaught.
Bottom: Men of the 26th Infantry Regiment move out to meet a German attack at Butgenbach on 17 December.

ally nothing now stood between himself and the northern arm of the 18th *Volksgrenadier* assault.

Nor was this the only German breakthrough in Manteuffel's sector, for the main emphasis of his assault, delivered by XLVII and LVIII Panzer Corps, was concentrated against 28th Division, with predictable results. Major General Cota had deployed his three front-line regiments as best he could, with the 112th in the north, linking with the right of 106th Division, the 110th in the center and the 109th in the south, bordering 9th Armored Division lines. In the event, the two flank regiments held firm during 16 December – the 112th denied two important bridges across the Our to 116th Panzer while the 109th held up an attack by three German infantry battalions – but the center cracked wide open. The 110th Regiment, only recently taken over by Colonel Hurley Fuller, a veteran of the Argonne Forest in World War I, was overstretched even by the generous terms of the time and was strung out in a number of isolated posts on what was known as 'Skyline Drive,' an exposed supply route running parallel to the front. These posts were hit by the infantry units of XLVII Panzer Corps, who quickly infiltrated through the defensive gaps in their advance to Clervaux. Despite Hitler's orders, however, they could not afford to leave the American positions intact in their rear and, in a series of close-quarter engagements in deep snow, the 110th Regiment inflicted heavy losses and did not collapse immediately. Hand-to-hand battles and costly sieges in villages such as Weiler, Holzthum, Munshausen and Marnach slowed down the German advance significantly. They could not stop it entirely. As Lüttwitz threw bridges across the Our at Gemund and Dasburg, pushing the first of his heavy tanks to the western bank soon after nightfall, the road to Clervaux and Bastogne lay open. The 110th Regiment, isolated and gradually succumbing to the pressure, virtually ceased to exist.

Meanwhile, further south, Brandenberger's Seventh Army, charged with the twin tasks of breaking through to protect Manteuffel's left flank and of demonstrating toward Luxembourg in an effort to tie down American reserves, had followed a pattern which Dietrich would have found familiar. Two divisions, 5th Parachute and 352nd *Volksgrenadier* of the LXXXV Infantry Corps, attacked on his right but the forward elements encountered difficult terrain and were held by the US 109th Regiment. According to the commander of the 109th, the regiment 'did not even consider giving up any ground,' a remarkable statement given the overwhelming odds and one which was to mean little once Colonel Fuller's regiment to the immediate north had collapsed late in the day. In Brandenberger's center a similar lack of headway ensued as the Combat Command of 9th Armored, holding a narrow sector and enjoying the support of an entire field artillery battalion, inflicted heavy casualties on the 276th *Volksgrenadier* Division of LXXX Infantry Corps. Things went slightly better in the extreme south, where the 12th Infantry Regiment of 4th Division bore the brunt of an assault across the Sauer river by the 212th *Volksgrenadiers*, for predawn infiltrations, coupled with overwhelming numbers, led to forward outposts being surrounded and besieged in a series of small villages. The 12th Regiment was the only element of 4th Division to be attacked and the divisional commander, Major General Raymond O Barton, was able to build up a strong reserve, including armor, and prepare it for commitment. The southern shoulder of the Ardennes had therefore not been broken, and although heavy fighting was still to take place, leading eventually to a breakthrough by 5th Parachute Division, Seventh Army as a whole was to make little further progress.

Thus, by the end of 16 December, German gains were quite small. Very little had been achieved on either of the two flanks and Dietrich's Army, upon which the main onus for the advance to the Meuse rested, had not made the expected breakthrough. In the center, elements of 28th Division seemed to be holding on. This was a superficial view. In both north and south important bridges had been captured or constructed, the Losheim gap and Skyline Drive were breached and, despite the traffic jams developing behind Dietrich's sector, the armor was about to be committed. As in so many modern battles, the first day had been one of probing, finding and opening lines of least resistance, ready for more dramatic advances thereafter. In short, the German forces were poised for breakthrough.

Even so, it would be wrong to see 16 December as a German victory. The American forces, even those completely new to battle, had not collapsed as soon as pressure was exerted upon them and in nearly all sectors had inflicted irreplaceable casualties, slowing the Germans down and delaying their advance. More significantly, the Allied High Command did not split or fail to react. Regardless of Hitler's beliefs, Eisenhower was making redeployments to answer the threat within the first 24 hours. News of the assault finally reached his HQ in Paris after dusk on 16 December. The Supreme Commander, aided by Bradley who happened to be visiting, ordered two armored divisions – the 7th in Ninth Army sector and the 10th with Patton in the south – to be withdrawn from the line and sent to the Ardennes. A few hours later XVIII Airborne Corps, under Major General Matthew B Ridgway, was directed to send its two European-based divisions, 82nd and 101st Airborne, to Bastogne. The strategic reserve which OKW had calculated did not exist had been created and committed in a very short time. It was an

Below: A German artillery battery lays down a barrage.
Right: The Panzerfaust antitank weapon, which fired a large hollow-charge bomb, gave an infantry section a measure of protection against enemy armor.
Below right: The Panzerschreck was similar to the Panzerfaust.

Right and below right: Men of Otto Skorzeny's 150th Panzer Brigade infiltrated Allied lines wearing American uniform. Here German troops dressed as GIs are guarded by military police. *Below:* A German tank drives past a column of captured US troops.

indication of Allied flexibility which the Germans had failed to recognize.

The importance of the initial American resistance to the attack may be seen throughout the ensuing battle, for although German armor was able to push forward in three key sectors – in the north to the Amblève river and around St Vith, and in the south around Bastogne – carefully laid down timings had been disrupted, in some cases decisively. As the battle progressed and American resistance hardened into more organized defensive lines, the crossing of the Meuse – which was only the *first* objective – gradually became less and less feasible. Nowhere was this more apparent than in the north, where Dietrich's Sixth Panzer Army found itself slowly but effectively hemmed in and denied the massive breakthrough it so desperately needed.

The first major setback took place in the far north of Dietrich's assault sector, in the area covered by the US 2nd and 99th Divisions. By the end of the first day they had managed to hold firm but were dangerously vulnerable, particularly as Hodges was insisting upon a continuation of the attack toward the Roer Dams. No military formation, however flexible, can be expected to attack and defend simultaneously and, fortunately, this was recognized at 0730 hours on 17 December. Hodges authorized General Gerow to defend his corps front as he saw fit, an order which Gerow thankfully took to mean that 2nd Division's attack could be cancelled. This changed the entire situation in the north, especially when Gerow delegated responsibility for defense to Major General Walter M Robertson, the experienced commander of 2nd Division. Robertson immediately reviewed the overall situation, recognized the confusion caused by the previous day's battle and ordered a withdrawal of both divisions to the strategically important Elsenborn Ridge, two miles to the rear. Here they would be joined by one of the most experienced formations in the European Theater – 1st Infantry Division, released by Gerow from Corps reserve.

Robertson faced a daunting and extremely difficult task. The withdrawal of units from the thick of a battle is fraught with danger, particularly if some of those units are new to combat. In addition, by 17 December the whole area was hopelessly confused. In the face of continuing German attacks, 2nd and 99th Divisions had become intermingled, fighting was taking place all over the area, command networks were overstretched and the roads were packed with equipment, while to the south the Losheim gap had been forced, exposing Robertson's flank. Displaying remarkable coolness, the new commander worked out and implemented a plan. His first priority was to recover those elements of 2nd Division concentrated in the northeast for the Roer Dams attack, and for this reason 99th Division was ordered to hold on to its current positions as a protective screen. This complex maneuver was completed during 17 December, with 2nd Division moving into Rocherath and Krinkelt, important locations as they controlled the roads leading up to the Elsenborn Ridge from the east. Once in position, the 2nd acted as a blocking force through which the remnants of 99th Division could withdraw. This was a dangerous move, for throughout 17–18 December the three front-line regiments of the 99th were under sustained attack from 12th SS Panzer, and 12th and 277th *Volksgrenadier* Divisions, and were being directed to disengage under fire. It was thus extremely fortuitous that Dietrich, frustrated by lack of progress in the north, chose just this moment to redeploy 12th SS Panzer, moving it from opposite Rocherath to help in the exploitation through the Losheim gap. The pressure was taken off 99th Division sufficiently to enable it to make a fighting withdrawal, through Rocherath–Krinkelt to the Elsenborn positions, late on 18 December. The 2nd Division followed on 19 December and, once up on the ridge, these units set up a solid defense line. They were joined by 1st Division and elements of 9th Division which had moved down from north of Monschau. This force successfully withstood repeated German infantry attacks. Casualties were heavy (99th Division alone lost 2200 men between 16–20 December) but a barrier had been created on the northern shoulder. It was a major contribution to eventual American victory.

Dietrich had no more luck with the 'specialist' forces attached to his command, for although both von der Heydte and Skorzeny committed their units during this early phase, neither achieved its allotted task. As early as 0300 hours on 17

FRONT LINES
26 DECEMBER 1944
2 JANUARY 1945
16 JANUARY
7 FEBRUARY
LIÈGE
VERVIERS
B E L G I U M
US XIX
MONSCHAU
Meuse
HUY
SPA
Amblève
LXVII
NAMUR
US V
Ourthe
US XVIII Abn
MALMÉDY
Fifteenth Army
STAVELOT
US First Army
DURBUY
STADTKYLL
US VII
Salm
LXVI
ISS Pz
CINEY
Sixth SS Pz Army
Br XXX
HOTTON
ST VITH
DINANT
II SS Pz
VIELSALM
MARCHE
PRÜM
CELLES
LVIII Pz
Our
ROCHEFORT
LAROCHE
GERMANY
GIVET
XLVII Pz
HOUFFALIZE
Fifth Pz Army
WELLIN
CLERVAUX
Meuse
A r d e n n e s
BASTOGNE
US 101 Abn Div
BITBURG
FRANCE
WILTZ
LXXXV
US VIII
Seventh Army
RECOGNE
VIII ALLIED CORPS
LXVI GERMAN CORPS
US 4 Armd Div
Sûre
LXXX
NEUFCHÂTEAU
ETTELBRUCK
US XII
MARTELANGE
ECHTERNACH
US III
0 MILES 20
0 KILOMETERS 30
US Third Army
LUXEMBOURG

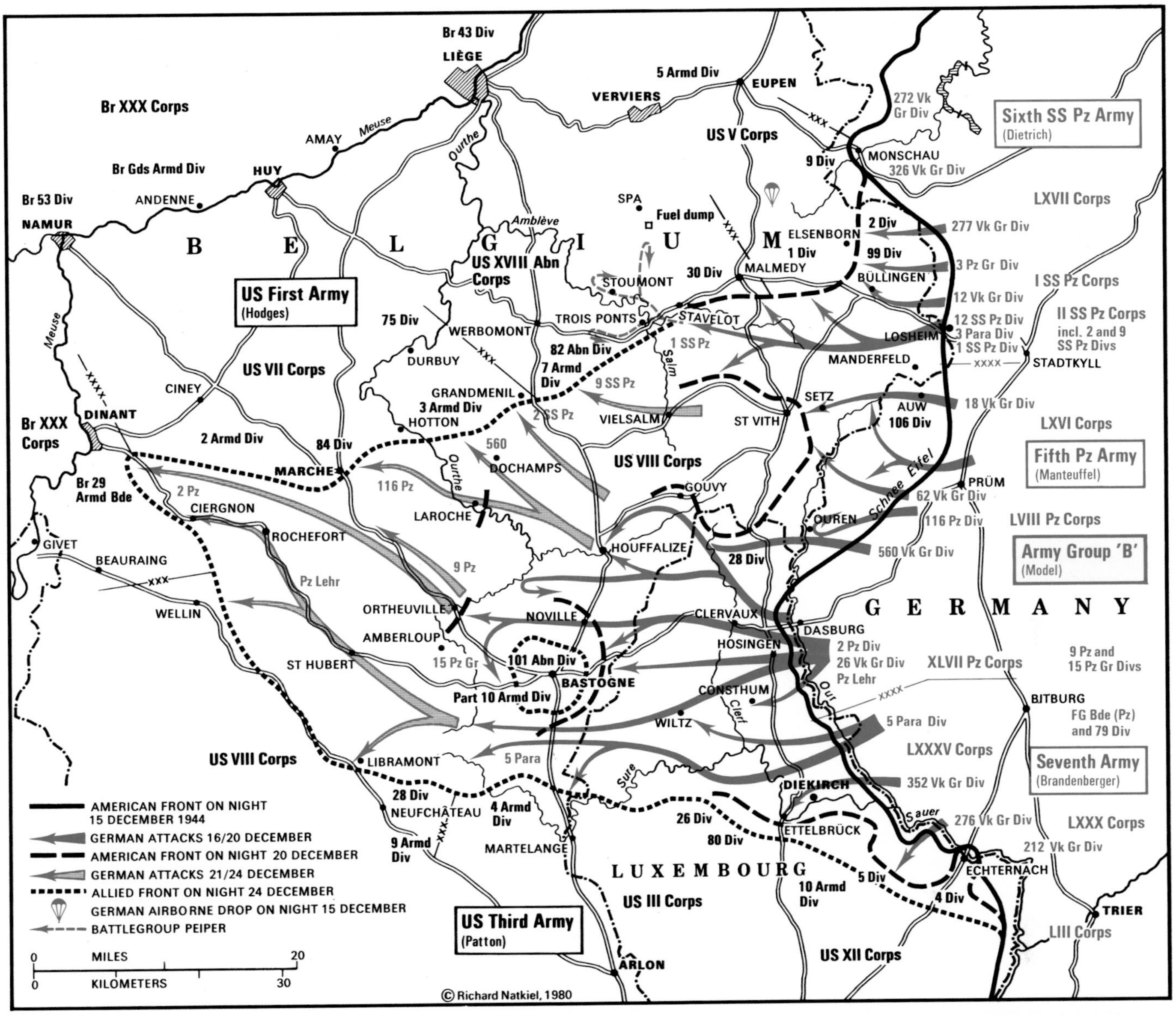

Br 43 Div
LIÈGE
5 Armd Div
EUPEN
Br XXX Corps
VERVIERS
272 Vk Gr Div
Sixth SS Pz Army (Dietrich)
AMAY
Meuse
Ourthe
US V Corps
9 Div
MONSCHAU
326 Vk Gr Div
Br Gds Armd Div
HUY
Br 53 Div
ANDENNE
SPA
Fuel dump
LXVII Corps
NAMUR
Amblève
2 Div
277 Vk Gr Div
B E L G I U M
ELSENBORN
1 Div
99 Div
US XVIII Abn Corps
30 Div
MALMEDY
3 Pz Gr Div
US First Army (Hodges)
STOUMONT
BÜLLINGEN
I SS Pz Corps
12 Vk Gr Div
75 Div
TROIS PONTS
STAVELOT
12 SS Pz Div
II SS Pz Corps incl. 2 and 9 SS Pz Divs
WERBOMONT
1 SS Pz
LOSHEIM
3 Para Div
1 SS Pz Div
82 Abn Div
Salm
MANDERFELD
STADTKYLL
DURBUY
7 Armd Div
US VII Corps
9 SS Pz
GRANDMENIL
SETZ
18 Vk Gr Div
CINEY
3 Armd Div
2 SS Pz
AUW
106 Div
Br XXX Corps
DINANT
HOTTON
VIELSALM
ST VITH
LXVI Corps
2 Armd Div
84 Div
560
Fifth Pz Army (Manteuffel)
MARCHE
DOCHAMPS
US VIII Corps
PRÜM
Br 29 Armd Bde
2 Pz
116 Pz
GOUVY
Schnee Eifel
62 Vk Gr Div
CIERGNON
LAROCHE
OUREN
116 Pz Div
LVIII Pz Corps
GIVET
ROCHEFORT
HOUFFALIZE
560 Vk Gr Div
Army Group 'B' (Model)
BEAURAING
9 Pz
28 Div
Pz Lehr
WELLIN
ORTHEUVILLE
NOVILLE
CLERVAUX
G E R M A N Y
AMBERLOUP
DASBURG
HOSINGEN
2 Pz Div
26 Vk Gr Div
Pz Lehr
XLVII Pz Corps
9 Pz and 15 Pz Gr Divs
ST HUBERT
15 Pz Gr
101 Abn Div
BASTOGNE
Our
CONSTHUM
BITBURG
Part 10 Armd Div
Clerf
WILTZ
5 Para Div
FG Bde (Pz) and 79 Div
LXXXV Corps
US VIII Corps
LIBRAMONT
5 Para
Seventh Army (Brandenberger)
Sure
DIEKIRCH
352 Vk Gr Div
28 Div
NEUFCHÂTEAU
4 Armd Div
26 Div
Sauer
276 Vk Gr Div
LXXX Corps
80 Div
ETTELBRÜCK
9 Armd Div
212 Vk Gr Div
MARTELANGE
LUXEMBOURG
5 Div
ECHTERNACH
10 Armd Div
4 Div
US III Corps
TRIER
US Third Army (Patton)
LIII Corps
ARLON
US XII Corps

AMERICAN FRONT ON NIGHT 15 DECEMBER 1944
GERMAN ATTACKS 16/20 DECEMBER
AMERICAN FRONT ON NIGHT 20 DECEMBER
GERMAN ATTACKS 21/24 DECEMBER
ALLIED FRONT ON NIGHT 24 DECEMBER
GERMAN AIRBORNE DROP ON NIGHT 15 DECEMBER
BATTLEGROUP PEIPER
0 MILES 20
0 KILOMETERS 30
© Richard Natkiel, 1980

Above: The German offensive on 16 December created a massive salient in the Allied line.
Above left: By 7 February Allied counterattacks had restored their position.
Left: Men of 325th Glider Infantry Company clear a street of enemy snipers. The XVIII Airborne Corps was among the few reserves available to Eisenhower in December 1944.
Right: German infantrymen cluster round an antitank gun.

German soldiers who were captured wearing American uniforms were treated as spies and executed by firing squad, as their *ruse de guerre* denied them the protection of the Geneva Convention on POWs.

December von der Heydte's parachute drop into the Baraque Michel area, postponed the day before, met with complete disaster. In atrocious weather conditions, which included ground winds of up to 50 feet per second, and plagued by problems caused by lack of recent jumping experience, the force was distributed far and wide, some of the men actually landing as far afield as Bonn. Von der Heydte himself found the dropping zone but, with less than 130 of his soldiers joining him by the end of the day, there was little he could do. He and his men went to ground, avoiding contact with American units, and finally surrendered on 22 December. At the same time, selected groups of Skorzeny's *Greif* commandos, dressed in American uniforms, infiltrated behind enemy lines, where they cut telephone wires, misdirected traffic and even reached the Meuse, but in the absence of a supporting advance all were soon captured, killed or withdrawn. Many of those captured were in fact shot by the Americans as spies, an inevitable consequence of their deception.

In purely military terms, none of these 'specialists' achieved a great deal and their use can be dismissed as a significant waste of German resources. However, they had a quite dramatic effect upon American rear-area morale, out of all proportion to their numbers. Convinced that paratroops and commandos were swarming all over the Ardennes, dressed as GIs, American soldiers added to the confusion of the battle by stopping everyone they met and demanding proof of identity. As normal identity cards were no longer sufficient, such proof was usually demanded through the medium of 'catch questions,' and if any American did not know 'the capital of Illinois' or the title of 'the man between center and tackle on a line of scrimmage' he was instantly suspect. Even General Bradley was delayed in this way on one occasion, while Eisenhower, believed to be the object of a special assassination squad, was surrounded by so many security men that he was virtually a prisoner in his own HQ. If a major German breakthrough had occurred, such incidents could have had a decisive demoralizing effect. As it was, they were merely irritants.

With the bulk of his infantry and all his 'specialist' units thus stalled or ineffective, Dietrich had no choice but to depend on his armor to achieve his aims. Two SS panzer divisions, the 12th on the right and the 1st on the left should have been committed by the end of the first day, exploiting gaps made in the American lines by the infantry and reaching the Meuse by 18 December. The failure of 12th SS Panzer against the 2nd and 99th Divisions was apparent relatively quickly, leading to its redeployment. This left the 1st to carry out the plan. Operating immediately behind 3rd Parachute Division, it should have been able to sweep through the Losheim gap with ease. In the event a significant proportion of it, commanded by SS Obersturmbannführer Jochen Peiper, did manage to break through, but was not supported and, in the face of growing American defenses, was not decisive. Its story illustrates the essence of the Ardennes battle, with its mixture of confusion, harshness and small-unit action. Its failure also marks the end of Sixth Panzer Army's efforts in the north.

Peiper was a natural choice to lead the spearhead assault. A committed Nazi with a record of ruthless action on the Eastern Front, where his tank unit was known as the 'Blowtorch Battalion' after the destruction of two villages and their inhabitants, he was briefed for his part in *Wacht am Rhein* on 14 December. *Kampfgruppe Peiper* comprised 100 Mark IV and V (Panther) tanks, a battalion of 42 King Tigers and a fully motorized Panzer Grenadier unit (a force which constituted about half the total strength of 1st SS Panzer Division). Peiper was ordered to push through the southern sector of 99th Division's lines around Buchholz Station and Honsfeld, penetrate down the Amblève valley to its junction with the Salm river at Trois Ponts and then race through Werbomont to cross the Meuse at Huy. A rigid, unalterable route was to be followed to avoid blocking roads earmarked for 12th SS Panzer to the north and Peiper was given strict instructions to keep moving at all times, regardless of events on his flanks. The idea was not only to effect a breakthrough which could then be widened by the rest of 1st SS Panzer, but also to create maximum chaos deep in the American rear, a process which, on the evidence of traditional Blitzkrieg, would quickly lead to collapse.

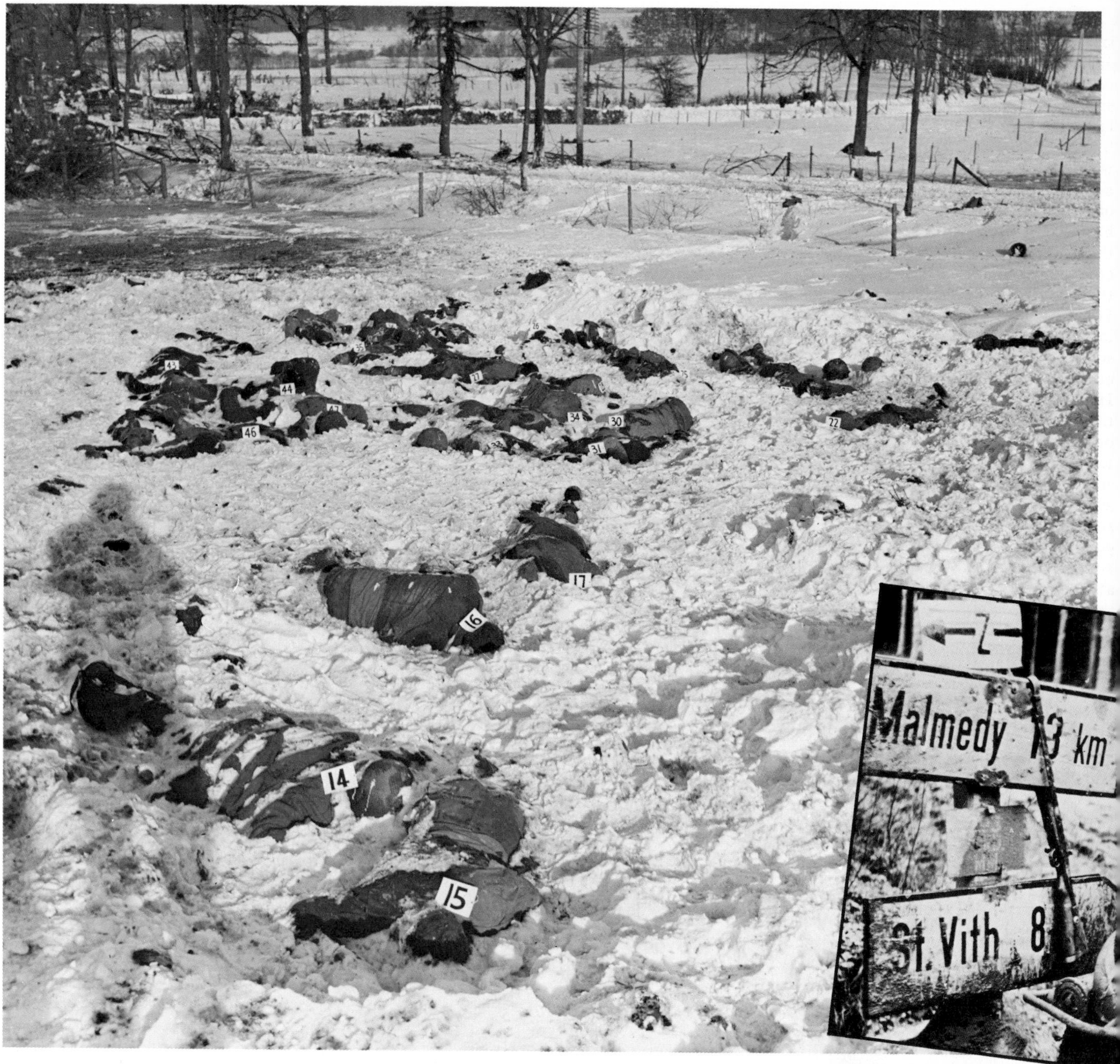
17
16
14
15
Z
Malmedy
km
St. Vith 8

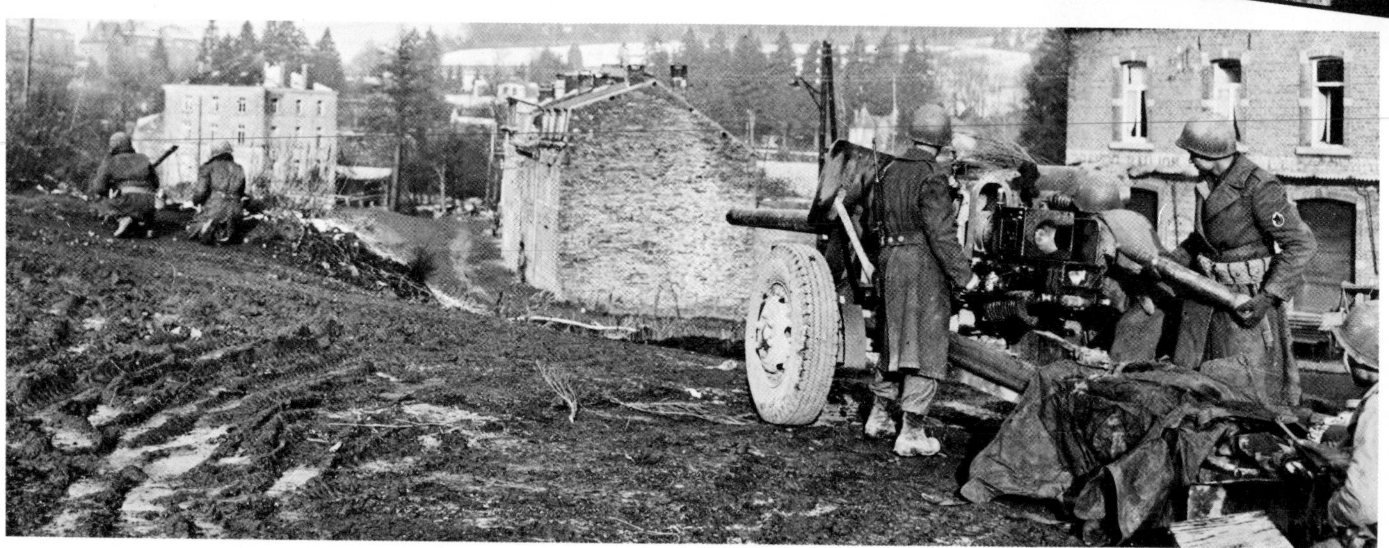

From the start, things did not run smoothly. On 16 December, as *Kampfgruppe Peiper* approached its start line near Losheim, it became embroiled in the enormous traffic jam behind the German lines. Peiper had to force his way through, by-passing a destroyed railroad bridge which was one of the causes of the chaos, and did not reach the newly captured town of Lanzerath until nearly midnight. There he should have been briefed and aided by the 9th Parachute Regiment of 3rd Parachute Division, but it was soon obvious that that unit was poorly led and confused. Peiper had to take personal command, leading the paratroops and his own men in a successful assault on Buchholz Station early on 17 December. He then moved on to Honsfeld, entering the town unopposed by the simple expedient of tagging on to a disorganized American column. Once in the town, he ordered 9th Parachute Regiment to stay put and, gathering his *Kampfgruppe* around him, pushed on alone. He had successfully turned the southern flank of 99th Division and was already in the American rear. Breakthrough seemed assured.

According to his orders, Peiper should now have headed due west as quickly as possible, but he was already aware of another problem – his lack of fuel reserves. As a result he decided to disobey his instructions, and headed north for a US gasoline dump at Bullingen on the route ascribed to 12th SS Panzer. He helped himself to an estimated 50,000 gallons of gasoline before moving back on to the Ligneuville road, hoping to capture an antiaircraft brigade HQ at that town. To ensure success, Peiper split his force, sending the Panzer Grenadiers under Major Josef Diefenthal along the main road while he led the bulk of the armor to envelope Ligneuville from the south. The maneuver was carried out easily and, although the American HQ did manage to escape, both groups had joined up again in the town by late afternoon.

Above left: Bodies of American soldiers lie in the snow at Malmèdy. They were shot by their German captors after surrendering.
Left: An American field gun covers the advance of forward troops.
Above: A Schwimmwagen of the 2nd Panzer Grenadier Regiment heads toward Malmèdy on 17 December.

It was during the course of this advance that Diefenthal's force was responsible for one of the more shocking atrocities of the war in western Europe – the Malmèdy Massacre. As the Panzer Grenadiers, with armor support, had followed the northern route to Ligneuville they had approached the vital crossroads at Baugnez, just south of Malmèdy, where they were to turn left to link up with Peiper. The road through to Ligneuville was packed with American traffic, much of it belonging to 7th Armored Division moving down from Ninth Army and, in order to clear a space, Diefenthal fired on the unfortunate 285th Field Artillery Observation Battalion. Lacking heavy weapons and incapable of stopping either tanks or half-tracks, about 120 men of that unit surrendered, whereupon they were herded into a nearby field and shot. Eighty-five unarmed, helpless prisoners of war did not survive. It was not the only atrocity committed by *Kampfgruppe Peiper* – American prisoners had already died at Bullingen, more were to be shot in Ligneuville and Stavelot – but it was the most sickening. The discovery of the unburied dead by other American units in the area later on 17 December was immediately publicized and probably did much to harden defensive efforts throughout the Ardennes.

Peiper left Ligneuville at about 1700 hours on 17 December, aiming for the important bridge across the Amblève at Stavelot. The road was narrow and poor (Peiper was later to complain that his entire route was fit 'not for tanks but for bicycles') and American defenses were hurriedly being prepared. One of these – a roadblock by a cliff just to the east of Stavelot which could not be by-passed – proved to be of the utmost importance. Although manned by only 13 soldiers of Company C, 291st Combat Engineer Battalion, armed with only a few mines and a bazooka, it succeeded in delaying Peiper for a crucial 13 hours. As his lead tanks approached, one was stopped by a bazooka shot and Peiper withdrew. He did not resume his advance until 0800 hours on 18 December and although he was then able to take Stavelot and the bridge without loss (it is presumed that the bridge demolitions were sabotaged by a *Greif* commando unit), the delay enabled Hodges to redeploy 30th Infantry Division from the north against the penetration. It was the first of the American blocking moves.

Peiper had not broken through entirely, however, for he still needed to cross the Salm river at Trois Ponts if he was to take Werbomont and get to the Meuse. Once again he was stopped, this time by a small task force belonging to the 51st Engineer Battalion, ordered to Trois Ponts late on 17 December. Once in position, they set up roadblocks and prepared two of the three bridges, across the Amblève and the Salm, for demolition. Both were destroyed as Peiper approached, blocking his direct route and forcing him to turn north toward La Gleize. He was beginning to lose both momentum and the initiative, as he was forced to react to a series of American moves designed to blunt his advance and contain his force. His luck changed momentarily at Cheneux, southwest of La Gleize, where an intact bridge across the Amblève was found, but almost immediately he was hit by American fighter-bombers, operating through a rare break in the weather. By late afternoon on 18 December, therefore, *Kampfgruppe Peiper* had been located and checked. Elements of 30th Division were rushed to the area, preventing any movement westward across the Lienne Creek, and by nightfall Peiper had no choice but to withdraw into La Gleize. Locating his men in that village and the neighboring one of Stoumont, he bivouacked for the night.

As Peiper rested, the remainder of 30th Division, aided by 82nd Airborne Division, newly released from strategic reserve by Eisenhower and redeployed to Werbomont while on their way to Bastogne, gradually closed in. Early in the morning of 19 December 1st Battalion, 117th Infantry (part of 30th Division) managed to recapture Stavelot, cutting Peiper off from the rear. Counterattacks by the remainder of 1st SS Panzer, trying desperately to exploit the spearhead breakthrough, led to bitter fighting in Stavelot on 20 December, but the Americans held on. Peiper was now completely isolated. Over the next three days American units slowly squeezed the La Gleize–Stoumont pocket, employing artillery, armor and infantry in overwhelming numbers. By 23 December, with his force decimated and out of gasoline, Peiper realized that all was lost and ordered a breakout on foot. Only a small proportion of his original *Kampfgruppe* survived to link up with friendly forces east of St Vith three days later. Sixth Panzer Army had run its course and, in the process, the Americans had built up a solid defensive line, facing south, from Elsenborn to Stoumont. The northern shoulder of the salient had been held.

3. THE BATTLE FOR THE NORTH

Dietrich's lack of progress was recognized by OKW as early as 20 December, and although it was never intended at this stage that his attack should be halted or his forces withdrawn, the emphasis of the assault was shifted to Manteuffel's army. Here the initial gains had been more dramatic, incorporating breakthroughs in two areas, on the right through 106th Division toward St Vith and on the left through 28th Division toward Bastogne. If Dietrich could not push through on the shortest route to the Meuse, it was therefore logical to reinforce Manteuffel in the hopes that his forces could exploit the gaps and open up the battle. On 20 December Dietrich's II SS Panzer Corps (2nd and 9th SS Panzer Divisions) was shifted southward to follow routes already opened up around St Vith, while Hitler's strategic reserve brigades (*Führer Begleit* and *Führer Grenadier*) were earmarked to support Fifth Panzer Army.

Manteuffel's breakthrough toward St Vith was by no means complete by this date. On 16 December his 18th *Volksgrenadier* Division had outflanked 106th Division in the Schnee Eifel and appeared to face little opposition in its projected sweep westward, yet four days later St Vith itself, defended by a hastily assembled collection of units centered upon 7th Armored Division, was still holding out. The existence of this 'fortified horseshoe' was to continue until 23 December, and although some German formations did by-pass it to both north and south, it stood like a rock which effectively broke the tide of the German advance for a full week. Even when 7th Armored Division and its attached units withdrew, they did so into a screen of strong well-ordered American regiments, rushed into the area to prevent a German exploitation. Such regiments had not been available during the first few days of the battle and without the defense of St Vith it is conceivable that Manteuffel would have made it to the Meuse, if not beyond. St Vith bought time in the northern sector and that time was not wasted.

As with so many other aspects of the Ardennes battle, early defensive efforts around St Vith were extemporized, using whatever forces were available, until more organized formations could be moved in. Thus, although 7th Armored Division was ordered to move south from Ninth Army late on 16 December, it did not begin to arrive at St Vith until 24 hours later, having been rerouted from its original destination of Bastogne by Middleton when he heard the news from the Schnee Eifel. During this crucial period Major General Jones, in his divisional HQ at St Vith, was forced to improvise an initial defense. As his three front-line regiments – the 422nd, 423rd and 424th – were still to the east and apparently surrounded (in the event a large proportion of the 424th was to escape westward), very few troops were immediately available. Those that were, comprising two engineer battalions, the 81st and 168th, and Jones' HQ companies, had to be organized into a scratch force. Under Lieutenant Colonel Tom Riggs, they moved due east toward Schönberg, about two miles out of town, to set up a roadblock through which, it was hoped, 7th Armored Division would attack to relieve the regiments in the Schnee Eifel. Riggs only got as far as Prümerberg, however, before he encountered German forces. There, on high ground overlooking Schönberg, his task force dug in.

Meanwhile, 7th Armored Division was not moving toward St Vith with a great deal of speed, for the closer to the area of battle they came, the more confusion they encountered. Led by Combat Command B (CCB) under Brigadier General Bruce Clarke (who arrived at Jones' HQ ahead of his troops early on 17 December), the division was delayed by traffic jams, particularly between Vielsalm and St Vith. It was split in two by Peiper's advance to Ligneuville and lost contact with its support artillery. The first elements of CCB did not join their commander until about 1600 hours. They were immediately ordered east to join Riggs at the roadblock. At about the same time Brigadier General Robert W Hasbrouck, commanding 7th Armored Division as a whole, arrived to confer with Jones and Clarke. Instantly recognizing the extent and danger of the German attack, he decided not to order a counterattack against the Schnee Eifel but to concentrate on denying St Vith to the enemy. The decision broke the last of Jones' resolve – he now had the dubious distinction of having lost an entire division faster than any other American in history – and although he should, by virtue of his rank, have taken command of the defense, he sensibly handed it over to the infinitely more experienced Clarke. Hasbrouck agreed before moving back to set up divisional HQ at Vielsalm from where he could direct the battle as a whole. By the end of 17 December, therefore, defensive measures were beginning to take shape, principally to the east of St Vith where a fairly strong mix of armor and engineer-infantry, supported by a Field Artillery Battalion (the 275th, available since the collapse of 14th Cavalry Group), was in position.

Fortunately for the Americans the next few days were not to see a concerted German effort against the town, which was by-passed as soon as its defense was recognized. Thus on 18 December probing attacks against the Prümerberg roadblock were beaten off, while to the north a potentially dangerous outflanking move by elements of 1st SS Panzer Division, advancing in support of *Kampfgruppe Peiper*, was countered by the commitment of Combat Command A (CCA) of 7th Armored Division around the village of Poteau. After hard fighting had persuaded the Germans that the Americans meant business, 1st SS Panzer decided to move westward, leaving St Vith to the infantry units which should have been following up. The fact that these units were still trying to break into defensive positions in front of the Elsenborn Ridge contributed significantly to the survival of St Vith.

The probing attacks continued on 19 December, but the lack of a decisive assault enabled Hasbrouck and Clarke to organize and consolidate their defenses. By this time the screen around St Vith was beginning to take on the appearance of a horseshoe with the open end facing west. In the north, between Vielsalm and Poteau, the defenses were light, for dense woods, made even more difficult to pass by the winter weather, acted as a useful barrier.

Top right: A German scans the snow-covered landscape from the cover of his foxhole.

Top far right: 'Sepp' Dietrich consults with his staff officers.

Right: An American supply column brings up reserve ammunition for a battery of self-propelled guns.

Far right: A Panther tank edges past a broken-down truck.

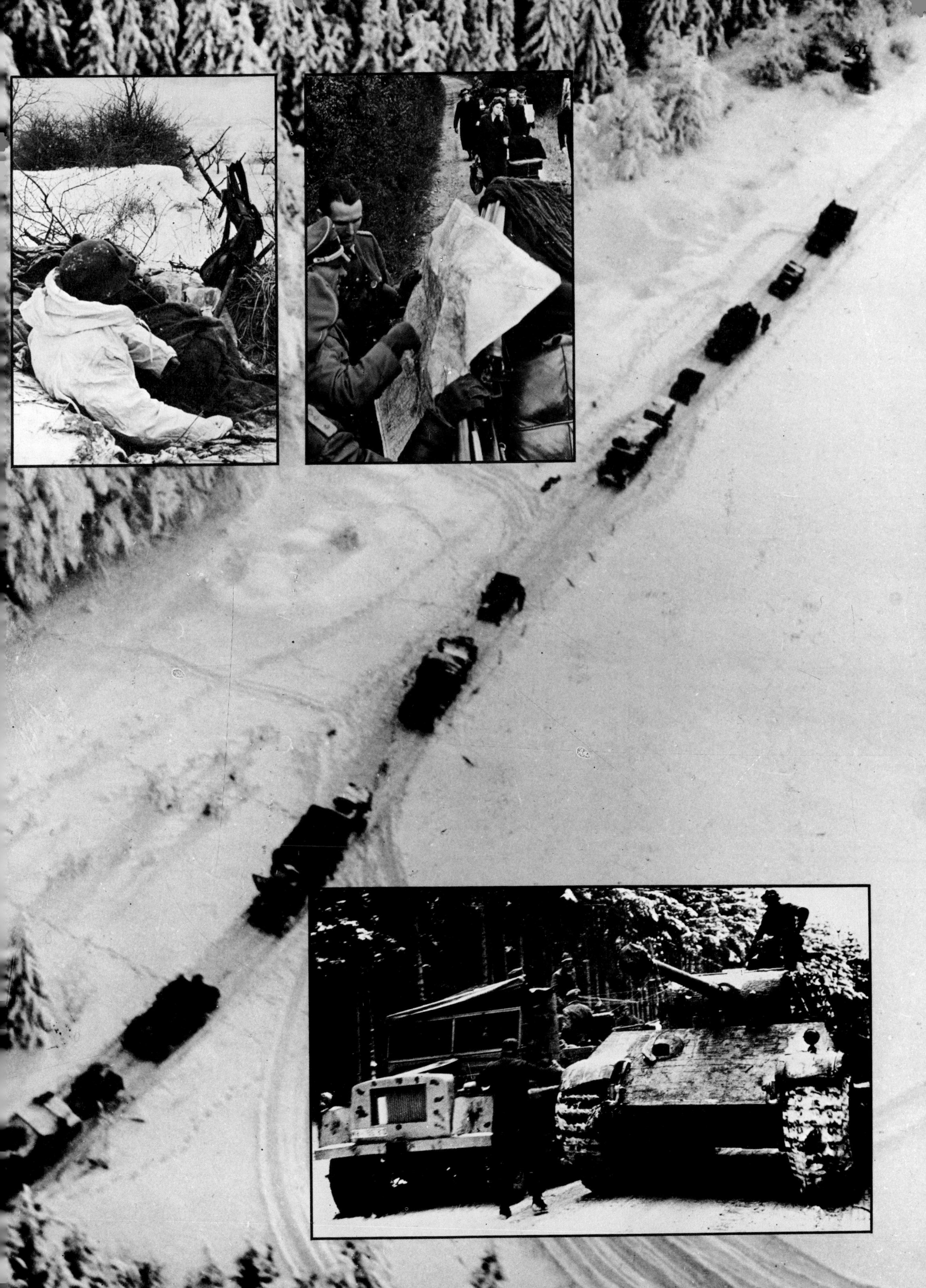

Around Poteau itself CCA of 7th Armored Division was in relatively strong positions, linked on their right to CCB and Riggs' task force on the high ground at Prümerberg. To their right, bending back slightly to the west, was CCB of 9th Armored Division, moved in by Middleton from his mobile reserve, together with the remnants of the 424th Infantry Regiment, recently extricated from the southern sector of the Schnee Eifel. Thereafter the flank was 'in the air,' although the gap was filled to a certain extent as far south as Trois Vierges when the 112th Regimental Combat Team (RCT) 28th Division, pushed northwestward by the German breakthrough on the Our River, suddenly appeared. It was closely followed by 116th Panzer Division, however, and gradually gave ground toward St Vith (thus completing the southern curve of the horseshoe) until the Germans decided to continue westward. Between Gouvry and Vielsalm there was no defense at all, it being hoped that other American units would be moved in from the west as a plug. If this did not happen, of course, it was also a useful escape route for the St Vith defenders. Finally, to bolster up the 424th Regiment and 112th RCT, Hasbrouck organized two mobile task forces, under Lieutenant Colonel Robert B Jones of the 814th Tank Destroyer Battalion and Captain Franklin P Lindsey of 14th Cavalry Group respectively, stationing them at Gouvry and Gruflange in the south. It was not an unbreachable defense – it was particularly vulnerable to encirclement and outflanking moves – but it was well organized and prepared. It was prepared only just in time.

The significance of St Vith altered dramatically on 20 December. Hitler's acceptance of Dietrich's failure and his decision to concentrate on Manteuffel's breakthroughs not only released fresh bodies of troops to add to the pressure but also made the capture of St Vith essential to the revised German plan. In American hands the town straddled vital north-south communications and acted as a block in the path of a broad advance. Under German control it would open up the northern approaches to Bastogne and, hopefully, break the logjam of American defense. As soon as he knew of Hitler's change of plan, therefore, Model ordered the swift destruction of Clarke's horseshoe, using 62nd and 560th *Volksgrenadier* Divisions as well as the *Führer Begleit* Brigade, released from OKW reserve. As an added bonus, he also received the 18th *Volksgrenadiers*, relieved of their mopping-up duties on the Schnee Eifel by the sudden surrender of the 422nd and 423rd Infantry Regiments late on 19 December, and could expect the arrival of II SS Panzer Corps as soon as it redeployed from Dietrich's sector. With such forces beginning to concentrate against him and with elements of 1st SS Panzer and 116th Panzer by-passing to north and south, Clarke faced overwhelming odds.

The 20 December was a day of decision for the Allies as well. Ever since the initial reports of the assault had trickled through to Eisenhower, the Supreme Commander and his staff had been aware of the need for fundamental command changes to deal with the situation. As Manteuffel's forces broke through they created a significant salient in the American lines (the 'bulge' from which the popular name for the Ardennes battle comes), which threatened to split Bradley's 12th Army Group in two. Bradley's headquarters was situated in Luxembourg, to the south of the salient. Communications all around the battle area were poor and control of the northern sector, by now in the process of being heavily reinforced to stop what the Allies imagined was a drive to Liège, was almost impossible. It therefore seemed logical to split the battle area in half along a line drawn between Givet in the west and Prüm in the east and give control of each sector to a different commander. The decision was made on 20 December and thereafter, for the duration of the battle, all forces north of the Givet–Prüm line (the entire Ninth Army and most

Above: The wreckage of a knocked-out Marder III self-propelled antitank gun lies by the road.
Top: An American tank destroyer takes cover behind a pillbox.

of Hodges' First) were transferred to 21st Army Group under Montgomery, leaving Bradley to concentrate on the south. Militarily it was a sound move, although politically it did seem to cause the sort of inter-Allied squabbling which Hitler had planned to exploit. Montgomery's appointment was unpopular with many Americans, particularly when both he and the British Press appeared to presume that the Ardennes front would have collapsed without his help, but it did rationalize the command structure. Once again, Hitler's presumption that the Allied reaction to *Wacht am Rhein* would be disjointed proved false.

Montgomery's new command area included St Vith and although his initial reaction was to order an immediate withdrawal of Clarke's forces to 'straighten the line,' he was persuaded that a defense of the horsehoe, however short, might impose some decisive delays upon the German advance. Consequently, late on 20 December, he ordered Ridgway's XVIII Airborne Corps at Werbomont to link up with Clarke using 82nd Airborne Division and a portion of 3rd Armored Division (the latter on attachment from VII Corps). Ridgway was to move into the gap between Vielsalm and Salmchâteau and keep it open as an escape route for 7th Armored Division, to be used after sufficient delay had been imposed.

The Germans attacked St Vith in force on 21 December, concentrating on the routes from the east and north. Heavy fighting ensued in very poor weather conditions and, not surprisingly, the American defenses began to crack. First to go was the roadblock at Prümerberg, hit by sustained artillery fire and determined assaults from the 18th *Volksgrenadiers*. By the end of the day Riggs' task force had been split from CCA of 7th Armored Division and surrounded. Riggs attempted to break out to the west after dark, but deep snow hampered his progress and he was forced to surrender. Early the next morning the *Führer Begleit* Brigade followed up in the same area, penetrating deeply between CCB at Poteau and CCA to its right. Clarke abandoned St Vith, pulling back his left flank as far west as Hindershausen, and asked for permission to withdraw. As Ridgway's forces had arrived at Vielsalm and Salmchâteau, Montgomery concurred, even though by now the battle area had been churned to mud, which made movement of any kind difficult.

Fortunately, by 0500 hours on 23 December, a sudden frost had hardened the ground and Clarke began to pull back. Protected by elements of 82nd Airborne Division, all the forces in the horseshoe had been successfully withdrawn by dusk, leaving the Germans in possession of St Vith and its surrounding area. It was a Pyrrhic victory, for although Model was now free to swing his divisions northwestward in a broad drive to the Meuse, American defenses had consolidated in his projected path. He was going to have to fight through them with exhausted troops.

Above: These Belgian children were forced from their homes.

German forces which had by-passed or were involved in the assault against St Vith – the infantry and armor of Manteuffel's right wing, plus some of the redeployed SS panzer units from Dietrich's army – were intent upon swinging toward the northwest, aiming for the Meuse between Huy and Liège. At the beginning of the battle this was an American rear area, virtually unprotected once the front line had been breached, and susceptible to the sort of panic and collapse which traditional Blitzkrieg caused. Fortunately for the Allies the successful holding action on the Elsenborn Ridge, together with the defense of St Vith for a week, prevented an immediate breakthrough and enabled the Americans to rush troops into the region in an attempt to create a defensive line. It was a crucial phase of the battle, developing into a race between American and German units to occupy key road networks and river crossings along an 80-mile front.

The area in question, running westward from the Elsenborn positions, is divided roughly down the middle by the river Salm. To the east of the river, following the Amblève valley to the original front line of 16 December, lay the sector which offered the quickest route to Liège, principally following the road through Malmèdy and Spa. This was the area which Dietrich had tried to break into on the first day, only to be stopped by the 2nd and 99th Divisions in front of Elsenborn. The western sector, bordered by the Salm on the east and the Ourthe on the west, offered a more usable road – Route 15, running from Bastogne, through Manhay and Werbomont, to Liège – but entailed potentially difficult river crossings and necessitated an early advance through the Losheim gap to the road network centered upon St Vith. Both sectors therefore had much to offer to the Germans, although American defensive measures did need to be preempted.

By 20 December the Allied commanders were trying desperately to create such defenses before the Panzers could outflank them. A degree of success had been achieved – 1st Division had moved into Elsenborn by 17 December, 30th Division had been deployed against Peiper's spearheads at Stavelot, Malmèdy and Stoumont by the 18th and 82nd Airborne had been redeployed to the west of the Salm, with a Combat Command of 3rd Armored on its right, between the Salm and the Ourthe, by the 19th – but the line was thin and, as yet, uncoordinated. Continuing German attacks could still be successful, particularly if the vital crossroads at Malmèdy in the east and Manhay in the west could be taken, for they would crack the American positions on the northern flank wide open.

Assaults on the eastern sector, and especially against the approaches to Elsenborn on the shoulder of the developing bulge, had been intense since the opening of the battle, but they reached a new, almost desperate, level of ferocity in the early hours of 21 December. At 0130 hours elements of 12th SS Panzer Division, redeployed to widen the corridor created by 3rd Parachute Division and *Kampfgruppe Peiper*, attacked the village of Don Burtgenbach from the direction of Bullingen, hoping to force a way into the Elsenborn defenses. They almost succeeded, hitting the 26th Infantry Regiment, 1st Division, with large numbers of tanks and infantry. However the superior, and underestimated, flexibility of the Americans was beginning to tell. By this time the 1st, 2nd and 99th Divisions had decided to combine their artillery, with devastating results. The approaches to Don Burtgenbach were blasted in a massed artillery strike, disrupting the German attack and inflicting significant casualties. The 12th SS Panzer tried again 24 hours later, only to suffer the same fate, and thereafter the Elsenborn Ridge was not seriously assaulted. The shoulder was clearly secure.

A similar degree of defensive success was enjoyed at the same time around Malmèdy. After Peiper's forces had come perilously close to the town on 17 December, the 120th Infantry Regiment, 30th Division, had been moved in. They were attacked on 21 December by 150th Panzer Brigade, the unit formed by Skorzeny for rear-area disruption but now used conventionally in the absence of a massive breakthrough. A two-pronged advance, designed to isolate Malmèdy from east and west, failed in the face of determined resistance. As Peiper's spearhead had by this time been contained, the area east of the Salm was holding firm.

The western sector, between the Salm and the Ourthe, was less secure, however, for in the light of the initial attacks against the shoulder, fewer troops had been pushed into it during the early days. By 21 December therefore, despite the arrival of Ridgway's XVIII Airborne Corps HQ at Werbomont, little more than a division was protecting the region and even that was deployed more to maintain contact with St Vith than to consolidate an east-west line. The 82nd Airborne was occupying positions running principally north-south along the west bank of the Salm from Trois Ponts to Vielsalm, with only a few of its units projecting westward to just above Salmchâteau and Baraque de Fraiture. This meant that they were covering little over half the sector, leaving the area up to the Ourthe to a single Combat Command (CCR) of 3rd Armored Division, under Colonel Robert L Howze Jr. He established his HQ at Soy, to the west of Manhay, and divided his inadequate force into three groups, sending them to protect the river crossing at La Roche (Task Force Hogan), the Samrée to Soy road (Task Force Orr) and Manhay itself (Task Force Kane). Even as these dispositions were being made, on 20 December, the bulk of LVIII Panzer Corps (116th Panzer and 560th *Volksgrenadier* Divisions), having by-passed St Vith to the south, was taking Samrée, while 2nd SS Panzer Division, redeployed from Dietrich's reserve, was crossing the upper reaches of the Ourthe at Houffalize and advancing northward toward Manhay. CCR of 3rd Armored, overstretched and unsupported, was all that stood between the Germans and the Meuse.

The inevitable attacks began on 21 December but, remarkably, were held. The 116th Panzer, ordered to advance from Samrée toward a river crossing at Hotton,

Left: American troops 'dig in.'
Above: As commander of Army Group B, Field Marshal Model was in overall charge of the Ardennes offensive.
Top: Model (center) talks to a group of infantrymen.

a few miles west of Soy, broke through the gap between Hogan and Orr but were stopped short of their objective by a scratch force of Howze's HQ troops. The Germans withdrew, convinced that a large American formation opposed them and shifted their probing assault to La Roche. Hogan's task force held out until the evening of 21 December, but was eventually forced to withdraw northward to Marcouray, allowing the Panzers to cross the Ourthe on the 22nd. To the surprise of the Americans, who still saw Liège as the main German objective, the 116th then swung westward toward Dinant, leaving 3rd Armored in possession of their existing locations. This was just as well, for almost immediately 2nd SS Panzer attacked from Houffalize toward the crossroads at Baraque de Fraiture and the vital road junction of Manhay. The crossroads, defended by a hastily assembled rear-area force under Major Arthur C Parker III (and so, inevitably, known as 'Parker's Crossroads') and recently reinforced by a company of the 325th Glider Infantry, 82nd Airborne Division, was hit by artillery, tanks and Panzer Grenadiers early on the morning of the 23rd. After an unequal struggle, the position fell, leaving the route to Manhay wide open.

Ridgway was now in a desperate situation, even when he received CCA of 3rd Armored as reinforcement, for his line was still extremely thin. Fortunately 2nd SS Panzer, finding that it was out on its own (too many German troops were involved in the final phases of the St Vith battle to offer support), did not exploit its success immediately. The pause was well-used by the Americans. On 24 December the survivors of St Vith were rested and, although the majority were in no condition to continue fighting, CCA of 7th Armored Division was still strong enough, on paper at least, to take over the defense of Manhay, joining Task Force Kane in plugging the gap. At the same time Montgomery ordered a 'straightening of the line,' withdrawing 82nd Airborne from Vielsalm–Salmchâteau to positions running east-west from Trois Ponts to Manhay and Hotton.

The 2nd SS Panzer renewed its attack at 2100 hours on 24 December (clearer weather was forcing the Germans to lie low during daylight for fear of Allied air attacks), advancing quite fortuitously straight down the interface between 3rd and 7th Armored Divisions. CCA of 7th Armored, exhausted after its gallant efforts around St Vith, broke under the pressure, leaving Kane isolated: Manhay fell. The Panzers promptly moved westward to outflank 3rd Armored at Soy and to cross the river at Hotton. Ridgway, surprised at the lack of northward advance, took the opportunity to fill the Manhay gap by moving in the first units to arrive of the redeployed 75th Infantry Division. They were in position by the early hours of 25 December, so that when 2nd SS Panzer tried to widen the flank of its penetration, it made little headway. Ridgway completed his blocking move by ordering a scratch force of St Vith survivers (a combined CCA/CCB of 7th Armored together with the 2nd Battalion, 424th Infantry Regiment) to retake Manhay, a task successfully carried out on the 26th. 2nd SS Panzer now had nowhere to go.

The Americans had thus managed, against considerable odds, to create a solid defensive line from Elsenborn all the way to Hotton. German attempts to swing northwestward to the Meuse had been blocked over an 80-mile front and if the maneuver was ever to be carried out it would have to be done by troops of Manteuffel's left wing, advancing by an extremely circuitous route from Bastogne in the south. With clearer weather, increased Allied air activity and a chronic shortage of fuel on the German side, the odds in favor of this were never good. The bulge was rapidly developing into a trap.

4. BASTOGNE BESIEGED

By nightfall on 16 December the troops of General von Lüttwitz's XLVII Panzer Corps, responsible for the assault on Manteuffel's left wing, appeared to be on the verge of a breakthrough. The initial infantry attacks, carried out by 26th *Volksgrenadier* Division, had crossed the Our, penetrated as far as Skyline Drive and punched large holes through Colonel Hurley Fuller's 110th Infantry Regiment. The 112th and 109th Regiments, to north and south respectively, had held firm, but with the Our crossings secure von Lüttwitz was able to begin deployment of 2nd Panzer and Panzer *Lehr* Divisions during the hours of darkness. Their objectives were the bridges over the Clerf river, particularly at Clervaux and Drauffelt, the road center of Wiltz where Fuller had his HQ, and the approaches to Bastogne.

An early occupation of Bastogne was essential to German success, for the town was the focal point for seven major roads (leading to Houffalize in the north, St Vith in the northeast, Luxembourg in the southeast, Arlon in the south, Neufchâteau in the southwest and Marche and La Roche in the northwest). Its importance was recognized during the planning stages of *Wacht am Rhein*, when OKW officers had managed to persuade Hitler to exempt the town from his 'no deviation' rule, for if the Americans held on, the entire road network of the Ardennes, so crucial in an advance through winter weather, would be denied. According to the plan, 26th *Volksgrenadiers* were to capture Bastogne by the third day of the assault, allowing 2nd Panzer and Panzer *Lehr* to by-pass it to north and south, using roads free from American interference. It was an ambitious schedule, particularly as the *Volksgrenadiers* were also responsible for the Our and Clerf crossings, but during the first few days of the battle, it was very nearly realized.

The first priorities on 17 December were for XLVII Panzer Corps to clear the area east of Bastogne and for the Panzer Divisions to begin a rapid exploitation to the Meuse. In both respects a degree of success was enjoyed. Despite a gallant counterattack by elements of the 110th Regiment east of Clervaux, 2nd Panzers captured that town by late afternoon, crossing the Clerf and heading for Houffalize preparatory to a swing northwestward, toward the Meuse. The 110th Regiment thereby ceased to exist and, as the gap left by it became apparent, the other units of 28th Division were forced to pull back: the 112th Regiment toward St Vith and the 109th toward 4th Division on the southern flank of the assault area. The latter movement allowed Panzer *Lehr* to cross the Clerf at Drauffelt and 5th Parachute Division (on the right wing of Brandenberger's Seventh Army) to deploy west of the Our. Both units joined 26th *Volksgrenadiers* in an attack against Wiltz and when the town fell on 19

Below: American troops advance at Bastogne, where the 101st Airborne Division was surrounded during the German advance until 26 December.
Left: An engineer plants a mine in a muddy roadway.
Above: This German tank was destroyed by the Bastogne defenders.

December, the southern approaches to Bastogne lay open. A major German breakthrough seemed inevitable.

The Americans had not been slow to appreciate the danger. General Middleton, whose Corps HQ was in Bastogne, had begun defensive deployments as early as 17 December, sending two task forces from his mobile reserve (CCR of 9th Armored Division) to cover the eastern approaches to the town. Task Force Harper (under Lieutenant Colonel R S Harper) had established a roadblock at Allenborn, on the road to St Vith, while Task Force Rose (under Captain L K Rose) had moved a few miles to the northeast, protecting the route from Clervaux and Trois Vierges. At the same time a thin defensive screen had been set up in an arc from Foy to Neffe, covering the northeast to the rear of Harper and Rose and manned by hastily-collected units of the 128th Combat Engineer Group. Task Force Harper did not survive for long. It was overrun by spearheads of 2nd Panzer Division late on 18 December, but as the Germans were intent upon exploitation toward Noville and Houffalize in the northwest, Bastogne itself was not directly threatened. This gave Middleton time to deploy the reinforcements being rushed to him under orders from the Supreme Commander.

The first of these formations to arrive was the CCB of 10th Armored Division under Colonel William L Roberts, released from Patton's Third Army by Eisenhower late on 16 December. As the troops drove

into Bastogne 48 hours later, they were divided into three 'teams' and hurriedly sent out to form strongpoints in an arc to the east. Team O'Hara (Lieutenant Colonel James O'Hara) pushed southeast to an area around Wardin on the Luxembourg road, Team Cherry (Lieutenant Colonel Henry T Cherry) moved toward Longvilly on the route to St Vith in the east, and Team Desobry (Major William R Desobry) travelled northeast to Noville on the road to Houffalize. They were supported by elements of 101st Airborne Division, under temporary command of Brigadier General Anthony C McAuliffe (the official divisional commander, Major General Maxwell D Taylor, was absent on leave), redeployed from their initial destination of Werbomont as soon as the threat became apparent. The first unit to arrive, the 501st Parachute Infantry Regiment, was sent due east, toward Team Cherry on the Longvilly road, late on 18 December. Unknown to them, spearheads of Panzer *Lehr* had already cut that road at Margeret, forming a solid block between the two American formations. The paratroops of the 501st were therefore stopped early on 19 December at Neffe and Team Cherry was forced to attempt a withdrawal to link up. Results were mixed. Team Cherry was caught in the open to the east of Neffe and destroyed, but the 501st, in a classic three-battalion attack, managed to push Panzer *Lehr* units out of Bizory to the north of Margeret, consolidating a defensive line which was to hold firm until the following day. Elsewhere the situation was much the same. In the northeast Team Desobry, supported by the 506th Parachute Infantry Regiment, beat off an attack by 2nd Panzer Division at Noville, while Team O'Hara was forced to give some ground, including Wardin itself, in the southeast. The Germans were clearly probing for weak spots, but a coherent defensive line was beginning to emerge by the end of 19 December. The period of American confusion, during which the major German advances should have been made, was already coming to an end.

This was seen to good effect elsewhere on the same day, for while the defenders of

Far left: When summoned to surrender at Bastogne, Brigadier General Anthony McAuliffe answered 'nuts.'
Left and below left: Airborne supply drops sustained the defenders of Bastogne.
Right: General Patton's Third Army fought its way through to Bastogne on 26 December.

Bastogne were sorting themselves out, top-level Allied commanders at a meeting in Verdun were making some far-reaching strategic decisions. Eisenhower was by now convinced that the only way to destroy the German assault was to contain it between the already-solidifying shoulders around Elsenborn and Echternach, preparatory to counterattacks from north and south. Bastogne was the key, so priority had to be given to the southern flank. Toward this end, the Supreme Commander cancelled Patton's projected attack in the Saar and extended the front to be defended by 6th Army Group northward. The Third Army, thus released from both offensive and defensive commitments, could then turn north, toward Bastogne. Patton had already appreciated this, and when Eisenhower directed him to redeploy on 19 December, he was able to oblige with remarkable speed. The 4th Armored Division was ordered to move toward Arlon and 80th Infantry Division toward Luxembourg, while 26th Infantry Division was directed to concentrate as a reserve, facing north. All three formations were earmarked for an advance toward Bastogne. Once again, American flexibility under pressure was superb.

Patton's forces could not be expected to begin their advance until 22 December at the earliest, so the Bastogne defenders still faced a difficult task against progressively stronger German assaults. On 20 December Team Desobry (now under Major Robert F Harwick of 101st Airborne since Desobry had been wounded the previous evening) came under sustained pressure from Panzer Grenadiers of 2nd Panzer Division, and although the initial attacks were repulsed, the American positions rapidly became untenable. Harwick was ordered to withdraw to link up with the 502nd Parachute Infantry Regiment to his south, a movement completed by 1700 hours. 2nd Panzer, unopposed, swept through Noville to Ortheuville and crossed the Ourthe river, outflanking Bastogne to the north. At the same time Panzer *Lehr* units managed to dislodge the paratroops of the 501st from their positions in Bizory in the east, forcing them back to within two miles of Bastogne itself. Brigadier General McAuliffe, appointed that day to command all American units involved in the defense, seemed to be facing a crisis.

Fortunately for the Americans the following day – 21 December – saw an easing of German pressure. This was partly due to a temporary break in the weather which allowed Allied aircraft to fly in supplies and hit ground targets, but it was also an indication of von Lüttwitz's growing frustration. Bastogne should have fallen on the 18th yet, despite Panzer Division breakthroughs to north and south, the town's defenses were still holding out, principally in an arc from Noville to Wardin. He therefore spent the day reorganizing his forces, sending the bulk of Panzer *Lehr* to the south of Bastogne but keeping back the 901st Panzer Grenadier Regiment as a reinforcement to 26th *Volksgrenadiers*, now charged with taking the town. In addition, he shifted the emphasis of attack from the east right round to the southwest and west, a policy which completed the encirclement of American defense. The siege of Bastogne began late on 21 December, with the odds theoretically in the Germans' favor. The 2nd Panzer was cutting off communications to the north and Panzer *Lehr* and 5th Parachute Division, newly positioned astride the Arlon road, were in the south. Therefore, 26th *Volksgrenadiers*, comprising a reconnaissance battalion, an engineer battalion, the 39th, 77th and 78th *Volksgrenadier* Regiments as well as the 901st Panzer Grenadiers, could devote all its energies to a quick victory. Opposing them, under McAuliffe, there were four airborne regiments (501st, 502nd and 506th Parachute and 327th Glider Infantry), four light artillery and two medium howitzer battalions, the 420th Armored Field Artillery Battalion, about 40 medium tanks and the 705th Tank Destroyer Battalion. They could not be expected to hold out indefinitely.

Bearing this in mind, the commander of the 26th *Volksgrenadiers*, General Heinz Kokott, offered to negotiate the surrender of the town early on 22 December. McAuliffe's terse reply – 'Nuts!' – has entered the folklore of the Ardennes battle, but it

was indicative of the high morale enjoyed by the American defenders at this time. This was doubtless reinforced by news that Patton's counterattack had begun that same morning and was manifested in successful actions against Kokott's troops in the south around Assenois and in the northwest around Champs. Once these attacks had been repulsed, Kokott seemed prepared to go over to the defensive, aiming for an investment of the town rather than a costly occupation. For this reason the next two days were relatively quiet. On 23 December limited German operations against Flamierge in the northwest and Marvie in the southeast were countered in improving weather conditions (the same freeze which enabled Clarke to escape from St Vith), and a major Allied airlift began. This continued on the 24th, together with ground-

attack air strikes which succeeded in preventing further German assaults. McAuliffe used the lull to rationalize his perimeter, drawing back the units deployed in a vulnerable salient around Flamierge and Marde St Etienne in the northwest. The ring around Bastogne was now only 16 miles in circumference.

Kokott resumed his offensive on Christmas Day, having been reinforced by elements of 15th Panzer Grenadier Division, taken from Manteuffel's reserve specially for operations against Bastogne. A major attack began to develop around Champs as early as 0300 hours. The plan was for the 77th *Volksgrenadier* Regiment to attack to the northwest of the village and tie down American units, whereupon the 115th Panzer Grenadier Regiment would break through to Hemroulle and into Bastogne itself. At first a degree of success was achieved – by 0530 hours the 77th had made significant penetrations and the 115th

Left: GI's inspect a King Tiger tank knocked out by fighter bombers.
Below left: Dead American paratroopers await burial during the siege of Bastogne.
Above: German soldiers who died assaulting Bastogne lie in the snow.
Right: Men of the 101st Airborne Division dig casualties out of a collapsed building.

had overrun two companies of the 327th Glider Infantry – but then disaster struck. As the Panzer Grenadiers moved in a pincer assault on Hemroulle they were caught in a specially prepared trap. As paratroops of the 502nd picked off the infantry with small-arms fire, the 705th Tank Destroyer Battalion took on the tanks. The German forces were wiped out, losing a total of 17 AFVs, and the attack ground to a halt. The immediate threat to Bastogne diminished as Kokott counted the cost, although, in the absence of a link up with Patton's forces from the south, the town was still not secure.

Patton had worked hard since 19 December to organize his counterattack. The three divisions initially moved northward toward the Ardennes sector – 4th Armored, 26th and 80th Infantry – were quickly formed into III Corps under Major General John Millikin and given the main task of relieving Bastogne. At the same time, however, Major General Manton Eddy's XII Corps (10th Armored – less CCB – and 4th and 5th Infantry Divisions) was prepared for a drive on the right toward

Left: A brief rest for two of the garrison during the Bastogne battle.
Below left: Men of the 101st Airborne Division relax after their relief by US armor.

Above: American troops advance to the relief of Bastogne.
Below: A patrol of 101st Airborne Division moves out of Bastogne on 29 December.

the Sûre river north of Ettelbrück. It was envisaged that this attack would eventually lead to Wiltz and even St Vith. This increased the workload on Patton's staff and, when combined with a total lack of knowledge about German dispositions, served to delay the start of the offensive until 22 December. Nevertheless, hopes ran high and an early link up with McAuliffe was predicted.

In the event, things did not go smoothly. Despite an initial advance all along the line of about seven miles on the first day, most of this proved to be over the no man's land between the opposing forces and as more difficult ground was encountered, particularly in the east toward the Sûre river, the advance rapidly bogged down. The 4th Armored Division, operating on the extreme left and charged with responsibility for the actual relief of Bastogne, found the going especially hard. The division was divided, as was normal practice, into three Combat Commands, of which two (CCA and CCB) were expected to attack while the third (CCR) was held in reserve. On 22 December CCA took the right wing of the

advance, operating along the Arlon–Bastogne road, while CCB followed secondary roads to the west emanating from Habay La Neuve, aiming to converge with CCA as Bastogne was approached. Little opposition was encountered to begin with, but by noon on this first day both commands had made contact with units of 5th Parachute Division. CCB had to fight its way through Burnon – an operation which took until the early hours of the 23rd – while CCA was forced to redeploy against entrenched opposition at Martelange. The attacks seemed in danger of petering out well short of their objective.

When a similar pattern of slow, costly advance was experienced on Christmas Eve, Millikin was forced to act. He reinforced both commands with infantry drawn from 80th Division and, more importantly, deployed CCR of 4th Armored to the west of CCB, on the Neufchâteau–Bastogne road. This was an astute move, for when CCR advanced from Cobreville toward Remonville on the morning of 25 December, significant advances were made. A bitter battle had to be fought in Remonville itself, but by dusk on Christmas Day the way was clear to Remichampagne, Clochimont and Bastogne. Twenty-four hours later the first tanks broke through to link up with McAuliffe's troops and the siege was over. With contact now regained, a dangerous salient had been forced across the German line of advance, threatening the security of those forces already heading westward. It was a turning point in the battle which, in conjunction with other events taking place at the same time, ensured eventual Allied victory.

Left: Two of Bastogne's German besiegers surrender.
Below: An American half-track rolls into Bastogne past a column of dejected German prisoners on 27 December.

5. THE FINAL RECKONING

The by-passing of Bastogne by 2nd Panzer Division to the north and Panzer *Lehr* to the south – a process well under way by 20–21 December – presented the Americans with a potentially dangerous situation. The battle area as a whole was in a state of considerable confusion, with holding actions being fought at Elsenborn, La Gleize, St Vith, Bastogne and on the southern shoulder, but with large, relatively undefended gaps in between. Admittedly the Germans were being slowed down – to a decisive extent as it turned out – but an advance to the Meuse was still a distinct possibility. Once the Panzers broke loose to the west, blocking moves at places such as Bastogne could become irrelevant, tying down valuable resources at a time when as many troops as possible would be needed in a mobile defensive role. It was therefore something of a gamble when Middleton, after consultation with his superiors, allowed McAuliffe to become encircled late on 21 December for, in reality, he had little left with which to prevent a Panzer advance. Reserves moved into the battle area had been devoted to the defense either of key locations or of the line from Elsenborn to the Ourthe, leaving a significant gap between that river and the Meuse at Dinant. If German forces, probably from XLVII Panzer Corps in the south, as all others had been or were in the process of being blocked, could swing into this gap, capturing the Ourthe river crossing at Hotton and the important road junction at Marche on Route 35, the way would be clear to Liège and the Allied rear, east of the Meuse. The first priority should therefore have been a rapid expansion of the northern defensive line westward, to close the gap, but with the heavy commitment of reserves elsewhere and a degree of Allied confusion about German aims, this was not an easy policy to carry out.

By 20 December most of the Allied commanders were convinced that the German plan was to swing northward to Liège, cutting off the left wing of Hodges' First Army facing the Siegfried Line; in other words, Rundstedt's 'little slam' strategy, rejected by Hitler earlier in the month. With this in mind, it was expected that all the German assault formations, once having broken through, would take the shortest route to Liège, cutting northward somewhere between Elsenborn and the

Above left: Soldiers of an SS unit stop for a smoke near an abandoned American armored car.
Left: Men of the US Army's 5th Infantry Division advance through the bitter winter weather.
Above: A gun crew of the 548th Antiaircraft Battalion watch the progress of a dogfight, which is etched in condensation trails.
Right: German prisoners carry a wounded comrade in a blanket.

Ourthe, ignoring Dinant and Namur to the northwest. Thus, although significant countermoves were initiated as early as 19 December, when Montgomery redeployed Horrocks' XXX Corps from Holland to an area between Brussels and Liège and Hodges withdrew Collins' VII Corps from Düren in the north to the Marche Plain, west of the Ourthe, there appeared to be little sense of urgency involved. Both were regarded as long-term moves, the former to create a defense in depth and the latter to begin the build up of a counterattack force designed to advance eastward, across the main German thrusts. The development of Panzer attacks toward Dinant and Namur, at right angles to the imagined German axis, was therefore something of a surprise, necessitating a hurried and piecemeal commitment of Collins' corps to close the Ourthe–Meuse gap.

Collins had been given four divisions with which to prepare his counterattack, but they were by no means a coherent force on 20 December. The 2nd Armored and 84th Infantry were situated on the front line around Düren, so they had to be withdrawn and sent south over poor roads in winter conditions. The 3rd Armored was split up and already involved in the battle on the northern sector of the Ardennes; CCA was chasing von der Heydte's paratroops around Baraque Michel, CCB was attached to 30th Division for operations against *Kampfgruppe Peiper*, and CCR was moving into defensive positions east of the Ourthe. The 75th Infantry was an inexperienced formation which had to be moved into the area from Hodges' reserve. Furthermore, as Collins' HQ also had to be moved south to its new location, those units which did arrive were placed temporarily under Ridgway's command, a policy which inevitably led to their use wherever the danger was greatest. Thus, for example, when the first elements of 75th Infantry came within XVIII Airborne Corps area on 25 December they were immediately committed to the defense of Manhay, east of the Ourthe, rather than to the Ourthe–Meuse gap. In the end, this important sector was covered by 2nd Armored and 84th Infantry only, occupying a series of strongpoints rather than a continuous line. The first units of 84th Infantry, 334th and 335th Infantry Regiments, in fact arrived on 21 December – a remarkable achievement in the prevailing conditions. They were deployed in battalion groups on the road between Hotton and Marche, with one battalion moving down to Rochefort, eight miles southwest of Marche, the following day. They were only just in time.

Responsibility for capturing Marche and opening the route to Namur lay with 2nd Panzer Division, aided on their left by Panzer *Lehr* and on their right by 116th Panzer from LVIII Panzer Corps. By 22 December all three divisions were converging on the Ourthe–Meuse gap, having successfully by-passed the defensive blocks

Left: US combat engineers work in icy water to build a bridge.
Below left: A well-clad patrol of the Queen's Own Rifles of Canada.

Above: Troops of the 82nd Airborne Division drag ammunition by sled.
Below: A heavily bearded sergeant of the 320th Infantry Regiment.

at Bastogne and St Vith. The 2nd Panzer was in the lead, pushing hard toward its objective despite a number of Allied air strikes against its lead formations. Indeed, so intent were they upon exploitation that they skirted Marche to the south, leaving the capture of the town to a detached Panzer Grenadier group, and headed straight for the Meuse. It was an ill-considered move, placing them between Marche to the north and Rochefort to the south, each defended by a relatively strong American force. When the lead units encountered probing Allied patrols late on 22 December they halted in a dangerously vulnerable 'finger' protruding northwestward for nearly seven miles. Nor were they fully supported on their flanks; Panzer *Lehr* was meeting opposition from the defenders of Rochefort while 116th Panzer was finding the going hard between Hotton and Verdenne. The 2nd Panzer Division was occupying a potential trap.

This seems to have been realized by the Germans before the Americans, for throughout 23–24 December enormous efforts were made to broaden the finger. They were not very successful. On the left, after heavy fighting, Panzer *Lehr* units managed to captive Rochefort, only to be held to the west at Ciergnon as they tried to link up with 2nd Panzer. The 116th Panzer on the right had no better luck, finding it impossible to break through the 84th Infantry defenses betwen Hotton and Verdenne, and reinforcement divisions – 9th Panzer and the bulk of 15th Panzer Grenadier – were kept away from the area by Allied air attacks. By late afternoon on the 24th, 2nd Panzer – by now running desperately short of fuel – should have been ordered to withdraw but, despite pleas from von Lüttwitz, Hitler characteristically refused permission. The lead units, occupying two separate areas, one around the village of Foy-Notre-Dame and the other around Celles and Conjoux, all within four miles of the Meuse, prepared for the inevitable American attack.

This did not materialize immediately. The first units of 2nd Armored Division, commanded by Major General Ernest N Harman, had arrived north of Marche as early as 22 December, but had received little information about either their role or the German dispositions. Harman therefore spent two days feeling his way, linking up with elements of the British XXX Corps on his right and sending probing patrols of his CCA southward from Ciney toward Rochefort, and it was not until late on 24 December that the vulnerability of 2nd Panzer was realized. Even then, a counterattack against the finger was by no means automatic, for with defense as the first priority Harman could find no one among his superiors prepared to sanction an offensive, however limited or guaranteed of success. In the end, he used a considerable amount of personal initiative, based upon the ambiguity of his orders, and moved cau-

Tongres on the 31st and explained the magnitude of the crisis to his superior. Montgomery, genuinely surprised at the furore caused by what he termed 'frank remarks,' immediately wrote an apology to Eisenhower, pledging his loyalty and support, and the crisis blew over. It was only a temporary *rapprochement*, for at a Press conference on 7 January 1945 relations were soured yet again when Montgomery, unintentionally but tactlessly, overstated the part played by himself and his British troops in the Ardennes battle. The British newspapers picked this up and gave it great prominence, with headlines proclaiming that Montgomery 'foresaw the attack' (when Bradley quite patently did not) and that he 'saved the day' as Middleton's VIII Corps collapsed. Inter-Allied relations reached a new low and, although once again the rift was healed by some hasty diplomatic actions on both sides, it was obvious that the British and American commanders were by no means united. The only consolation was that all this took place after the 'high-water mark' of the German offensive had passed, so denying the enemy any advantage.

Meanwhile the fighting in the Ardennes sector continued with undiminished ferocity, with the emphasis firmly on the Bastogne salient. Although McAuliffe and Millikin had managed to link up on 26 December the corridor created by 4th Armored Division was narrow and extremely tenuous, attracting forces from both the opposing armies like a magnet. Just as the Allied priority was to expand and consolidate this link, turning Bastogne into a springboard for an offensive to the north and east, so the German aims were to cut the corridor, eliminate the American defense and clear the way for a fresh offensive toward the west. What had been a diffuse and widespread battle was suddenly concentrated into a relatively small area in the southern sector.

The initial American moves were made on 28 December. Eisenhower spent much of that day conferring with Montgomery about the organization of a counterattack from the north, designed to link up with Patton's army at Houffalize and so split the bulge down the middle, but when it became apparent that regrouping would take at least until 3 January, he shifted his attention to the south. By this time a new strategic reserve had been created, com-

Below: Soldiers of a British airborne unit carry out a reconnaissance patrol in Belgium, January 1945.
Right: The US 87th Division entered St Hubert, Belgium, on the heels of retreating Germans.

Below right: A group of dispirited and poorly clad German POWs are paraded by their captors.

prising the 11th Armored and 87th Infantry Divisions, and this was immediately released to help in the expansion of the Bastogne corridor. Patton deployed the new troops to the west of the original breakthrough line, aiming to use them to flush out the salient toward Flamierge and Champs, timing their advance to coincide with one by 35th Infantry Division in the east, driving toward Margeret and Longvilly. If all three divisions could push forward until they were in line with the 101st Airborne, still protecting Bastogne itself, then a solid wedge would be established deep into the enemy flank, enabling 26th Infantry Division, even further to the east, to advance to Wiltz or even Clervaux. The attacks were scheduled to begin in the early hours of 30 December.

They met with little success, smashing straight into the flanks of German assault formations attempting to cut the corridor from west and east. The 11th Armored Division, with 87th Infantry on its left, hit and was hit by elements of Panzer *Lehr* and 26th *Volksgrenadiers*, recalled to the Bastogne battle from their positions to the west by Hitler. The 35th Infantry Division, stretched out between Lutrebois and Harlange on the eastern shoulder of the salient, encountered tank and infantry units from 1st SS Panzer Division. The results were predictable. After heavy preliminary fighting, particularly in the east where two companies of 35th Infantry held out against wave after wave of determined German troops in the village of Villers-La-Bonne-Eau, the attacks bogged down. Neither side achieved its objective – the Americans had not widened the corridor to any appreciable extent and the Germans had not cut it. The battle rapidly devolved into a slogging match, made worse by deteriorating weather conditions. At the same time, 26th Infantry Division made little headway in the hills and forests to the southwest of Wiltz, grinding to a halt around the small but important crossroads known as Café Schumann, dominated by the German-held Hill 490.

The pattern so painfully established on this day continued until well into the New Year, with anything up to 17 separate German attacks against Bastogne being experienced daily. Casualties were heavy on both sides and, inevitably, more and more units were drawn into the fray. On the American side 6th Armored Division reinforced the corridor on 30/31 December, followed a few days later by 17th Airborne, the third of the divisions belonging to Ridgway's XVIII Airborne Corps. Also in early January 90th Infantry Division joined the 26th around Hill 490 and the approaches to Wiltz. On the German side, as Manteuffel tried desperately to eliminate the salient – a process which reached even greater heights of ferocity on 3–4 January when he shifted his attacks away from the corridor to the original defensive perimeter, still held by 101st Airborne – units from as many as eight different divisions were involved. Bastogne was in danger of becoming another Verdun.

The pattern was eventually broken by a number of apparently unconnected events, many miles apart. The first of these occurred just before midnight on 31 December, when Hitler's offensive against 6th Army Group began. Code named Operation *Nordwind*, this was an attempt to pinch out the Allied salient in the Vosges Mountains by a number of coordinated attacks from north and south. The plan was conceived in outline at much the same time as *Wacht am Rhein* but only recently put together in detail. Infantry and armored divisions were to punch through the overstretched American defenses west of the Vosges and along the north-south spine of the mountain chain itself, outflanking the US VI Corps and sealing the Saverne Gap. At the same time units of the Nineteenth Army were to break out northward from the Colmar Pocket to surround .Strasbourg and complete the encirclement of the salient. On paper the idea was feasible and could act as a significant diversion, forcing the Allies to withdraw troops from the Ardennes and so release the pressure on Model's units. This, in turn, would enable the drive on Antwerp to continue, with all its expected results.

In reality, however, *Nordwind* never stood much chance of success and, far from breaking the Allied will to resist in the Ardennes, its subsequent failure undoubtedly demoralized Model's already tired and dispirited men. By 3 January the initial German assaults in the Vosges region had been blunted, partly by American defensive efforts and partly because the divisions allocated to *Nordwind* were not well equipped. Although fighting was to continue until the 20th, particularly between the Nineteenth Army in the Colmar Pocket and the French defenders of Strasbourg, the offensive was contained without upsetting the Ardennes counterattack too dramatically. Eisenhower would probably have liked to use more of Devers' divisions around Bastogne, but when those divisions were inflicting considerable losses on the Germans in their own area, this was hardly a cause for major concern. What was more important to the Allies was that Hitler had committed the small reserve he had left in the West to a battle away from the Ardennes sector. Before the New Year was three days old it was apparent that the bulge contained as many German units as it was ever likely to, at a time when American reinforcements were still pouring in.

It was not just the German ground forces that were dissipated in this way. On 1 January 1945 the Luftwaffe committed a similar strategic error. At 0745 hours more than 1100 fighters and fighter-bombers took off in four massive formations to attack American forward airfields. The aim was to

Below: These German troops were captured in Luxembourg.

Bottom: Germans captured during the American advance to the Rhine.

Below: Eisenhower confers with Generals Somervell and Devers.

destroy air opposition to a renewed land drive on Antwerp, but it was a forlorn and costly gesture. Although considerable damage was imposed – a number of airfields were unusable for a week and almost 300 American aircraft were destroyed on the ground – the losses inflicted upon the Luftwaffe in the process were crippling. By the end of the day over 100 German planes had been lost and perhaps twice that number severely damaged while, of far greater significance, experienced pilots had been killed. The losses were irreplaceable and from then until the end of hostilities five months later the Luftwaffe was no longer a force to be reckoned with.

Thus when Montgomery's counterattack on the northern flank of the Ardennes bulge began on 3 January, the odds had shifted decisively in favor of the Allied armies. Responsibility for the assault lay with Collins' VII Corps, comprising the four divisions originally assigned to him in December. They were concentrated to the east of the Ourthe river with 82nd Airborne protecting their left. British troops had been moved in to relieve 2nd Armored and 84th Infantry Divisions west of the river, and these two units joined 3rd Armored and 75th Infantry with the intention of driving down the Bastogne–Liège road from Manhay to Parker's Crossroads at Baraque de Fraiture, preparatory to a link up with Patton's forces at Houffalize. In the event 75th Infantry Division was kept in reserve and replaced in the frontline by the 83rd. Opposing them were 2nd SS Panzer and 12th and 560th *Volksgrenadier* Divisions, occupying defensive positions in rapidly deteriorating weather conditions.

The attack began at 0830 hours on the 3rd but because of icy roads and deep snow made little initial headway. By the end of the first day's fighting an advance of two miles only had been achieved and it was not until 7 January that units of 2nd Armored managed to take Baraque de Fraiture. This was sufficient to cause grave concern at OKW headquarters, where Hitler was at last forced to recognize the failure of *Wacht am Rhein.* In a series of meetings on 8–9 January he redeployed his forces accordingly. Fifth Panzer Army was ordered to withdraw to occupy a north-south line between Dochamps and Longchamps, west of the Bastogne–Liège road, and Sixth Panzer Army was pulled back to east of St Vith and Wiltz, with II SS Panzer Corps (comprising the remnants of 1st, 2nd, 9th and 12th SS Panzer Divisions) being extracted entirely from the Ardennes sector for refitting as a future reserve. These moves took until 22 January to complete in conditions of chaos and continued fighting, but the fact that they were ordered at all marked the end of any remaining hopes for German success.

Thereafter the blows fell thick and fast upon Manteuffel's hard-pressed men. On 9 January Patton launched his counterstroke northward from the Bastogne salient with a total of eight divisions, 4th and 6th Armored, 26th, 35th, 87th and 90th Infantry and 17th and 101st Airborne. At first the emphasis was on the German pocket concentrated against the eastern shoulder of the corridor, west of Bras. For this a combined assault, delivered by 6th Armored and 35th Infantry from within the Bastogne perimeter and by 90th Infantry from the Café Schumann crossroads, was put into effect. The fighting was hard, particularly to the northwest of Café Schumann where 90th Infantry suffered heavy casualties. However, by 11 January the two arms of the pincer had linked up at Bras, trapping an estimated 15,000 enemy soldiers, most of them belonging to 5th Parachute Division, in a pocket which was rapidly cleared. At the same time 4th Armored and 101st Airborne began to move out of the Bastogne perimeter to the north, pushing toward Noville and Houffalize. News of a major Soviet offensive on the upper Vistula river, launched on 12 January, caused Hitler to transfer what remained of Sixth Panzer Army to the Eastern Front on the 14th, and this relieved the pressure significantly in the Ardennes. By 15 January the northern and southern arms of the Allied counteroffensive were within patrolling distance of each other and the link up was effected at Houffalize the following day.

As soon as this took place, Bradley resumed responsibility for Hodges' First Army and the subsequent mopping-up operations were a purely American affair. As the combined forces turned eastward to push the last of the German troops out of the bulge, further counterattacks were launched from the original shoulders, heading north from Echternach and south from Elsenborn. On 23 January, as the German retreat degenerated into a disorganized exodus, Brigadier General Clarke led CCB of 7th Armored Division back into St Vith and by the 28 January American soldiers stood once again along the lines they had occupied on 16 December. It had been a long, hard road to eventual victory.

The Ardennes battle – the 'Battle of the Bulge' – cost the Americans over 75,000 men (8497 killed, 46,000 wounded and 21,000 missing or in German POW camps), but in the process they destroyed the cream of Hitler's remaining formations. German losses were nearly 120,000 (12,652 killed, 57,000 wounded and 50,000 captured), a loss rate which prevented the creation of any future reserve within the Reich to stand against the remorseless assaults from both east and west. Thus, although *Wacht am Rhein* may have succeeded in delaying Allied advances by about six weeks, the battle left Germany poorly defended and vulnerable, characteristics which undoubtedly contributed to her early defeat. The 'master stroke' in the West had failed, the odds cut short by the stubbornness and courage of the American soldier. The Bulge was his hardest European battleground; it was also his finest hour.

APPENDIX

1. Units Involved, 16 December 1944–28 January 1945

A. **Allied**

(Organization, often extemporized, during the battle)

US First Army
- V Corps
  - 1st Infantry Division
  - 2nd Infantry Division
  - 9th Infantry Division
  - 99th Infantry Division
- VII Corps
  - 2nd Armored Division
  - 3rd Armored Division
  - 75th Infantry Division*
  - 84th Infantry Division
  - (*75th replaced by 83rd Infantry Division from 3 January 1945)
- VIII Corps
  - 9th Armored Division
  - 14th Cavalry Group (from 2nd Infantry Division)
  - 28th Infantry Division
  - 106th Infantry Division
- XVIII Airborne Corps (created as reinforcement from reserve)
  - 7th Armored Division (from Ninth Army)
  - 30th Infantry Division (from Ninth Army)
  - 17th Airborne Division (from SHAEF reserve)
  - 82nd Airborne Division (from SHAEF reserve)
  - 101st Airborne Division (from SHAEF reserve)

US Third Army
- III Corps
  - 4th Armored Division
  - 26th Infantry Division
  - 80th Infantry Division
- XII Corps
  - 10th Armored Division
  - 4th Infantry Division
  - 5th Infantry Division

The following units were committed to the Bastogne salient in the final stages of the battle:
- 6th Armored Division
- 11th Armored Division
- 35th Infantry Division
- 87th Infantry Division
- 90th Infantry Division

Also involved:
- British XXX Corps (British Second Army, 21st Army Group): 29th Armored Brigade

B. **German**

Sixth SS Panzer Army
- I SS Panzer Corps
  - 1st SS Panzer Division
  - 12th SS Panzer Division
  - 3rd Parachute Division
  - 12th *Volksgrenadier* Division
- II SS Panzer Corps (Reserve)
  - 2nd SS Panzer Division
  - 9th SS Panzer Division
- LXVII Corps
  - 246th *Volksgrenadier* Division
  - 277th *Volksgrenadier* Division
  - 326th *Volksgrenadier* Division

Fifth Panzer Army
- XLVII Panzer Corps
  - 2nd Panzer Division
  - Panzer *Lehr* Division
  - 26th *Volksgrenadier* Division
- LVIII Panzer Corps
  - 116th Panzer Division
  - 560th *Volksgrenadier* Division
- LXVI Corps
  - 18th *Volksgrenadier* Division
  - 62nd *Volksgrenadier* Division
- Reserve
  - 9th Panzer Division
  - 15th Panzer Grenadier Division

Seventh German Army
- LXXX Corps
  - 212th *Volksgrenadier* Division
  - 276th *Volksgrenadier* Division
- LXXXV Corps
  - 5th Parachute Division
  - 352nd *Volksgrenadier* Division
- Reserve
  - 79th Infantry Division
- OKW Reserve
  - 3rd Panzer Grenadier Division
  - 9th *Volksgrenadier* Division
  - *Führer Begleit* Brigade
  - *Führer Grenadier* Brigade

Also involved (attached to Sixth Panzer Army)
- 150th Panzer Brigade (Skorzeny's commandos)
- Von der Heydte's Parachutists

2. Chains of Command, 16th December 1944

A. **Allied**

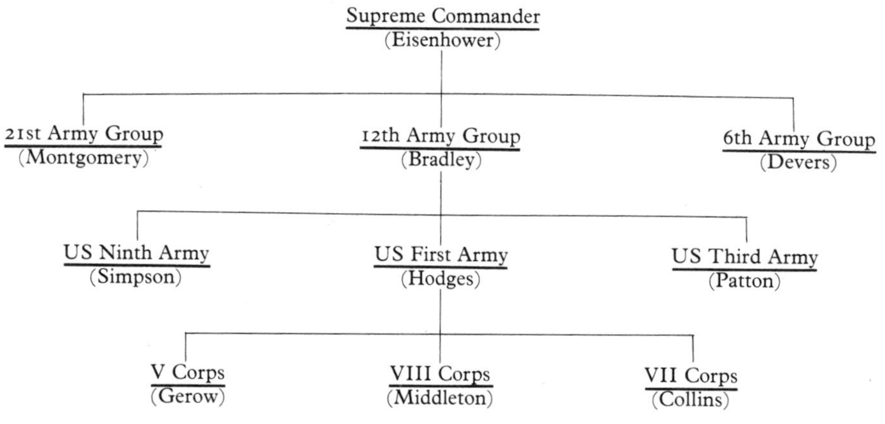

B. **German**

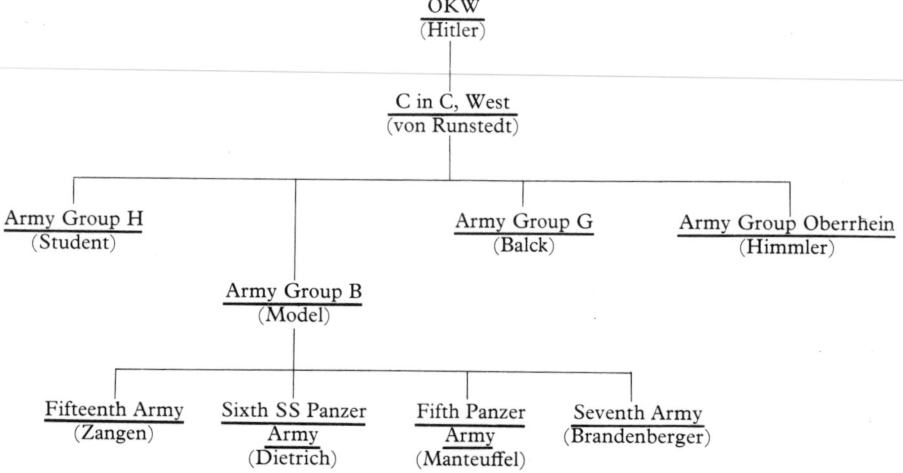

3. Casualties 16 December–28 January 1945

A **American**
- Killed: 8497
- Wounded: 46,000
- Missing: 21,000

B **German**
- Killed: 12,652
- Wounded: 57,000
- Captured: 50,000

One of the 50,000 German soldiers captured during the Battle of the Bulge surrenders.

OKINAWA

OKINAWA

LT.-COL. A. J. BARKER

Page 328: US Marines practice jungle warfare during a training exercise held on a south Pacific island.
Page 329: Troops from the 5th Marines were held up for as long as 48 hours on this ridge, two miles north of Naha.
Pages 330/331: The battleship *USS New Mexico* bombards Okinawa, April 1945.
These pages: Transports gather off the coast of Okinawa, 13 April, 1945.

70
70
70

1. ISLAND HOPPING

By October 1944 the tide of war had very definitely turned against Japan, and the Americans in the Pacific were confounded by their successes. The question was not what to do next but how to do it. The US Air Force believed that bombing the home islands would bring Japan to her knees, but the US Army considered that an invasion would be necessary. The US Navy's job was virtually completed. Command of the sea had been won and sea lines of communication to the Western Pacific were secure. Naval forces could now be used to support ground and air operations.

In July, after the Battle of the Philippine Sea, Admiral Raymond A Spruance, the Commander of the US Fifth Fleet in the Central Pacific, had recommended the capture of Okinawa as the next step on the road to Tokyo. He was overruled, as the flamboyant General MacArthur wanted to return to the Philippines and Admiral Ernest J King, Chief of Naval Operations, advocated the invasion of Taiwan. However, the US Army Chiefs of Staff claimed that for such an invasion nine more divisions than were available in the whole Pacific Theater before the fall of Germany would be required. In the event a plan proposed by Admiral Chester W Nimitz, the US Naval Commander of the Pacific Ocean Area, was ultimately accepted. Luzon in the Philippines would be liberated first by MacArthur's forces; then the Ryukyu group islands – the largest one of which was Okinawa – would be occupied by Lieutenant General Simon Bolivar Buckner's Tenth Army transported by Spruance's

Left: Fleet Admiral Ernest J King was the commander in chief of the US Fleet and the leading proponent of the United States' Pacific offensives, which often contradicted the Allied 'Europe-first' strategy.
Below left: The Combined Chiefs of Staff Committee brought together British and American top-level strategic planners.

Above: American GIs in action on Luzon, where mopping-up operations continued until September 1945.
Below: American commanders pictured at lunch. From left, General H Arnold, Admiral W Leahy, Admiral E King and General G Marshall.

Fifth Fleet. Initially MacArthur's forces were scheduled to help out in the Okinawa campaign but they were subsequently diverted to mopping-up operations in the Philippines and Borneo.

The overall plan changed slightly when it became apparent that possession of the pear-shaped, rocky island of Iwo Jima in the Volcano Islands was essential to the US advance toward Japan. Iwo Jima has an area of only eight square miles, but in Japanese hands it menaced US bombers from Saipan that were harassing the Japanese mainland at extreme range, while in American hands it could become a splendid forward air base. In the event D-Days were set for Luzon, 9 January 1945, Iwo Jima, 19 February and Okinawa, 1 April.

Meantime the Japanese had been working on a new defense line to keep the Allies well away from the Japanese home islands. This defense line included Iwo Jima, Okinawa, Taiwan, Shanghai and South Korea. In these areas Japanese ground forces were to hold out to the end without reinforcements. Suicide aircraft – called Kamikaze after the 'divine wind' which had thwarted the last attempted invasion of Japan in the thirteenth century – would be used against the advancing enemy. The final battle would be fought in Japan itself, and bloody attrition was expected to bring the Americans to terms.

On Iwo Jima Major General Tadamichi Kuribayashi commanded a garrison of some 22,000 Japanese army and naval troops. The island itself was honeycombed with concealed gun emplacements, concrete pillboxes and expertly interlaced minefields. An elaborate underground cave system protected Kuribayashi's men against the incessant bombardments which preceded the American assault. This began at 0900 hours on 19 February when men of the 4th and 5th US Marine Divisions landed without much opposition until they got clear of the beaches. Then the Japanese artillery opened up and the Marines suffered heavy casualties – 2420 men on the first day. However the attackers inched forward, under cover of naval gunfire which provided continuous and accurate support. Mount Suribachi, the dominant feature of the island, was stormed on 23 February and the photograph of the American flag being raised on its crest became one of the best-known pictures of the war. By 11 March the remnants of the defenders were pinned on the northern tip of the island and organized resistance ended on 16 March.

The Kamikaze corps was four months old when the Iwo Jima campaign opened and it had made its debut in the Philippines. There, in terms of men and materiel, the Kamikazes had exacted a terrible toll from the Americans – not so great as they believed at the time, but nonetheless formidable. Nothing like this had ever been known before and although the

Americans were not daunted they were shocked by such savage tactics. On 21 February a massive suicide attack was launched against the American invasion fleet off Iwo Jima. Early in the morning 32 Kamikazes took off from airfields near Tokyo and launched their attack. That night Tokyo radio announced that a US aircraft carrier and four transports had been sunk and another carrier and four other warships had been damaged. Subsequently the Americans confirmed that the carrier USS *Bismarck Sea* had been sunk and the carriers *Saratoga* and *Lunga Point*, together with a cargo ship and two landing ships, had been damaged.

The attacks were an indication of things to come. By the way Japanese resistance was mounting the Americans could look forward to nothing less than a suicidal blood bath on their way to Tokyo. Iwo Jima cost the lives of 6891 US Marines and 18,070 others were wounded. Japanese casualties were even heavier. Only 212 of the garrison surrendered and more than 21,000 dead were counted; many others were sealed in their underground shelters. It is hardly surprising therefore that the

Left: A Coast Guard-manned LST heads for the beach at Leyte in the Philippines, where an American force landed in October 1944.
Below: Iwo Jima was assaulted in February 1945. Men of the 5th Marine Division are having an especially difficult time in establishing themselves ashore.
Above: A Japanese position at the base of Mount Suribachi is bombarded.

occupation of Okinawa, the next step to Japan, was viewed with some trepidation. Okinawa is the central and largest island of a long chain commonly known as the Ryukyu Archipelago. It is only 340 miles from both the Japanese home island of Kyushu, and Taiwan; 900 miles from Leyte, and 1200 miles from Ulithi and Guam which, early in 1945, were the three nearest US bases. Pearl Harbor lies 4000 miles to the east. Strategically Okinawa dominated the East China Sea and the Chinese coast from Foochow to Korea. It sat astride Japan's sea lanes to the oil-rich East Indies. Furthermore, from Okinawa American B-29s would be able to range over the Yellow Sea and Straits of Shimonseki and return with fuel to spare.

Okinawa was a natural defensive stronghold. Sixty-seven miles long and from 3–20 miles wide, its terrain was cut up in a maze of ridges, cliffs, and limestone and coral caves. Divided into two by the narrow Ishikawa Isthmus, the larger, northeastern portion of the island is barren, mountainous and thickly wooded. Immediately south of the isthmus the terrain is undulating and lightly wooded and the southwestern end is rugged and hilly. In 1945 three-quarters of the island's population of 435,000 lived in the area south of the isthmus. The capital was located there and in this southern part of the island the Japanese had constructed three airfields – at Naha, Yontan and at Kadena close to the west coat. In addition there were two other airstrips, at Yonabaru and Machinato. Nakagusuku Wan (Buckner Bay) and Chimu, the two extensive bays on the eastern side of Okinawa, were considered suitable for development into an advanced naval base since both were protected from the sea by clusters of small islands and barrier reefs. Across the straits, some 11 miles west of Naha, lies a group of 10 small islands known as the Kerama Retto, and off the point of the Motobu Peninsula in the northern part of Okinawa, is the island of Ie-Shima on which there was another small airfield.

The people of Okinawa are descended from a mixture of Chinese, Malays and Ainus. At one time they were an independent kingdom whose ruler paid tribute to the emperor of China. In 1875, however, the Ryukyu islands were invaded by the Japanese who deposed the king, stopped the tribute to China and formally annexed the territory. The colonial-type regime which was then introduced did not endear the islanders to their Japanese masters, who treated them as inferior beings. In the event this eased the task of the US troops in dealing with the Okinawans when they discovered that the stories of American brutality told to them by the Japanese were untrue.

Compared with Japan the islands were underdeveloped and overpopulated. There were only three towns of any size – Naha, the capital; Shuri, the ancient capital; and Toguchi on the Motobu Peninsula.

Above: Vice-Admiral Marc Mitscher commanded the aircraft-carrier task force which supported the Okinawa landings.
Above left: Rear Admiral Jesse Oldendorf on the bridge of the battleship USS *Tennessee*. He was an exponent of traditional surface-ship action.
Below left: Admirals C Nimitz (right) and R Spruance tour Kwajalein.

Most Okinawans lived in thatched huts, clustered in villages of a few hundred or so inhabitants. They were predominantly farmers, raising barley, sugar cane, cabbages and sweet potatoes – the latter providing the staple of their diet while pork was the principal luxury. (An ancient law still in force in 1945 required each family to keep four pigs.)

Such, in sum, is the nature of the island which was needed as a springboard to Japan, and the invasion of which would cost the United States more casualties than had been incurred in taking any other of the islands in the Pacific.

Preparations for Operation Iceberg, the invasion of the Ryukyus, started in October 1944 and from the very beginning it was clear that this would be the most daring and the most complex operation ever undertaken by American amphibious forces. Lieutenant General Buckner's Tenth US Army, consisting of the III Amphibious Corps (1st, 2nd and 6th Marine Divisions) and the XXIV Corps (7th, 27th, 77th and 96th Divisions with the 81st held in reserve in New Caledonia) would be put ashore on Okinawa on 1 April. Most of the troops concerned were seasoned veterans, having already taken part in similar operations elsewhere in the Pacific. As the objective was so far from the Allied airfields and was surrounded by Japanese airfields within a 350-mile radius, Buckner planned to make the initial landing on the west of the island on the Hagushi beaches, in order to secure the Yontan and Kadena airfields quickly. As soon as they had been captured and the middle of the island cleared, the Marines would fan out east and north to occupy the island as far as the Motobu Peninsula and capture Ie-Shima with its airfield. Meantime the men of the XXIV Corps would turn south. Their task was to mop up the southern end of the island and occupy the cluster of islands on the east coast masking the entrance to the Chimu and Nakagusuku bays. About a week before the main assault, the Kerama Retto group of islands, which provided a large anchorage, was to be seized for use as an advanced fuelling and repair base and as a refuge for ships damaged during operations.

Below: Lieutenant General Simon Bolivar Buckner (left) talks with amphibious-warfare expert Vice-Admiral R Kelly Turner.

Under the overall command of Admiral Spruance the greatest invasion fleet ever to operate in the Pacific now began to assemble – 1440 warships and merchant ships of all kinds and sizes. This included Vice-Admiral Marc Mitscher's fast-carrier force of 11 fleet carriers, six light carriers, seven battleships, 15 cruisers and 64 destroyers, the British Pacific Fleet under the command of Vice-Admiral Sir Bernard Rawlings, and Vice-Admiral Turner's Joint Expeditionary Force.

The British Pacific Fleet comprised the battleships *King George V* and *Howe*, the fleet carriers *Indomitable, Victorious, Indefatigable* and *Illustrious,* five cruisers and 11 destroyers.

The Joint Expeditionary Force consisted of the Gun-Fire and Covering Force under command of Rear Admiral M L Deyo, Rear Admiral W H P Blandy's Amphibious Support Force, the Western Islands Attack Group carrying the 77th Division for the assault on the Kerama Retto, the Northern Attack Force carrying the 1st and 6th Marine Divisions, and the Southern Attack Force carrying the 7th and 96th Divisions. There were also two other small, self-contained forces – one to set up a seaplane base at the Kerama Retto when the islands had been captured, and the other carrying part of the 2nd Marine Division which was to make a diversionary landing on the east coast opposite Yonabaru airfield. Aboard this vast armada there were approximately 182,000 soldiers and Marines together with all their stores and supplies.

Before D-Day the Iceberg planners reckoned that a week of air bombardments would be necessary to 'soften up' the objective. Kamikaze air attacks were expected and so it was necessary to pare down Japanese air power as much as possible before the invasion of Okinawa started. The softening-up bombardments and air strikes against the Japanese airfields would be carried out mainly by planes from Mitscher's and Deyo's fast carriers. However, to assist them in the bombing program and in the formidable task of protecting the invasion armada against attack by Kamikazes the Joint Chiefs of Staff in Washington authorized Nimitz to call on the Superfortress B-29 bombers of the Strategic Air Command based in the Marianas. (This, in fact, was not a popular arrangement so far as Generals 'Hap' Arnold and Curtis LeMay of the Strategic Air Command were concerned. They were reluctant to have the costly B-29s employed like this. In the event Nimitz got his way.)

The preliminary 'softening-up' program that was eventually agreed included attacks on airfields in Kyushu, shipping in Japan's Inland Sea and targets on Okinawa by the carrier-borne planes. The Superfortresses would thicken up the bombardments with attacks on Kyushu. They would also drop mines in the Shimonseki Strait through which most of Japan's remaining shipping then passed, as well as the approaches to Sagebo, Hiroshima and Kure. At the same time planes from the carriers of the British Pacific Fleet would bomb the airfields in the Sakishima Islands. The program would start on 18 March and continue through to the 26th when the Gunfire and Covering Force would join the lists to add their contribution to the forthcoming *Götterdämmerung* with an intensified bombardment of Okinawa. Minesweepers, in the van of the Joint Expeditionary Force, were to begin to clear the approaches to Okinawa of mines on 22 March and the Western Attack Group was to assault the Kerama Retto on the 26th. Finally on D-Day the 1st and 6th Marine Divisions were to be landed just north of, and the 7th and 96th Divisions immediately south of, the Bisha River on the Hagushi beaches.

The Japanese knew the Americans would invade Okinawa, and indeed they guessed the correct date of D-Day. They were under no illusions – they had to defend successfully this malaria-ridden island or lose the war. Okinawa was so important that they were prepared to risk everything to hold it. Two divisions and two brigades of the Imperial Army under command of Lieutenant General Mitsura Ushijima were deployed mainly in the southern part of the island. There was also a naval force under Rear Admiral Minoru Ota, which included seven sea raiding companies manning *Shinyo* suicide boats (boats powered by a gasoline engine with an explosive charge in the bow), three companies were stationed in the Kerama Retto and the remainder in Okinawa. Originally there were seven battalions of *Shinyo*, but Ushijima reduced them to form three infantry battalions to supplement the army battalions. About 7000 airmen commanded by Captain Tanamachi were also available. These in fact were ground crews who had no aircraft to service. An Okinawa Home Guard some 20,000 strong provided labor units. All in all the total strength of the Japanese garrison – excluding civilians – was about 80,000 men.

That Kamikaze air attacks would be mounted against the invading force was a foregone conclusion. In addition to suicidal

Above left: Curtiss SB2C Helldivers take off from the carrier USS *Enterprise* (CV-6) for a strike on Okinawa, October 1944.
Left: The escort carrier USS *St Lo* (CVE-63) under Kamikaze attack on 25 October 1944. The carrier sank later that day.

Above: The naval equivalent of the Kamikaze was the Kaiten human torpedo. This example was discovered on Ulithi Atoll in 1945.

attacks from the skies the Japanese also planned to strike under the sea with human torpedoes. In February 1944 they had developed a type of one-man midget submarine which its designers called the Kaiten (literally, 'Heaven shaker'). In essence it was simply an oversized torpedo which had an additional section between the warhead in the nose and the oxygen motor. This was the pilot's compartment, fitted with a periscope and a set of controls enabling a man to direct the torpedo run. The Kaiten had a range of 40 nautical miles and tests had shown that its 9000-pound high explosive warhead was capable of breaking the back of a heavy cruiser. The original design had included an escape hatch, giving the pilot a chance to get away once he had put his weapon on a sure course to the target. In mid-1944 the Naval General Staff decided to simplify the design to permit crash production of these weapons, and the Kaiten became another suicide weapon.

Like the Kamikaze airmen Kaiten pilots were all volunteers. Until they started their training none of them knew what they had volunteered for. They were merely told that they would operate a *Kyukoko heiki* – a new national salvation weapon – on missions from which they were not expected to return alive. Even when it was learned that their probable fate was an unseen death beneath the waves there were plenty of volunteers. Indeed, it appears that the first ones were grateful at being accepted. Selection was supposedly based on three qualifications: physical and moral strength, evidence of a strong sense of patriotism, and a minimum of family responsibilities. Married men were excluded and very few eldest or only sons were chosen. The accent was on young fit men who would have little tendency to look over their shoulders.

The Kaitens were carried to the operational area in big I Class fleet submarines, each of which was fitted to carry six. During the approach to the target the Kaiten pilots climbed into their tiny craft through a special hatch which was then sealed off. As the submarine closed on its victim, a telephone link between the submarine's conning tower and the Kaiten enabled the captain to keep the pilots informed of the relative position of the target. At the optimum moment the Kaiten's engines were started and they were released at five-second intervals from the mother ship. Once in motion the pilot could observe the target through his own periscope, and make the necessary corrections to his course. At about 500 yards distance he would switch his craft to automatic control for the final dash at full speed, submerged to a depth of about 12 feet.

The first Kaiten attack was made in November 1944 at Ulithi Atoll. Three fleet submarines, each carrying four Kaiten, set out for the vicinity of Ulithi where large numbers of American ships were reported to be concentrating. En route the *I-37* was spotted by the American destroyer *Nicholas* and sunk. The *I-36* reached the position designated for launching its four Kaitens, just off the eastern entrance to the Ulithi lagoon, soon after midnight on 20 November. The pilots were ordered into their craft and everything seemed set for the attack when it was found that Numbers One and Two Kaiten were stuck in their racks, and Number Four reported his craft was leaking badly. Only Number Three, manned by Ensign Imanishi, could be dispatched and it was launched shortly before 0500 hours.

The third fleet submarine, the *I-47*, was more successful. All four of its Kaiten were launched successfully at about 0500 hours. Judging by the three explosions which were heard by the crew of the *I-47*, at least three of the Kaiten had scored hits on something. Nobody knew what damage they had done but one thing was certain; all five Kaiten pilots were dead. Both *I-36* and *I-47* got safely back to their home port of Kure and on 2 December a special conference was held on board the *Tsukushi Maru*, flagship of the Sixth Fleet, to consider the reports of the two submarine captains on the Kaiten attacks. Over 200 staff officers and specialists attended, and there was a lot of discussion before the results were summarized by a staff officer of the Sixth Fleet. Men on board *I-47* had seen two fires, he said, and the crew of *I-36* had heard explosions. Photographs of Ulithi taken by a reconnaissance plane from Truk on 23 November, three days after the Kaiten operation, were then produced. 'From these,' declared the speaker, 'we can estimate that Lieutenant Nishina sank an aircraft carrier, as did Lieutenant Fukuda and Ensign Imanishi. Ensigns Sato and Watanabe sank a battleship apiece!'

This was the conclusion the audience wanted to hear, and there was a great outburst of banzais. The Japanese High Command had ordered Kaiten to be produced in quantity, and news that the first strike had been an outstanding success was a great boost to the morale of the scores of young men in training. 'Die for the Emperor, but not in vain' was a good motto. Every embryo Kaiten pilot was positively

I-18
KEEP OUT

Left and below: Japanese midget submarines were used for local defense of strategically important bases in the closing years of the Pacific War. *Below left:* The Yokosuka MXY-7 Ohka was a rocket-propelled suicide plane, which was carried to the vicinity of its target by a Mitsubishi G4M parent aircraft.

looking forward to his death-dealing mission after the news was circulated.

However the Japanese estimate of ships destroyed was a complete fabrication. The only ship sunk in the operation was the US tanker *Mississinewa*. Nevertheless the Kaiten represented yet another serious menace to the Allied armada currently assembling for the invasion of Okinawa.

Among other Japanese preparations to stop the seemingly irresistible American advance was the development of a new, simpler Kamikaze aircraft to supplement the dwindling stocks of fighter aircraft and reconnaissance planes that had been used up to this time. During the summer months of 1944 Ensign Ohta had come up with the idea of a piloted bomb which could be carried into action by a Type-O Betty bomber. The idea was taken up by the Japanese Naval Command and the first of the new piloted glide bombs started to roll off the production lines in October 1944. Named Ohkas, they were tiny single-seater aircraft which had rocket motors, and 2640 pounds of high explosive packed into the nose. As airplanes their performance was strictly limited and the mother aircraft had to launch them within 10 miles of their target. From an altitude of 20,000 feet an Ohka had a range of about 15 miles and the pilots were taught to correct their glide path with short blasts of the rocket motors. The system was comparatively simple. En route to the combat zone the Ohka pilot travelled in the mother bomber. Approaching the target area he would climb through the bomb bay into his bomb, and when the pilot of the bomber had confirmed the target and aligned his plane the Ohka would be released. When this happened there was no return. It was a one-way ride for the Ohka pilot.

Like the more conventional Kamikaze pilots and the men who manned the Kaiten, the young men who flew the Ohkas were all volunteers. Most of them were youngsters who had only the minimal training necessary for their mission. However, as D-Day for Operation Iceberg approached they were joined by a few hard-bitten veterans from experienced units.

2. PRELIMINARY OPERATIONS

To isolate the battlefield the Americans planned to neutralize the Japanese airfields in southern Japan, and on 14 March Admiral Marc Mitscher's fleet – designated Task Force 58 – sailed from Ulithi and headed toward Kyushu. By dawn on the 18th Mitscher's carriers had reached their flying-off position some 90 miles southeast of Kyushu, and the planes took off to strafe the airfields on Kyushu. The Americans had expected to run into considerable opposition, but much to the surprise of the pilots there were very few Japanese planes either in the air or on the ground – for a very good reason. A Japanese reconnaissance plane had shadowed Task Force 58 from Ulithi, and Vice-Admiral Matome Ugaki, the Commander of the Fifth Air Fleet, had decided to launch a devastating air attack on the American carriers. In consequence when the US planes were flying toward Kyushu to drop their bombs on deserted airfields, all the available aircraft of the Fifth Air Fleet – including 50 torpedo bombers – were winging their way toward Mitscher's fleet. In the ensuing action the two fleet carriers *Enterprise* and *Yorktown* were hit by bombs. However neither ship suffered serious damage – although some men were killed or wounded. The Fifth Air Fleet not only lost many aircraft, it also became considerably disorganized as its surviving planes landed on airfields all over southern Japan.

The following day, 19 March, Mitscher's planes struck at Japanese shipping in the Inland Sea and at Kure and Kobe, and when they returned to their carriers they reported hits on 17 ships including such monsters as the battleship *Yamato* and the carrier *Amagi*. In fact, except for a cruiser, which was severely damaged, only minor damage had been inflicted. Meantime the Japanese had counterattacked and their efforts had been more successful. Two American carriers, the *Wasp* and the *Franklin* ('Big Ben' as her crew called her) had been hit by bombs and badly damaged. *Wasp* was attacked shortly after sunrise, soon after most of her aircraft had taken off on strikes. A solitary Japanese bomber was undetected until it was over the ship and dropped a bomb which smashed through to the lower deck where the cooks were preparing breakfast. A few minutes later a Kamikaze plane dived on the carrier and exploded as it crashed alongside. Casualties were heavy – 101 killed and 269 wounded – and the *Wasp* eventually had to retire for repairs. 'Big Ben' was caught soon after 0700 hours as she was launching her second strike of the morning. Two bombs from a Japanese aircraft which also made an undetected approach were dropped to explode on the hangar and flight decks, creating a fire which quickly enveloped the entire ship in flames and a pall of heavy smoke. Everyone on the hangar deck was killed and in the blaze the bombs in the planes which were about to be launched blew up. The 'Tiny Tim' rockets, with which a dozen fighter bombers on the flight deck were armed, were also ignited and these produced a spectacular display. According to Commander Joe Taylor, the *Franklin*'s executive officer:

'Some screamed by to starboard, some to port, and some straight up the flight deck. The weird aspect of this weapon whooshing by so close is one of the most awful spectacles a human has ever been privileged to see. Some went straight up and some tumbled end over end. Each time one went off the fire-fighting crews forward would instinctively hit the deck.'

Before the fires were brought under control all the ammunition stored on the flight deck and in the hangar had exploded.

For a while it appeared as if the *Franklin* was doomed and the skipper, Captain Leslie H Gehres, ordered all but a skeleton crew to abandon ship. Many men dived overboard and were rescued by destroyers which had closed in on the stricken carrier. The wounded were taken off by the cruiser *Santa Fe* which ran alongside the blazing and exploding *Franklin* for that purpose.

In the event the men who remained aboard the crippled *Franklin* managed to bring the fires under control and by the morning of 21 March she was able to move under her own power. Her flight deck looked rather like a half-eaten Shredded Wheat biscuit, according to Captain Gehres, who reported 'Down by the tail but reins up.' To this Admiral Spruance signalled back that 'the ability, fortitude and sheer guts of skipper and crew in saving their ship were in the highest degree praiseworthy.'

The *Franklin* was the most heavily damaged Allied carrier in World War II to

Above: General Kazushige Ugaki was foreign minister in the first cabinet of Prince Konoye.
Right: USS *Intrepid* (CV-II) belches smoke after a Japanese air attack on 18 March 1945.
Above right and above far right: The carrier *Franklin* was severely damaged by Kamikazes on 19 March, but despite casualties of 724 killed and 265 wounded the ship remained afloat.

be saved; she was in far worse shape than the *Lexington* had been at the Coral Sea or the *Yorktown* at Midway. But she managed under her own power – with only one stop at Pearl Harbor – to make the 12,000-mile voyage to New York. She was lucky in the initial stages of her withdrawal. Following the Inland Sea strikes on 19 March the whole of Mitscher's Task Force 58 began slowly to retire, sending fighter sweeps over Kyushu to deter any Japanese aircraft.

The morning of 20 March was quiet, but the situation was brewing up. During the afternoon Kamikaze planes crashed down on the destroyer *Halsey Powell*. Fortunately the Kamikaze's bomb went right through the *Halsey Powell*'s hull without exploding, but 12 men were killed and the ship's steering gear put out of action.

Soon after this between 15-20 Japanese aircraft swooped down on Mitscher's fleet and one plane bombed and strafed the carrier *Enterprise*. The bombs missed and little damage was done. The climax was yet to come.

Task Force 58 was shadowed during the night and early on the morning of 21 March. Vice-Admiral Ugaki at Kyushu was handed a report from the pilot of one of the reconnaissance planes which had been following the US fleet. Three US carriers appeared to be wallowing in the water about 320 miles off Japan, the pilot reported. All three appeared to have suffered damage and, surprisingly, no fighter cover was being maintained; indeed they appeared to be completely unprotected.

Ugaki decided that this was the ideal opportunity to try out the Ohka. Eighteen bombers began to load Ohka weapons, and every available fighter in the whole of southern Japan was ordered up to escort the bombers. Carrying the heavy Ohkas the ponderous bombers would be slower than ever, and a powerful escort was necessary to make sure they got through to where the carriers had been sighted. Only 55 Zeros could be mustered, and because this was considered too few the operation was very nearly called off. According to the official report it was the enthusiastic determination and keenness of the Ohka pilots which resulted in the decision to take the risk and let the operation proceed.

Commanding the bombers was a certain Lieutenant Commander Goro Nonaka, one of the few veterans who remained. He was said to be a hard man, 'who placed great emphasis on the traditional Samurai spirit.' Nevertheless his unit was a happy one, and Nonaka was respected as an able leader.

Nonaka's senior was the 45-year-old Captain Okamura, who had grown gray in the service of the Imperial Navy's fleet air arm. It was he who had raised and organized the first Ohka unit, and he was determined to vindicate his work by taking part in the very first Ohka mission. When the aircraft were warming up Okamura announced that he was going to lead the attack. Nonaka was furious. He too was anxious to be the first Ohka martyr, and apparently there was a somewhat unseemly argument on the airstrip before Okamura gave way.

Nonaka had obviously prepared his last speech and before climbing into the cockpit of his bomber he announced enigmatically, 'This is Minatogawa.' (The reference was to the shrine of that name at Kobe, which was erected to immortalize the fourteenth-century patriot Masashige Kusunoki who said before his death '*Shichisei hokoku!*' – Would that I had seven lives to give for my country!)

The 18 bombers took off at 1135 hours with Nonaka leading. All the pilots were wearing the customary *hachimaki* and as this was one of the biggest and most important operations for some time, the

Below: Firefighters at work on the flight deck of USS *Enterprise* spray foam around the Hellcats of Air Group 90.
Right: A formation of Grumman TBM Avengers approaches the coast of Okinawa during the preinvasion bombardment phase.
Bottom: A destroyer escort drops depth charges near a Japanese submarine, which penetrated Ulithi Harbor in November 1944.

edge of the runway was lined with spectators from the base. Admiral Ugaki himself was there to see the Kamikazes off, with tears in his eyes, it was said. Maybe his tears were for the brave men who would not return; possibly his thoughts were centered on the wretched depths to which his country had sunk. The takeoff was a depressing spectacle. Of the 55 Zeros assembled for escort duty, eight could not even get off the ground to follow the lumbering bombers, and 17 others were forced to turn back along the way because of engine trouble. No sooner were the planes airborne than a reconnaissance plane reported that the American carriers, surrounded by many more warships than was originally believed, had separated and the various groups were heading southwest.

With news like this the chance of the Kamikazes' success was considerably reduced, and there was some argument on whether the operation should be called off before the planes got any further. While Ugaki hesitated, 50 Grumman fighters settled the issue. The escorting Zeros tried in vain to drive off the interceptors, who concentrated their efforts on the Ohka-laden bombers. In consequence the bombers, powerless to fight back effectively, had to jettison their Ohkas to lighten their load and increase their maneuverability. Even so, 14 of them were shot down in quick succession, and nothing more was seen or heard of the others after they dived into a cloud bank hotly pursued by Grummans.

So ended the first of the Ohka sorties. The American airmen claimed to have destroyed 528 aircraft in the air and on the ground in these operations and the Japanese admitted later that 'losses had been staggering': 161 planes was their figure. Indeed they were so staggering that the Japanese Air Force was not able to participate effectively in the defense of Okinawa until 6 April. Admiral Ugaki, however, claimed that his 'eagles' had sunk five carriers, two battleships and three cruisers, and that the Americans would have to postpone their attack on Okinawa.

Although they must have known better, the Japanese appear to have accepted Ugaki's claim. On 23 March planes from Admiral Mitscher's carriers started their prelanding bombing program of targets on Okinawa and Admiral Blandy's ships appeared in the Kerama Retto. The Japanese High Command assumed that the bombing was a Parthian shot from crippled carriers returning to Ulithi and that Blandy's force was some sort of diversion. Within two days they knew better and an all-out air attack on Blandy's ships was ordered. By that time it was too late to interfere with the landings and the concentrated air attack did not materialize until 6 April.

Meantime the battlefield-isolation program was continuing as planned. On 27 and 31 March the B-29s of the US Army Air Force hammered the airfields in Kyushu, Taiwan and Honshu; they also dropped mines in the Shimonoseki Strait, effectively closing the main Japanese supply line for over a week. Finally the part played by the British Pacific Fleet deserves a brief mention. On 26 and 27 March and again from 30 March-2 April planes from the four British carriers attacked airfields in the Sakishima Islands and coastal shipping. During the time the British fleet was in action it was attacked by Kamikaze aircraft, and the carrier *Indefatigable* and the destroyer *Ulster* were both hit. The steel decks of the carrier prevented serious damage, but the destroyer had to be towed back to Ulithi for repairs. Operation Iceberg was now under way and during and after the landings the British carriers provided a flying buffer between the American amphibious forces and the Japanese airfields on Sakishima.

Concentrating Vice-Admiral Kelly Turner's invasion fleet during the latter half of March was no mean feat of organization. No single assembly area was big enough for this vast armada. Leyte Gulf was ample for the Northern Attack Force which was to land the Marines on the northern Hagushi beaches, but even the big lagoon at Ulithi was insufficient to hold the Southern Attack Force which was to land the troops on the southern Hagushi shoreline. The fact that other ships supporting the operation could only use the facilities at Ulithi served to complicate matters still further. So components of the invasion fleet had to move according to a

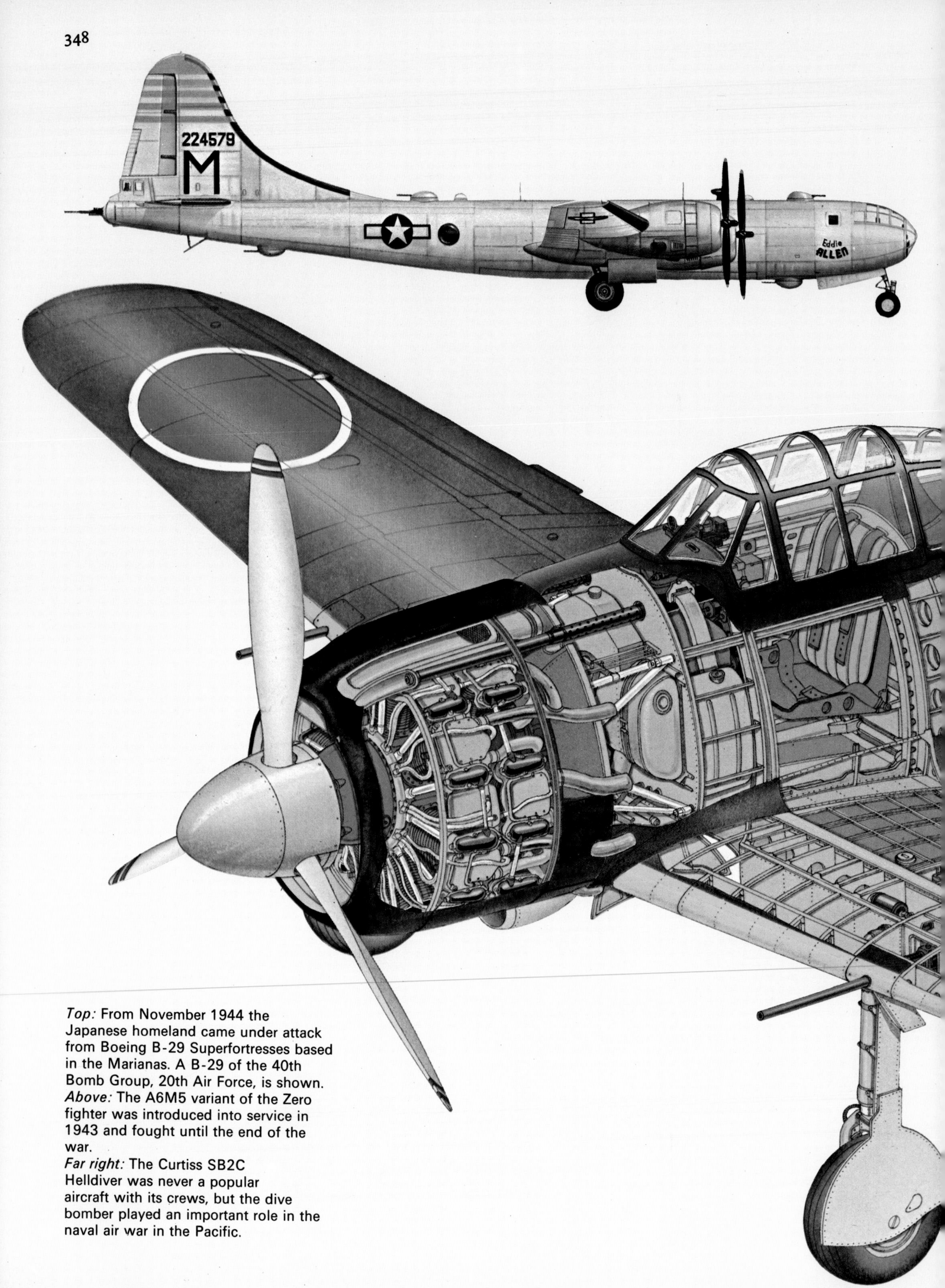

Top: From November 1944 the Japanese homeland came under attack from Boeing B-29 Superfortresses based in the Marianas. A B-29 of the 40th Bomb Group, 20th Air Force, is shown.
Above: The A6M5 variant of the Zero fighter was introduced into service in 1943 and fought until the end of the war.
Far right: The Curtiss SB2C Helldiver was never a popular aircraft with its crews, but the dive bomber played an important role in the naval air war in the Pacific.

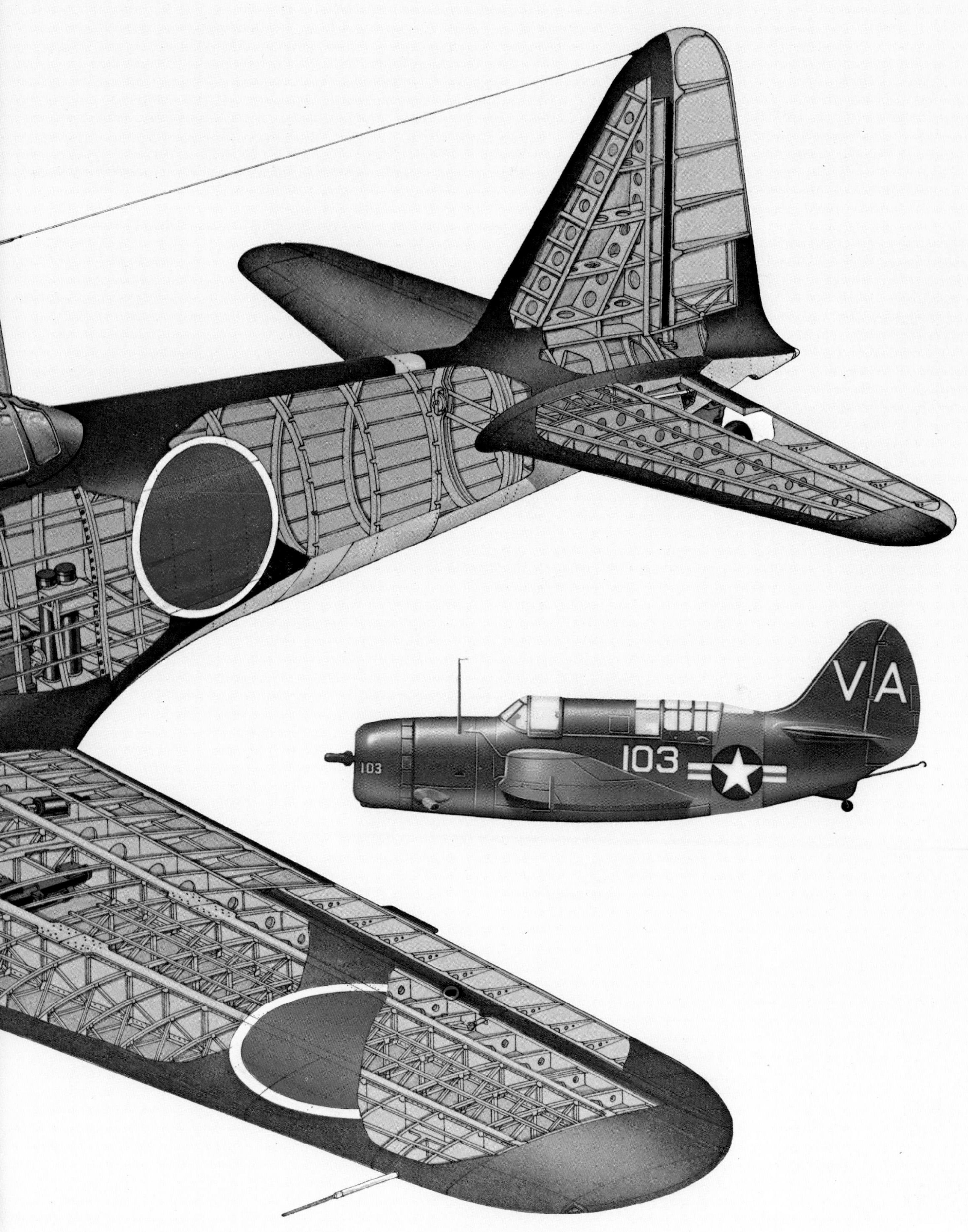
VA
103
103

strict schedule. Some of the ships which had been supporting the operation on Iwo Jima were badly in need of overhaul, and their crews needed rest and time to recuperate. There was no time; ships were refuelled and replenished and then they had to leave their berths for other vessels to take their place. Ulithi lagoon at this time was, in US Navy parlance, a 'hot bunk.'

Every effort was made to give the men who passed through Ulithi a memorable break and the atmosphere at the crowded officers club on the atoll on 20 March has been compared to the famous ball at Brussels on the eve of Waterloo. To boogie-woogie music played by a band of colored Seabees, officers of the US Navy and a few of their British counterparts danced with nurses from the three hospital ships, *Solace, Relief* and *Comfort*, lying in the lagoon. For some of them it would be their last dance, except for a dance of death with the Kamikaze Samurai. Next morning Rear Admiral 'Spike' Blandy's fire-support fleet, preceded by the minesweeping flotilla and its escort ships sailed for the Ryukyus, and were followed by the two assault forces – one of which had previously assembled in Leyte Gulf.

From Ulithi it was a run of only four days and the leading minesweepers sighted the peak of Kuba Shima in the Kerama Retto shortly after dawn on 24 March. From then on their task began in earnest, although some mines had already been encountered before they reached this point. Working in groups of four or five – each group under the protection of a destroyer – the minesweepers started methodically to sweep the ocean off Okinawa. The importance of their work may be gauged from the slogan coined by the minesweepers themselves: 'No Sweep, No Invasion.' If any warning were needed of the awful hazards associated with mines, what happened to the destroyer *Halligan* provided it. Venturing into unswept waters close to the shore, the *Halligan* hit a mine which blew up the ship's forward magazines. Altogether 153 men were killed and another 39 wounded out of a total complement of 325.

Nor were mines the only hazards the vessels of the minesweeping flotilla had to contend with. They were under constant air attack, day and night, and as the operation progressed more and more of them were sunk or damaged by Kamikazes. A number of submarine 'contacts' were also detected. Most of these were written off as false alarms, but it is possible that an attempt was made to pick off the odd destroyer with a Kaiten. The Japanese fleet submarine *I-44* captained by Commander Genbei Kawaguchi was sent out with a full complement of Kaiten to inflict as much damage as possible. He failed. According to the report Kawaguchi submitted on his return to the submarine's base at Otsujima the American antisubmarine patrols were operating everywhere and every time he tried to surface the *I-44* was detected. After US planes and ships had compelled him to remain submerged for 48 hours Kawaguchi called off the operation. For this he was relieved of his command; the Imperial Navy had little patience with officers who failed. Kawaguchi had thought it better to live and fight another day; his superiors did not agree with him.

Left: An infantry patrol from the US Army's 77th Division carries out a search on the island of Aka Shima, off the southwest coast of Okinawa.

While the minesweepers were still sweeping channels toward the main objective, the next phase of Operation Iceberg was initiated. This was the occupation of the group of mountainous islands known as the Kerama Retto which lies 15 miles west of southern Okinawa. The islands were thinly populated and the Japanese garrison was estimated to be about a thousand strong. (In the event this proved to be an exaggeration.)

An approach to the islands had been cleared by the minesweepers by 25 March when a couple of cruisers, the *San Francisco* and *Minneapolis*, and five destroyers moved in to bombard the beaches and Japanese defense works on the central island. Under cover of this bombardment frogmen went in to reconnoiter the approaches to the beaches which men of the US 77th Division would assault the following day. Landing craft lifted the frogmen to points about 500 yards from the shore where they took to the water from where they swam in toward the beach taking soundings at regular intervals.

Early next morning the *San Francisco* and *Minneapolis* and their accompanying destroyers resumed the bombardment of the beaches and defenses, and the fire from their guns was augmented by the 12-inch guns of the 33-year-old battleship *Arkansas*. Then shortly after first light planes from the escort carriers screamed in to bomb and strafe the landing zones. Meanwhile the amphibious and landing craft carrying the troops were moving in and the landings were effected exactly as planned, and without the loss of a single man. The Japanese had been taken completely by surprise; they had never thought that the Americans would be interested in the Kerama Retto. The Japanese soldiers there – and there were only a few hundred of them – herded the local population into caves and tunnels and prepared to die fighting. They did attempt two counterattacks during the first day, but the American beachheads were firmly established and the Japanese suffered heavy casualties and gained nothing. After that there was no organized resistance and such as there was was sporadic. On one of the smaller islands a dozen local women and a few children were found dead in a cave. They had been strangled by their own menfolk who had been told that a fate worse than death awaited them at the hands of the brutal and licentious American soldiers. The murderers were captured and when they found out what the Americans were really like they begged their guards to permit them to 'take it out' on the Japanese prisoners.

All the islands of the Kerama group had been occupied by the afternoon of 26 March, and work began on the establishment of a seaplane base. Nets covering the entrances to the roadstead were quickly laid also, to protect the vessels at anchor there from Kaiten attacks. Priority was given to the installation of antiaircraft and radar defenses, it appeared they were going to hit back with their Kamikazes. Sure enough the first attack came in the early evening of 26 March when nine Kamikaze aircraft attempted to crash dive on to ships of the invasion force. Next morning two other Kamikaze pilots flying obsolescent aircraft arrived on the scene and the destroyer *Kimberley* was slightly damaged but not disabled.

There was only one attempt to use a 'suicide boat' and one of the unexpected and welcome bonuses for the Americans was the capture of about 250 of these boats which had been camouflaged and concealed in caves on the Kerama Retto. The one attack that was made took place on the night of 28 March against the tender *Terebinth*. The crew saw the suicide boat racing toward them and prepared for the worst. However, it seemed that the Japanese pilot had no stomach for glory. After merely dropping one of the two 250-pound depth charges which these boats carried he veered away and raced off into the darkness – presumably to rejoin his comrades on Okinawa.

Back in Japan however, the staff of the Japanese Sixth Fleet were planning a more determined attack. The Japanese naval command still believed that the Kaiten could inflict enormous damage if employed properly. Following Kawaguchi's abortive mission, however, the commander and staff of the Sixth Fleet – responsible for the coordination and organization of Kaiten operations – had decided that a mass attack was called for. Only four of the fleet submarines capable of carrying Kaiten now remained. But it was proposed to fit them out to take as many as possible and they would all sail together to attack the American armada off Okinawa. A kind of underwater Banzai charge was envisaged, and the Japanese planners were convinced that some of the Kaiten must get through to their targets.

The operation was scheduled for the end of March, and the so-called Tatara Group (Tatara beach in northern Kyushu is where the Mongol armada was wrecked by the Kamikaze typhoon) of Kaiten pilots was embarked on the *I-44, I-47, I-56* and *I-58*. The *I-47* was designated the flagship for the Tatara operation. Three of the submarines carried four Kaiten, and the *I-56* had been refitted to take six.

The Kaiten pilots were given a party on the night of 26 March. A lot of sake was drunk, and Admiral Nagai, the commander of the Sixth Fleet, wished the Kaiten men 'every success.' 'I hope each of you will strike our enemy,' he said. 'At that moment your souls will fly to Yasukuni, there to watch forever over God's country, Japan. Please be assured that the rest of us in Sixth Fleet will do everything possible to comfort those you leave behind. . . .' Other senior officers made similar speeches exhorting the 'Samurai of the Sea' to 'do a good job.' Next morning, when they embarked, there were a few thick heads in the group.

In the event, like the previous operation, the Tatara affair was a complete and utter failure. Even as the submarine pack approached the target area the Americans were storming ashore at Okinawa, and no less than 150 destroyers were screening the vast invasion fleet. Through this formidable barrier of antisubmarine patrols the Japanese submarines had little hope of penetrating. *I-44* and *I-57* were sunk in the attempt. *I-47* managed to escape and limp back to Japan, and *I-58* was chased off and compelled to withdraw. There were now not enough submarines to take out all the men who were being trained to handle Kaiten, and by April most of them were

Below right: Inshore fire support was provided by suitably modified LCIs, such as this rocket-armed craft of the amphibious support force.
Below: A cruiser of the naval bombardment force in action. The landings on Okinawa were preceded by five days of naval and air bombardment.

scheduled to be employed in what was fancifully called 'base Kaiten attack.' A plan was drawn up for Kaiten to be deployed along Japan's coast, at points where an amphibious assault could most likely be expected. The Kaiten pilots were expected to hide their weapons and wait. When the Americans were just offshore, they would receive a signal from Imperial Headquarters. Then, the base Kaitens would roar out to sea and sink as many troopships as possible. Japanese naval strategy had not changed – give the Americans a blood bath and smash them in one single decisive action. This was the strategy that had been used at Midway, the Marianas and the Philippines. Soon it would be used again at Okinawa. It had not yet worked to Japan's advantage but as the Americans closed in, and the suicidal patriotic fervor increased, hopes that it might do so remained high.

The final 'softening-up' barrage of Okinawa began on 26 March and continued through until the 31st. The 16-inch guns of three *Maryland* Class battleships, 14-inch guns of two *New Mexico* Class and the old *New York, Texas* and *Tennessee,* augmented by the 12-inch armament of the *Arkansas* all combined fearsome firepower. To this was added the guns of seven heavy cruisers, three light cruisers and 24 destroyers and over 50 rocket and mortar ships. Plenty of fire support for the prelanding bombardment was thus available. The problem was to select profitable targets. Clearly it was not possible to destroy every Japanese installation on such a big island before the troops landed even if it was feasible to pinpoint them. A study of the air photographs taken in March revealed that the Japanese appeared to have very few defensive works immediately behind the beaches on which the Americans would land. Consequently it was decided that the ships' gunfire would best be directed by aerial spotters flying over the island.

The Fire Support Force, as this prelanding bombardment fleet was called, closed on Okinawa during the late evening of 26 March. It was under the command of Rear Admiral Morton L Deyo, a 57-year-old dynamic character, and to date it was the biggest gunfire and covering force that had ever been concentrated for an operation in the Pacific. Steaming at 10 knots in four close columns it moved through the 10-mile wide channel between Tonaki and the Kerama Retto which the minesweepers had cleared and marked with radar reflecting buoys. It was a pleasantly cool night and only the distant roll of artillery fire somewhere in the Kerama Retto indicated the presence of the Japanese. Those who had taken part in some of the earlier island-hopping expeditions knew that the enemy rarely showed his hand at the start of an operation.

At dawn the four columns of ships deployed for their bombardment tasks, with the battleships and cruisers remaining well offshore in waters that had been swept clean by the minesweepers. When they opened fire the only response evoked from the island's defenders was a burst of antiaircraft fire which damaged one of the spotter planes. However, it became clear that Japanese submarines were somewhere around lying in wait when lookouts on board one of the cruisers reported seeing the wake of a torpedo; soon after the two other cruisers reported near misses by torpedoes.

Both submarines and Kamikaze air attacks had been expected, and to cope with the latter it had been arranged that the escort carriers would provide an umbrella of fighter aircraft – first over the Fire Support Force and subsequently over the ships carrying the troops who were to land on the beaches. (This fighter cover was in addition to the bombing and strafing missions carried out by other carrier-based

Above: A Vought F4U-ID Corsair of VF-10 'The Grim Reapers' from USS *Intrepid* patrols off Okinawa on 10 April 1945.

Right: A US Marine watches landing craft assemble for the assault on Okinawa. The Kerama Retto islands provided a jumping-off point for the main landings.

aircraft.) This arrangement was to continue until one or other of the Japanese airfields was captured and put into commission so enabling land-based planes to take over. It worked well, not quite so well at the very beginning perhaps, but on and after 6 April when the Kamikazes attacked in alarming strength the carrier-based fighters accounted for more Japanese planes than did the ships' antiaircraft fire. Without them the invasion fleet would undoubtedly have suffered appalling casualties.

Unfortunately the air umbrella was not in position at dawn on the morning of 27 March when seven Kamikazes attacked. Diving through the curtain of antiaircraft fire one crashed onto the main deck of the battleship *Nevada*, knocking out two 14-inch guns, killing 11 men and wounding 49. A second Kamikaze narrowly missed the *Tennessee*, a third splashed down near the cruiser *Biloxi*, just before a fourth crashed into the side of the *Biloxi*. Fortunately for the crew the Kamikaze's bomb failed to explode and there were no casualties – other than the Japanese pilot. The destroyer *O'Brien*, hit by the fifth Kamikaze, was not so lucky; she lost 28 men killed, 22 missing and 76 wounded and had to return to the United States for repairs. The sixth Kamikaze crashed onto the deck of the minesweeper *Dorsey* but she got off with minor damage and only a few casualties. What happened to the seventh Kamikaze is not recorded, but it is presumed that the pilot joined his ancestors at Yasukuni.

During the six days of softening-up bombardment there was little variation in the routine followed by the Fire Support Force. Soon after sunrise, which was about 0630 hours, the ships would take up their positions and steam slowly down parallel to the shore, firing at targets behind the landing beaches – the targets being observed by the spotter aircraft who radioed back corrections to the gunlayers. Sunset was about 1845 hours, and about two hours before this the battleships and cruisers would retire seaward zigzagging to a rendezvous some 10-15 miles off Okinawa. There they would form a kind of seaborne laager for antiaircraft protection. The following morning they would return and resume the bombardment.

Between midnight on 28 March and dawn the following morning Japanese aircraft based on the Okinawa airfields tried to knock out the minesweepers working close to the coast. Only one of the US craft was damaged but the raiders caused a few casualties – at a cost to themselves of 10 aircraft. In the morning the crew of one of the minesweepers saw a man on the beach waving frantically. He appeared to be a European so the word was passed back and a seaplane was sent to pick him up. The seaplane alighted on the water just beyond the reef which precluded boats getting really close in, taxied in toward the beach and the rescue was successfully accomplished. The man concerned was a Lieutenant F M Fox of the *Yorktown* who had crashed while on a mission and had spent three days hiding near Kadena airfield.

That same day (29 March) a reconnaissance was made of the Hagushi beaches where the assault troops proposed to land and the beaches where they would pretend to land. The same technique was used as at Kerama Retto. Frogmen were taken to the reef in landing craft and from there they swam forward, taking soundings as they went. Except for some desultory mortar fire and sniping the Japanese did not respond. The fact that they did not do so made the Americans uneasy; this was not the way the enemy had reacted elsewhere. However, the frogmen returned and the results of the reconnaissance were assessed. The amphibious vehicles with which the vanguard of the invaders would charge onto the beaches should be able to negotiate the reef without difficulty. In some places there would be enough water over the reef at high tide to float landing craft. The only obstacles the frogmen had encountered were about 3000 antiboat stakes which had been driven into the coral in an attempt to make it more of an obstacle. Next day, 30 March (Good Friday) the frogmen went back and under cover of a bombardment put down on the beaches by the destroyers and cruisers, they set about destroying these stakes. Working their way systematically along the reef the frogmen placed explosive charges timed to explode when they had returned to their landing craft. Once again the operations of the frogmen evoked no response from the Japanese.

Okinawa at this time appeared to be

completely deserted. The fields had been neatly cultivated but not a single human being or animal was to be seen either from the ships or from the air. Nobody moved on the roads and the villages appeared to be empty. If there were any military installations on the island it looked as if they had been most effectively camouflaged. American Intelligence said that there were at least 60,000 Japanese troops on Okinawa, but there was no indication of where they were. In consequence the invaders had the uncomfortable feeling that the Japanese were preparing a very nasty surprise.

Judging by Air reconnaissance reports, Ie Shima, the tiny island with the airfield lying north of Okinawa, was also deserted, and a Japanese officer rescued from a motor torpedo boat sunk in the area supported the delusion by insisting that it had been evacuated. Air photographs indicated that the airfield had taken a severe pounding and could not be used. As at Okinawa there was nobody to be seen and American planes flying low over Ie Shima were not fired upon. Two weeks later the US 77th Division had to kill about 3000 Japanese to secure the island.

Locating military installations on Okinawa seemed to be like seeking the proverbial needle in the haystack. However on 30 March air photographs of Unten-Ko – the reef-ringed harbor on Okinawa's Motobu Peninsula – disclosed the existence of a midget-submarine base. An immediate attack by planes from the escort carriers was ordered and the submarine pens were duly destroyed together with the midget submarines and motor torpedo boats housed in them. For the Americans the success was marred only by the fact that two aircraft failed to return from the raid. The attack wiped out all the midget submarines in the area.

All the evidence suggested that the Japanese had pulled back from the shoreline. Nevertheless the Americans expected the landing to be opposed. The Hagushi beaches were bisected by the Bishi River which flowed into the sea between two high and steep limestone banks, the faces of which were honeycombed with caves and tunnels. Machine guns emplaced in these caves could rake the landing beaches from end to end and were inaccessible to naval gunfire or air attack. Another limestone outcrop also honeycombed with caves commanded the southern beaches, and a concrete pillbox had been constructed to cover the beaches north of the river. Behind each of the beaches there was a thick six–10 feet high wall of masonry and concrete on which the naval gunfire had made little impression. One or two other concrete emplacements which were visible from the air had been badly battered, but the Americans felt that they had only touched the tip of the iceberg so far as military installations were concerned, and it looked as if the landings on the Hagushi were going to be a bloody business.

Below left: Antiaircraft gunners aboard the battleship *West Virginia* keep watch by their 40mm weapons off Okinawa.
Bottom: Landing craft head for the Okinawa beaches on L-day, the first day of the assault.
Below: Lookouts scan the skies for incoming Kamikaze aircraft from their post aboard an American battleship.

3. OPERATION ICEBERG

At 0830 hours on the morning of Easter Sunday, 1 April 1945 the Americans stormed ashore on the Hagushi beaches. The weather had been slightly overcast and cool at 0630 hours when the assault troops prepared for H-Hour, and peered at the island which they had been told was likely to prove a tougher nut to crack than Iwo Jima. The cool weather was in fact a pleasant change for Marines and GIs who were accustomed to fighting in the steaming heat of the Philippines. As they climbed into their landing craft and amphibious vehicles however, the sun rose over the low-lying cloud. It was a beautiful morning and a perfect day for an amphibious operation: a calm sea and just enough wind to blow away the smoke of battle.

Four divisions were committed to the initial assault – two Marine (the 1st, veterans of Guadalcanal and Peleliu and the 6th, going into battle for the first time), and two infantry divisions (the 7th, veterans of Attu, Kwajalein and Leyte and the 96th, veterans of Leyte). The two Marine divisions each landed on five selected Hagushi beaches north of the Bishi River which served as an easily recognizable boundary between the Marine and Army divisions; the two infantry divisions landed on a total of 11 specified beaches south of the river.

Like previous Pacific-island invasions the landings had to be made over the fringing coral reef that extended seaward to a distance of eight to 12 hundred yards. There was one gap in the reef where the Bishi River flowed into the sea, but the Japanese were expected to have this so well covered with fire that it would be unusable until the suspected strongpoints in the bluff overlooking the gap had been cleared. The frogmen's reconnaissance had also shown that it would be possible to float small boats over the shelf-like reef at or near high

water around 0900 hours. In the event the Americans went over the reef in amphibious vehicles and so well had the technique been developed as a result of previous operations that 700 odd amtracs landed some 8000 men in the first 20 minutes.

The landings followed the pattern which had been worked out for Saipan. Experience there and elsewhere had proved that ferrying troops from ship to shore in several hundred landing craft required a well-trained traffic-control group to supervise the operation. Officers and men of this group were naval personnel and they were equipped with motor boats. The selected beaches were all designated by colors and numbered – Green 1 and Green 2 for example. The 6th Marines were allotted two 'green' and three 'red' beaches, the 1st Marines two 'blue' and three 'yellow,' the 7th Infantry Division two 'purple' and two 'orange' and the 96th Division three 'white' and four 'brown' beaches. Control boats flying a flag corresponding to the beaches they controlled were deployed and anchored in front of the beaches an hour or so before the landings to indicate the direction in which the waves of landing craft should steer. To make absolutely certain that the first waves got to their correct beaches they were marshalled and led by fast motor boats flying appropriately colored pennants. Every landing craft of the initial waves also had the color of the beach for which it was destined painted on its topsides. The first troops ashore also set up colored beach markers, brightly painted canvas screens about 10 feet high.

While the landing craft and amphibious vehicles were moving in toward the beaches the ships of the naval support force bombarded the beach area along a 10-mile front lifting their fire only when the first wave of amtracs were some 75 yards from the shore. Meantime carrier-based strike aircraft continued the bombardment, raining bombs on targets which had been selected because they looked as if they might constitute Japanese strongpoints. The air was filled with noise – the sound of exploding bombs and drone of the aircraft motors being punctuated by repeated crashes as the battleships fired broadsides from their main armament. On board the *Tennessee* Admiral Deyo sniffed the yellow cordite fumes appreciatively and commented, 'That has a good offensive smell!'

The amphibians of the first wave hit the beaches at approximately 0830 hours, and waddled up toward the seawall. Behind them the second wave had already touched the shore; behind the second wave the third wave was crossing the reef and behind the third wave, the fourth, fifth, sixth and other waves were plowing in toward the reef. As far as the eye could see waves of landing craft were moving in toward Okinawa with majestic, precise deliberation.

Up to this point Japanese interest in the landing operations had been confined to a single Kamikaze attack on the naval armada.

Below: At 0832 hours the first assault wave hit the beaches.
Left: US Marines take cover after crossing the beaches.
Right: Marines move away from the beaches. By 1030 hours on L-day 50,000 men were ashore.

This was made at first light and the plane was shot down. There was nothing to indicate the presence of Japanese soldiers on the island until the landings were well under way. Then the first signs that the Japanese were there somewhere came when mortar bombs raised plumes of white water just off the beaches. Some of these bombs fell close to landing craft but none was hit and the warships went quickly into action. The fire was coming from mortars on the bluffs of the Bisha River, and a few ferocious salvos of naval gunfire quickly silenced them forever.

Apart from this minor bombardment the landings were completely unopposed. By 0900 hours the early morning mist had been completely dispersed and the sun was shining down on an incredible scene. Off shore the transports were continuing to discharge more men and vehicles to join the swarms of men and amphibians already on the beaches. Behind the beaches men and tanks were moving up the slopes toward the tableland of the interior; above them spotter planes circled, radioing back the troops' progress to headquarters.

By about 1030 hours some 50,000 men had landed on the island and the first waves of Marines had overrun both Yontan and Kadena airfields. They did not meet any opposition and had not suffered any casualties. Everybody was astounded and the questions on everybody's lips were: 'Where are the 60,000 or so Japanese that are supposed to be defending the island? And what about the elaborate defenses they were supposed to have constructed? Are we walking into some sort of trap – into a killing ground?' Throughout the afternoon

Left: Fleet Admiral Nimitz (left foreground) and Admiral Spruance tour the Okinawa beachhead.
Below left: LST-829 heads for the beaches with a floating causeway lashed alongside.

Below and bottom: As US troops moved inland on Okinawa they discovered that the Japanese garrison had withdrawn to the interior, leaving the old and sick and women and children to the invaders.

while the troops set about securing the hills dominating the two airfields, the total lack of opposition continued to puzzle the invaders. Behind the southern beaches there were a few bursts of mortar fire and some light artillery shells fell in the area through which the GIs of the 7th Division were advancing. On the northern beaches there was nothing, and intensive air reconnaissance failed to pick up any Japanese troop concentrations. In the late afternoon there was some sniping around Yontan airfield and three Japanese tanks were discovered concealed in a cave. By dusk the Marines in the northern sector had encountered and dealt with only 15 Japanese soldiers, but they had rounded up some 675 Okinawa civilians – mostly old people and children. Even the Kamikazes failed to put in an appearance until dusk. However a few did appear as the light failed and one succeeded in crashing into the battleship *West Virginia*, killing four men and wounding 23. The remainder were either shot down or their pilots decided the time for their supreme sacrifice was not yet opportune.

Further south the force under Rear Admiral Jerrault Wright which carried out the decoy landings on D-Day and 2 April received more attention from the Japanese air force than did the real landings. As dawn was breaking and the ships maneuvered into position for the landings, the Kamikazes arrived and one succeeded in crashing his plane into a tank landing craft with 300 Marines on board. The vessel burst into flames, ammunition exploded and 24 sailors and Marines were killed; 21 others were wounded. Another Kamikaze which smashed into the side of the transport *Hinsale* caused 55 other casualties. The landings did not in fact deceive the Japanese but enabled them to claim on Radio Tokyo that they had 'forced "Jerry" Wright and his men to withdraw . . . after being mowed down one after the other.'

While the landing of stores, equipment and still more men continued unabated, the absence of Japanese soldiers continued to puzzle even the American Intelligence experts. To abandon two valuable airfields without a fight seemed inconceivable. The Japanese must surely be dug in somewhere waiting to give the invaders hell when they came up to their positions. Where were the defenses? Some of the captured civilians who were interrogated said that the Japanese had withdrawn to the east, still others said they had pulled back south. Most of the experts concluded that they were holed up in the rugged terrain of the northern part of Okinawa.

In fact General Ushijima had concentrated his troops in two areas – east and south of the town of Naka, and on the Motobu Peninsula. He had been hoping reinforcements would reach him from Japan before the island was invaded, but even without them he had about 100,000 men, if the Okinawa Home Guard was counted in. This was greatly in excess of American Intelligence estimates. Ushijima had studied the American technique of island invasions, and had seen that in earlier campaigns the forces deployed by the invaders came in overwhelming strength. The old ideas of annihilating the enemy on the beach as the Japanese commanders at Tarawa, Saipan and Iwo Jima had tried to do were no longer valid, and Imperial General Headquarters had laid down a new code of tactics. Ushijima was to allow the enemy to 'land in full' and be 'lured into a position where he cannot receive cover and support from the naval and aerial bombardment . . .

Right: From the second day of the landing US troops began to encounter serious resistance. Okinawan women help to load wounded Americans on to a truck for evacuation.
Below: Supplies are unloaded on 13 April 1945. The development of Okinawa as an American base began soon after L-day, although Japanese resistance lasted for nearly three months.

(and) where the most effective fire power can be brought to bear. His force is then to be wiped out.' Such tactics, the Japanese High Command reckoned, would gain time and inflict maximum casualties; in fact the end was the same – the extermination of the Japanese garrison on Okinawa, and ultimately the defeat of Japan.

Ushijima decided that his best bet for prolonging the defense and inflicting maximum casualties was to abandon the Hagushi beaches and the two airfields. He had originally intended to put both airfields out of commission but the invasion took place before the demolitions his engineers had planned could be put into effect. In the last-minute rush to pull back to the two concentration areas they were abandoned. So far as the Americans were concerned Yontan and Kadena were the most important territorial gains of D-Day. On 2 April the Kadena strip was being used as an emergency landing ground, and next day two strips of the Yontan field could also be used. One of the stories that went the rounds at this time told of a Japanese plane landing on the Yontan airfield on the night of 1/2 April. The pilot taxied up to the filling station, climbed out and asked for fuel in Japanese. A Marine sentry replied and the Emperor lost one pilot.

On 2 and 3 April men of the 7th Infantry Division and Marines of the 1st Marine Division reached the east coast of the island and on 4 April the 1st and 6th Marine Divisions occupied the Katchin Peninsula and a large stretch of the east coast. The operation was now 20 days ahead of the schedule the planners had forecast. Next day the advance was resumed with the Marines moving into the northern half of Okinawa and meeting no serious resistance until they crossed into the Motobu Peninsula.

South of the Bisha River on the second day the GIs of the 96th Division began to encounter increasing resistance in rugged terrain. This resistance, by a rear guard covering the withdrawal of Ushijima's Naha force, was swept aside on 4 April when air reconnaissance flights spotted Japanese troops moving toward Shuri, the ancient capital of Okinawa east of Naha. At long last the aircraft and the battleships had some positive targets, although nobody had yet seen any great concentration of Japanese or pinpointed their defense works. Their real whereabouts was still a mystery. That night however the GIs were subjected for the first time to a heavy artillery bombardment and, although they resumed the advance the next morning, the intensity of the storm of fire that greeted them brought them up short. They had reached the so-called Machinato Line of the Japanese Shuri Zone – an interlocking system of mountain defenses organized in great depth. Here the GIs were destined to remain for the next two weeks.

For the Japanese 3 April was a significant date – it was 'Jimmu Day' – the day

Above: Marine artillerymen hunt for Japanese snipers who have infiltrated their position.
Below: This bulldozer follows close behind advancing Marines and so an infantryman rides shotgun to protect the driver.
Above right: Marines scramble over a stone wall during their advance. Note the flame thrower carried by the man in the center.
Right: Marines raise the Stars and Stripes on Okinawa.

when 2500 years earlier the Emperor Jimmu had initiated a policy of Japanese expansion when he declared that he wished '. . . to make the universe our home.' Jimmu Day was supposed to be a happy occasion and for many years it had always been possible to find some cheerful news in keeping with the spirit of the day. Following the landings on Okinawa, the constant bombing of the home islands and the virtual destruction of Japan's major cities, the Japanese Government had to admit the situation was extremely serious. If Okinawa was lost, Admiral Takahashi pointed out in a broadcast from Radio Tokyo, Japan would be cut off from all the territories she had conquered in the South Pacific. However, there was no need for despair, he said; the Imperial Navy was going to go on the offensive and all would soon be well. In the Japanese Parliament – the Diet – the wizened General Kuniaki Koiso blustered that 'our Japanese heroes' would drive the Americans off Okinawa and then 'retake Saipan and other points.' But the sands were running out for Koiso. In a few days time he was to resign and the aged Admiral Suzuki, charged by the Emperor with the task of finding some honorable way of ending the war, became Premier. Meantime, since the finding of a formula for peace without loss of face would take time and require circumspection and caution to avoid a military coup d'état, there was no question but that Okinawa would be defended vigorously and to the last man.

After the Battle of Leyte Gulf, which saw the beginning of the Kamikaze Corps, the Imperial Japanese Navy had ceased to exist as a practical fighting force. Most of the cruisers had been lost, and the battleships *Yamato, Nagato* and *Haruna*, which had limped home, had been bottled up in the Inland Sea. The *Yamato* (863 feet long) and her sister ship the *Musashi* (which had been sunk in October 1944) were the world's biggest battleships. Laid down in 1937 and completed in 1941 they were armed with nine 460mm (18.1-inch) guns capable of hurling a shell of 3200 pounds 42,000 meters (22.5 miles). The *Yamato*'s crew totalled 2800 men.

Shortage of fuel precluded the *Yamato, Nagato* and *Haruna* being used for operations. During March, however, an attempt had been made to resuscitate the Second Fleet, by allocating what remained of the dwindling fuel stocks to the *Yamato*, the cruiser *Yakagi* and five destroyers. In an effort to cripple the American invasion fleet off Okinawa Admiral Toyoda, Commander in Chief of the once proud Combined Fleet, decided to use these ships in an operation called 'Ten-Go.' There was little if any coordination between the services as to how the army, navy and air force would act and when. Ten-Go was supposed to be a combined and coordinated triservice operation with mass Kamikaze attacks from the air, Kaiten and other submarines attacking under the sea, and what was left of the Imperial Navy took part. A series of Kaiten and Kamikaze attacks had already been scheduled for 6 April under the code name Kikusui. Literally 'floating chrysanthemum,' Kikusui was the crest of the Kusukoni family. In the fourteenth century Mazashige Kusukoni had led a Japanese army to certain death in a suicide operation. However, Kikusui Operation Number 1 was to be the grand attack which could make the other operations superfluous.

The warships of the reconstituted Second Fleet were commanded by Vice-Admiral Seeichi Ito, who had been Vice-Chief of Naval Operations in 1941 and who was considered to be an outstanding officer. Realizing that desperate circumstances called for desperate action, Ito was willing to accept orders for a suicidal operation without questioning them. He was one of the few senior officers of the Imperial Navy who did. In Tokyo the Naval General Staff were against Toyoda's Kikusui, maintaining that although Japan faced total defeat it was inhuman to order men into an operation of this magnitude which was so uncertain of success. In their view the fleet would never reach Okinawa, so the loss of men and ships was a wasteful sacrifice. Toyoda's own Combined Fleet Headquarters refuted this argument. The loss of Okinawa would be disastrous, they said, and it was the navy's job to cooperate with the army. The fleet might not reach Okinawa but it would attract the attention of a large number of American aircraft. A lull in the land fighting would follow, during which a counterattack by General Ushijima's troops would have considerable chance of success.

Toyoda's order called for the Second Fleet to beach itself in front of the Americans on Okinawa and to fire every gun of every ship until the last shell had been expended or the last ship destroyed. Individual survivors were told that they could join in the land fighting and 'find glory.'

The order was received aboard Ito's flagship, the *Yamato*, during the afternoon of 5 April, as the operation was scheduled for 8 April. Ito promptly summoned his captains to a conference, and there was a storm of protest. Nearly all the commanding officers objected to the operation – not because it meant certain death, but because they considered it meant squandering what was left of the Imperial Navy for a very dubious return. There was no question of Ito's subordinates not being prepared to give their lives, and those of their men, for the Emperor. But they were dominated by a philosophy that had come to them long ago through their association with Britain's Royal Navy: 'Fight bravely, but not in vain.' The conference lasted for five hours, during which some heated comments were passed about the planning capabilities of Combined Fleet Headquarters, safe in its air-raid shelter. But discipline held. When Ito said that the order must be obeyed, the

Above and top: In a vain attempt to open communications with the defenders of Okinawa, the huge battleship *Yamato* sortied from Japan. On 7 April she was sent to the bottom by carrier planes.

argument stopped and the commanders returned to their ships to prepare for the forthcoming action.

On board the ships the return of the captains spelled feverish activity. Bayonets were sharpened ready for the hand-to-hand fighting many of the crews expected to see ashore. Fuel sufficient only for a one way passage was taken on, and the crews were weeded out, only those needed to man the ships remaining. (Among those who were disembarked was a batch of midshipmen, fresh from the Naval Academy, who had arrived only a few days earlier. Many of these young men wished to take part in the operation but they were not permitted to do so.) Finally there were the farewell parties, at which many bottles of sake were consumed. These broke up with the singing of *Doki no Sakura* ('Cherry Blossoms of the same rank') – an old Naval Academy song.

The Second Fleet steamed out of the Inland Sea that night, and by 0600 hours on 6 April it was southwest of Kyushu, heading due south for Okinawa on a zigzag course. If all went well it was scheduled to reach the American landing beaches just before daylight on the 8th. An antisubmarine formation was assumed after the ships passed through the Bungo Strait, and for some hours 20 Zeros of the Fifth Air Fleet provided an aerial umbrella. However, as land receded the Zeros returned, and the reconnaissance seaplanes from the *Yamato* and *Yahagi* were flown off to prevent their destruction in the forthcoming battle. There was no need for reconnaissance; the whereabouts of the Americans was well known – just as the Americans knew of Ito's approach. Five miles behind Ito's fleet the US submarines *Threadfin* and *Hackleback* trailed the fleet and watched in fascination as the monstrous *Yamato* moved across their periscopes. At dawn on 7 April US flying boats arrived to tighten the watch.

Low, heavy clouds provided perfect protection for the attackers when the Americans struck at 1230 hours. Shortly after noon the *Yamato*'s radar had picked up two large formations of planes converging on her, and the first of them appeared overhead even before the message had been relayed to the other ships. There was no question of changing course, but the fleet speeded up to 27 knots, swung into two lines with 5000-yard intervals between ships, and opened fire. From start to finish Ito's fleet stood little chance. Although the *Yamato*'s AA guns put up a formidable curtain of steel, it was of little use. Planes were shot down but new attack waves came on incessantly. This was the fourth time the Americans had attacked the giant battleship and they were determined to sink her on this occasion.

The first bomb struck the *Yamato* at 1240 hours, and 10 minutes later a torpedo found its mark. Thereafter many more bombs and at least 15 torpedoes struck home. Three hours of steady attack finally doomed the great battleship. In all 300 US carrier-based planes struck at Ito's ship. According to Ensign Yoshida who survived the action:

'. . . bombs, bullets and torpedoes reduced the mighty battleship to a state of complete confusion. . . . The desolate decks were reduced to shambles, with nothing but cracked and twisted steel plates remaining. . . . . Big guns were inoperable because of the increasing list, and only a few machine guns were intact. . . . One devastating blast in the emergency dispensary killed all its occupants including the medical officers and corpsmen. . . .'

The ship was listing at an angle of 35 degrees when, shortly after 1400 hours, American Hellcats and Avengers returned to the attack. According to Yoshida:

'. . . the enemy came plunging through the clouds to deliver the coup de grace. . . . It was impossible to evade. . . . I could hear the Captain vainly shouting, "Hold on, men! Hold on, men! . . ." I heard the Executive Officer report to the Captain in a heartbroken voice, "Correction of list hopeless! . . ." Men were jumbled together in disorder on the deck, but a group of staff officers squirmed out of the pile and crawled over to the Commander in Chief for a final conference. Admiral Ito struggled to his feet. His Chief of Staff then arose and saluted. A prolonged silence followed during which they regarded each other solemnly. Ito looked around, shook hands deliberately with his staff officers, and then went resolutely into his cabin. The Captain concerned himself with saving the Emperor's portrait.'

At 1423 hours the ship slid under completely, followed by the blast, rumble and shock of compartments bursting from air pressure and exploding magazines already submerged. By 1500 hours not only *Yamato*, but the *Yahagi* and two destroyers *Asashimo* and *Kamakaze* had all been sunk. Two other destroyers the *Isokaze* and *Kasumi*, dead in the water, were sunk by other Japanese destroyers, after their crews had been rescued. Of the fleet only five destroyers now remained, and they returned to port next day. This greatest of suicide actions which was aborted had cost Japan six out of 10 ships and the lives of more than 2500 men.

After the battle Combined Fleet Headquarters issued a communiqué which read: 'Owing to the brave and sacrificial fighting of the Second Fleet, our Special Attack planes achieved great result.' The truth was that this last desperate fleet sortie of the Imperial Navy had ended in a miserable failure. The once glorious Combined Fleet, which had prided itself on commanding the entire Western Pacific, had been driven ignominiously from the seas around Japan.

4. STALEMATE

Left: Marines smoke out the Japanese defenders from their strongpoint in a cave.
Below left: A heavy machine gun of the US Army's 96th Division fires on Japanese positions, 4 April 1945.
Right: Major General Lemuel Shepherd commanded the 6th Marine Division on Okinawa.
Below: Marines detonate a satchel charge in the entrance of a Japanese cave.

With the rapid advance of the Marines in the northern half and that of the GIs in the south, Ushijima's forces on Okinawa were effectively cut in two. The main part of the Japanese garrison was in the south, and by 8 April the advance toward Shuri and Naha had ground to a halt. The GIs of the 96th Division had driven in the Japanese outposts but they could not pierce the elaborate and carefully prepared defenses of the Machinato Line. The Japanese had made full use of the geological structure of the island – coral-limestone caves occurring naturally as a result of the upward pressure of volcanic forces which had created Okinawa and broken much of its surface into sharp ridges and ravines. These caves provided splendid defensive positions – particularly to a people with the endless patience of the Japanese. They occurred usually in the faces of cliffs and ridges in defilade from naval gunfire and all but invulnerable from the air. The Machinato Line had been constructed by linking together a series of the caves. They were of course susceptible to manmade improvements, but fortunately on Okinawa there had been little time or materials available for such work. Here were few of the reinforced concrete bulkheads, steel doors and elaborate galleries that had been encountered on Iwo Jima. But many of the natural positions had been developed to obtain scientifically interlocking fields of fire for mutual protection, so it was not possible to bypass the Machinato positions.

The Americans brought up artillery and pounded the Jap positions but the point has been made that many of them were in an acute defilade. Moreover there was an acute shortage of ammunition. On 6 April Kamikaze bombers had sunk two of the three ammunition ships which had just arrived off Okinawa and this probably contributed to the shortage. Bad weather also hampered the unloading of stores over the beaches between the 4th and 6th and this also added to the problems of the troops.

It was now the turn of the Japanese. Imperial General Headquarters in Tokyo had radioed a 'suggestion' to Ushijima that the time was ripe for a counterattack, and Ushijima duly passed it on to his subordinate commander in Shuri. Four battalions took part and the attack was planned in considerable detail In fact it took practically everything into consideration – except the terrain. As a result of this omission and some hard fighting by the GIs the effort ended in complete frustration.

The attack began at midnight on 12 April when the Japanese left the safety of their caves and advanced toward the entrenched Americans. They had been given a slogan for the occasion: 'Seven lives to repay our country' – meaning, evidently, that each man was supposed to kill seven Americans before going to join his ancestors. In the event they were singularly unsuccessful. Not only did they fail to kill seven for one but when they were driven back in the early hours of the morning they left 200 dead behind them.

Bottom: Phosphorus shells explode on an enemy-held ridge as Marines wait to move in and assault it.
Right: A flame-throwing tank of the 7th Infantry Division attacks a Japanese bunker on Hill 178.
Below: The corpse of a Japanese soldier caught by a flame thrower.

The next night (13 April), however, they tried again. This time the attack began shortly after 2100 hours with a fire fight followed by several assaults in considerable strength, and it flickered intermittently all night. The GIs were well dug in and the Japanese were unable to penetrate their defenses. One feature was notable about this attack. For once the Japanese failed to display the spirit and determination that generally characterized their soldiers. The fact was they were close to exhaustion and their morale was low before the assault started.

The next few days on the southern front were relatively quiet. The Kamikaze attacks on the armada off the island also appeared to have tapered off. To a large extent this was due to the rapid buildup of a land-based air force on Yontan and Kadena. The shipping congestion was also being reduced as men and stores were unloaded, so enabling the transports to disperse to safer waters. Now that the invasion force was well established ashore it was also possible to reduce the numbers of warships, although five battleships, five cruisers and 17 destroyers were retained to back up the fire support now provided by the GIs' and

Marines' own artillery. Every night, until the Japanese on Okinawa were finally silenced, the naval vessels stood by off southern Okinawa to shell or illuminate targets indicated by shore fire-control parties. Star shell proved to be one of the best ways of uncovering Japanese attempts to infiltrate the American lines and this was expended liberally.

As a prelude to its capture the island of Ie-Shima was subjected to a naval bombardment and air attack which lasted until 15 April when Minna-shima, four miles to the south, was occupied and three artillery battalions deployed there to support the main landing. After a heavy naval bombardment and air strike men of the 77th Division landed on the south and southwest coasts of Ie-shima without difficulty, and by the evening its airfield was in American hands. The Japanese garrison of two battalions of infantry supplemented by a large number of civilian 'Home Guard' had wrecked the runways and airfield installations and then retired to elaborately prepared defensive positions on the high ground east of the airfield and north of the town of Ie. Many of the defenses were underground networks of tunnels and caverns burrowed below the ridge of high ground. There were scores of hiding places and every hole in the ground had to be poked into since the Japanese had a habit of lying low and coming to life when least expected. Some of the holes needed treatment with hand grenades and flamethrowers, while others were sealed with demolitions. It was 26 April before the last of the defenders had been accounted for and the GIs suffered 1120 casualties of whom 172 were killed; 4716 Japanese were killed and 149 taken prisoner.

When the 27th Division was landed on 10 April there were approximately 160,000 American troops ashore on Okinawa and yet the situation on both the northern and southern fronts remained more or less the same. Men in the ships, shaken by the repeated Kamikaze attacks, grumbled that the men ashore were 'dragging their feet.' The trouble was the formidable strength of the Japanese defense works, especially on the southern front, and the fact that the GIs and Marines had been trained to conserve their strength – to rely on artillery and air strikes to knock out major obstacles before infantry was committed to an assault. It was a technique which kept the casualty list short, but on Okinawa it meant waiting until heavy artillery was brought ashore and deployed for action.

In the event the northern front was cleared up fairly quickly. Having sealed off the northern end of Okinawa the 6th Marine Division set about clearing the Motobu Peninsula. The Japanese were in position on the 1500-foot high Yae Take hills in the center of the peninsula. These hills dominated the surrounding countryside but they had not the same potential for defense as the coral-limestone caves of the

Above: A mortar crew of the 7th Infantry Division pictured in action against Japanese positions on 19 April 1945.

Below: An eight-inch howitzer of the 749th Field Artillery Battalion fires on Japanese positions. This was that weapon's first use in the Pacific war.

Above: A Marine offers comfort to a comrade who broke down after the death of his buddy.
Above right: Men of the 6th Marine Division advance.

Machinato Line. By 19 April the Marines had driven the Japanese from their positions. From then until the end of the month when they were moved to the southern front they were engaged in mopping up in the north of the island.

At 0640 hours on 19 April three US divisions attacked the Machinato Line. The night before the attack took place the ships providing fire support had deliberately refrained from illuminating the battle zone. This, it was thought, would enable the GIs to deploy for the attack unseen and – in view of the intense bombardment which went on throughout the night – unheard. Every naval gun that could be ranged on the enemy positions was included in the fire plan. Ashore 27 battalions of artillery rained 19,000 shells on the Japanese positions for 40 minutes before the assault, and 650 aircraft added bombs, rockets, napalm and strafing to the general din. The infantry assault then went in, the GIs hoping that if the Japanese had not been blown to smithereens then at the very least they would have been so stunned by the bombardment as to be helpless. The Americans were soon disillusioned. Their advance came to a standstill when Japanese troops – seemingly untouched by the great mass of explosive material that had been showered down on them – emerged from their caves to take up their battle positions. Only on the extreme right was the Machinato Line pierced.

For the next five days bitter fighting continued and the Americans' progress was measured only in yards. The Japanese fought tenaciously, stubbornly contesting every inch of ground. Their positions were bombed from the air, strafed and subjected to tremendous artillery bombardment. Yet they clung to them until the sheer weight of attack penetrated and force them to abandon them and fall back. Then the process was repeated. The battle for Okinawa – essentially an infantry battle despite the weight of artillery and air support that was deployed – was the toughest and most prolonged of any in the Pacific war with the exception of Guadalcanal. It was also distinguished by the fact that naval gunfire was:

'employed longer and in greater quantities in the battle of Okinawa than in any other in history. It supported the ground troops and complemented the artillery from the day of the landing until action moved to the extreme southern tip of the island, where the combat area was so restricted that there was a danger of shelling American troops.'

Night illumination with star shell, usually delivered by destroyers, was also a great help to the troops, thwarting Japanese tactics of infiltration and night attack. The US Army historians wrote in *Okinawa: The Land Battle*:

'Time and time again naval night illumination caught Japanese troops forming or advancing for counterattacks and infiltration, and made it possible for the automatic weapons and mortars of the infantry to turn back such groups. It was very difficult for the Japanese to stage a night counterattack of any size without being detected.'

5. MORE KAMIKAZES

The major phase of Kikusui Operation No 1 had achieved nothing, but the subsidiary operations which continued throughout April, May and June scored some minor successes. Ohnishi's planes came down from Kyushu and 1465 Kamikaze planes took part in day and night attacks on targets at Okinawa. These attacks accounted for the heaviest of all Kamikaze-inflicted damage. According to the official report of the Commander in Chief US Pacific Fleet 26 American ships were sunk, and 164 damaged by suicide attacks between 6 April and 22 June. This figure included the victims of sporadic small-scale suicide efforts which occupied another 200 Japanese army and navy planes.

During April the Ohkas scored their first hit. After the Ohka sortie of 21 March had ended so ignominiously, there was some hesitation about selecting the right moment and proper conditions for using this weapon again. The opportunity presented itself on 12 April when Ohka sorties were ordered as part of Kikusui Operation No 2. Eight Ohkas participated in an attack during the morning, along with 80 Kamikaze planes and more than 100 escort fighters. They headed for Okinawa by varying courses to converge on the island from different directions. The bombers carrying them also flew low, in order to take advantage of the high cliffs which surrounded the American anchorages off the island.

Of the eight mother planes in this attack, six were shot down after making their release and only one returned to base to relate the dramatic story of how the pilot of one Ohka, Lieutenant Saburo Dolii, had performed his mission. Dolii, 22 years old, appears to have been a placid and somewhat taciturn individual. During the flight out to Okinawa he slept on a pile of sacks in the back of the Betty bomber. Wakened as they approached the target area, he shook hands with the crew before climbing through the bomb bay into his tiny rocket-powered craft. A battleship was selected as his objective and he was released 20,000 yards from his target at an altitude of about 7000 feet. Last seen by the crew of the bomber as it turned west for safety, Dolii was plummeting down toward the American ships surrounding his battleship. Later, they said, a column of black smoke could be seen belching from the general location of the target. Whether Dolii hit a US ship, or whether the damage should be attributed to one of the other Ohka pilots will never be known, but that day the destroyer *Mannert L Abele* was sunk and the destroyer *Stanley* damaged by piloted 'Baka bombs,' as the Americans called the Ohkas.

This operation proved the worth of the Ohka to the Japanese and after this the piloted bombs were used regularly. All in all a total of 74 Ohka missions were dispatched before the war came to an end. Of these 56 were either released from their carrier planes, or shot down while still attached to them. While many Ohka dives were reported as successful, confirmation was questionable. After the war the Americans estimated that only four ever hit a target, and claimed that the weapon was a fiasco. 'It failed,' wrote Admiral J J Clark, 'because it was a one shot mission – the pilots never got any practice!' Yet, even if the Ohka failed to do much material damage, there can be little doubt that the appearance of piloted suicide bombs had a telling effect on the morale of the American sailors.

The Ohka bomb attacks were, of course, supplementary to what might be termed the more 'conventional' Kamikaze strikes. These scored other successes on 12 April. Two fell on the destroyer minelayer *Lindsey*, and although she managed to stay afloat she lost 56 men killed and 51 wounded. The destroyer *Zellars*, the minesweeper *Gladiator* and the antisubmarine patrol vessel *Rall* also suffered extensive damage and casualties.

During the afternoon the Kamikazes set their sights on the battleship *Tennessee* and a formation of Kamikazes made a determined effort to knock out Admiral Deyo's flagship. The first was shot down at a range of 4000 yards; three others were destroyed at a distance of between 500 and 100 yards from the ship, a fifth which was seen to be on fire plunged into the sea close to the vessel's bows. Possibly this Kamikaze was intended as a decoy to distract the *Tennessee*'s crew from the one that really meant business, for at the same time another was seen heading directly for the battleship's bridge. All the antiaircraft guns concentrated on this fresh menace and one of the Kamikaze aircraft's wheels was shot off; this upset the plane's balance and slightly deflected its course. Missing the bridge it crashed onto one of the antiaircraft guns and slithered along the deck scattering flaming gasoline until it was brought to a shuddering halt when it hit one of the ship's 14-inch gun turrets. The blazing fuel caused the deaths of many of the gunners and the Kamikaze's 250-pound bomb went through the deck to explode and created fires in the interior of the ship. One sailor, blown into the air, landed on top of one of the big gun turrets where he calmly stripped off his burning gasoline-soaked clothes while waiting for someone to turn a fire hose on him. Another sailor, trying to dodge the plane as it slithered across the deck, tripped and fell overboard. When he came to the surface he found himself near burning pieces of the plane. Diving to avoid the flames he came up close to a life raft. Climbing on to it he found he had company – the decapitated body of the Japanese Kamikaze pilot which had been tossed into it by the explosion. In this grisly company the sailor remained for several hours until he was picked up by a destroyer.

When the damage was totted up it was found that although the *Tennessee* had suffered little damage her casualties totalled 23 killed and 106 wounded – of whom 33 were horribly burned. All the crew of the gun on which the Kamikaze first crashed were among the casualties. However, the battleship was still capable of continuing her support mission and she was not withdrawn.

At least three other ships were hit or suffered casualties from near misses on 12 April. The next two days were relatively quiet but the Kamikazes returned with a vengeance on the 16th. That day all hell broke loose when the Japanese launched another Kikusui attack with 220 planes. The destroyers on radar picket duty and the minesweepers – isolated and away from the main force – bore the brunt; one destroyer, the *Pringle*, was sunk, while three other destroyers and two minesweepers were badly damaged. One of the ships concerned was the *Laffey*, whose radar operator spotted 50 aircraft closing in on her at 0827 hours. Some of these were shot down or driven off by planes of the air umbrella over the invasion fleet before they were within range of the *Laffey*'s guns. However, within the space of 80

Left and above: On 11 May 1945 a Kamikaze crashed through the flight deck of USS *Bunker Hill* resulting in nearly 400 deaths before the fires were controlled.
Below: Not all kamikazes reached their target. A Japanese aircraft explodes over the carrier USS *Bennington*. In the foreground are USS *Hornet*'s Hellcats.

minutes the ship was attacked from all sides by 22 aircraft. Although all but one of the attackers were destroyed, she was hit by four bombs and six Kamikazes crashed on her decks. Despite this the *Laffey* remained afloat, and was towed back to the Kerama Retto where she was patched up; six days later she was able to sail to Guam under her own steam but was out of action for the rest of the war. American casualties amounted to 31 killed and 72 wounded, and the cost to the Japanese was at least 21 aircraft.

By the middle of April 1944 there could be little doubt that the Kamikazes were spreading flaming terror as well as scorching burns and searing deaths. The crews of the vessels off Okinawa had shown tremendous courage and fighting spirit. Nevertheless the attacks were causing considerable alarm and despondency; casualties and losses in ships were heavy and there seemed to be no real answer to Kamikaze tactics. Admiral Nimitz therefore once again called for the Superfortress B-29s of the Strategic Air Command to bomb the Japanese airfields in southern Japan from which the Kamikazes were operating. Thus it was that from 17 April to the middle of May three-quarters of all the available Superfortresses were diverted from bombing industrial targets and Japanese cities to supporting the Okinawa campaign. Over 2000 B-29 sorties were flown against 17 airfields during which 24 of the Superfortresses were lost and 233 damaged, but it was reckoned that they had destroyed 134 Japanese aircraft. This offensive diminished but did not stop the mass attacks on the ships around Okinawa. However, by 11 May there were then sufficient US aircraft operating from the airfields on Okinawa and Ie-Shima, and Admiral Nimitz told Strategic Air Command that the Superfortresses were no longer needed to support the Okinawa operations.

Back in Japan at this time the respective Imperial Navy and Japanese Army High Commands were arguing about the conduct of the war. The Navy saw the Okinawa operations as the decisive battle and wanted to devote their entire resources to it, while the Army, realizing that Okinawa could not be held, wanted to keep as many aircraft as possible for repelling the inevitable attack on the Japanese mainland. In the event a form of compromise was agreed – with Admiral Toyoda withdrawing (on 17 April) the Tenth Air Fleet with about half the total number of aircraft deployed for the Okinawa operation. This left the Fifth and Third Air Fleets with about 600 aircraft to continue the battle for Okinawa. These were the planes used in the attacks between 6 April and 22 June which took such a heavy toll of the fast carrier force and the shipping around Okinawa.

One of these attacks, toward the end of May, included a new feature: a number of twin-engined bombers, each with 14 Japanese aboard were detailed to land on the Yontan airfield and do as much damage as possible. Four of these raiders were brought down by antiaircraft fire before they reached the airfield, but a fifth made a belly landing and, before its crew was disposed of, seven American planes had been destroyed and 26 others damaged, and two dumps containing 70,000 gallons of aviation fuel had been set on fire.

The last two mass Kamikaze attacks took place in June as the Okinawa campaign was drawing to a close. Meantime the Kaiten operations had been stepped up although they were in fact no more successful than the flamboyant lemming-like self-destruction of the Second Fleet. After the ill-conceived *Tatara* operation the *I-58* was ordered to support the Second Fleet action with Kaiten attacks on the US ships lured out by the *Yamato*. Spotted by American aircraft she never got near any of the American capital ships. Harried and chased day and night by destroyers and aircraft, its captain eventually called off the operations and returned to port with his Kaiten intact.

I-58 was lucky to get back to Japan. Eight other Japanese submarines were sunk during April and, with the Sixth Fleet's Kaiten carriers reduced to four, a heated argument developed on how the 'Heaven-shakers' should be employed in future operations. The Naval General Staff in Tokyo, and Combined Fleet Headquarters, still believed that the best way was against American fleets and fleet bases. Commander Tennosuke Torisu, the torpedo expert on the staff of the Sixth Fleet Headquarters, argued fiercely against this. He claimed that Kaiten should be sent well out to sea to disrupt the Americans' lines of communications. Eventually Tokyo agreed to let two submarines make attacks on supply lines. Their performance would be evaluated and a final decision would be taken on how the Kaiten would operate in the future.

I-47 and *I-36* were selected for the experiment, and they sallied forth on 20 and 23 April respectively. Each was carrying six Kaiten. *I-47* headed for an area through which US ships bound for Okinawa from Ulithi would have to pass, while *I-36* made for a similar interception zone between Okinawa and Saipan. *I-36* drew the first blood. Soon after dawn on 27 April she ran into a convoy of 30 ships bound for Okinawa. At 8000 yards distance orders were given for all six Kaiten to be fired. Four got away, but two were jammed in their racks. Ten minutes later four successive explosions shook the submarine. That night a report was radioed to Tokyo claiming 'four victims,' 'estimated to be transports or cargo ships.' Coming when it did, this success seemed an appropriate sacrifice to the Emperor, whose birthday was on 29 April. In fact only one vessel was sunk, the SS *Canada Victory*, so it must be assumed that all four Kaiten pilots had aimed for the same ship.

During the night of 1 May, *I-47*'s captain, Commander Orita, also encountered a convoy. Because the Kaiten were virtually blind in the dark, he decided to attack with conventional torpedoes. Twelve hours later, however, an opportunity came to use the suicide weapons and two Kaiten (Lieutenant Kakizake and Petty Officer Yamaguchi) were fired at targets reported to be a transport escorted by a destroyer. When two explosions were heard in quick succession it was assumed that both targets had been hit. When Orita raised his periscope he could see a destroyer about three miles away. Another Kaiten was launched and a long-delayed explosion eventually suggested that Petty Officer Furukawa had gone to Yasukuni. Four days later two of the three remaining Kaiten, Lieutenant Maeda and Petty Officer Shinkai, were fired at a 'cruiser.' Orita's intention had been to fire all three, but when the telephone link to the last Kaiten broke down, Petty Officer Yokota lived to tell the tale. 'To live, at times, is much more difficult than to die. . . . A lot of patience is required to wait until the best possible moment for dying comes.' These words were used by Orita as consolation when Yokota protested at being deprived of the opportunity to give his life.

I-47 now followed *I-36* back to Japan. After their return a conference in Tokyo concluded that the success of the two most recent sorties justified Commander Torisu's views. Submarine operations would now be left entirely in the hands of the Sixth Fleet Headquarters. Admiral Nagai promptly ordered every available I Class submarine, a total of nine, to be dispatched on Kaiten operations in the western Pacific. By mid-July six had been sunk, but the Japanese claimed that the Kaitens sank 15 tankers and transports, two cruisers, five destroyers, one seaplane tender and six unidentified ships in the last three months of the war. These figures were subsequently declared by the Allies to be spurious. Eighty Kaiten pilots were killed in action, and even if they had sent down 80 ships it is doubtful whether they could have changed the outcome of the land battle for Okinawa.

Left: The night sky is crisscrossed with tracers during a Japanese air raid on Yontan airfield. In the foreground F4U Corsairs are parked.
Bottom: The remains of two transport aircraft destroyed on Yontan.

The raiders were flown in by Mitsubishi Ki-21s on 24 May.
Below: The charred remains of one of the Japanese commandos killed during the raid on Yontan airfield.

6. CLIMAX

By 23 April the GIs of General Hodge's XXIV Corps had battered their way through the Machinato Line at several points and General Ushijima, fearing that the weakened line would break, withdrew to a second and even stronger one covering Shuri. This line extended from the southwestern end of the Machinato airstrip through Maeda and Kochi to Gaja.

There was now a brief pause while both sides regrouped and prepared for the next round. On 30 April the Americans brought up the 1st Marine Division to relieve the 27th Division and 77th Division to take over from the hard-pressed 96th Division. On their side the Japanese brought their 24th Division into action for the first time. The stage was now set, with both sides in contact along the new Japanese defense line.

At dawn on 4 May General Ushijima hurled the fresh 24th Division supported by tanks and artillery against the center of the American line – held by the US 7th Division. A second minor attack, launched simultaneously, hit the 1st Marine Division on the western flank. At the same time squads of Japanese engineers were landed on the west and east coasts behind the American forward troops to disrupt communications. It was an all-out offensive which Ushijima hoped would inflict a

Right: Bazookas support an infantry attack on a ridge two miles north of Naha, the capital of Okinawa.
Below right: Infantrymen follow a tank into an attack on Japanese caves and pillboxes on 6 May.
Below: A flame-throwing tank of the 713th Tank Battalion goes into action on Coral Ridge.

major defeat on the American invaders. According to plan it was to be supported by Kikusui mass attack No 5 from Kyushu, with the Japanese Navy alone contributing 280 planes, and although only 115 aircraft were actually committed they did a lot of damage. As in other such attacks the isolated vessels on radar picket bore the brunt and two destroyers and two tank landing ships were sunk. Moreover, other Kamikaze 'floating chrysanthemums' which broke through the picket line crashed themselves into several other ships in the bay.

Ashore however the engineer commando raids failed completely, the raiders being wiped out, and the 24th Division's attack soon broke down. Caught by American artillery and strike aircraft supplemented by naval gunfire, the Japanese infantry could make no progress. They tried again that night (4/5 May) but their efforts were equally unsuccessful. The offensive cost Ushijima some 5000 men and many guns, for these had been dragged out of their emplacements and caves into the open; other hidden Japanese artillery positions had also been disclosed in the attack. For the Japanese all this amounted to a serious setback and Ushijima now clearly recognized the writing on the wall. So too did the Japanese High Command in Tokyo who judged that the launching of the offensive had been a serious mistake since it greatly diminished the length of time that the Japanese garrison on Okinawa could hold out. After it units had to be amalgamated and reorganized with men doing administrative duties being posted to fighting units; ammunition expenditure also had to be rationed.

Ushijima's offensive more or less coincided with the transfer of the 6th Marine Division from the northern part of Okinawa to the southern front. The Marines had completed their mission of mopping up the Motobu Peninsula, and General Buckner, the Tenth Army commander, was anxious to resume the offensive and destroy what was left of Ushijima's forces. With the 77th Division and the 1st and 6th Marine Divisions still in hand Buckner was faced with a dilemma: he could either launch a frontal attack in the hope that the sheer weight of the assault would smash through the Japanese defenses; alternatively he could try to envelop Ushijima's force by amphibious landings on the southern tip of the island behind the Japanese. In the event Buckner decided on a frontal attack – two attacks in fact, one on each flank – and his forces were organized into two corps, with the Marines (6th and 1st Divisions) on the right and the 77th and 96th Divisions on the left. (The 6th and 1st Marine Divisions constituted the Marine III Amphibious Corps; the 77th and 96th Divisions formed the XXIV Corps.) To back up the attack the five support ships were also divided into two groups, one stationed off the Hagushi beaches and one in Nakagusuku Wan.

For a week there was a lull in the fighting – broken on the 8th when the news of Germany's unconditional surrender was flashed to Okinawa. Turner reported:

'It was the most quiet day yet experienced by our forces in this area. Many ships conducted Divine Services in Thanksgiving for Victory in Europe. At exactly 1200 hours one round from every gun ashore accompanied a full gun salvo from every possible fire support ship directed at the enemy, as a complimentary and congratulatory gesture to our Armed Forces in Europe.'

Three days later in appalling weather General Simon Bolivar Buckner launched his offensive. Torrential rain turned the country, except for the rocky outcrops, into a sea of mud. Tanks bogged down, wheeled transport could not move at all and even amphibious tractors were often useless. In consequence the Americans had to carry up all their supplies and bring back their wounded. To add to this the Japanese resisted bitterly. However, both flanks of the Japanese line were finally pierced and on 21 May Buckner's men reached the outskirts of Shuri. The line of defenses covering the town still held, but American pressure was so great that Ushijima judged

Far left: A party of Marines strings up communications lines behind advancing troops.
Above left: An M-18 of the 77th Division's 306th Antitank Company fires into enemy lines.
Left: A caterpillar tractor pulls a Marine ambulance jeep out of the mud which made roads almost impassable during the rainy season.

that his troops would not be able to hold the line much longer. Casualties had reduced the two divisions and mixed brigade which had originally been deployed on the southern front, to about a third of their strength, and so the Japanese commander decided to withdraw to a ridge which, with its caves, dugouts and tunnels gave his force a better chance of prolonging resistance on the island. By the end of the month the Japanese had completed their withdrawal and the Americans occupied the shattered town of Shuri on 31 May. Ushijima's depleted army was now in a sorry state; its strength was down to about 30,000 men of whom only a third were fighting troops, most of its artillery had been lost, there were insufficient rifles and machine guns to go round, a paucity of ammunition and there was a critical shortage of food. The end could not long be delayed.

There was fierce fighting early in June but by the 12th the Americans had gained control of the ridge and driven off a counter-attack by Ushijima's last reserve. The Japanese fought on but as their account of the battle says:

'By the 17th organized resistance was no longer possible and nothing remained but to fight it out around the caves, rocky crags and broken ground at the southern tip of the island. Individual fighting of a desperate nature continued for a while with rifles, grenades and swords but, against enemy superiority, particularly in flame-throwing tanks, human beings were helpless.'

Realizing that resistance was no longer possible, Ushijima ordered the remnants of his army to disperse and individuals to travel north and to form guerrilla bands.

The struggle for Okinawa was almost over, yet General Buckner did not live to see the end. On 18 June an observation post to which he had gone to watch an attack by the 8th Marine Regiment came under fire from one of the few remaining Japanese guns. In the bombardment one of

Bottom: Marines cover the tower of a Christian church, which provided a vantage point for Japanese snipers. *Below:* Lieutenant Colonel Richard Ross attaches the Stars and Stripes to a Japanese flagpole, after the 5th Marine Regiment captured Shuri castle in May 1945.

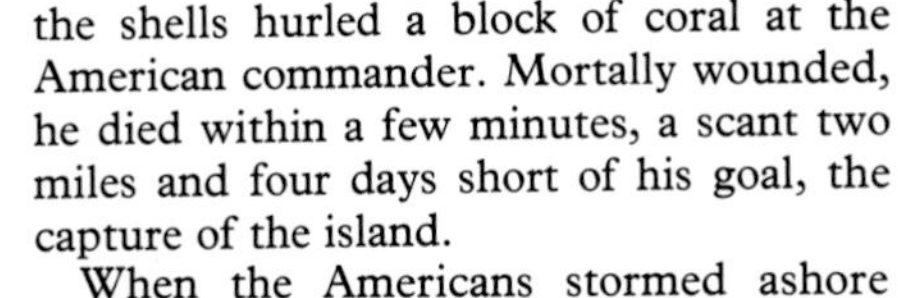

the shells hurled a block of coral at the American commander. Mortally wounded, he died within a few minutes, a scant two miles and four days short of his goal, the capture of the island.

When the Americans stormed ashore on Okinawa they had expected an immediate and vicious response from the garrison. To everybody's surprise the defenders offered little resistance, and the landing beaches were secured in the face of only a mild defense. Not until the American troops started to move inland was the pattern of previous assaults repeated. Then the Americans experienced another version of the storming of Iwo Jima. The defenders fought desperately, inflicting heavy casualties on the invaders. Gradually they were pushed back to the hills in the southern part of the island. By VE Day, 8 May, the Japanese were beaten.

In the next three weeks General Ushijima managed to perform a minor miracle by organizing another line of defense, but he knew the end was close. By this time the

Above left: After their surrender, three Japanese soldiers carry a wounded comrade from their cave.
Left: The funeral of Lieutenant General Simon Bolivar Buckner, commander of the US Tenth Army, who was killed in action by shellfire on 18 June.
Below: The bodies of Japanese defenders lie in the ruins of Shuri castle after its capture.

Above: Marines cross into Naha over a footbridge thrown across the river by American engineers.
Top left: A bazooka pictured in action from the shelter of a tomb.
Left: A patrol from the 6th Marine Division searches the streets of Naha, Okinawa's capital.
Top: Engineers scan a roadway with a mine detector in June 1945.

Japanese troops knew it also. Bombarded by millions of leaflets which assured them of fair treatment, a few considered surrendering. Most decided against it and committed suicide instead.

Admiral Ota's naval force made a final Banzai charge on 13 June against the forces which had landed in the vicinity of Oroku. Nothing more is known of Ota and his men. The last message received from him was sent on 6 June:

'More than two months have passed since we engaged the invaders. In complete unity and harmony with the army, we have made every effort to crush the enemy.
. . . I tender herewith my deepest apology to the Emperor for my failure to better defend the Empire, the grave task with which I was entrusted.

The troops under my command have fought gallantly, in the finest tradition of the Japanese navy. Fierce bombing and bombardments may deform the mountains of Okinawa but cannot alter the loyal spirit of our men. We hope and pray for the perpetuation of the Empire and gladly give our lives for that goal.

To the Navy Minister and all my superior officers I tender my sincerest appreciation and gratitude for their kindness of many years. At the same time, I earnestly beg you to give thoughtful consideration to the families of my men who fall at this outpost as soldiers of the Emperor.

With my officers and men I give three cheers for the Emperor and pray for the everlasting peace of the Empire.

Though my body decay in remote Okinawa, my spirit will persist in defense of the homeland.

Minoru Ota
Naval Commander'

Before he perished Ota is known to have issued one order which typifies the suicidal attitude of his kind. A huge cave inside the Japanese lines was serving as a field hospital and 300 badly wounded Japanese Marines of Ota's detachment lay there. Fearing that the Americans would flush out the cave with flame throwers before asking questions, Ota ordered the senior medical officer to make sure the patients had an honorable death without any further suffering. The doctor and his orderlies walked along the long rows of sick men and methodically squeezed hypodermic syringes into 300 outstretched arms.

No one appears to know quite what happened to Tanamachi's 7000 airmen. Like many of the army units they probably fought on until they were annihilated. That at least was what happened to one isolated detachment whose commanding officer reported in a final message:

'My men are in high spirits and fighting gallantly. We pray for the final victory of the motherland. We will fight to the last man in defense of this outpost. . . .'

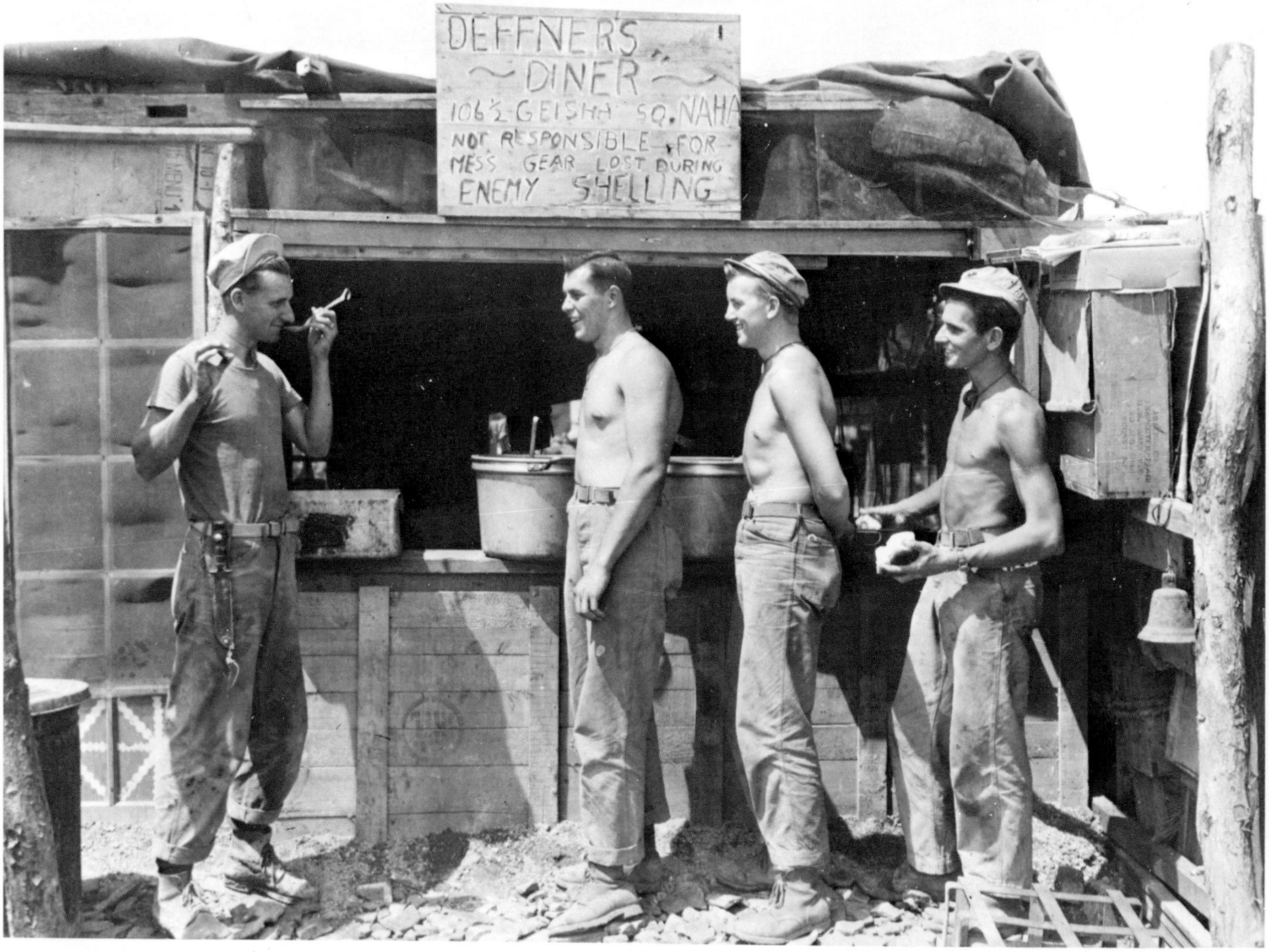
DEFFNER'S
DINER
106½ GEISHA SQ. NAHA
NOT RESPONSIBLE FOR
MESS GEAR LOST DURING
ENEMY SHELLING

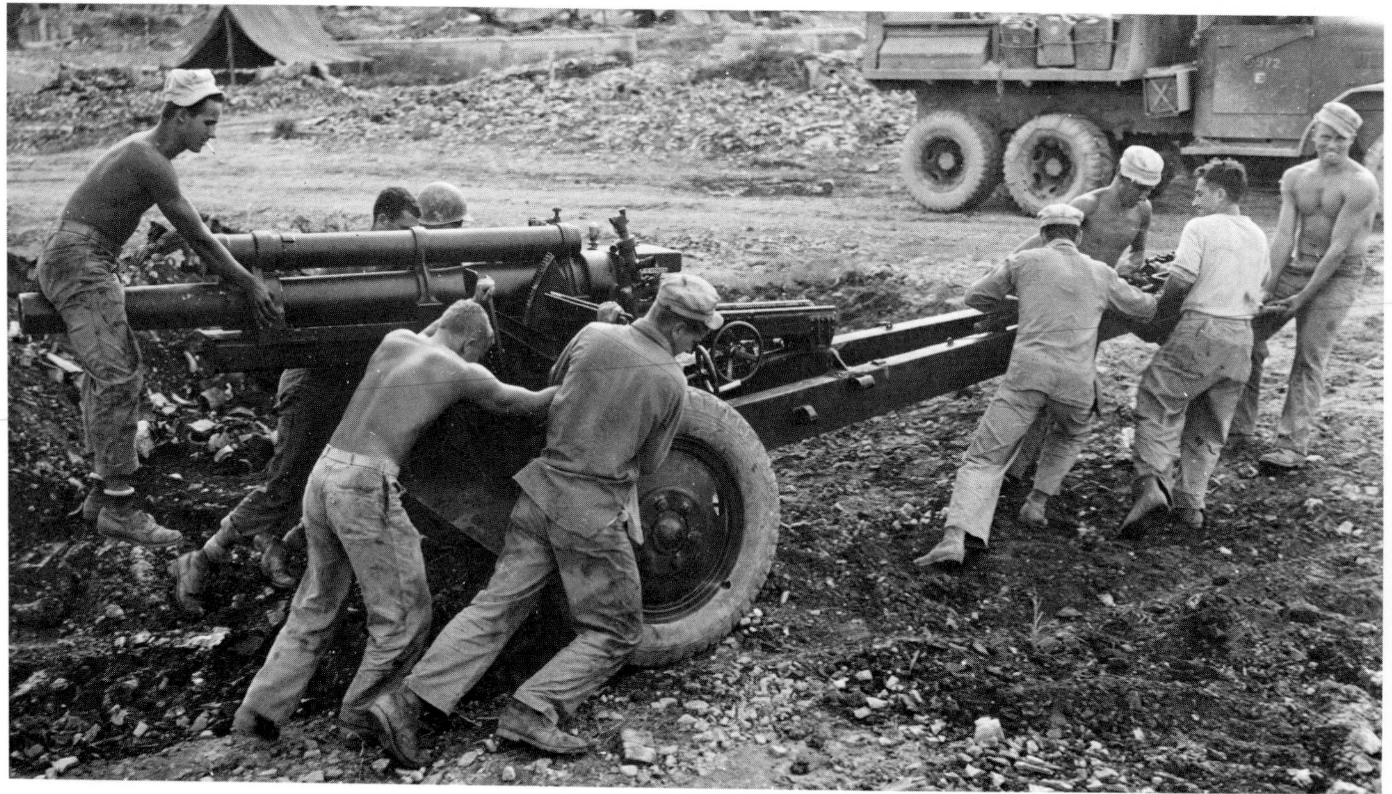

Left: A Marine 'chow line' near Naha.
Below left: Marine artillerymen manhandle a 105mm howitzer into position on 9 June.
Right: Japanese naval troops surrender to the Americans.
Bottom: Japanese are flushed out of a cane field.
Below: Men of the 15th Marine Regiment move into the outskirts of Naha on 6 June 1945.

Inside the cave which sheltered his headquarters, General Ushijima relaxed with a bottle of whiskey while he listened to the reports coming from his scattered units. His last defense line had disintegrated and the Japanese troops had become a disorganized rabble, skulking in holes, hungry and without hope. Ushijima was a realist and he knew that it was finished. Quietly he dictated a farewell message to Tokyo:

'To my great regret we are no longer able to continue the fight. For this failure I tender deepest apologies to the Emperor and the people of the homeland. We will make one final charge to kill as many of the enemy as possible. I pray for the souls of men killed in battle and for the prosperity of the Imperial Family.

Death will not quell the desire of my spirit to defend the homeland.

With deepest appreciation of the kindness and cooperation of my superiors and my colleagues in arms, I bid farewell to all of you forever.'

A poetic postscript to his letter read:

'Green grass dies in the islands without waiting for fall,
But it will be reborn verdant in the springtime of the homeland.
Weapons exhausted, our blood will bathe the earth, but the spirit will survive,
Our spirits will return to protect the motherland.'

In the early morning of 22 June, Ushijima and his chief of staff, General Isama Cho, dressed themselves in their best

Right: A US Navy Grumman Avenger commences its bombing run on a target on Okinawa, June 1945.
Below: Infantrymen of the 7th Division take cover during the final stages of the fighting on Okinawa, 18 June 1945.

uniforms and pinned their medals to their tunics. A quilt had been laid out on a narrow ledge of rock just outside the cave. Over it was a white sheet symbolizing death. The two generals knelt. According to the Samurai code hari-kiri is supposed to be committed facing toward the Imperial Palace in Tokyo. Because of the narrowness of the ledge Ushijima and Cho had to face west to the Pacific. A staff officer handed the two generals each a knife. Then came *seppuku* – the slash across the abdomen. Behind Ushijima another officer raised his sword and quickly struck off Ushijima's head. Cho was decapitated in the same way a few moments later.

The battle for Okinawa was over, but not the dying, since Ushijima's example was followed by the most grotesque series of suicides. Naked Japanese soldiers would dash out of their caves, hurl rocks at the Americans and then race back behind the rocks and slit their throats or blow themselves up with grenades. A particularly bizarre incident occurred when a patrol of US Marines suddenly found themselves in a clearing surrounded by a strong force of Japanese accompanied by a number of women. With unusual presence of mind, the patrol commander smiled, pulled out his cigarettes and offered them around. A few of the Japanese soldiers dropped their weapons and reached for the cigarettes. Their officers not only refused but turned away. Then one drove his sword straight through his woman companion, handed his sword and wristwatch to one of the Americans, stepped back and blew off his head with a grenade. This infected the others who promptly killed the other women and then committed suicide. For two hours the US patrol was compelled to watch a suicidal blood bath.

In the fighting for Okinawa Japanese casualties amounted to more than 100,000 killed. Of these deaths at least half were incurred in suicidal operations. Strategically the Americans had won a great victory, for they were now on Japan's very doorstep. Their losses were also high – more than 12,500 killed and missing, twice the casualty rate of Iwo Jima.

Okinawa was now to become the final base for the invasion of Japan.

7. EPILOGUE

The Okinawa campaign has been compared to that of Iwo Jima. In fact the comparison is incorrect and unfair to the gallant US Marines who secured Iwo Jima at a terrible cost to themselves. The Okinawa terrain had none of the natural defensive qualities of Iwo Jima; the Japanese had no previously prepared defenses between Yontan and Shuri. Only the incredible fanaticism of the Japanese soldier held the line, and that fanaticism for almost two months was sufficient against an invader who held absolute command of the air, who had the equivalent of two armored divisions, who, to an overwhelming strength in artillery, had added the stupendous power of the guns of a great fleet, and who had an almost unlimited superiority in men, equipment and supplies.

It is always easy to be wise after the event and to oversimplify the problems facing a commander. Any serious student of war will question the wisdom of General Buckner's decision to launch a frontal attack at the beginning of May rather than try to break the deadlock by landing more Marines in the rear of the Japanese – as the Marines themselves suggested. No doubt Buckner saw the situation as analogous to that in Italy in 1943, and considered that the proposed Marine amphibious landing, like the Anzio operation, would have been beyond range of support from the main front. Against this it can be argued that he had the finest body of amphibious troops in the Pacific and Buckner's critics believe that his decision to opt for a frontal attack was an error of overcaution.

In the event Buckner's strategy worked, but at a heavy price in men. Moreover, instead of the 40 days estimated by the original planners, the Okinawa campaign took 82. On the other hand the tactical handling of the US Fifth Fleet – the armada which carried the assault force to Okinawa and set it down there so successfully – was

Below: The official Japanese surrender ceremony on Okinawa.

Left: A Japanese prisoner is interrogated by an intelligence specialist on Okinawa.
Below: Japanese POWs march to the dock from where they will be shipped to Hawaii. Organized resistance on Okinawa ceased on 21 June.

nothing short of brilliant. The logistical support of the great fleet at sea over a protracted period was unprecedented, and a most remarkable demonstration of efficiency.

The object of the Okinawa campaign was to secure a base for the invasion of Japan. It succeeded in doing far more than this, for the campaign cost Japan the remainder of her effective navy. Apart from the loss of the *Yamato*, sunk in the abortive sortie against the invasion force, innumerable minor vessels were sunk, and by mid-June the once proud Imperial Japanese Navy had ceased to exist as a fighting force.

The same was true of the Japanese air force. Coupled with the toll taken of Japanese aircraft in the Philippines and during the Iwo Jima campaign, the numbers destroyed in the covering operations for Okinawa crippled the striking power and the defensive power of that part of the Japanese air force which was to protect the home islands. Only the suicide tactics of the Kamikaze organization kept Japanese airmen in the picture and even that by the end of the Okinawa campaign was becoming a diminishing asset. Although the Japanese military forces involved were not large in relation to the actual size of the Japanese armies, the loss in military prestige and in material was considerable.

Meanwhile the tremendous achievement of American production was now beginning to play its full part in the war against Japan. The material losses of the campaign – and of the operations to secure Iwo Jima and recapture the Philippines – were quickly made up. By the end of Okinawa the Philippines were already a vast base for the invasion of Japan. Even while the fighting was continuing, the work of preparing Okinawa for its eventual role as a staging area for the invasion was well under way.

The military operations that followed the capture of Okinawa were small and unimportant. They consisted of the seizure and consolidation of other small islands in the Ryukyus. The vital factor in this period was the 'buildup' and that proceeded unhampered by the Japanese – swiftly and inexorably.

The three campaigns – to liberate the Philippines, capture Iwo Jima and Okinawa – were in combination the greatest successes in the great successes of the Pacific war. With the earlier capture of the Marianas they made possible, first, the wiping out by incendiary bombing of the great cities of Japan and second the provision of all that was necessary for the staging of the eventual descent on the Japanese mainland. They, and not the atomic bomb, were the decisive factor in the subsequent Japanese surrender.

APPENDIX

The Kikusui (floating chrysanthemum) operations

In addition to a number of minor raids by up to 20 planes on 'off' days the Japanese launched 10 major Kamikaze attacks on the US armada off Okinawa. These are detailed in the following table.

Attack No	*Date*	*Navy*	*Army*	*Total*
		*Number of Aircraft**		
1 (*TEN-GO*)	6– 7 April (1945)	230	125	355
2	12–13 April	125	60	185
3	15–16 April	120	45	165
4	27–28 April	65	50	115
5	3– 4 May	75	50	125
6	10–11 May	70	80	150
7	23–25 May	65	100	165
8	27–29 May	60	50	110
9	3– 7 June	20	30	50
10	21–22 June	30	15	45
	Total	860	605	1465

* These figures do NOT include the aircraft which escorted the Kamikazes to the battle zone.

Together with individual Kamikaze attacks not listed in the table it is estimated that approximately 1900 suicide sorties were made against the US naval forces during the Okinawa campaign. Apart from these there were hundreds of attacks by conventional dive bombers and torpedo bombers.

INDEX

Page numbers in italics refer to illustrations

Aachen, Germany 276, 278, 280
Abe, Capt 178
Abe, Chief Petty Officer 172
Abe, Rear Admiral 182, 198
Abukuma, light cruiser 97, 132, 134
airborne troops, role of in Normandy 216, 218
aircraft, American
Boeing B-17 95, 99, *101*, 104, *109*, 119, *129*, *151*, 161, 163, 164, 165, 170, 184, *185*, 194, 195, *230–31*
Boeing B-29 237, 337, 339, 347, *348*, 376
Brewster Buffalo 163
Consolidated PBY Catalina 154, *155*, 161, 163, 168, 184, 186
Curtiss Helldiver *340*, *349*
Douglas Dauntless *146*, *157*, *160*, 163, *164*, 164, 166, 167, 168, 177, *177*, 178, *184*, *189*, 191, *193*, *194*
Douglas Devastator *116*, 146, *155*, 166, 167, *167*, 168
Grumman Avenger 164, *165*, *186*, *193*, *347*, 367, *388*
Grumman Hellcat *346*, 367, *375*
Grumman Wildcat 166, 167, *173*, 175, 176, 177, *192*
Lockheed Hudson *17*
Lockheed Lightning 233
Martin Marauder *151*, 233, *286*
North American B-25 *137*, *148*, 149
North American Mustang *230*, *286–7*
Republic Thunderbolt 233
Vought Corsair *354*, *376*
Vaught Vindicator *191*, 191–2
aircraft, British
Avro Lancaster 229
Boulton-Paul Defiant 21, 62
Bristol Blenheim 62
de Havilland Mosquito 224, 229
Gloster Gladiator 17
Handley Page Halifax 229
Hawker Hurricane *11–13*, *18*, *23–5*, *27*, 30, 32, *33–4*, 34–6, 39, 41, 43, 44, 46–7, 50, *55–6*, 59–62, *64*, 65, *66*, *69*
numbers in 1939–40, 17, 19
Hawker Typhoon 248, 255
Short Stirling 224, *226–7*
Supermarine Spitfire *15*, 26, *27*, 28, 30, 32, *35*, 39, 40, *43*, *47*, 50, 59, 61, 62, *232*, 233
numbers in 1940 19
aircraft, German
Dornier Do17 22, *22*, 26, 41, 46, 50, *50–51*, 52, *57*, 58
Dornier Do215 40, 58
Heinkel He111 9, *20*, 22, 26, 30, *31*, 36, 41, *45*, *56*, 57, 60–61
Junkers Ju87 22, 30, 35, 37
Junkers Ju88 *21*, 22, 30, *31,–2*, 36, 59
Messerschmidt Bf109 *21*, 22, *23*, 26, 28, 30, *31*, 34–7, 58–63, *63*, 65, 67
Messerschmidt Me110 22, *22*, 25, 30, *32*, 34–6, *37*, 40–41, 46, 52, 60–61, 67
aircraft, Italian
Fiat BR 20 65, *65*
Fiat CR 42 65
aircraft, Japanese
Aichi D3A Val *91*, *98*, 99, 106, 117, *119*, 121, *125*, *126*, 163, *167*, 173, *192*
Kawanishi flying boat 159
Mitsubishi A5M Claude *90*
Mitsubishi A6M Zero 90, 91, *96*, *98*, 99, *100*, 104, 117, 119, 121, 154, 163–6, 168, *169*, *170*, 173, 175, 177, 185, *185*, *193*, 346–7, *348*, 367
Mitsubishi G3M Nell *93*
Mitsubishi G4M Betty *93*, 343, 374
Mitsubishi Ki-21 Sally *109*
Nakajima B5N2 Kate 99, 106, *108*, 109, 117, 121, 162, 163, *163*, *176*
Nakajima Ki-43 Oscar *81*
Nakajima Ki-49 Helen *81*
Yokosuka MXY-7 Ohka *342*, 343, 346–7, 374
aircraft carrier/battleship controversy 123, 126–7
Aitken, W/Cdr Max *37*
Ajax, HMS, cruiser 233
Akagi, carrier *84*, 87, 88, 97, 132, 134, 150, 153, 157–9, 162–6, 168, 170, 171, 173, 177, 182, 184, 197
Akebonu Maru, tanker 161, 197
Akigumo, destroyer 132, 134
Aleutian Islands 87, 88, 150, 151, 153, 156
Alexander, Gen Sir Harold 212
Allard, F/Lt G *42*, 43, 44
Allied Armies in Normandy
12th Army Group 212, 272, 276, 302, 326
21st Army Group 212, 261, 272, 273, 303, 321, 326
see also British Army, United States Army
allied dissension in NW Europe 207, 270, 272, 276, 303, 321–2
Allied Tactical Air Forces 211, 213
see also Royal Air Force, United States Army Air Force
Amagai, Cdr T 171–2
Amagi, carrier 344
Amblève river, Belgium 293, 299
valley of 297, 303
Ambrose (RAF 46 Sqn) *63*
anti-aircraft units in Battle of Britain *25*, 62
Antwerp, Belgium 272, 273, 276, 321
Aoki, Capt 166, 170, 171
Arare, destroyer 132, 134
Arashio, destroyer 191, 197
Ardennes 270, 273, 276–8, 280, 287
Ardennes offensive 270–325 *passim*
allied counter-attacks 309–15, 318–19, 321–5
allied defensive measures 293, *294*, 300, 302–5, 307, 309
attack, the 281, *282–5*, 284–5, 289, 293, 297, 299–300, 302–9, 311–12, 316, 318–19, 321
casualties 325, 326
German strategy 276–8, 280
German weaponry *290–91*, *295*

maps 294, 295
Argonaut, HMS, cruiser 233
Arizona, US battleship 109, *110–11*, *116–17*, 117, 121, *127*, 131
Arkansas, US battleship *240–41*, 351, 353
Arnhem 212, *272–3*, 273
Arnold, Commodore J 237
Arnold, Gen H *335*, 339
Asakaze, destroyer 132, 134
Asashimo, destroyer 367
Asashio, destroyer 191, 197
Astoria, US cruiser 178
Atlanta, US cruiser *138–9*
Atlantic Wall *206*, 261
Attu, Aleutian Is 153, 159, 357
Auchinleck, Gen Sir Claude 208
Avranches, France 271, 272

Bader, S/Ldr D 25, *45*
'Baka bombs' 374
Baker, Maj Gen Ray W 209
Balck, Gen 326
Ball, S/Ldr Eric *45*
Baraque de Fraiture, Belgium 304, 305, 325
Baraque Michel, Belgium 284, 297, 318
Barclay, P/O R G A 60
Barton, Maj Gen R O 289
Bastogne 285, 289, 293, 299, 300, 302, 303, 305, 306, 316, 319, *320*, 322, 323, 324, 325
siege of 306–15, *306–16*, 321
Battle of Britain *see* Britain, Battle of
Bayerlein, Lt Gen F 254
Bayeux, France 216, 248, *255*, 258, 261
Bayne, F/Lt A W A *25*
Beamish, W/Cdr F V 26, *27*
Bedell Smith, Lt Gen W 211, *215*
Belgium 15. 272, 273, 284
Belfast, HMS, cruiser 248
air force 17
Resistance 212
Bellinger, Rear Admiral P 93, 95
Bennington, US carrier *375*
Bennion, Capt Mervyn 117
Bennions, P/O G H 62
Beresford, F/Lt H R A 52
Berlin, bombing of 41, 48
Biloxi, US cruiser 354
Bird-Wilson, P/O H A C 38, 39
Bismarck 123, 126
Bismarck Islands 135
Bismarck Sea, US carrier 336
Blandy, Rear Admiral W H P 339, 347, 351
Blatchford, F/Lt H P 65, 67
Blitzkrieg 15, 22, 207, 208, 270, 276, 277, 281, 284, 297, 303
Blumentritt, Gen Gunther 207
Bodyguard deception plan 213
Boulogne, France 216
Bourne, Gen A G B 209
Bradley, Gen Omar N 212, *212*, *215*, 217, 256, *256*, 270–72, 273, 276, 289, 297, 302, 303, 321, 322, 325, 326
Brand, AV-M Sir C Q 21
Brandenberger, Gen Erich 280, 289, 306, 326
Breese, US destroyer/minelayer 119
Britain, Battle of 15–70, 211
airfields attacked 30, 32, 35–7, 40–41, 43–4, 46, 48, 52
convoys attacked 26
German intelligence in 29, 30, 32, 58, 59
German objectives 25, 29, 30, 59
invasion possibility 29, 30, 57, 59
London bombed 41, 48, *48*, 50–51, *51*, 52, 57, *57*, 59, 62, *66*
radar stations attacked 32, 35
British/Canadian army
First Canadian Army 212, 272
Second Army 212, 272, 273, 326
'Fourth Army' 213
XXX Corps 273, 318, 319, 326
Divisions
1st 251
1st Airborne 273
3rd Infantry 222, 250, 251, 254–5, 256, 262
3rd Canadian Division Group 248, 250, 262
4th 251, 253
6th Airborne 218, *220*, 224, 246, 252, 255, 256, 261, 262
50th 248, 262
79th Armored 262
Brigades
1st SS Commando 218, 222, 224, 246, 252, 254, 255, 261, 262
1st RE Assault 262
1st Tank 262
3rd Parachute 220, 221–4, 262
4th SS Commando 246, 251, 252, 261, 262
5th Parachute 220–21, 262
6th Airlanding 262
7th Canadian 250, 262
8th British 252, 254, 262
8th Canadian 250, 262
9th British 254, 262
9th Canadian 250, 262
29th Armored 326
30th Armored 262
56th 248
69th 248, 262
151st 248, 262
185th 254, 262
231st 248, 262
Regiments, Battalions
Durham Light Infantry *254*, 262
Green Howards 248, 262
Lincolnshire 252, 262
North Nova Scotia Highlanders 250, 262
North Shore 250, 262
Nottinghamshire Yeomanry 248
Staffordshire Yeomanry 254
Queen's Own Rifles 250, 262, *318*
Regina Rifles 248, 262
Royal Marine Support 252, 262
Westminster Dragoons 248, 262
Winnipeg Rifles 250, 262
27th Canadian Armored 250
1st Dorset 248, 262
4th/7th Dragoon Guards 248
2nd East Yorkshire 252, 254, 262
5th East Yorkshire 248, 262
7th Field Regt, RA 252, 262
33rd Field Regt, RA 252, 262
76th Field Regt, RA 252, 262
1st Hampshire 248, 262
1st Hussars 251
13th/18th Hussars *246*, 252
2nd King's Shropshire Light Infantry 254, 262
9th Lancers 253
2nd Oxfordshire and Buckinghamshire Light Infantry 220, 262
9th Parachute Bn 223, 255, 262
1st Royal Norfolk 254, 262
2nd Royal Warwickshire 254, 262
1st South Lancashire 252, 262
1st Suffolk 254, 262
other units
3 Commando 224, 252, 256
4 Commando 224, 246, 252
6 Commando 224, 252
41 RM Commando 224, 252
45 RM Commando 246
46 RM Commando 246, 252
47 RM Commando 246
48 RM Commando 246, 251
10 Interallied Commando 252
249th Field Coy, RE 220
591st Parachute Sqn, RE 221
British Broadcasting Corporation 212
Brittany 261, 272
Brockman, Lt Cdr William 171
Brooklands, Surrey 46, 52
Brothers, P (RAF 52 Sqn) *24*
Brussels 272, 318
Buchholz Station, Belgium 284, 297, 299
Buckmaster, Capt Elliott 178, 180
Buckner, Lt Gen Simon Bolivar 334, *338*, 339, 380–83, *383*, 389
'bulge, the' 302, *see* Ardennes
Bullingen, Belgium 299, 303
Bulolo, allied HQ ship 233
Bunker Hill, US carrier 375

Caen, Normandy 216, 246, 254–5, *255*, 256, 259, 261, 270, 272
Cairo Conference 208
California, US battleship *106*, 113, 120, 131
Canada Victory, SS 377
Canadian troops *see* British/Canadian army
Canham, Col 245
Carpenter, P/O J M V 47
Caroline Islands 80, 85, 90
carried-borne aircraft, use of 85–6, 88, 93,

123, 126, 142
Casablanca Conference 209, *209*
Cassin, US destroyer 120, *124*, 132
Castor, US minesweeper 99
Ceylon 142, 143, 145, 153
Chiang Kai-shek 78
Cherbourg, France 210, 214, 216, *219*, 224, 256, 271
Cherry, Lt Col Henry T 308
Chikuma, carrier 97, 132, 134, 158, 162, 178, 180, 182, 183, 184
Chimu Bay, Okinawa 337
China, Japanese in 78, *79*, *81*, 90
Cho, Gen Isama 387–8
Churchill, Winston 19, 67, 129, 209, *209*, 210
Churchill tank *250*
Clark, Admiral J J 374
Clarke, Brig Gen Bruce 300, 302, 303, 310, 325
Clervaux, L'bourg 285, 289, 306, 307, 323
Collins, Maj Gen J L 234, 271, 318, 325, 326
Colmar pocket, France 276, 324
Colorado, US battleship 97, 121
Combined Operations HQ 207, 209–10
Comfort, US hospital ship 351
Condor, US minesweeper 89
Condor Legion 22
Cooke, P/O C A 26
Coral Sea battle 132, 145, *147*, 154, 157, 168, 177, 344
Corry, destroyer 235
COSSAC 209, 210, 211
Cota, Maj Gen Norman D 280, 289
Cotentin peninsula 216, 224–5, 229, 234, 256, 271
Coventry, bombing of *49*, *67*
Crerar, Lt Gen H D G 212, 272
Curtiss, US aircraft tender 119, 120
Czernin, F/O Count M B 26, *27*, 40, 67

Daigo, Rear Admiral T 197
Davis, F/O C R 47
Davis, Sgt J 43
D-Day (Tute) 225
Deere, W/Cdr A C 25, *42*, 43
de Gaulle, Gen Charles 212
de Guingand, Maj Gen Francis 321
Dempsey, Gen Sir Miles 212, 217, 254, 256, 272
Desobry, Maj W R 308, 309
Detroit, US cruiser 109
Devers, Gen J L 272, 273, 321, 324, *325*, 326
Dewar, W/Cdr J S 52, 57
Deyo, Rear Admiral M L 339, 353, 358, 374
Diadem, HMS 250
Diefenthal, Maj Josef 299
Dieppe, France 207, 208, 252, 261
Dietrich, Gen Sepp *274*, 277, 280, 284, 285, 289, 293, 297, 300, *301*, 302, 303, 304, 326
Dinant, Belgium 305, 316, 318, 321
Dives, river, Normandy 216, 220, 224
Dobbin, US destroyer-tender 120
Doe, P/O R F T 62
Dolii, Lt Saburo 374
Dollmann, Gen 254, 256
Don Burtgenbach, Belgium 303–4
Donaldson, S/Ldr E M *27*
Doolittle, Col J H *146*, 149
Dorsey, US minesweeper 354
Dowding, ACM Sir Hugh 15, *15*, 17, 19, 21, 25, 30, 41, 43, 65
Downes, US destroyer 120, *124*, 132
Dundas, F/Lt J C 58, *66*, 67
Dunkirk 15, *16–17*, 17, 19, 25, 211, 251
Dutch Harbor, Aleutians 153, 156, 161, 182

Eagle Day 30, 32
Earp (RAF 46 Sqn) *63*
Echternach, Luxembourg 270, 276, 309, 325
Echford, A (RAF) *24*
Eddy, Maj Gen Manton 312
Edsall, P/O E F 43
Eifel, Germany 276, 280
Eindhoven, Holland 273
Eisenhower, Gen D D *146*, 208–9, *210*, 210–11, 212, *215*, 217, *218*, 270, *271*, 272–3, 276, 289, 297, 299, 302, 307, 309, 321–2, 324, *325*, 326
El Alamein, N Africa 208, 212
Elliott, Pte G 97
Ellis, L F 222
Elsenborn Ridge 284, 293, 299, 300, 303–4, 305, 309, 316, 321, 325
Emerald, HMS 248
English, Rear Admiral R H 186, 189
Enterprise, US carrier 97, 104, 109, 132, *138–9*, 149, 153, 154, 156, *157*, 162, 163, 166, *167*, 168, 175, 177, 178, 183, 184, 192, 194–5, 196, *340*, 344, 346, *346*
Eyre, F/O A 35

Falaise Pocket, Normandy 272
Falley, General 228
Fast Carrier Task Group concept 126
Feric, M (RAF 303 Sqn) *53*
Feuchtinger, Maj Gen Edgar, 216, 254, 255, 256, 259
Finucane, W/Cdr B E *28*, 29, 32
Fitch, Rear Admiral Aubrey *143*
Fleet Air Arm, British 39, 69
Fleming, Capt Richard 191–2
Fletcher, Rear Admiral Frank 156, 161, *161*, 162, 163, 166, 167, 173, 177, 178, 184, 199
Fopp, Sgt D 46
Forbes, F/Lt A S 52
Fortitude deception plan 213
Fox, Lt F M 354
France 15, 17, 22, 78, 80
Franklin, US carrier 344, *345*
Frantisek, Sgt Josef *57*, 62
Frederick the Great 207, 277
Fuchida, Cdr M 97, 101, 117, 120, 131
Fujita, Rear Admiral R 198
Fukudome, Admiral S 86, 91
Fuller, Col Hurley 289, 306
'funny tanks' 248, 261
Fuso, battleship 156, 159

Gale, Maj Gen Richard N 221
Galland, Adolf 25, *30*, *59*, 67
Gamelin, General M 8
Gardner, P (RAF 32 Sqn) *24*
Gehres, Capt Leslie H 344
Genda Cdr Minoru 84, 86–8, 95, 97, 101, 131
George VI, King 217, *253*, *271*
German Air Force *see* Luftwaffe
German Armed Forces High Command (OKW) 228, 276, 277, 278, 280 289, 300, 302, 306, 321, 325, 326
German army
- General Staff 208, 277
- strength in 1944 208
- strength in Norway 213
- Army Group B 208, 217, 228, 254, 256, 278, 326
- Army Group G 321, 326
- Army Group H 326
- Armies
  - Fifth Panzer 272, 278, 285, 300, 325, 326
  - Sixth Panzer 277, 293, 397, 299, 325, 326
  - Sixth SS Panzer 285, 326
  - Seventh 254, 255, 256, 272, 278, 280, 289, 306, 326
  - Fifteenth 278, 280, 326
  - Nineteenth 276, 324
- Corps
  - I SS Panzer 254, 277, 326
  - II Panzer 277, 300, 302
  - II SS Panzer 325, 326
  - XLVII Panzer 285, 289, 306, 316, 326
  - LVIII Panzer 285, 289, 304, 318, 326
  - LXVI Infantry 285, 326
  - LXVII Infantry 326
  - LXXX Infantry 289, 326
  - LXXXIV 216, 225, 233, 256, 258
  - LXXXV Infantry 289, 326
- Divisions
  - 1st SS Panzer 280, 297, 299, 300, 302, 323, 325, 326
  - 2nd Panzer 280, 285, 306, 307, 309, 316, 318–19, 321, 326
  - 2nd SS Panzer 280, 300, 304, 305, 325, 326
  - 3rd Panzer Grenadier 280, 284, 326
  - 3rd Parachute 280, 284–5, 297, 299, 303, 326
  - 5th Parachute 280, 289, 306, 309, 314, 325, 326
  - 6th Parachute 239

7th Panzer 208
9th Panzer 280, 319, 321, 326
9th SS Panzer 280, 300, 325, 326
12th SS Panzer 216, 254, 280, 284, 285, 293, 297, 299, 303–4, 325, 326
15th Panzer Grenadier 280, 311, 319, 326
21st Panzer 216, 221, 250, 254–5, 256, 259, 261
77th Field 216, 261
79th Infantry 280, 326
84th Field 261
91st Airlanding 216, 224, 228, 238
116th Panzer 216, 280, 285, 289, 302, 304–5, 318–19, 321, 326
352nd Infantry 216, 239, 245, 258
353rd 261
709th Infantry 216, 239
711th 216
716th Infantry 216, 220, 250, 255, 258
Panzerlehr 216–17, 254, 280, 285, 306, 308, 309, 316, 318–19, 321, 323, 326
Volksgrenadier divns 277
9th 280, 326
12th 280, 284, 293, 325, 326
18th 280, 285, 289, 300, 302, 303, 326
26th 280, 285, 306, 323, 326
62nd 280, 303, 326
212th 280, 289, 326
246th 280, 326
276th 280, 289, 326
277th 280, 284, 293, 326
326th 280, 326
352nd 280, 289, 326
560th 280, 285, 302, 304, 325, 326
Brigades
150th Panzer 278, 304, 326
Fuhrer Begleit 280, 300, 302, 303, 326
Fuhrer Grenadier 280, 300, 326
Regiments
3rd Panzer 321
6th Parachute 216, 258
9th Parachute 299
39th *Volksgrenadier* 309
77th *Volksgrenadier* 309, 311
78th *Volksgrenadier* 309
115th Panzer Grenadier 311–12
125th Panzer Grenadier 221
304th Panzer Grenadier 321
736th Grenadier 220, 221, 250, 251, 254
901st Panzer Grenadier 309
915th Infantry 248, 258–9
1716th Artillery 250
Kampfgruppe Peiper 297, 299, 300, 303, 318
Greif Commandos 278, 297
German naval forces 208, 233
Gerow, Maj Gen L T 234, 280, 293, 326
Gillman, K (RAF 32 Sqn) *24*
Gladiator, minesweeper 374
Gleave, S/Ldr T P 41, 46
Gleed, F/Lt Ian R *12*, 35
Goering, Reichsmarschal H W *16*, 17, 22, 30, 48, 59, *60*
Gold Beach, Normandy 246, 262
Gray, P/O Colin *18*, *42*
Grice, D (RAF 32 Sqn) *24*
Gruska, F/O F 37
Guadalcanal 132, 134, 135, 357, 373
Guam 80, 159, 337
Gwin, US destroyer 180

Hackleback, US submarine 367
Hagikaze, destroyer 171
Hagushi beaches, Okinawa 339, 347, 354, 355, 357, 364, 380
Hall, Rear Admiral 234, 243
Halligan, US destroyer 351
Halsey, Admiral W F 88, 149, *154*, 156
Halsey Powell, US destroyer 344
Hamaka, destroyer 172
Hamakaze, destroyer 132, 134
Hamlyn, W/Cdr R F 40, *40*
Hamman, US destroyer 180, 196
Hanson, P/O D H W 26, 46
Hara, Admiral Chuichi 129
Harman, Maj Gen Ernest N 319
Harper, Lt Col R S 307
Harrison, G A 224
Haruna, battleship 150, 158, 162, 178, 197, 365
Harwick, Maj R F 309
Hasbrouck, Brig Gen R W 300, 301
Hashimoto, Toshio 176, 183
Hawaii 80, 142, 184
Helena, US cruiser 109
Helm, US destroyer 97, 119
Henneberg, Z (RAF 303 Sqn) *53*
Hermes, HMS, carrier 143
Hiei, battleship 95, 97, 132, 134, 182
Hillary, P/O R H 44, 46
Himmler, Reichsfuhrer 326
Hinsale, US transport 362
Hiroaki, Rear Admiral 158
Hiroshima 129
Hiryu, carrier 97, 132, 134, 150, 158, 163, 165, 166, 168, *170*, 173, 175, 176, 177, 178, *178*, 182, 183, 184, 185, 194, 197
Hitler, Adolf 25, 29, 48, 57, 59, 207, 208, 213, 214, 216, 217, 270, *274*, *275*, 276–8, 280, 281, 289, 302, 303, 306, 316, 319, 321, 323, 324, 325, 326
Hobart, Maj Gen Sir Percy 261
Hodge, General 378
Hodges, Gen Courtney H 272, 276, 284, *289*, 293, 299, 303, 316, 318, 325, 326
Holland 15, 17, 272, 284, 318
Holmes, Sgt R T 58
Hollis, Sgt Maj S E 248
Honolulu, USS 120
Honsfeld, Belgium 297, 299
Hood, HMS, battlecruiser 123
Hornet, US carrier (1) 97, 132, *148–9*, 149, 153, 154, 156, *157*, 162, 166, 168, 175, 177, 178, 183, 184, 194–5; (2) 132, *375*
Horrocks, Lt Gen Sir Brian 273, 318
Hosho, carrier 151, 159, 178, 183, 195
Hosogaya, Vice-Admiral M 151, 157, 158, 198
Howard, Maj R J 220, 221
Howe, HMS, battleship 339
Hotton, Belgium 304, 305, 316, 318, 319
Houffalize, Belgium 285, 304, 306, 307, 308, 322, 325
Howze, Col R L Jr 304, 305
Huebner, Maj Gen C R 245
Hughes, F/Lt P C 36, 52
Hughes, US destroyer 178, 180
Hull, F/Lt Caesar *41*, 44, 51
Hull, Cordell 92
Hurtgen Forest 276, 280
Hyuga, battleship 156, *158–9*, 159

I-36 Jap submarine 341, 377
I-37 341
I-44 351–2
I-47 341, 351–2, 377
I-56 351
I-57 352
I-58 351–2, 377
I-168 163, 180, *180*, 182, 186, 197
Ichiki, Col K 157, 159, 161, 162, 187
Ie-Shima island, Okinawa 337, 339, 355, 372, 376
Iida, Lt Fusata 104
Illustrious, HMS, carrier 339
Imaizumi, Capt 135
Imanishi, Ensign 341
Indefatigable, HMS, carrier 339, 347
Indianapolis, US cruiser *90*
Indo-China 89, 90
intelligence
American 92–3, 95, 145, 153, 262, 355
German 217
Japanese 85, 87, 93, 97, 153, 156, 159, 162
Indomitable, HMS, carrier 339
Intrepid, US carrier 345
Ise, battleship 156, 159, *172*
Isokaze, destroyer 172, 367
Italian air force 65
Ito, Cdr 178
Ito, Vice-Admiral Seeichi 366–7
Iwo Jima 131, 335, 351, 357, 362, 370, 383, 389, 390
assault on 335–6, *336–7*

Japan
Air Self-Defense Force 131
alliance with Axis powers 80
bombing of *148*, 149, 334, 335, 339, 344, 347, 376
invasion of advocated 334, 339, 390
merchant shipping 127–8
mission in Asia of 78, 81, 90
war strategy 129, 142, 335
Japanese army
at Midway 150, 151
High Command 142, 362, 364, 370, 376, 379

in China 78, *79*
on Okinawa 339, 370–73, 378–82
24th Division 378–9
Japanese Navy 82, 365
ambitions in SE Asia 78, 80, 90
manoeuvres 157
submarines 163, 377
I class 341, 377, *see also* midget submarines
suicide tactics 104, 341, 343, 353, 365–7
war games 85, 91, 153, 186
war losses 133, 365
war strategy 80, 81, 83, 90, 91, 128, 142, 353, 376
Second Fleet 143, 157, 159, 182, 183, 184, 187, 365–7, 376–7
Sixth Fleet 341, 351, 352, 377
First Air Fleet 143
Fifth Air Fleet 344, 367, 376
Tenth Air Fleet 376
Eleventh Air Fleet 86
1st Carrier Division 131, 134
2nd, 5th Carrier Divns 134
3rd Battle Division 134
1st Destroyer Flotilla 88, 134, *152*
1st, 2nd, 3rd Submarine Flotillas 88, 135
Carrier Striking Force 150, 157, 158, 161, 162, 198
Combined Fleet 81, 85, 86, 142, 150, 153, 183, 187, 365–7, 377
'Main Body' 150, 151, 153, 157, 161, 198
Midway Occupation Force 150, 151, 153, 198
Northern Area Force 150, 151, 153, 157, 158, 198
Submarine Advance Expeditionary Force 150, 151, 197
Support Force 157, 159
Tatara Group 351–2, 377
Jefferies, F/Lt A *53*
Jimmu Day 364–5
Jiutsu, cruiser 159
Jodl, Gen Alfred 216, 276, 278, 280
Joint Chiefs of Staff 321, 339
Jones, Maj Gen Alan 280, 285, 300
Jones, Lt Col R B 302
Juno Beach, Normandy 251, 262
Junyo, carrier 151, 153, 157, 161, 182, 183

Kadena airfield, Okinawa 337, 339, 354, 359, 364, 371
Kaga, carrier 88, 97, 132, 134, *150*, 150, 158, 162, 163, 164, 166, 168, *169*, 170, 171–2, 177, 182, 184, 197
Kagero, destroyer 132, 134
Kaiten midget submarine 341, *341*, 343, 351–3, 365–6, 376–7
Kakikaze, Lt 377
Kaku, Capt Tomeo 177, 178
Kakuda, Rear Admiral K 151, 153, 182, 184, 198
Kamakaze, destroyer 367
Kamikaze
aircraft 335–6, *342*, 343, 344, 347, 351, 353–4, 361, 362, 370, 374
attacks 339, *340*, 346–7, 358, 365–6, 371, 372, *375*, 376–7, 379, 391
Corps 365, 390
Kasumi, destroyer 132, 134, 367
Katori, light cruiser 197
Kawaguchi, Cdr Genbei 351
Kazaguma, destroyer 178
Keitel, FM Wilhelm 228, 256
Kellet, S/Ldr R G 47
Kent, J A (RAF 303 Sqn) *53*
Keough, P/O 'Shorty' *44*
Kerama Retto islands 337, 339, 347, 351, 353, 354
Kesselring, FM Albrecht 22
Keyes, Admiral of the Fleet Sir Roger 209
Kieffer, Commandant 252
Kikusui,
Operation No 1 366, 374
Operation No 2 374
Mass Attack No 5 379
Kimberley, destroyer 351
Kimmel, Admiral Husband E *130*, 131, 142
Kimura, Rear Admiral S 158, 198
King, Fleet Admiral Ernest J. 334, *334*, *335*
King George V, HMS, battleship 339
Kirishima, battleship 97, 132, 134, 150, 158
Kirk, Rear Admiral Alan G *216*, 217, 234
Kiska, Aleutian Is 153, 159
Kobayashi, Lt M 173, 175
Koiso, Gen Kuniaki 365
Kokott, Gen Heinz 309–12
Konatsu, Vice-Admiral T 197
Kondo, Admiral Nobutake 143, 151, 153, 157, 159, 161, 182, 183, 184, 187, 191, 195, 198
Kongo, battleship *151*
Konishi, Capt 134
Kono, Rear Admiral Chimaki 197
Konoye, Prince 80, *81*, 92
Korea, 335, 337
Kraiss, Gen Dietrich 258–9
Krancke, Vice-Admiral 208, 217, 233
Krebs, Gen Hans 278
Krinkelt, Belgium 284, 293
Krosnodebski, F/Lt Z 47
Krüger, Gen Walter 285
Kumano, cruiser 182, 191
Kunisada, Lt Cdr Yoshio 171
Kuribayashi, Maj Gen T 335
Kurile Islands 88, 97
Kurita, Rear Admiral T *156*, 157, 159, 187, 191, 198
Kuroshima, Rear Admiral 186
Kusaka, Rear Admiral Ryunosuke 97, 120, 121, 153, 170, 171
Kwajalein 88, 97, *338*, 357

Lacey, J H 'Ginger' 25, *42*, 43, 44, 57
Laffey, destroyer, 374, 376
La Gleize 299, 316
Lane, S/Ldr B J E 40, *40*, *42*, 50
La Roche, Belgium 304, 305
Last Enemy, The (Hillary) 46
Laval, Pierre 212
Leahy, Admiral W *335*
Lefevre (RAF 46 Sqn) *63*
Leggett, P/O P G 63, 65
Leigh-Mallory, ACM Sir Trafford 21, 40, 211, *215*, 217
LeMay, Gen Curtis 339
Lewis, P/O A G 60, 61
Lexington, US carrier *94*, 97, 132, *144*, *147*, 149, 154, 344
Leyte Gulf 337, 347, 351
battle 131, 132, 133, 134, 357, 365
landings *336*
Liege, Belgium 276, 284, 302, 303, 305, 316, 318, 325
Ligneuville, Belgium 299, 300
Lindsey, Capt Franklin P 302
Lindsey, US destroyer-minelayer 374
Lockard, Pte Joseph 99
Lofts, P/O K T 35
London, bombing of 41, 48, *48*, 50–51, *51*, 52, 57, *57*, 59, *60–61*, 62, *66*
Losheim Gap 280, 284–5, 289, 293, 297, 303
Lovat, Brig Lord 224, 255
Lucht, Gen Walter 285
Luftwaffe 16–70 *passim*
aircraft armament 25
aims in Battle of Britain 25, 29, 30, 48
fighter tactics 25, 35
in Ardennes offensive 324–5
in Normandy 208
losses in Battle of Britain 29, 30, 32–41 *passim*, 46, 47, 52, 58, 60–63, 65, 68
organization and role 25
strength in 1940 17, 21, 22, 29, 30
Luftflotte 2 17, 21, 22, 35
Luftflotte 3 17, 21, 22, 35, 40
Luftflotte 5 21, 22, 35
units 70
EG210 67
JG2 67
JG51 26
KG2 32, 58
KG3 26, *51*
IIJG3 *58*
IIKG2 26
IIIKG53 26
ZG79 *22*
Lunga Point, US carrier 336
Lurline, liner 95
Lüttwitz, Gen H von 285, 289, 306, 309, 319
Lützow, Gunther 25
Luxembourg 272, 289, 302, 306, 309
Luzon 80, 93, 334, *335*

MacArthur, Gen Douglas 211, 334–5
McArthur, F/Lt J H G 50
McAuliffe, Brig Gen A C 308, *308*, 309, 311, 315, 316, 321, 322
McClintock, P/O J A P 36
McClusky, Lt Cdr C 168, 170
McDowell, Archie (RAF 602 Sqn) 43

McGregor (RAF 46 Sqn) *63*
Machetski, Hauptmann 26
Machinato airstrip, Okinawa 337, 378
Machinato Line 364, 369–70, 373, 378
McKnight, F/Lt W L *45*
McNab, S/Ldr E A 41
Maeda, Lt 377
Maikaze, destroyer 171
Makigumo, destroyer 172
Malan, S/Ldr A G 25, 26, *29*, 32, 39
Malmedy, Belgium 284, 299, 303, 304
massacre at *298*, 299
Mamedoff, P/O 'Andy' *44*
Manhay, Belgium 303, 304, 305, 318, 325
Mannert L Abele, destroyer 374
Manteuffel, Gen Hasso von *276*, 278, 280, 285, 289, 300, 302, 303, 305, 306, 311, 321, 323, 325, 326
Marcks, Gen Erich 216, 228, 245, 256, 259
Mariana Is 80, 85, 90, 339, 353, 390
Marrs, P/O E S 67
Marshall, Gen G C 211, *335*
Marshall Is 80, 85, 86, 90, 91
Martin, Maj Gen Frederick 93, 95
Martin, Maj J E 253
Maryland, US battleship 109, 113, *113*, 117, 120, 132, 353
Matapan Cape battle 123
Maxwell, P/O M C 60
Medusa, US repair ship 119
Meuse, river 270, 276, 278, 285, 289, 293, 297, 299, 300, 303, 304, 305, 306, 316, 319
Middleton, Maj Gen Troy 276, 280, 300, 302, 307, 316, 322, 326
Midget submarines 88, *89*, 99, 119, *119*, 121, 135, 233, *342–3*, 355
see also Kaiten
Midway 87, 88, 97, 142, 149, 153–4, 156, 161, 353
battle 120, 128, 132, 133, 134, 149, 344
action 161–8, 170–73, 175–8, 180, 182–6
maps 150, 171
planning 142–3, 150–51, 153–4, 156–9
Mikawa, Vice-Admiral 134
Mikuma, cruiser 182, 186, *187*, *190*, 191–2, 194, 195, 197
Millikin, Maj Gen J 312, 314, 322
Minneapolis, US cruiser 351
Mississinewa, tanker 343
Mitscher, Vice-Admiral Marc 149, *338*, 339, 344, 346, 347
Miura, Cdr 171
Miwa, Rear Admiral 135
Miyazaki, Capt Takeharu 197
Model, FM Walther 278, 280, 302, 303, *305*, 324, 326
Mogami, cruiser 182, 186, 191–2, 194, 195, 197
Mölders, Werner 25, 26, *59*
Monaghan, US destroyer 97, 119, 180
Monschau, Germany 270, 276, 277, 284, 293
Montgomery, Gen Sir Bernard 208, 210, 212, *212*, *215*, 217, 251, 256, *256*, *271*, 272, 303, 305, 318, 321–2, 325, 326
Morgan, Lt Gen F E 209, 210, 211
Motobu peninsula, Okinawa 337, 339, 355, 362, 364, 372, 380
Mount, F/Lt J C 63
Mountbatten, Vice-Admiral Lord Louis 207, 209–10
Mulberry Harbor *249*, *260*, 261
Mungo-Park, J C *36*, *38*
Musashi, battleship 151, 365
Mutsu, battleship 156, *158–9*, 159, *183*

Nagai, Admiral 352, 377
Nagano, Rear Admiral Osami 84, *84*, 90, 91, 93, 142, 150, 184
Nagara, light cruiser 158, 173, 178, 183
Nagasaki 129
Nagato, battleship 85, 120, 156, 159, 365
Nagumo, Vice-Admiral Chuichi 88, *88*, 97, 120, 121, 128, 131, 132–3, 134, 143, *143*, 145, 150, 153, 154, 157–8, 159, 162–8 *passim*, 170, 171, 173, 178, 183–4, 191, 195, 198
Naha airfield, Okinawa 337
town 337, 362, 364, 369, *384–5*, *387*
Nakagusuku Wan, Okinawa 337, 380
Namur, Belgium 276, 285, 318
Nautilus, US submarine 171
Neosho, fuel carrier 120
Nevada, US battleship *112*, 113, 117, 119–20, 131, 132, *135*, *216*, *235*, 243, 354
New Guinea 145, 149
New Mexico, US battleship 330–31
class 353
New York, US battleship 353
Nicholas, US destroyer 341
Nicholson, F/Lt E J B 36, *36*
Nijmegen, Holland 273
Nimitz, Admiral Chester 121, 131, 142, *142*, 153–4, *154*, 156, *156*, 159, 161, 162, 195, 334, *338*, 339, *360*, 376
Nishibayashi, Lt Cdr 171
Nishina, Lt 341
Nonaka, Lt Cdr Goro 346
Normandy invasion 132, 207, 214, 216, 270
Allied preparation 209–14, 216–17
airborne assault 218, *219*, *220*, 220–25, *224–5*
assault fleet 229, 233
casualties 228, 245, *248–9*, 261
German anticipation 214, 216–17
German coastal defences *202–3*, *206*, 207, 208, *210–11*, *214*, 222–4, 229, 233, 239
landings 234–5, *234–5*, *236–7*, 237–9, *240–45*, 241, 243, 245–6, *246–9*, 248, 250–55, *258–60*, *271*
map 222–3
training *201*, *213*
North, P/O H L 41
Norway 19, 21, 22, 213, 214
Noville, Belgium 307, 309, 325
Nowake, destroyer 171

Oahu, Hawaii 85, 88, 93, 95
map 99
O'Brien, S/Ldr J 52
O'Brien, US destroyer 354
Oesau, Walter 25
Ogawa, Lt Shoichi 163
Oglala, US minelayer 109, 132
O'Hara, Lt Col James 308
Ohka piloted bomb *342*, 343, 346–7, 374
Ohta, Ensign 343
Okada, Capt Jisaku 171
Okamura, Capt 346
Okinawa 131, 132, 133, 134, 334–5, 337, 366
bombardment *330–31*, 347, *347*, 351, *352–3*, 353–4, 373
casualties 372, 388
description 337, 339, 354–5
final US offensive 381–3
Jap air attacks on 374
Jap counter-attacks 370–71, 378–9
Jap defense 362, 364, 365–7, 369–70, 372–3, 383
Jap presence on 339, 359, 362, 364
landings on 351–2, *355–7*, 357–9, *358–9*, *360*, 362, *362–3*
map 356
planning capture 339
surrender at *389*
Okinawa: The Land Battle 373
Oklahoma, US battleship 109, *113*, 120, *121*, 131
Oldendorf, Rear Admiral J *338*
Omaha Beach, Normandy *204–5*, 225, 233, 238, 239, *240–41*, 241, 243, *244–5*, 245, *246*, 259, 261, 262, 270
Omori, Rear Admiral S 134, 198
Onishi, Rear Admiral Takajiro *85*, 86, 91
Operation Cobra 271
Operation Dragoon 272
Operation Epsom 270
Operation Garden 273
Operation Goodwood 270
Operation *Greif* 278
Operation Iceberg 339, 343, 347, 351
Operation Market 273
Operation *Nordwind* 324
Operation Overlord 209–10, 212, 218, 270
Operation Ten-Go 365–6
Oppeln-Bronowski, Col von 259
Orion, HMS 248
Orita, Cdr 377
Ota, Rear Admiral Minoru 339, 385
Otway, Lt Col Terence 222–4
Our river, L'bourg 285, 289, 302, 306
Ourthe river, Belgium 285, 303, 304, 305, 309, 316, 318, 325

Park, AM Sir Keith *20*, 21, 22, 30, 37, 40, 41, 52, 59, 65
Parker, Maj Arthur C III 305

Parker's Crossroads 305, 325
Pas de Calais 213–14, 217, 228, 256, 259, 270
pattern bombing 88
Patton, Lt Gen George S. 210, 212, *256*, *271*, 272, 273, 276, 289, 307, 309, *309*, 310, 312, 313, 322, 323, 325, 326
Pearl Harbor 81, *96*, 142, 151, 159, 337
  airfields at 101, *101–5*, 104, 119, 120, *128*
  American, Japanese losses 121
  assessment of effects 126–7, 128–9
  attack on 99–120
  effect on Jap strategy 142
  effect on US strategy 126, 142
  map 99
  objections to attack 89–91
  planning 81, 83, 84–91
  preparation 87–8, 92, 93, *98*
  strike force details and fate 132–5
Peel, Johnny (RAF) 25
Peiper, SS Obersturmbannführer J 297, 299, 300, 303, 304
Pemsel, Maj Gen 256
Pennsylvania, US battleship *107*, 109, 120, *126*, 132
Pétain, Marshal 212
Philippine Sea battle 132, 133, 134, 334
Philippines 80, 91, 93, 95, 134, 135, *152*, 334, 335, 353, 390
Pingel, Rolf (Luftwaffe) 25
PLUTO 261
Port Moresby 145, 149
Portsmouth, bombing of 40, 41, 52
Poteau, Belgium 300, 302, 303
Proctor, J (RAF 32 Sqn) *24*
Prince of Wales, HMS, battleship 93
Pringle, US destroyer 374
Pye, Admiral 88
Pyle, Ernie 212

Quadrant meeting 210
Queen Beach, Normandy 246, 251

Radar defense systems 21, 32, 35, 57, 95, 99
  German *209*, 233
radar stations, English *20*, 32, 35
Raleigh, US cruiser *108*, 109, 120
Rall, US patrol vessel 374
Ramillies, HMS, battleship 233, 253
Ramsay, Admiral Sir Bertram 211, *215*, 217
Rawlings, Vice-Admiral Sir Bernard 339
Reid, Ensign Jewell 161
Relief, US hospital ship 351
Remagen bridge 280
Rennie, Maj Gen T G 251
Repulse, HMS, battle-cruiser 93
Resistance 212, 258
Reynell, F/Lt R C 51
Rhine, river 272, 273, 276, 280, 321
Rhodes-Moorhouse, F/Lt 'Willie' 37, *37*, 47
Richter, Lt Gen 228
Ridgway, Gen Matthew B. 225, 289, 303, 304, 305, 318, 323
Riggs, Lt Col Tom 300, 302, 303
Roberts, Col W L 307
Roberts, HMS, monitor 233
Robertson, Maj Gen Walter M 293
Robertson, Sgt F N 26
Robinson, S/Ldr M L 62, *62*
Rocherath, Belgium 284, 293
Rodney, HMS, battleship *229*
Roer dams, Germany 276, 280, 284, 293
Rommel, FM Erwin *206*, 207–8, 212, 246, 255, 256, 259
Roosevelt, President 80, *90*, 129, *129*, 149, 208, *209*, 210, 211
Roosevelt, Brig Gen Theodore Jr 237
Rose, Capt L K 307
Roseveare, Maj J C A 221
Ross, Lt Col Richard *382*
Royal Air Force
  in Battle of Britain 15–70
  in France 1939–40 17, 19
  in Normandy invasion 224
  Air Defence of Great Britain 224
  Allied Tactical Air Forces 211
  School of Army Cooperation 211
  Second Tactical Air Force 255
Royal Air Force Army Cooperation Command 39
Royal Air Force Bomber Command 39, 41, 224, 229
Royal Air Force Fighter Command
  aircraft armament 25, *34–5*, 40
  Headquarters, Bentley Priory *39*
  losses in Battle of Britain 29, 30, 32, 34, 35, 36, 37, 40–41, 43, 46, 51, 52, 58, 60–63, 65, 69
  squadron routine 28–9, 38–9
  strength 1939–40 17, 19, 21, 22, 30, 59
  tactics 25, 37, 40, 41, 47, 52, 59, 62
  10 Group 21, 35, 41, 43, 57, 69
  11 Group 21, 22, 35, 41, 43, 50, 57, 59, 65, 69
  12 Group 21, 26, 35, 40, 43, 50, 57, 58, 59, 69, 211
  Squadrons
    1 Canadian: 41, *52*
    17: 26, 38, 40, 46, 65, 67
    19: *35*, 40, *40*, *42*, 43, 47, 50
    32: *24*, *33*, 35, 41, *69*
    41: 47, 62
    43: *40*, 41, *41*, 44, 51
    46: *63*, 65
    54: *18*, *42*, 43
    56: *18*, *27*, 34, 44, 60, 61
    65: 28, 32, 37
    66: 26, *27*, 47
    74: 26, *29*, 32, *38*, 39
    79: 44
    85: 26, *42*, 43, 44, *66*
    87: *12*, 35, 40–41, 52, 57
    92: 59
    111: 35, *50*
    145: 30, *37*, 63, 65
    151: 26, *27*, 44
    152: 37, 61, 67
    213: 35
    222: 47, 63
    229: 61
    234: 36, 37, 52
    238: 62
    242: 26, *45*, 50, *55*, 58, *62*
    249: 36, 52, 60
    253: 41, 43, 46–7
    257: *18*, 52, *64*, 65, 67
    303: 47, 52, *52–3*, *56–7*, 62
    310: 50, *53*
    501: 42, 43, 44
    504: 58
    601: 37, *37*, 47, *64*
    602: 37, 41, 43, *47*, 63
    603: 44, 65
    609: 32, 35, 40–41, 50, 62, *62*, 66
    610: *29*, *34*, *38*, 40, *40*, 44
    615: 35, 36, 37, 41, *64*
    616: 41
  Stations
    Biggin Hill *33*, 35, 36, *38*, 41, 44, 59
    Brize Norton 36
    Coltishall 26, *27*, *45*
    Croydon 35, 36, 41
    Debden 26, 38, 44
    Detling 41, 44
    Duxford *35*, 40, *42*, *53*, 59
    Eastchurch 32, 35, 44
    Ford 37
    Gosport 35
    Hawkinge *24*, 32, 34, 35, 44, *69*
    Hemswell *33*
    Hornchurch 28, 43, 44, 47, 59
    Kenley 35, 36–7, 41, 47
    Lee-on-Solent 36
    Lympne 35, 44
    Manston 26, 28, 29, 32, 35, 40
    Martlesham Heath 26, 35, *64*
    Middle Wallop 35
    North Weald 26, *27*, 40, 41, 44, 52
    Northolt 41, *52*, 58, 59, *64*
    Odiham 35
    Portsmouth 40, 41
    Rochford 28, 29, 37, 44
    Stapleford Abbots *63*
    Tangmere 35, 36, 47, 52, 59
    Thorney Island 37
    West Malling 35, 36
    Westhampnett 36
    Worthy Down 35
Royal Marines 262, *see also* British/Canadian army, other units
Royal Navy
  Far Eastern Fleet 142
  Pacific Fleet 339, 347
  see also names of specific ships
Royal Observer Corps 21
Ruhr area, Germany 273, 321
Rundstedt, FM K R G von *206*, 207, 208, 212, 214, 216, 217, 228, 256, 259, 261, 277, 278, 280, 316, 326
Russo-Japanese War 81, *82–3*, 83

Ryujo, carrier 151, 153, 157, 161, 182, 183
Ryukyu islands 334, 337, 339, 351, 390

St Lô, Normandy 216, 225, 261, 270
St Lo, US carrier *340*
St Nazaire, France 207
St Vith, Belgium *266–7*, 277, 278, 285, 293, 299, 300, 302, 303–8 *passim*, 310, 313, 316, 319, 325
Saipan 335, 358, 362, 377
Sakamaki, Ensign 119
Sakishima islands 339, 347
Salm river, Belgium 297, 299, 303, 304
Salmachâteau, Belgium 303, 304, 305
Sample, S/Ldr J 58
San Francisco, US cruiser 196, 351
Santa Cruz battle 132
Santa Fe, US cruiser 344
Saratoga, US carrier 97, 132, 153, 154, 336
Sato, Ensign 341
Sato, Rear Admiral 135
Satterlee, US destroyer 245
Sazanami, destroyer 134
Schnee Eifel region 280, 285, 300, 302
Settsu, battleship 153
Shannon, Lt Col Harold 153–4
Shaw, US destroyer *74–5*, 120, *124–5*, 132
Sherman tanks *250–51*, 251, *266–7*
Shepherd, Maj Gen Lemuel 369
Shimonoseki Strait 337, 347
Shinyo suicide boats 339
Shiranuhi, destroyer 132, 134
Shoho, carrier *145*, 149
Shokaku, carrier *85*, 87, 97, 131, 132, *145*, 149, 153, *195*
Shuri, Okinawa 337, 364, 369, 370, 381–2 *383*, 389
Siegfried Line *273*, *275*, 278, 316
Simard, Cdr Cyril 153–4
Simpson, Lt Gen, W H 276, 326
Simpson, F/Lt John *40*
Sino-Japanese wars 81, 83
Skorzeny, SS Obersturmbannführer Otto 278, 293, 297, 304, 326
Slim, FM Sir W J 92
Smythe, R (RAF 32 Sqn) *24*
Solace, US hospital ship 351
Solomon Islands 159
  battles 131, 132, 133, 134
Somervell, General *325*
Soryu, carrier 97, 132, 134, 150, 158, 163, 165, 166, 168, 170, 172, 173, 175, 177, 178, 182, 184, 197
Southampton, bombing of 52, 63
Soviet Union
  and Japan 93
  Vistula offensive 1945 325
Soyi, Capt Akira 191
Spanish Civil War 22, 25
Special Operations Executive (SOE) 212
Speidel, General 256
Sperrle, FM Hugo 22, 208
Spruance, Admiral Raymond 156, *156*, 163, 166, 167, 168, 184, 185, 186, 191, 194–5, 199, 334, *338*, 339, 344, *360*
Stanley, US destroyer 374
Stavelot, Belgium 299, 303
Stevenson, P/O P C F 32
Stoumont, Belgium 299, 303
Strasbourg, France 276, 321, 324
Studd, P/O J A P 26
Student, General 326
Stumpf, Generaloberst H-J 22
Suganomai, Lt Masaharu 163
Suribachi, Iwo Jima 335, *337*
Suzuki, Admiral 365
Suzuya, cruiser 182, 191
Svenner, Norwegian warship 233
Sword Beach, Normandy 262
Szcesny, Henryk (RAF 74 Sqn) *38*

Taiwan 334, 335, 337, 347
Taiyo Maru 87
Takagi, Vice-Admiral 157
Takahashi, Admiral 365
Takao class destroyers *188–9*
Takasu, Vice-Admiral S 153, 198
Talybont, HMS, destroyer 245
Tambor, US submarine 186, 187, 191
Tampo, Cdr 171
Tanabe, Cdr Yahachi 163–4, 180, 182, 186
Tanaka, Read Admiral R *157*, 198
Tanamachi, Capt 339, 385
Tanikaze, destroyer 132, 134, 194, 195, 197
Taranto, attack on 85, 86, 87, 123
Tataro operation, Okinawa 351–2, 377
Taylor, Cdr Joe 344
Taylor, Lt Kenneth 104
Taylor, Maj Gen Maxwell D 308
Tedder, ACM Sir Arthur 211, *215*, 217
Tennessee, US battleship 109, 113, 117, 132, *338*, 353, 354, 358, 374
Terebinth, US tender 351
Texas, US battleship *216*
Thorne, Lt Gen Sir A F A N 213
Threadfin, US submarine 367
Tide, US minesweeper *246*
Tobin, P/O 'Red' *44*
Togo, Admiral 97, 157
Toguchi, Okinawa 337
Tojo, Gen Hideki 92, *92*
Tomano, Lt 159
Tomioka, Capt Sadatoshi 142
Tomonaga, Lt Joichi 163, 164, 165, 166, 175, 176, 177, 178, 182, 184
Torisu, Cdr Tennosuke 377
Tone, heavy cruiser 97, 133, 134, 158, 162, 164, 165, 166, 182
Townsend, S/Ldr P W 41, *41*, 43, 66
Toyoda, Admiral 365–6, 376
Trident Conference 209
Trois Ponts, Belgium 299, 304, 305
Trois Vierges 302, 307
Tsukahara, Vice-Admiral N 199
Tsukushi Maru 341
Tsu-shima battle 97, 157
Tuck, W/Cdr R R S *18*, 25
Tulagi, Solomon Is 149
Turner, P/O P S 58, *62*
Turner, Vice-Admiral R Kelly 339, 347, 380
Tute, Warren 225
Two-Ocean Naval Expansion Act 80, 91, 132
Tyler, Capt Marshall 191
Udet, Ernst *59*
Ugaki, Gen Kazushige *344*
Ugaki, Rear Admiral Matome 142, 153, 184, 186, 197, 344, 346, 347
Ulithi atoll 337, 341, 344, *346*, 347, 351, 377
Ulster, HMS, destroyer 347
United States
  Pacific War strategy 142, 334–5
  relations with Japan 80, 89–90, 91
United States army
  and invasion of Japan 334
  Chiefs of Staff 334
  First Army 212, 224, 270–72, 276, 203, 316, 321, 325, 326
  Third Army 212, 272, 276, 289, 307, 309, 321, 326
  Sixth Army Group 272, 276, *282*, 309, 321, 324, 326
  Ninth Army 276, 289, 299, 300, 302, 321, 326
  Tenth Army 334, 339, 380
  Corps
    III 312, 326
    III Amphibious 339
    V 234, 238, 245, 280, 326
    VI 324
    VII 234, 238, 271, 303, 318, 325, 326
    VIII 276, 280, 322, 326
    XII 312, 326
    XVIII Airborne 289, 294, 303, 304, 318, 323, 326
    XXIV 339, 378, 380
    Rangers 245, 262
  Divisions
    1st Inf 244, 245, 262, 293, 303–4, 326
    2nd Inf 280, 284, 293, 297, 304, 326
    2nd Armored 318, 319, 321, 325, 326
    3rd Armored 303, 304–5, 318, 325, 326
    4th Inf 235, 238, *238*, *259*, 280, 289, 306, 312, 326
    4th Armored 309, 312, 313–15, 322, 325, 326
    5th 312, *316*, 326
    6th Armored 323, 325, 326
    7th 339, 357–8, 361, 364, *371*, *372*, 378, *388*
    7th Armored 289, 299, 300, 302, 303, 305, 325, 326
    8th 258
    9th Armored 280, 289, 302, 307, 326
    9th Inf 293, 326
    10th Armored 289, 307, 312, 326
    11th Armored 323, 326
    17th Airborne 323, 325, 326
    18th Airborne 303

26th Inf 309, 312, 323, 325, 326
27th 339, 372, 378
28th Inf 280, 285, 289, 300, 302, 306, 326
29th Inf 245
30th Inf 299, 303, 304, 318, 326
35th Inf 323, 325, 326
75th Inf 305, 318, 325, 326
77th 339, *350*, 351, 355, 372, 378, 380, *381*
80th Inf 309, 312, 314, 326
81st 339
82nd Airborne 224, 225, 238, 258, 262, 270, 273, *288*, 289, 299, 303, 304, 305, *319*, 325, 326
83rd Inf 325, 326
84th Inf 318–19, 325, 326
87th Inf *322*, 323, 325, 326
90th Inf *320*, 323, 325, 326
96th 339, 357–8, 364, *368*, 369, 378, 380
99th Inf 280, 284, 293, 297, 299, 304, 326
 101st Airborne 224, *224*, 225, *238*, 238–9, 258, 262, 273, 289, 308, 309, *311*, *312–13*, 323, 325, 326
 106th Inf 280, 285, 289, 300, 326
Regiments
 12th Infantry 289
 26th Infantry *289*, 303
 109th Infantry 289, 306
 110th Infantry 289, 306
 112th Infantry 289, 306
 117th Infantry 299
 120th Infantry 304
 320th Infantry *319*
 334th Infantry 318
 335th Infantry 318
 422nd Infantry 300, 302
 423rd Infantry 300, 302
 424th Infantry 300, 302, 305
 501st Parachute Inf 308, 309
 502nd Parachute Inf 309, 312
 506th Parachute Inf 308, 309
Battalions
 6th Marine Defense 153
 51st Engineer 229
 81st Engineer 300
 168th Engineer 300
 275th Field Artillery 300
 285th Field Artillery 299
 291st Combat Engineer 299
 420th Armored Field Artillery 309
 548th Antiaircraft *317*
 705th Tank Destroyer 309, 312
 713th Tank *378*
 749th Field Artillery *372*
 814th Tank Destroyer 302
other units
 14th Cavalry Group 280, 284, 285, 300, 302, 326
 128th Combat Engineer Group 307
 Task Forces Harper, Rose 307
 Task Forces Hogan, Kane, Orr 304, 305
 Team Cherry 308
 Team Desobry 308, 309
 Team O'Hara 308
United States Marine Corps *364–5*, *368–70*, *380*, *382*, *384–7*, 389
 III Amphibious Corps 380
 Divisions
 1st 339, 357–8, 364, 378, 380
 2nd 339
 4th 335
 5th *329*, 335, *336–7*
 6th 339, 357–8, 364, *369*, 372–3, *373*, 380, *384*
 Regiments
 5th *382*
 8th 382
 15th *387*
United States Navy
 battleship/carrier controversy 123, 126–7
 casualties/losses Pearl Harbor 121
 prewar expansion plans 80
 submarine campaign 127–8, 142
 Atlantic Fleet 121
 Fifth Fleet 334–5, 389
 Joint Expeditionary Force 339, 347, 351, 353–4
 Pacific Fleet 81, 95, 127, 128, 129, 131, 142, 150, 151, 154, 156, 159, 184, 374
 Task Force 16 156, 162, 166, 199
 Task Force 17 156, 162, 166, 184, 199
 Task Force 58 132, 344, 346
 Western Task Force 234
 Air Group 90 *346*
 Squadron VCS-7 *230*
United States Strategic Air Command 339, 376
Unwin, F/Sgt 'Grumpy' *42*, 43
Urakaze, destroyer 132, 134
Ushijima, Lt Gen Mitsura 339, 362, 364, 366, 369, 370, 378–83, 387–8
Ushio, destroyer 134
Utah, US battleship *108*, 109, 131
Utah, assault area, Normandy 217, 225, 233, 234–5, *234–6*, 238, 239, 258, 262, 270

Vaagso raid 213, 252
Valentine tanks *251*
Vestal, US repair ship 109, 117
Victorious, HMS, carrier 339
Victory in the West (Ellis) 222
Vielsalm, Belgium 300, 302, 303, 304, 305
Vincent, G/Capt S F 58
Vireo, US fleet tug 180
von der Heydte, Col F-A 258, 284, 293, 297, 318, 326

Wacht am Rhein plan 278, 280, 284, 297, 303, 306, 321, 324
Wada, Cdr Yoshio 182
Wake Island 80, 97, 131, 159, 192, 195
Wakeling, Sgt S R E 41
Waldron, Lt/Cdr John 168
Ward, US destroyer 99
Warspite, HMS, battleship 233
Wasp, US carrier 344
Watanabe, Ensign 341
Watanabe, Cdr Yasuyi 142
Watson, P/O A R 67
Weir, P/O A N C 30, *37*, 63, 65
Welch, Lt George 104
Werbomont, Belgium 297, 299, 303, 304, 308
Werra, Oberleutnant Franz von 47
West Virginia, US battleship *73*, *107*, 109, *112*, 113, 117, *118*, 131, *356*, 361
Westphal, Gen Siegfried 278
Whitworth, Lt P 253
Wick, Helmut (Luftwaffe) 25, 66, 67
Wiltz, L'bourg 278, 306, 313, 323, 325
Woods-Scawen, F/O Anthony 44
Woods-Scawen, F/O Patrick 44
Wright, Rear Admiral J 362

X20, X23, RN midget submarines 233

Yakagi, cruiser 365, 367
Yamaguchi, Petty Officer 377
Yamaguchi, Rear Admiral T 158 173, 175, 176, 177, 178, 182, 198
Yamamoto, Admiral Isoruku 81, 83, 84–7, 88, 89, 90–91, 97, *99*, 120, 131, 132, 142, *143*, 149, 151, 153–61 *passim*, 166, 168, 171, 177, 178, 180, 182, 183, *183*, 184, 186, 187, 191, 195, 197, 198
Yamashiro, battleship 156, 159
Yamato, battleship 132, 142, *143*, 151, 153, 156, 157, 159, 182, 183, 184, 186, 195, 197, 344, 365, 366–7, *366–7*, 377, 390
Yamazuka, Rear Admiral 135
Yanagimoto, Capt Ryusaku 172
Yokota, Petty Officer 377
Yonabaru airstrip, Okinawa 337, 339
Yonai, Admiral Mitsumasa 80
Yontan airfield, Okinawa 337, 339, 359, 361, 364, 371, 376, *376*, *377*, 389
Yorktown, US carrier *94*, 97, 132, 149, 153, 154, *155*, 156, 157, 162, *163*, 165, 166, 167, 168, 170, 173, *174–5*, 175, 176–7, 178, *179*, *181*, 183, 184, 186, 196, *197*, 344, 354
Yoshida, Ensign 367
Young, (RAF 46 Sqn) *63*
Young, Lt Col Peter 253, *253*
Yukikaze, destroyer *188–9*

Zanger, General 326
Zellars, US destroyer 374
Zuiho, carrier 151, 159, 183, 195
Zuikaku, carrier 87, 97, 131, 132, 134, 149, 153

PICTURE CREDITS

AELR Museum, Brussels: pp 16 (center), 48 (bottom left)
Archiv Schliephake: pp 16 (top), 30, 59 (top)
Archiv exemplar: pp 321 (top), 324–5 (bottom)
Associated Press: pp 24 (top), 271 (bottom left)
R Athey: pp 10–11, 15 (top), 18 (top), 19, 22 (top), 42, 54–5, 68–9
Mike Badrocke: pp 286–7 (center)
John Batchelor: pp 188–9 (top and bottom)
Beaumont Aviation: pp 20 (top right), 21 (top), 23 (top)
Bildarchiv Preussischer Kulturbesitz: pp 285 (bottom), 301 (bottom)
Graham Bingham (artwork): pp 250 (both), 251 (bottom)
BIPPA: p 27 (top)
Bison: pp 15 (bottom), 46, 50 (bottom), 57 (bottom right), 61 (bottom), 66 (bottom), 206 (top right and bottom), 209 (top), 210 (below), 211 (top), 212 (top), 214 (both), 217, 237 (top), 248 (below), 249 (top), 257 (center right)
Bison Picture Library: pp 82 (both), 83, 94 (left), 97 (top), 98, 100 (bottom), 120, 130 (top), 151 (center), 152 (top), 185 (top), 192, 272 (top), 273 (center), 274 (bottom), 275, 278–9 (bottom), 282, 283, 286 (top), 290–91 (bottom), 295 (bottom), 308 (top left), 309, 312 (top)
Bundesarchiv: pp 206 (top left), 208, 257 (top left and bottom), 274 (top right), 302 (bottom), 323 (bottom), 324 (top)
CB Collection: pp 21 (center), 22 (bottom), 23 (bottom), 26, 27 (center right), 31 (center and bottom), 32 (bottom), 33 (bottom), 34 (top right), 36 (top left), 37 (center right), 38 (bottom), 40 (all four), 44 (center), 45 (top left and top right), 49 (top), 51 (top), 53 (bottom), 56 (top), 57 (top right), 58, 60 (top three), 61 (top), 63 (top and bottom left), 64 (bottom left and right)
J B Cynk: pp 52 (top), 56 (bottom), 57 (top left), 62 (top)
Helen Downton: pp 192–3 (center)
via H L R Franks: pp 27 (center left), 37 (center left)
Grp Capt C F Gray: pp 18 (bottom), 43 (top center)
Robert Hunt: pp 24 (bottom), 49 (center), 59 (bottom), 99 (top), 213 (bottom), 220 (bottom two), 224 (top), 225 (top), 226–7, 228 (bottom), 233, 248 (top), 249 (bottom), 252 (top and center), 253 (top), 255 (all three), 257 (center left), 344, 355
Robert Hunt Library: pp 143 (center left and center right), 146 (bottom), 151 (top), 154 (bottom), 157, 158–9 (top), 162, 173, 175 (top), 177 (top), 182–3, 187, 270–71 (center), 271 (top), 274 (top left), 276, 276–7 (bottom), 288 (top left), 298 (bottom), 301 (top left and center), 303, 305 (center), 306–7 (bottom), 308 (top right), 310 (top), 313 (top), 315 (top), 316 (top), 318 (top), 320, 321
Imperial War Museum: pp 16 (bottom), 17, 20 (top left), 21 (bottom), 25 (bottom), 26 (bottom), 28–9 (all three), 31 (top), 32 (top), 34 (bottom), 39 (top), 43 (top left, top right and bottom), 45 (top right), 51 (bottom), 53 (top and center), 60 (bottom), 62 (bottom), 64 (top), 65 (top), 66 (center left and right), 67 (bottom), 73, 89 (top), 145, 148–9 (bottom), 150 (bottom), 151 (bottom), 152 (bottom), 158–9 (bottom), 164, 176 (bottom), 179 (top), 181 (top), 201, 209 (below), 210 (top), 213 (top), 218 (bottom), 220 (main pic), 221, 229, 253 (center and bottom), 254 (both), 257 (top right), 260 (center), 268–9, 277, 285 (top), 288 (top right), 292 (top and center), 296 (top, center left and bottom), 297, 298–9 (center), 302 (top), 322 (bottom), 324–5 (top), 342 (bottom), 345 (top left), 353, 370–71
Kantosha Company: p 169 (bottom left)
via Koku-fan: pp 169 (center), 170 (bottom), 185 (bottom)
P G Leggett: pp 63 (bottom right), 65 (bottom)
McDonnell-Douglas Corporation: p 155 (top left)
Manchini Newspapers: pp 79 (all three), 129 (top)
Masami Tokoi: pp (both), 92 (center and right), 93 (all three)
MOD (Air): p 64 (center)
National Archives: pp 73–5, 76–7, 100 (top), 104 (both), 105 (bottom), 106–7 (both), 110–11 (both), 112–13 (all four), 114–15 (all three), 116–17 (all three), 118 (both), 119 (top), 121, 122, 124–5 (all three), 126–7 (all three), 128 (both), 132 (main pic), 133, 134, 218 (top), 232 (bottom), 235 (all three), 236–7 (bottom), 239 (bottom), 240 (top), 240–41 (bottom), 241 (top), 242 (top), 244–5 (bottom), 246 (center and top), 247 (top), 251 (top), 258 (both), 259 (top), 260 (top and bottom), 340 (top), 340 (bottom), 341, 342–3, 345 (top right), 346 (top), 346–7 (bottom), 361 (bottom), 362–3, 365 (bottom), 366 (top), 366 (bottom), 368 (top), 375 (top right), 375 (top left), 375 (bottom), 383 (bottom), 390 (top)
Richard Natkiel: pp 150 (top), 171, 294 (top), 295 (top)
Wiley Noble: p 155 (top right)
C Order: p 37 (top)
PNA: p 41
Pilot Press: pp 191, 193 (top and center), 266–7
Public Archives of Canada: pp 45 (bottom), 52 (bottom), 318 (bottom)
J K Ross: p 25 (top)
SADO, Brussels: pp 273 (bottom), 301 (top right), 305 (top)
M Sargant: pp 37 (bottom), 47 (top left)
Shizuo Fukui: p 85 (top)
Signal Corps: p 287
courtesy 32 Squadron: p 33 (top)
courtesy 56 Squadron: p 18 (center)
courtesy 74 Squadron: pp 34 (top left), 36 (top right), 38 (top)
Mike Trim: pp 192–3 (bottom)
US Air Force: pp 96 (top), 101 (top), 102–3 (all three), 129 (bottom), 146 (top), 170 (top), 219, 225 (bottom), 230 (both), 232 (top)
US Army: pp 101 (below), 105 (top), 212 (center), 215 (both), 224 (center), 228 (top two), 234 (bottom), 236 (top), 238 (all three), 239 (top), 242–3 (bottom), 243 (bottom), 244 (top left), 247 (bottom), 256, 259 (center), 265, 271 (bottom right), 272 (bottom right), 280, 281, 282–3 (bottom), 314–15 (bottom), 316 (bottom), 317, 319, 322–3 (top), 335 (top), 351, 363 (top), 368 (bottom), 370 (top), 371 (top), 372 (top and bottom), 377 (top), 378, 381 (top), 383 (center), 388 (bottom), 389, 390 (bottom)
US Coast Guard: pp 244 (top right), 332–3, 336 (top)
US Marine Corps: pp 329, 336–7 (bottom), 337 (top), 347 (top), 358 (top), 358–9 (bottom), 359 (top), 361 (top), 364 (top), 364 (bottom), 365 (top), 369 (top and bottom), 373 (top left), 373 (top right), 376, 377 (bottom), 379 (top and bottom), 380, 381 (center), 382 (top and bottom), 383 (top), 384 (top and bottom), 385 (top and bottom), 386 (top and bottom), 387 (all three), 388 (top)
US National Archives: pp 143 (bottom), 147, 154 (top), 155 (bottom), 156 (top right), 156–7 (bottom), 160–61, 163, 164–5, 166–7, 169 (bottom right), 174 175 (bottom), 176 (top), 177 (bottom), 179 (bottom), 181 (bottom), 184, 186, 190–91, 194–5
US Navy: pp 81 (all three), 84 (both), 85 (bottom), 88, 89 (bottom), 90 (top), 94–5 (both), 96–7 (bottom), 108 (all three), 119 (bottom), 137, 138–9, 140–41, 142, 143 (center), 144, 144–5 (bottom), 148, 148–9 (top), 156 (top left), 169 (top), 172, 178, 180, 183 (top), 188–9, 204–5, 216, 240 (center), 246, 330–31, 334 (top and bottom), 335 (top and bottom), 338 (all), 342 (top), 345 (bottom), 352, 354–5, 356 (top and bottom), 357, 360 (top and bottom)
R F Watson: p 12–13
Peter Young: p 253 (right)